'Artificial intelligence is no longer a future consideration—it is a present-day governance, risk, and leadership challenge. This book provides a clear, disciplined framework for understanding how AI reshapes cybersecurity, enterprise risk, and regulatory accountability. What makes this work stand out is its practical grounding: it connects strategy to execution, and innovation to responsibility. For executives, board members, and policymakers seeking to deploy AI with confidence rather than optimism alone, this book is an essential guide.'

Dr. Yoav Intrator, *Former CEO, JPMorgan Chase Israel*

'AI has pervaded all industry sectors, and businesses face a multitude of challenges when implementing it. *AI Governance: The Executive Handbook for Safe and Responsible AI* uniquely equips readers to integrate AI safely, with real-life guidance from top executives on overcoming regulatory, governance, cybersecurity, and risk challenges.'

Dr. Shariq Nisar, *Fellow at the Harvard Law School and Distinguished Management Professor at the University of Luxembourg*

AI GOVERNANCE

AI Governance: The Executive Handbook for Safe and Responsible AI is a book researched and written by cyber experts Ariel Evans and Ajay Singh with contributions from leading members of Cyber Intelligence 4U advisory board, including top CISOs, CIOs, CTOs, DPOs, and cyber attorneys to help businesses prepare for the safe and intelligent use of AI.

This book is a comprehensive handbook that bridges the gap between the complex world of artificial intelligence and its practical applications for business. Covering regulation requirements, governance, cyber controls, explainability, and privacy in easy-to-understand language, it is an essential resource to navigate and address the opportunities, complex challenges, and responsibilities associated with AI technologies and provides a roadmap for businesses to implement a safe AI program. Each area is explored from a business perspective to allow the reader to understand how this relates to their role in a company and to harness the power of AI in their respective fields and concludes with a section on how to create a step-by-step AI program. In addition, real-life examples of the challenges that any business needs to address as it rolls out AI-based applications are presented throughout.

This book will empower readers, whether they are IT professionals, tech enthusiasts, business leaders, or students, with the necessary knowledge and insights to create a safe and responsible AI program.

Ariel Evans is a senior cybersecurity and AI governance expert, serial entrepreneur, and award-winning author. She is CEO and Co-Founder of RiskQ Inc., a cyber risk quantification and AI governance platform, and founder of Cyber Intelligence 4U, an executive education and thought leadership initiative, where she has educated more than 5,000 global business leaders. She is the author of *Managing Cyber Risk*, *Enterprise Cyber Risk in Digital Business*, and *Navigating Supply Chain Cyber Risk*.

Ajay Singh is a globally recognized cybersecurity and AI governance expert, Professor of Practice, former Chief Executive Officer, and award-winning author.

A Fellow of the Institute of Directors, he advises boards, governments, and regulators on enterprise cyber resilience and AI governance strategy. He has authored several internationally acclaimed books on cyber risk management, including *Cyber Strong*, an International Book Awards Finalist (2022).

AI GOVERNANCE

The Executive Handbook for Safe and Responsible AI

Ariel Evans and Ajay Singh

Routledge
Taylor & Francis Group
LONDON AND NEW YORK

Designed cover image: Getty images

First published 2027
by Routledge
4 Park Square, Milton Park, Abingdon, Oxon OX14 4RN

and by Routledge
605 Third Avenue, New York, NY 10158

Routledge is an imprint of the Taylor & Francis Group, an informa business

British Library Cataloguing-in-Publication Data
A catalogue record for this book is available from the British Library

ISBN: 978-1-041-16057-1 (hbk)
ISBN: 978-1-041-13529-6 (pbk)
ISBN: 978-1-003-68253-0 (ebk)

DOI: 10.4324/9781003682530

Typeset in Joanna
by codeMantra

CONTENTS

ACKNOWLEDGMENTS

The journey of creating *AI Governance: The Executive Handbook of Safe and Responsible AI* has been both deeply rewarding and intensely collaborative. This book is the result of countless conversations, workshops, panels, and reviews by experts across cybersecurity, privacy, compliance, risk management, academia, policy, and technology. We are profoundly grateful to everyone who contributed their time, insight, and encouragement along the way.

We would like to especially recognize the ongoing support and intellectual leadership of our Advisory Board members. Their diverse expertise and real-world experience helped us ground this work in practical relevance while challenging us to think more broadly about the future of AI governance.

Advisory Board Members who contributed to this publication include:

- Ahsan Sheikh, CISO, Societe Generale
- Alex Shalger, CEO, Iceberg.ai
- Amit Basu, CISO, International Seaways
- Anne Higgins, Global Head of Cyber Controls, Information Security, BNY Mellon
- Jo Ann Davaris, CPO, Booking Holdings
- Brittany Sakson, Arch Insurance
- Chad Viola, CISO, AMBest

- Charles Golliday, CISO, Ellkay
- Chris Baker, TTS Business Disruption and Safety Risk, Citi
- Chris Drake, CTO, iconnectiv
- Emile Nasseh, Global Privacy Counsel, Kimberly Clark
- Frank Gonello, Associate General Counsel, Shopify
- Fred Eslami, Director, Alternative Risk Transfer and Cyber Security, AMBest
- Mark Gibson, GM of Banking, Prove
- Mike Battistella, CEO, Solutions^3
- Moe Hassan, Cybersecurity, Confidential
- Neal Goldstein, CIO, Mutual of America
- Ninad Purohit, Managing Partner Cybersecurity, CFGI
- Steve Fouchong, Cybersecurity, Tradeweb
- Orrie Dinstein, CPO, Marsh
- Peter Rosario, CISO, USI
- Rafi Buchnick, Head of US IT Risk, RBC
- Scott Aurnou, Cybersecurity Attorney, The Security Advocate
- Tohru Watanabe, CISO, Lazard
- Vito Sardanopoli, Head of IT and Information Security, Spire Ortho
- Will Shu, CIO, Riverstrong
- Yossi Barkalifa, CISO, Confidential

We also wish to thank:

- Industry Practitioners who provided case studies, operational insights, and constructive critique. Their frontline experience shaped many of the recommendations in this book.
- Legal and Regulatory Experts whose guidance helped us navigate the evolving global landscape of AI-related laws and ethical frameworks.
- Academic Partners who offered research support, peer reviews, and helped bridge theory with practice.
- Conference Panelists and Workshop Participants whose feedback during key sessions (including those hosted at Seton Hall, Pace University, and the CIU Advisory Boards) sharpened our understanding of pressing challenges and priorities.

- Technical Contributors who helped frame complex topics such as model drift, adversarial attacks, and explainability in a way that is accessible for executive audiences.

A special thanks goes to the entire team at Cyber Intelligence 4U, RiskQ, and our university collaborators who supported us through writing, editing, designing, and promoting this book. Your dedication is deeply appreciated.

Finally, we thank our readers—executives, CISOs, policymakers, data scientists, and board members—who are leading the charge in deploying AI with integrity. We hope this book helps guide your journey toward safer, more transparent, and responsible AI systems.

PREFACE

Artificial intelligence is no longer emerging—it is executing. It is writing code, negotiating contracts, diagnosing illnesses, approving financial transactions, and influencing national security strategies. In parallel, the world is grappling with a fundamental question: Who controls AI—and under what governance?

The acceleration of AI has outpaced traditional regulatory, cybersecurity, and IT governance models. Decisions once made in quarterly strategy cycles are now being made in milliseconds by autonomous systems. For boards, executives, and regulators, the conversation is no longer about AI adoption, but about AI accountability—assurance that these systems are safe, defensible, compliant, transparent, and recoverable under failure or attack.

This book is written as a strategic playbook for leaders, not as a technical manual. It bridges regulation, cybersecurity, legal responsibility, risk quantification, and operational execution—unifying AI governance as a board-level discipline. Whether your organization is adopting AI, building AI, or auditing AI, this handbook offers the structured, practical frameworks needed to move from uncertainty to control.

The goal is not to slow down innovation—but to make it responsible, measurable, and trusted. AI will define the next decade of economic power. Governance will determine who survives it.

SECTION 1

THE IMPORTANCE OF DEFINITIONS IN AI

Precise definitions are foundational to the study, regulation, and deployment of artificial intelligence (AI). In AI, terminology is not merely descriptive—it shapes governance frameworks, technical implementation, legal accountability, and even public perception. Ambiguity or inconsistency in definitions can lead to misaligned expectations between developers, regulators, enterprises, and end users, resulting in compliance failures, ethical risks, or flawed system design.

This section provides a structured grounding in the critical role of definitions in AI across four chapters:

- **Chapter 1: Why Definitions Matter in AI**—establishes how definitions influence governance, risk management, interdisciplinary communication, and societal trust.
- **Chapter 2: AI Terminology and Definitions for Non_technical Readers**—identifies high-impact terms such as "autonomy," "explainability," "AI system," and "risk," and explains why their clarity is essential.

DOI: 10.4324/9781003682530-1

- **Chapter 3: Challenges in Defining AI Concepts**—explores why differing academic disciplines, cultural contexts, regulatory approaches, and technical architectures make consensus difficult.
- **Chapter 4: The Future: Standardizing AI Definitions**—examines emerging efforts by bodies such as ISO, NIST, the EU AI Act, and OECD to create standardized terminology for global alignment.

Together, these chapters demonstrate that establishing a shared vocabulary is the first necessary step toward safe, interoperable, and ethically governed AI systems.

1

WHY DEFINITIONS MATTER IN AI

The Importance of Definitions in AI

In the rapidly evolving world of artificial intelligence (AI), definitions are not mere semantics; they are foundational. Clear and precise definitions are critical to ensuring that AI systems are transparent, fair, consistent, and safe. As AI technologies increasingly influence societal systems, from healthcare and finance to criminal justice and transportation, the need for standardization in terminology and conceptual clarity becomes ever more urgent.

AI is built on foundations of mathematics, logic, data, and human judgment—but none of these can function without shared, precise definitions. Definitions determine how systems interpret the world, how developers build models, how regulators write rules, and ultimately how society experiences the outcomes of AI.

In a domain where technologies evolve faster than laws, norms, and organizational capabilities, definitional clarity is not a luxury—it is a fundamental requirement for transparency, fairness, safety, compliance, and

DOI: 10.4324/9781003682530-2

trust. As AI becomes embedded in healthcare, finance, insurance, education, policing, national security, and consumer products, inconsistent or ambiguous definitions can lead to catastrophic consequences.

This chapter explains why definitions matter and why establishing standardized, stable terminology is a critical first step in building responsible and reliable AI systems.

Clarity and Understanding

At the core of every AI system lies a structured understanding of the world, expressed through data, models, and objectives. These systems rely heavily on well-defined inputs and outputs to function effectively. When key terms are ambiguous or poorly articulated, AI systems are prone to misinterpretation and failure.

Example: Consider a fraud detection algorithm in financial services. If the system lacks a precise definition of "fraud," it may erroneously flag legitimate transactions, leading to customer dissatisfaction, revenue loss, or regulatory scrutiny. Conversely, vague definitions may allow actual fraudulent activities to go undetected (Chouldechova & Roth, 2018).

At the most basic level, definitions allow AI systems—and the humans who develop and operate them—to share a common understanding of what key concepts mean. Machine learning algorithms rely on data labels, feature definitions, operational goals, and success metrics. When those underlying terms are vague, contradictory, or poorly understood, the resulting models become unreliable and unpredictable.

Humans may tolerate ambiguity; AI systems cannot.

Why definitional clarity is essential in practice:

- Training data requires consistent labeling.
- Models require well-defined optimization goals.
- Business stakeholders need common terminology to interpret outputs.
- Regulators require clarity to enforce compliance.

Illustrative Example:

A fraud detection system is only as effective as its definition of "fraud." Vague or overly broad definitions can lead to false positives, false negatives, inconsistent reporting, and regulatory scrutiny.

Fairness and Bias Reduction

Fairness in AI is deeply connected to how we define concepts such as bias, discrimination, equity, and justice. These terms are often socially and culturally contextual, which adds complexity. Without agreed-upon definitions, efforts to reduce bias in machine learning models can be misguided or ineffective.

Example: An AI-based hiring tool must have a clear and measurable definition of "fair hiring." Without it, the tool may reinforce existing systemic biases—such as favoring candidates from certain educational backgrounds—rather than correcting them (Barocas et al., 2019).

Definitional ambiguity can also lead to ethical pitfalls. For instance, different definitions of fairness—such as demographic parity versus equal opportunity—can lead to conflicting decisions in the same dataset (Friedler et al., 2019).

AI fairness is fundamentally determined by how we define fairness-related concepts. Bias, discrimination, protected classes, equity, opportunity, and harm all require explicit, measurable definitions before they can be operationalized in algorithms. Without standardized definitions, fairness interventions become inconsistent, model evaluation becomes subjective, regulators struggle to assess compliance, and organizations reach different conclusions about the same dataset.

Example in Hiring AI

If an AI hiring system lacks a precise definition of "fair hiring," the model may reinforce systemic biases or discriminate unintentionally.

Regulatory Compliance

AI regulation is expanding globally. Laws such as the EU AI Act, General Data Protection Regulation (GDPR), CCPA, and emerging AI laws depend on precise terminology to enforce compliance.

Definitions enable legal enforcement. Terms like automated decision-making, high-risk AI system, explanation, consent, profiling, and transparency all carry legal implications. If these terms remain undefined, organizations face unpredictable regulatory risk.

As regulators around the world introduce AI-specific laws and policies, the importance of standardized definitions has become paramount.

Regulatory language must be interpretable and enforceable, which is only possible when terms are clearly defined.

Example: The European Union's GDPR includes a "right to explanation" for individuals subject to automated decisions. However, what constitutes an "explanation" remains legally and technically contested. Without a clear definition, compliance becomes a moving target (Wachter et al., 2017).

Consistency Across Systems

AI models are increasingly integrated across geographic and organizational boundaries. However, when models are trained using different definitions for the same term, inconsistencies and misalignments can arise—leading to potentially dangerous outcomes.

Example: A medical AI system trained in one country may use a specific threshold to define "high risk" for a disease, while another country may use a different standard. This divergence can result in conflicting diagnoses for the same patient, depending on where the AI was developed or deployed (Rajkomar et al., 2019).

In a world of interconnected data flows and cross-border AI deployments, definitions ensure consistency across models, regions, and organizations.

Human–AI Interaction

Humans must be able to understand, trust, and effectively interact with AI systems. Definitions shape how AI communicates decisions and how users interpret those decisions.

Example: In autonomous vehicles, the distinction between a "pedestrian" and an "obstacle" must be unambiguous. Misclassification could result in accidents with serious consequences for human safety (Kalra & Paddock, 2016).

AI systems must communicate decisions to humans clearly. Definitions shape how models describe events, how humans interpret outputs, and how decisions are justified.

Strategic and Organizational Alignment

Definitions are essential for business alignment, governance, and risk reporting. Clear terminology ensures consistent governance and accountability.

Conclusion

Definitional clarity is not a theoretical exercise; it is a prerequisite for building AI systems that are ethical, lawful, and effective. The absence of clear definitions can lead to serious consequences, including biased outcomes, safety risks, non-compliance, and erosion of public trust. As AI becomes more embedded in critical infrastructures and everyday life, stakeholders—including developers, policymakers, and users—must prioritize the development and adoption of standardized, transparent definitions.

Bibliography

Barocas, S., Hardt, M., & Narayanan, A. (2019). *Fairness and Machine Learning: Limitations and Opportunities*. MIT Press. https://fairmlbook.org

Chouldechova, A., & Roth, A. (2018). The frontiers of fairness in machine learning. *arXiv preprint arXiv:1810.08810*. https://arxiv.org/abs/1810.08810

Friedler, S. A., Scheidegger, C., Venkatasubramanian, S., Hamilton, E. P., Roth, D., & Bartley, N. (2019). A comparative study of fairness-enhancing interventions in machine learning. In *Proceedings of the 2019 Conference on Fairness, Accountability, and Transparency* (pp. 329–338). Association for Computing Machinery. https://doi.org/10.1145/3287560.3287589

Kalra, N., & Paddock, S. M. (2016). Driving to safety: How many miles of driving would it take to demonstrate autonomous vehicle reliability? RAND Corporation. https://www.rand.org/pubs/research_reports/RR1478.html

Rajkomar, A., Dean, J., & Kohane, I. (2019). Machine learning in medicine. *New England Journal of Medicine*, 380(14), 1347–1358. https://doi.org/10.1056/NEJMra1814259

Wachter, S., Mittelstadt, B., & Floridi, L. (2017). Why a right to explanation of automated decision-making does not exist in the General Data Protection Regulation. *International Data Privacy Law*, 7(2), 76–99. https://doi.org/10.1093/idpl/ipx005

2

AI TERMINOLOGY AND DEFINITIONS FOR NON-TECHNICAL READERS

Introduction

Welcome to the World of Artificial Intelligence (AI)! AI might sound like a complex, technical subject, but at its core, it's all about machines learning to think, decide, and help us in everyday life. Whether it's your smartphone recognizing your face, an online store suggesting what to buy next, or a virtual assistant answering your questions, AI is becoming a part of our daily routines.

AI comes to life through different categories—each representing how it thinks, learns, and interacts with the world. In this glossary, we break AI down into practical groups: Core AI Concepts, Learning Methods and Algorithms, AI Tasks and Functions, Data and Model Behavior, Ethics and Governance, and Security and Risk.

DOI: 10.4324/9781003682530-3

Core AI Concepts

Artificial Intelligence

AI is the ability of machines to perform tasks that normally require human intelligence, such as recognizing patterns, making decisions, or understanding language.

Example: A customer-service chatbot that can answer questions and route issues without a human agent.

Machine Learning (ML)

ML is a way of building AI systems that learn from data and improve over time, instead of being explicitly programmed step-by-step.

Example: A fraud detection system that gets better at spotting suspicious transactions as it sees more examples.

Neural Network

A neural network is a type of machine-learning model inspired by the way neurons connect in the human brain. It uses layers of interconnected "nodes" to detect complex patterns in data.

Example: A system that can recognize different types of vehicles in traffic camera footage.

Deep Learning

Deep learning is a form of neural networks with many layers, allowing the system to learn very complex patterns from large volumes of data such as images, audio, or text.

Example: A speech-to-text engine that can accurately transcribe spoken conversations in noisy environments.

Large Language Model (LLM)

An LLM is a deep learning model trained on massive amounts of text so it can generate and interpret human language, answer questions, summarize documents, or write content.

Example: Using an LLM to summarize a 50-page regulatory report into a one-page briefing for the board.

Narrow AI (Weak AI)

Narrow AI is an AI system designed and optimized for a single task or narrow set of tasks; it does not have general intelligence.

Example: A system that only reads medical images for cancer detection but cannot handle any other type of task.

Artificial General Intelligence (AGI)

AGI is a hypothetical form of AI that could understand, learn, and perform any intellectual task a human can, across domains. It does not exist today but is used as a reference point in debates about long-term AI risk.

Example: An AGI would be able to learn law, medicine, finance, and engineering at human expert levels without being retrained from scratch for each.

Hybrid AI

Hybrid AI combines different approaches—such as ML plus rules-based logic—to get the benefits of both.

Example: A compliance tool that uses rules to enforce regulatory requirements and ML models to detect unusual behavior that rules might miss.

Learning Methods and Algorithms

Supervised Learning

In supervised learning, models are trained on data where the correct answer (label) is already known, so the system learns to map inputs to outputs.

Example: Training a model on past loan decisions labeled "approved" or "denied" to predict future approvals.

Unsupervised Learning

Unsupervised learning finds patterns and groupings in data without pre-labeled answers. It is used for discovery and segmentation.

Example: Grouping customers into segments based on behavior, without knowing in advance which groups exist.

Reinforcement Learning

Reinforcement learning trains an AI agent by letting it act in an environment and giving it rewards or penalties based on the results, teaching it which actions work best over time.

Example: A warehouse robot that learns the most efficient route to move goods by trial and error.

Generative AI

Generative AI creates new content—such as text, images, audio, or code—based on patterns it has learned from training data.

Example: Generating draft policy language or risk reports that a human expert can then refine.

Semi-Supervised Learning

Semi-supervised learning uses a small amount of labeled data and a large amount of unlabeled data to train more efficiently when labels are expensive or time-consuming to create.

Example: Labeling a few hundred legal documents and using thousands of unlabeled ones to improve contract classification.

Few-Shot Learning

Few-shot learning allows a model to learn a new task from just a handful of examples, rather than needing thousands.

Example: Showing an AI system only a few examples of a rare fraud pattern and having it start to recognize similar cases.

Zero-Shot Learning

Zero-shot learning is when a model performs a task it was never explicitly trained on, by relying on its general understanding of language or concepts.

Example: Asking an LLM to classify emails by urgency, even though it was never specifically trained on that exact label.

Transfer Learning

Transfer learning takes a model trained on one task and adapts it to a related task, saving time and computational cost.

Example: Starting with an image model trained on generic photos and fine-tuning it to identify specific manufacturing defects.

Foundation Model

A foundation model is a very large, general-purpose AI model trained on broad data, which can then be adapted to many downstream tasks.

Example: Using one foundation model as the base for customer support, document search, and translation tools across the enterprise.

Embeddings

Embeddings are numerical representations of data (such as words, sentences, or images) that capture their meaning and relationships in a way AI can use.

Example: Finding all documents semantically related to "third-party cyber risk" even if they use different words.

AI Tasks and Functions

Natural Language Processing (NLP)

NLP is the branch of AI that enables machines to understand, interpret, and generate human language.

Example: Automatically extracting key clauses and obligations from vendor contracts.

Computer Vision

Computer vision allows machines to interpret and make decisions based on visual information such as images and video.

Example: Monitoring a production line to detect damaged products in real-time.

Speech Recognition

Speech recognition converts spoken language into text that machines can process.

Example: Transcribing customer-service calls for quality monitoring and sentiment analysis.

Recommendation Systems

Recommendation systems analyze past behavior and patterns to suggest items or actions a user is likely to value.

Example: Suggesting relevant training modules to employees based on their role and learning history.

Classification

Classification is the task of assigning items into predefined categories.

Example: Flagging incoming emails as "phishing," "marketing," or "business-critical."

Regression

Regression models predict a continuous numerical value rather than a category.

Example: Estimating the expected financial loss of a cyber incident given certain conditions.

Clustering

Clustering groups of similar items together without predefined labels, revealing natural structure in the data.

Example: Discovering distinct risk profiles across vendors based on their controls, geography, and incident history.

Sentiment Analysis

Sentiment analysis estimates the emotional tone of text, such as positive, negative, or neutral.

Example: Monitoring social media and support tickets to detect rising customer frustration after a product change.

Entity Recognition (Named Entity Recognition, NER)

Entity recognition identifies and labels key information such as names, organizations, dates, and locations in text.

Example: Automatically pulling out company names, jurisdictions, and contract dates from legal agreements.

Data and Model Behavior

Training Data

Training data is the set of examples an AI model learns from. Its quality, diversity, and representativeness directly shape the model's behavior and risk profile.

Example: If your training data only includes large enterprises, the model may perform poorly on small business customers.

Feature

A feature is an individual measurable property used by a model to make predictions.

Example: Credit utilization rate, number of recent logins, or number of third-party connections can all be features in different models.

Overfitting

Overfitting occurs when a model learns the training data too closely, including noise and quirks, and performs poorly on new, unseen data.

Example: A risk model that looks excellent in testing but fails in production because it learned patterns unique to last year's data.

Hallucination

A hallucination is when an AI system, especially a generative model, produces confident but incorrect or fabricated information.

Example: An LLM inventing a case law citation that looks plausible but does not exist.

Bias

Bias in AI is systematic unfairness in model outcomes, often caused by skewed data, poor design choices, or historical inequities reflected in the training set.

Example: A hiring model that down-ranks candidates from certain schools or zip codes in ways that correlate with protected characteristics.

Drift (Data Drift / Concept Drift)

Drift is the gradual change in real-world data or relationships over time that causes models to become less accurate or fair if not updated.

Example: Payment patterns changing after a new product launch, leading to a higher false-positive rate for fraud.

Label Leakage (Data Leakage)

Label leakage happens when a model has access to information during training that it would not have in real use, making performance look better than it actually is.

Example: Including a field like "chargeback issued" while trying to predict whether a transaction will be fraudulent.

Confidence Score

A confidence score is the model's estimated level of certainty in a particular prediction or output. High confidence does not guarantee correctness, but it is a key input to risk-based decision thresholds.

Example: Requiring human review for all model decisions below a 70% confidence score.

Tokenization

Tokenization is the process of breaking text into smaller units (tokens) such as words, subwords, or characters so that models can process it.

Example: Splitting a policy document into tokens before feeding it into an LLM for summarization.

Benchmarking

Benchmarking evaluates a model against standard tests or datasets so its performance can be compared over time or against alternatives.

Example: Testing different models on the same labeled dataset to choose the safest and most accurate one for production.

Ethics, Governance, and Trust

Fairness

Fairness means that AI systems do not systematically disadvantage certain individuals or groups, especially those protected by law or ethics policies.

Example: Ensuring that a credit model does not disproportionately reject applications from a particular demographic group without valid, explainable reasons.

Transparency

Transparency is the ability to see and understand how an AI system works at a level appropriate to the audience—developers, regulators, or end users.

Example: Providing clear documentation and user-facing explanations describing what data is used and how decisions are made.

Explainability

Explainability is the capability to describe, in human-understandable terms, why an AI system produced a particular output or decision.

Example: Showing which factors most influenced a vendor's risk score and how they changed over time.

Accountability

Accountability means clearly assigning responsibility for the design, deployment, and outcomes of AI systems to specific roles or teams.

Example: A named executive owning the AI risk register and reporting regularly to the board.

Autonomy

Autonomy refers to the degree to which an AI system can act on its own without real-time human control. Higher autonomy usually requires stronger safety and governance measures.

Example: An autonomous trading system executing orders directly in the market versus a decision-support tool that only provides recommendations.

Responsible AI

Responsible AI is the practice of designing, building, and using AI in ways that are lawful, ethical, safe, and aligned with human values and organizational goals.

Example: A governance program that requires impact assessments, bias testing, and human oversight for all high-risk AI use cases.

Human-in-the-Loop (HITL)

Human-in-the-loop means humans remain actively involved in reviewing, approving, or overriding AI decisions, especially in high-risk contexts.

Example: A clinician making the final diagnosis after reviewing AI-suggested results.

Alignment

Alignment ensures that an AI system's goals and behaviors stay consistent with human intentions, organizational policies, and societal norms.

Example: Guardrails that prevent a chatbot from providing self-harm instructions even if prompted to do so.

AI Safety

AI safety focuses on preventing AI systems from causing unintended harm, whether through accidents, misuse, or emergent behavior.

Example: Defining and testing failure modes for an AI-enabled medical device before deployment.

AI Governance Framework

An AI governance framework is the set of policies, processes, roles, and controls used to manage AI risk across the organization.

Example: A framework that requires registration of all AI systems, formal risk assessments, documentation, monitoring, and periodic audits.

Security and Risk in AI

Adversarial Attack

An adversarial attack manipulates inputs to an AI system so that it makes incorrect predictions, often in ways that are hard for humans to notice.

Example: Slightly altering an invoice image so an OCR model misreads the amount.

Evasion Attack

An evasion attack specifically targets the way a model classifies inputs, modifying them to "slip past" detection.

Example: Modifying malware just enough to avoid being flagged by an AI-based security scanner.

Data Poisoning

Data poisoning corrupts the training data so that the model learns harmful or misleading patterns.

Example: Injecting fake user behavior into logs so a recommendation engine promotes the wrong content.

Model Theft (Model Stealing)

Model theft occurs when an attacker recreates or copies a proprietary model by repeatedly querying it and learning how it responds.

Example: A competitor replicating your high-value risk model via an exposed API.

Model Extraction

Model extraction is a form of model theft focused specifically on recreating the model's internal logic or parameters from its outputs.

Example: Using carefully designed queries to reconstruct a chatbot's underlying model so it can be reused without permission.

Deepfake

A deepfake is synthetic media—such as video, images, or audio—created by AI to convincingly mimic real people or events.

Example: An AI-generated audio clip that sounds like your CEO asking finance to wire funds.

Synthetic Data

Synthetic data is artificially generated data that mimics the patterns of real data without directly exposing sensitive records.

Example: Creating synthetic patient records to test models without revealing actual personal health information.

Shadow AI

Shadow AI refers to employees or teams using AI tools and models outside official governance, security, or compliance processes.

Example: Staff pasting regulated data into consumer AI tools without legal or security approval.

Prompt Injection

Prompt injection attacks manipulate the instructions given to an AI system—often via user input or external content—so that it ignores prior rules or reveals sensitive information.

Example: A user embedding hidden instructions in a website that cause an AI assistant to exfiltrate internal data when it summarizes that page.

Safety Guardrails

Safety guardrails are technical and policy-based constraints that prevent AI systems from performing high-risk or prohibited actions.

Example: Blocking an AI assistant from generating discriminatory content or providing step-by-step instructions for cyberattacks, regardless of user prompts.

Bibliography

European Commission. (2021). *Proposal for a Regulation Laying Down Harmonised Rules on Artificial Intelligence (Artificial Intelligence Act)*. https://artificialintelligenceact.eu/

Floridi, L., & Cowls, J. (2019). A unified framework of five principles for AI in society. *Harvard Data Science Review*. https://doi.org/10.1162/99608f92.8cd550d1

ISO/IEC 22989:2022. *Information Technology — Artificial Intelligence — Artificial Intelligence Concepts and Terminology*.

NIST. (2023). *Artificial Intelligence Risk Management Framework (AI RMF 1.0)*. National Institute of Standards and Technology. https://www.nist.gov/itl/ai-risk-management-framework

OECD. (2023). *OECD Framework for the Classification of AI Systems*. https://www.oecd.org/sti/ieconomy/oecd-framework-for-the-classification-of-ai-systems.pdf

3

CHALLENGES IN DEFINING AI CONCEPTS

Subjectivity, Evolving AI Capabilities, and Legal/Ethical Ambiguities all play significant roles in several areas of AI, particularly where human values, context, culture, or law are involved. These areas often require not just technical correctness, but alignment with ethical, social, or emotional expectations.

Subjectivity in AI

Subjectivity in AI refers to the influence of human values, perspectives, cultural contexts, and individual judgment in the design, implementation, and interpretation of AI systems. While AI is often perceived as objective and data-driven, many of its applications require handling ambiguity, ethical dilemmas, and personal or societal values. The following sections outline key areas where subjectivity plays a critical role, supported by academic and industry references.

Here are key areas in AI where subjectivity is important:

DOI: 10.4324/9781003682530-4

Ethical Decision-Making

AI systems in domains such as healthcare, criminal justice, and autonomous vehicles must frequently make decisions with ethical implications. These decisions often require balancing conflicting values such as safety, fairness, and autonomy, which are inherently subjective.

Example: An autonomous vehicle must choose between two actions in a crash scenario, each with potential harm. The selection depends on subjective priorities (e.g., saving the most lives vs. protecting the vehicle's passengers).

Citation: Lin, P. (2016). Why ethics matters for autonomous cars. In Maurer, M. et al. (Eds.), *Autonomous Driving*. Springer.

Fairness and Bias Mitigation

Defining fairness in AI is complex and varies based on legal, cultural, and social norms. Whether to prioritize equal outcomes, equal treatment, or equal opportunity often involves subjective trade-offs.

Example: A loan approval algorithm may meet one definition of fairness (equal approval rates) but fail another (equal false positive rates).

Citation: Barocas, S., Hardt, M., & Narayanan, A. (2019). *Fairness and Machine Learning*. fairmlbook.org.

Natural Language Understanding (NLU)

Language is rich in nuance, context, and ambiguity. Interpreting intent, emotion, or sarcasm depends heavily on subjective human understanding and varies across cultures.

Example: The phrase "Thanks a lot" can express gratitude or irritation depending on the tone and context.

Citation: Bender, E.M., & Friedman, B. (2018). Data statements for natural language processing: Toward mitigating system bias and enabling better science. *TACL*.

Sentiment Analysis and Emotion Recognition

These tasks aim to detect human emotions, but emotional perception is inherently subjective. Disagreements among human annotators are common, leading to noise in training data.

Example: Annotators may classify the same review as positive, neutral, or negative based on personal interpretation.

Citation: Mohammad, S.M. (2016). Sentiment analysis: Detecting valence, emotions, and other affectual states from text. In *Emotion Measurement*.

Content Moderation

Moderating online content involves subjective judgments about what is acceptable or offensive. Cultural, political, and individual differences make consistent moderation challenging.

Example: What counts as hate speech in one region may be protected speech in another.

Citation: Gillespie, T. (2018). *Custodians of the Internet: Platforms, Content Moderation, and the Hidden Decisions That Shape Social Media*. Yale University Press.

Explainability and Interpretability

Users and stakeholders often demand explanations for AI decisions, but what constitutes a satisfactory explanation varies by audience (e.g., regulator vs. layperson).

Example: A physician might want detailed feature weights, while a patient may prefer a simple reason in plain language.

Citation: Doshi-Velez, F., & Kim, B. (2017). Towards a rigorous science of interpretable machine learning. *arXiv*:1702.08608.

Recommender Systems

Relevance and usefulness in recommendations are subjective and change depending on personal tastes, cultural background, and even mood.

Example: A user's preference for music or movie genres can shift over time, and models must adapt to these nuanced changes.

Citation: Jannach, D., Adomavicius, G., & Tuzhilin, A. (2021). Recommender systems: Challenges, insights and research opportunities. *Machine Learning*, 110(8), 2551–2590.

Human–AI Collaboration

Designing AI tools for collaboration requires accounting for human trust, cognitive load, usability, and subjective satisfaction.

Example: An AI writing assistant might suggest grammatically correct text that the user feels doesn't fit their personal voice or tone.

Citation: Shneiderman, B. (2020). Human-centered artificial intelligence: Reliable, safe & trustworthy. *International Journal of Human–Computer Interaction.*

Evolving AI Capabilities: Developments from 2023 to 2025

Artificial Intelligence (AI) is no longer a static field—it is dynamic, rapidly advancing, and constantly redefining its boundaries. Over the past two years, AI has evolved from producing text and images to driving autonomous agents, powering real-world robotics, and reshaping industries at scale. These advancements demand a continuous re-evaluation of how we define and understand AI. As models grow more capable, efficient, and integrated into daily life, it becomes essential to track not just what AI can do, but how its applications are shifting across business, society, and technology.

Below are key examples from the past two years that highlight the rapid transformation of AI capabilities across various domains.

Generative AI Adoption in Business (2023–2024)

Generative AI tools like GPT-4 and DALL·E have moved beyond experimental phases and into active business use. By 2024, McKinsey reported that 65% of companies were regularly using generative AI tools—nearly double the figure from the year before.

Citation: McKinsey & Company. (2024). *The state of AI in early 2024: Gen AI adoption spikes and starts to generate value.* https://www.mckinsey.com/capabilities/quantumblack/our-insights/the-state-of-ai-2024

Rise of AI Agents (2024–2025)

AI agents have evolved from passive assistants to autonomous systems capable of multi-step planning and execution. OpenAI's Operator and similar systems now browse the web, book appointments, and perform tasks independently.

Citation: Wired. (2025). *Unpacking AI Agents.* https://www.wired.com/story/uncanny-valley-podcast-unpacking-ai-agents

Physical Intelligence and Robotics

AI is now capable of adapting in physical spaces. Google DeepMind's Gemini Robotics project enables robots to perform tasks like unscrewing jars or folding clothes with minimal prior training.

Citation: The Verge. (2025). *Google DeepMind's New AI Models Help Robots Perform Physical Tasks.* https://www.theverge.com

AI Boosting Workforce Productivity

AI tools are now directly integrated into workflows, improving efficiency in domains like sales, diagnostics, and content creation. Stanford's 2025 AI Index confirms that AI enhances productivity and reduces skill gaps across job functions.

Citation: Stanford HAI. (2025). *AI Index Report.* https://hai.stanford.edu

Breakthroughs in Algorithm Discovery and Drug Design

DeepMind's AlphaDev discovered new sorting algorithms now included in C++ libraries. In healthcare, AI-driven platforms dramatically accelerated drug screening for conditions like Parkinson's disease.

Citation: Nature (2024). *AlphaDev and AI in Drug Discovery.*

Foundation Model Optimization

OpenAI revealed that GPT-4.5 can be rebuilt by a team of 5–10 engineers, indicating massive improvements in training efficiency. Meanwhile, Google's Gemini 2.5 introduced a Deep Think mode for enhanced reasoning and coding.

Citation: Business Insider. (2025). *OpenAI Says It Could Rebuild GPT-4 from Scratch.* https://www.businessinsider.com

Consumer-Level Integration

At WWDC 2025, Apple introduced system-wide AI features, including visual intelligence, smarter messaging, and personal assistants embedded across iOS and macOS, marking a new level of consumer AI integration.

Citation: TechRadar. (2025). *WWDC 2025 Recap*. https://www.techradar.com

These shifts demonstrate a clear trajectory from model innovation → enterprise tools → physical autonomy and social AI agents → highly efficient, integrated AI systems.

Legal and Ethical Ambiguities: Laws struggle to keep up with new AI developments.

As AI advances rapidly, legal and ethical frameworks are struggling to keep pace. Traditional laws and regulations were not designed with autonomous systems, generative content, or algorithmic decision-making in mind. This gap creates significant uncertainty for developers, users, and policymakers, raising difficult questions about responsibility, consent, transparency, and fairness. As AI systems increasingly make or influence real-world decisions—often in high-stakes domains like healthcare, law enforcement, or finance—new challenges emerge around accountability and regulation. Below are key examples illustrating these ongoing legal and ethical ambiguities.

1. **AI-Generated Content and Copyright**

   AI systems like GPT or DALL·E generate text, images, and music, but current copyright laws in most jurisdictions do not clearly address whether these outputs are protected, or who owns them—if anyone. This creates uncertainty for artists, creators, and businesses using generative AI commercially.

   Citation: U.S. Copyright Office. (2023). *Copyright Registration Guidance: Works Containing Material Generated by Artificial Intelligence.*

2. **Autonomous Vehicles and Liability**

   When a self-driving car is involved in an accident, determining who is legally responsible—the manufacturer, the software developer, the passenger—remains unclear in many jurisdictions. Few legal systems have established consistent liability standards for autonomous systems.

   Citation: Lin, P. (2016). *Autonomous Cars and Ethical Dilemmas.* In *Autonomous Driving*. Springer.

3. **Algorithmic Discrimination in Hiring and Lending**

   AI systems used in hiring and credit scoring have been shown to reproduce or even amplify societal biases, yet legal mechanisms for auditing and redressing these harms are often reactive or nonexistent. Many countries lack specific AI audit or accountability requirements.

Citation: Barocas, S., Hardt, M., & Narayanan, A. (2019). *Fairness and Machine Learning*. fairmlbook.org.

4. **AI in Law Enforcement and Surveillance**

   The use of facial recognition and predictive policing algorithms raises concerns about racial profiling, surveillance overreach, and due process violations. However, regulation is uneven or absent, particularly in countries with fewer data protection laws.

   Citation: EFF (Electronic Frontier Foundation). (2023). *The Case Against Facial Recognition Technology in Law Enforcement.*

5. **Medical AI and Informed Consent**

   In clinical settings, AI is increasingly used to assist with diagnosis or treatment decisions. Yet, patients are often unaware when AI is involved, and informed consent laws rarely require disclosure of algorithmic involvement.

   Citation: Price, W. N., & Cohen, I. G. (2019). *Privacy in the Age of Medical Big Data. Nature Medicine.*

Summary: Navigating the Complex Landscape of Modern AI

The landscape of AI is marked by rapid technological advancement, profound ethical questions, and increasing reliance on systems that must navigate human values. As AI capabilities evolve, from generative models and autonomous agents to robotics and real-world applications, new challenges emerge that require more than technical solutions.

Subjectivity plays a critical role in shaping how AI is designed, interpreted, and deployed. From fairness and bias in algorithmic decision-making to cultural differences in content moderation and user expectations, many AI systems operate in gray areas where objective correctness isn't enough. Systems trained on human data inevitably absorb human nuances, making it essential to incorporate ethical reasoning, transparency, and cultural sensitivity into development processes.

Meanwhile, the **evolving capabilities of AI,** seen in the rise of agentic systems, multi-modal models, and integration into business and consumer platforms—have outpaced traditional definitions and frameworks. AI is no longer just about classification or prediction; it's about generation, autonomy, and dynamic interaction with the physical and digital world. These advances require continuous updates to both technical understanding and operational oversight.

This evolution has outstripped the speed at which laws and regulations are developed, exposing gaps in **legal and ethical governance**.

Copyright, liability, informed consent, and algorithmic accountability remain unresolved in many jurisdictions. Regulators struggle to define and enforce standards for AI-generated content, autonomous decision-making, and fairness in high-stakes applications like hiring or law enforcement.

Together, these three dimensions highlight the pressing need for **interdisciplinary governance**, flexible regulatory frameworks, and inclusive dialogue. AI is not just a technical field; it is a societal force that must be guided by ethics, adapted through policy, and informed by human values.

4

THE FUTURE—STANDARDIZING AI DEFINITIONS

As artificial intelligence (AI) becomes increasingly embedded in everyday life, the need for a shared, precise, and universally accepted vocabulary grows more urgent. Differing definitions of AI-related concepts—such as fairness, autonomy, or explainability—can lead to inconsistencies in deployment, misinterpretations in regulation, and even ethical missteps. This chapter explores the global efforts to standardize AI terminology, the role of international organizations like ISO and IEEE, the impact of emerging regulations, and the importance of interdisciplinary collaboration in shaping a coherent AI future.

ISO and IEEE Standards: Building a Common AI Language

Two of the most influential bodies leading the charge in standardizing AI terminology are the **International Organization for Standardization (ISO)** and the **Institute of Electrical and Electronics Engineers (IEEE)**. Their ongoing efforts aim to establish global consensus on how AI systems should be defined, designed, and deployed.

DOI: 10.4324/9781003682530-5

ISO/IEC JTC 1/SC 42, the international committee on AI under ISO, has developed several standards including: **ISO/IEC 22989:2022**—Terminology and concepts for AI.

Supplement: ISO/IEC 22989:2022—Terminology and Concepts for AI

The ISO/IEC 22989:2022 standard, developed by the Joint Technical Committee ISO/IEC JTC 1/SC 42, provides a foundational vocabulary for the development and governance of AI. Its purpose is to ensure a shared understanding of basic AI terms across international contexts, helping to reduce ambiguity and support interoperability in technical and legal systems.

Key terms defined in ISO/IEC 22989:2022 include:

- Artificial Intelligence (AI): The capability of a system to acquire, process, and apply knowledge and skills.
- Machine Learning (ML): A subset of AI whereby systems improve their performance on a task through experience.
- Autonomous AI System: A system capable of performing tasks or making decisions without human intervention.
- Ethical AI: AI systems that are developed, deployed, and maintained in ways that align with ethical norms and values.
- Transparency: The degree to which a human can understand the internal mechanics or decision-making process of an AI system.
- Trustworthiness: The extent to which an AI system behaves reliably, safely, and in alignment with user expectations and legal norms.

ISO/IEC 22989:2022 serves as a baseline for global AI governance and is referenced by other technical standards (e.g., ISO/IEC 23053) and regulatory efforts, such as the EU AI Act. The standard is instrumental in enabling cross-border cooperation and benchmarking by providing a consistent conceptual framework.

As you can see, these definitions are too generic in our opinion and need more clarity.

ISO/IEC 23053:2022—Framework for AI system life cycle management.

Framework for Artificial Intelligence (AI) Systems Using Machine Learning (ML) was developed by the **ISO/IEC JTC 1/SC 42** subcommittee, which focuses on standardization in AI. This standard provides a structured

framework for understanding and managing AI systems that utilize ML, from development to deployment.

Key Purpose—ISO/IEC 23053:2022 establishes:

- A common framework and terminology for AI systems using ML.
- A **functional perspective** on components, data flows, and processes in ML-based AI systems.
- **Guidance for developers, regulators**, and **stakeholders** on structuring AI system lifecycles.

Core Elements in the Standard

1. **Functional Architecture**
   It defines a high-level **modular architecture** for ML systems, including:
   - Data collection
   - Data preparation
   - Model training
   - Evaluation
   - Inference
   - Feedback loops for retraining.
2. **Roles and Responsibilities**
   It outlines key actors involved in the system lifecycle:
   - Data providers
   - Model developers
   - System integrators
   - End users
   - AI governance authorities.
3. **System Lifecycle Stages**
   The standard aligns with ML development phases:
   - Design
   - Development
   - Deployment
   - Operation and Monitoring
   - Retirement or re-engineering.
4. **Trustworthiness Principles**
   The framework is designed to support AI that is:
   - Transparent
   - Explainable

- Robust
- Fair
- Secure and privacy-preserving.

Why It Matters—ISO/IEC 23053:2022 complements **ISO/IEC 22989:2022** by not only defining **what AI is**, but **how to practically structure, build**, and **oversee** ML-based systems. It helps ensure systems are consistent, reliable, and fit for international and multi-sector use.

These documents provide structured definitions for AI-related terms such as "autonomous systems," "machine learning," "neural networks," and "bias," supporting consistency across nations and sectors (ISO, 2022).

Similarly, **IEEE's Global Initiative on Ethics of Autonomous and Intelligent Systems** has produced influential guidelines under its *Ethically Aligned Design* framework. It advocates for technical standards that account for societal and ethical values and includes working groups focused on algorithmic transparency and data governance (IEEE, 2021).

"Without a standardized framework, stakeholders across countries and sectors cannot reliably align on what is meant by core AI concepts"—ISO/IEC SC 42.

Regulatory Definitions: Law Catching Up to Code

Governments are increasingly recognizing the importance of precise legal definitions for AI. One of the most ambitious efforts is the **European Union's AI Act**, which is the first major attempt to regulate AI systems based on their risk profiles.

The **EU AI Act (2021/0106)** defines key terms such as:

- **AI System**: Software developed using ML, logic-based, or knowledge-based approaches.
- **High-risk AI**: Systems that pose significant risks to health, safety, or fundamental rights.

These legal definitions are not just semantic, they carry legal consequences for compliance, enforcement, and liability. They also influence how AI is classified in cross-border trade and governance (European Commission, 2021).

Other jurisdictions such as Canada, Singapore, and Brazil have also begun drafting or adopting AI governance frameworks with their own interpretations, highlighting the global need for alignment (OECD, 2023).

Interdisciplinary Collaboration: Bridging Technical and Social Understandings

Standardizing AI terminology is not only a technical challenge—it's a **social and ethical one**. Terms like "fairness" or "transparency" differ depending on cultural values, disciplines, and stakeholder perspectives.

This is why interdisciplinary collaboration is critical. Initiatives like:

- The **Partnership on AI** (which includes companies, academics, and civil society groups)
- The **AI4People framework** (Floridi et al., 2018)
- Global ethics panels from UNESCO and OECD

...are working to define key AI principles in ways that balance **technological precision with ethical clarity**.

Ethicists and legal scholars stress that if AI systems are to be trusted and widely adopted, the terms we use to describe their behavior must be **understandable, agreed upon,** and **actionable** across sectors.

"Interdisciplinary consensus is not a luxury in AI governance—it is a necessity" (Floridi et al., 2018).

Challenges and the Path Forward

Despite momentum, challenges remain. Definitions must remain:

- **Flexible**, to adapt to rapid technological evolution
- **Culturally aware** to accommodate different global values
- **Technically grounded** to support implementation and compliance.

Continued cooperation among international standards bodies, regulatory agencies, and academic communities will be essential to ensure that **AI evolves responsibly and coherently**.

Conclusion

The standardization of AI definitions is foundational to building trustworthy, equitable, and legally sound AI systems. With global entities like ISO and IEEE setting technical baselines, regulators like the EU codifying legal clarity, and interdisciplinary collaborations shaping ethical guidance, we are moving toward a more harmonized AI ecosystem. But this future depends on maintaining ongoing dialogue and a shared commitment to defining AI not just by what it can do—but by what it should do.

Bibliography

European Commission. (2021). Proposal for a regulation of the European Parliament and of the Council laying down harmonised rules on artificial intelligence (Artificial Intelligence Act) and amending certain Union legislative acts (COM(2021) 206 final). *Publications Office of the European Union*. https://eur-lex.europa.eu/legal-content/EN/TXT/?uri=celex:52021PC0206

Floridi, L., Cowls, J., Beltrametti, M., et al. (2018). AI4People—An ethical framework for a good AI society. *Minds and Machines*, 28(4), 689–707. https://doi.org/10.1007/s11023-018-9482-5

IEEE. (2021). *Ethically Aligned Design: A Vision for Prioritizing Human Well-being with Autonomous and Intelligent Systems*. https://ethicsinaction.ieee.org/

ISO/ IEC. (2022). *Artificial Intelligence – Concepts and Terminology* (ISO/IEC 22989). International Organization for Standardization.

ISO/ IEC. (2022). *Artificial Intelligence – Framework for AI Systems Using Machine Learning* (ISO/IEC 23053).

ISO/ IEC. (2022). *Framework for Artificial Intelligence (AI) Systems Using Machine Learning (ML)*. ISO/IEC 23053:2022. https://www.iso.org/standard/77610.html

OECD. (2023). *AI Governance Initiatives*. https://www.oecd.org/going-digital/ai/

SECTION 2

AI REGULATIONS—A GLOBAL OVERVIEW

As artificial intelligence rapidly permeates critical sectors such as finance, healthcare, national security, and infrastructure, governments and international bodies have accelerated the development of regulatory frameworks to ensure responsible deployment. However, these regulations vary significantly in scope, philosophy, and enforcement mechanisms—reflecting differing national priorities, cultural values, and risk tolerances. Understanding this evolving regulatory landscape is essential not only for compliance, but also for strategic innovation, market entry, and long-term governance planning.

This section offers a structured global overview of AI regulation across three chapters:

- **Chapter 5: Key AI Regulations and Frameworks**—examines major regulatory efforts, including the EU AI Act, US Executive Orders, NIST AI Risk Management Framework, OECD AI Principles, ISO standards, China's AI governance policies, and more.

DOI: 10.4324/9781003682530-6

- **Chapter 6: Common Themes in AI Regulations**—identifies shared regulatory priorities such as transparency, accountability, human oversight, safety, risk classification, and data protection—despite differing implementation models.
- **Chapter 7: AI Regulatory Case Studies**—analyzes real-world enforcement and compliance examples to illustrate how regulations are being applied in practice across finance, healthcare, consumer technology, and critical infrastructure.

This section equips readers with both a comparative understanding of global AI regulation and the analytical framework needed to evaluate future policy developments with strategic clarity.

5

KEY AI REGULATIONS AND FRAMEWORKS

Introduction

As artificial intelligence (AI) becomes central to digital innovation, governments and industry bodies worldwide are developing regulatory frameworks and governance models to guide its responsible development and deployment. These regulations aim to address growing concerns around privacy, safety, bias, accountability, and ethical use. For organizations leveraging AI in products, services, or internal operations, understanding these frameworks is critical for compliance, trust-building, and long-term viability.

This chapter reviews key AI regulatory developments and voluntary frameworks that shape global AI governance today.

The EU Artificial Intelligence Act (EU AI Act)

The EU AI Act is the world's first comprehensive regulatory framework specifically designed to govern AI across all sectors. Officially adopted by the

DOI: 10.4324/9781003682530-7

European Parliament in 2024 and was expected to take full effect starting in 2025–2026 (with phased implementation), the Act sets a global benchmark for AI governance, accountability, and trust.

It introduces a risk-based approach to regulating AI systems, classifying them into four categories:

- Unacceptable risk (banned)
- High risk (heavily regulated)
- Limited risk (transparency obligations)
- Minimal risk (largely unregulated).

Key Provisions and Requirements

1. Prohibited AI Practices (Unacceptable Risk)
   The Act strictly prohibits AI systems that pose a clear threat to safety, livelihoods, or rights. These include:
   - Real-time biometric surveillance in public spaces (with narrow exceptions)
   - Social scoring by governments or companies
   - AI systems that manipulate human behavior or exploit vulnerabilities (e.g., targeting children or vulnerable populations)
   - Predictive policing based solely on profiling or behavioral analysis
2. High-Risk AI Systems
   These include AI used in critical sectors such as:
   - Employment (e.g., resume screening, candidate ranking)
   - Education (e.g., grading systems)
   - Healthcare (e.g., diagnostic AI tools)
   - Finance (e.g., credit scoring)
   - Critical infrastructure (e.g., power grids, transport)
   - Public services (e.g., benefits eligibility, justice systems).

   Providers of high-risk systems must:
   - Conduct conformity assessments before market deployment
   - Maintain risk management systems
   - Ensure human oversight
   - Provide detailed technical documentation
   - Implement robust cybersecurity and data governance measures.

3. Transparency Obligations (Limited Risk AI)

   For AI systems that interact with humans, such as chatbots or content generators:

   o Users must be clearly informed that they are interacting with AI
   o Systems must disclose deepfakes or AI-generated content.

4. Minimal Risk AI

   Most applications (e.g., AI in spam filters or recommendation engines) fall under this category and are permitted without heavy regulation, though voluntary codes of conduct and best practices are encouraged.

Enforcement and Penalties

The EU AI Act introduces strict enforcement mechanisms with tiered penalties:

- Up to €35 million or 7% of global annual turnover for violations of banned AI practices
- Up to €20 million or 4% for non-compliance with high-risk obligations
- Lesser penalties for failing to meet transparency or cooperation requirements.

National supervisory authorities and a newly established EU AI Office will oversee implementation and coordinate enforcement across member states.

Global Implications

- The Act is extraterritorial, meaning it affects any company offering AI systems within the EU market, regardless of origin.
- It's expected to become a model regulation, influencing AI governance frameworks globally—similar to how the GDPR shaped global data privacy laws.
- Organizations developing or deploying AI systems that touch the EU market must now audit, document, and potentially redesign their AI tools to meet these new requirements.

US Executive Order on Safe, Secure, and Trustworthy AI (2023)

This Executive Order directs US federal agencies to establish guidelines and testing standards for AI, promote safety, prevent discriminatory outcomes, and protect privacy. It outlines mandatory evaluations for foundation models and AI used in national security, critical infrastructure, and federal procurement.

The US Executive Order 14110, titled "Safe, Secure, and Trustworthy Development and Use of Artificial Intelligence," was signed by President Biden on October 30, 2023. Its goal was to establish a federal framework for ensuring AI systems developed or deployed in the United States follow principles of safety, security, transparency, equity, and accountability.

Key Provisions and Requirements

1. Safety, Security and Standardized Evaluations:
   - AI systems must undergo robust evaluations, testing, and resilience measures before deployment.
   - Post-deployment monitoring and performance testing required to ensure systems resist misuse.
2. Reporting and Disclosure for High-Stakes AI Systems:
   - Developers of foundation models or powerful AI systems must notify the US government if systems pose significant risks.
   - Share red-teaming and safety test results with federal agencies.
   - Use of the Defense Production Act to require such reporting.
3. Standards, Guidelines, and Coordination:
   - Directed NIST to develop AI-specific safety, security, and trustworthiness standards.
   - Required federal agencies to align with those standards and coordinate interagency efforts.
4. Content Provenance and Watermarking:
   - Called for labeling or watermarking AI-generated content to distinguish from human-generated materials.
   - Explore transparent disclosure of AI outputs.

5. Equity, Civil Rights, and Public Trust Safeguards:
   - o Enshrined equity, civil rights protection, consumer/workforce safety, and innovation as guiding principles.
   - o Ensure AI systems do not exacerbate discrimination or disadvantage marginalized groups.
6. Cross-Sector and Critical Infrastructure Risk Mitigation:
   - o Agencies to assess AI risks in biotech, infrastructure, cybersecurity, and develop mitigation strategies.
   - o Evaluation of AI risks in biological synthesis and dual-use applications.
   - o Standards to manage AI-based cybersecurity threats.

Implications for Cybersecurity Controls

- Pre-deployment risk testing and red-teaming, with mandatory disclosure.
- Ongoing system monitoring and anomaly detection.
- Strong model provenance, encryption, and integrity protections.
- Transparency mechanisms and watermarking of AI outputs.
- Interoperable testing protocols and compliance with NIST standards.
- Equity and bias controls, fairness testing, explainability.
- Cross-domain risk assessments, including cybersecurity and infrastructure.

Effectiveness and Revocation Status

EO 14110 was rescinded on January 20, 2025, by the new administration. While its direct legal force no longer applies, many of its frameworks and policy positions continue to influence future legislation and standardization.

NIST AI Risk Management Framework (AI RMF)

The NIST AI Risk Management Framework (AI RMF 1.0), released in January 2023, is a voluntary guidance framework intended to help organizations manage risks associated with AI systems. It emphasizes trustworthy AI as its foundation and is structured to promote flexibility, usability, and alignment with existing enterprise risk frameworks.

Core Components of the AI RMF

The AI RMF is divided into two parts:

1. Foundational Information: Outlines key terms, definitions, and characteristics of trustworthy AI.
2. The Core: Organized into four risk management functions—GOVERN, MAP, MEASURE, and MANAGE.

Four Core Functions

1. GOVERN:
   - Establish risk management policies and accountability structures.
   - Assign roles, responsibilities, and authority across AI lifecycle.
   - Foster an organizational culture of risk awareness and responsible innovation.
2. MAP:
   - Contextualize AI systems, including their intended purpose and potential risks.
   - Identify and document risk factors and stakeholder expectations.
   - Understand system limitations and dependencies.
3. MEASURE:
   - Use qualitative and quantitative tools to assess AI risks.
   - Evaluate trustworthiness characteristics (e.g., accuracy, reliability, robustness).
   - Track performance drift and unintended outcomes.
4. MANAGE:
   - Implement controls, safeguards, and governance mechanisms.
   - Prioritize and address risks across the AI lifecycle.
   - Incorporate feedback loops and continuous improvement practices.

Trustworthiness Characteristics

- Valid and Reliable
- Safe
- Secure and Resilient

- Explainable and Interpretable
- Privacy-Enhanced
- Fair—with Harm Mitigation
- Accountable and Transparent.

Cybersecurity Control Implications

- Risk identification processes for adversarial and misuse risks
- Secure development practices (robustness, resilience)
- Monitoring for bias, drift, and operational deviations
- Data protection and privacy engineering
- Human oversight mechanisms and system transparency
- Integration with cybersecurity frameworks (e.g., NIST CSF, ISO 27001).

References

- NIST AI RMF 1.0 (https://www.nist.gov/itl/ai-risk-management-framework)
- NIST Special Publication 1270 (Companion Playbook)
- NIST SP 800–53 Rev. 5 (Security and Privacy Controls)
- OECD AI Principles (2019).

Comparative Analysis of Global AI Regulations and Governance Frameworks

AI governance has rapidly evolved into a multilayered global ecosystem composed of binding regulations, national policy directives, voluntary frameworks, and ethical principles. While each instrument varies in scope, enforcement, and technical depth, together they represent a converging global understanding of what constitutes responsible AI. This comparative analysis synthesizes the major frameworks shaping the regulatory landscape today—the EU AI Act, US Executive Order 14110, NIST AI RMF, ISO/IEC AI standards, and the OECD AI Principles—and highlights where they diverge, where they reinforce each other, and what organizations must implement to remain compliant and trustworthy across jurisdictions.

Regulatory Scope and Legal Force

- EU AI Act—Global Reach and Hard Law

  The EU AI Act is the world's first comprehensive, binding AI regulation. Its risk-tiered approach (unacceptable, high, limited, minimal) and sweeping sector coverage make it the most consequential framework for global organizations. It is legally enforceable across the EU, extraterritorial in effect, and backed by penalties reaching up to 7% of worldwide annual revenue—placing it on par with or exceeding GDPR in regulatory weight.
- US Executive Order 14110—Policy Direction & Sector Activation

  Although rescinded in 2025, EO 14110 set durable expectations for AI safety testing, red-teaming, content provenance, civil-rights protections, and federal procurement requirements. Its concepts continue to influence agency rulemaking, risk guidance, and sector-specific regulations. Unlike the EU AI Act, EO 14110 imposed no direct financial penalties; its strength lies in shaping standards and expectations in regulated industries, national security, and US government contracting.
- NIST AI RMF—Voluntary, but Industry-Defining

  The NIST AI Risk Management Framework is voluntary and non-regulatory, yet highly influential. Organizations adopt it to structure their governance programs, and regulators increasingly reference it when evaluating AI risk practices. Once an enterprise declares alignment with the RMF, failure to meet its expectations can pose audit, litigation, and reputational risks. It is emerging as the de facto "how-to" operational framework for implementing trustworthy AI.
- ISO/IEC Standards—Global Alignment and Certifiable Governance

  ISO/IEC standards—particularly ISO/IEC 42001:2023 (AIMS)—offer a certifiable blueprint for AI governance. Where NIST provides process guidance, ISO mandates documented controls, audits, and management-system rigor. ISO integration with ISO 27001, 31000, and 9001 strengthens accountability, security, and lifecycle oversight. These standards do not impose fines but strongly influence procurement decisions and cross-border trust.
- OECD and Other Ethical Frameworks—Foundational Principles

  The OECD AI Principles, UNESCO AI Ethics Recommendations, Singapore's Model Framework, and the G7 Hiroshima Process define the global normative baseline: human-centered values, fairness, transparency, robustness, and accountability. These frameworks shape the values and policy objectives embedded in binding regulations. They have no punitive mechanisms, but their influence on national legislation and international cooperation is profound.

Requirements and Obligations Across Frameworks

A. Risk Management and Lifecycle Governance

All major frameworks converge on the requirement for structured, lifecycle-based AI risk management:

- EU AI Act: Risk management file and conformity assessments for high-risk systems
- NIST: GOVERN–MAP–MEASURE–MANAGE cycle
- ISO/IEC: Lifecycle controls across design, development, deployment, monitoring, and decommissioning
- OECD: Emphasis on continuous oversight and responsible stewardship.

The message is clear: AI risk management must be ongoing, proactive, and evidence-based.

B. Documentation, Transparency, and Traceability

Across the ecosystem, documentation is mandatory or strongly expected:

- Technical documentation, logs, data governance, system descriptions (EU AI Act)
- Data cards, model cards, decision records (NIST AI RMF)
- Audit logs, model traceability, documented governance processes (ISO 42001)
- Transparency and explainability requirements (OECD, EU, Singapore).

An AI system without documentation is effectively non-compliant under every major framework.

C. Human Oversight, Rights Protection, and Equity.

Human oversight is universally required for high-stakes applications:

- EU AI Act mandates human-in-the-loop controls for high-risk systems
- EO 14110 emphasized civil-rights protections and fairness requirements
- NIST and ISO embed oversight, harm mitigation, and stakeholder engagement
- OECD and UNESCO frame fairness, dignity, and human-centered design as essential values.

Organizations must show not only *that* oversight exists, but *how* it is exercised and monitored.

D. Cybersecurity, Robustness, and Safety Testing

Security requirements are converging across frameworks:

- EU AI Act mandates resilience against data poisoning, model manipulation, adversarial attacks
- EO 14110 required red-teaming, adversarial testing, and monitoring
- NIST and ISO detail secure development, threat modeling, and robustness evaluation
- OECD principles call for continuous safety and security across the AI lifecycle.

AI security is no longer optional; it is central to governance.

Synthesis: How These Frameworks Work Together

Despite differences in legal force, all frameworks share a common architectural logic:

Ethical Principles (OECD, UNESCO)

→ Legal Obligations (EU AI Act, US sector rules)
→ Operational Guidance (NIST AI RMF)
→ Governance Management Systems (ISO/IEC 42001)
→ Enterprise Controls (risk assessments, oversight, monitoring, documentation).

Organizations that adopt a unified governance model—built on risk classification, lifecycle controls, documentation, oversight, and monitoring—can satisfy all major frameworks with one operational approach.

What This Means for CISOs, CROs, CEOs, and Boards

1. AI Governance Is Now a Board-Level Responsibility

   Regulators expect boards to oversee AI risk with the same rigor as cybersecurity, privacy, and financial controls. Directors must understand the AI systems in use, their risk categories, and the governance mechanisms in place.

2. One Global AI Operating Model Is Required

   Fragmented, country-by-country compliance approaches will fail. Enterprises must build a unified governance system that maps cleanly to the EU AI Act, NIST, ISO/IEC 42001, and other frameworks.

3. Documentation and Traceability Are Non-Negotiable

   No documentation = no compliance. Boards must ensure the enterprise maintains:

   - Model inventories
   - Data governance records
   - Testing and evaluation evidence
   - Risk assessments and decision logs
   - Human oversight documentation.

4. Human Oversight and Rights Protections Must Be Operationalized

   Boards are accountable for ensuring systems do not introduce discrimination, harm, or rights violations. This now requires:

   - Bias testing
   - Civil-rights reviews
   - Explainability protocols
   - Human-in-the-loop controls.

5. AI Security Must Be Built Into the Model Lifecycle

   Each model must be protected from training-time and inference-time threats:

   - Adversarial testing
   - Red-teaming
   - Secure MLOps
   - Monitoring for attacks and drift
   - Incident response and rollback plans.

   AI security is becoming inseparable from AI governance.

6. High-Risk AI Requires Continuous Monitoring, Not One-Time Review

   Boards must insist on real-time monitoring for drift, degradation, or harmful impacts. Once-a-year audits are no longer sufficient.

7. Vendor and Third-Party AI Systems Present Significant Compliance Exposure

   Under EU AI Act and ISO/IEC 42001, companies are responsible for the AI they procure—not only what they build.

Every AI vendor must pass governance, transparency, and security assessments.

8. Liability Is Shifting Upward

   Where AI harms occur—bias, safety failures, misinformation, or rights violations—boards and executives will increasingly be held responsible for oversight failures, poor governance, or lack of controls.

9. Competitive Advantage Comes From Governance Maturity

   Organizations that demonstrate trustworthy AI:
   - Win customer trust
   - Accelerate procurement approvals
   - Reduce regulatory friction
   - Qualify for more markets (especially the EU)
   - Improve resilience and reduce operational risk.

   Governance is not a cost—it is an enabler of scale.

10. Platforms Like ValuRisQ / RiskQ Become Essential Infrastructure

    Boards need systems that automate:
    - AI inventory
    - Risk classification
    - Testing and evidence collection
    - Documentation
    - Monitoring and alerts
    - Regulatory mapping.

    This is where AI governance platforms deliver strategic value.

ISO/IEC AI Standards

The ISO/IEC Joint Technical Committee 1/Subcommittee 42 (JTC 1/SC 42) is responsible for international standards related to Artificial Intelligence (AI). These standards provide a global framework for the development, governance, and use of AI systems, focusing on trustworthiness, risk management, safety, interoperability, and ethical principles.

Key ISO/IEC AI Standards

1. ISO/IEC 22989:2022—AI Concepts and Terminology
   - Defines foundational concepts and establishes common terminology for AI.

Framework / Instrument	Scope & Jurisdiction	Legal Status	Primary Focus Areas	Penalties / Enforcement
EU Artificial Intelligence Act (EU AI Act)	Applies to providers, deployers, importers, and distributors of AI systems placed on or used in the EU market, regardless of where they are developed. Risk-based coverage: unacceptable, high, limited, minimal risk systems.	**Binding regulation** (EU law). Phased application starting~2025–2026.	Safety, fundamental rights, risk management, governance, transparency, high-risk lifecycle controls, documentation, human oversight.	**Severe administrative fines:** up to €35M or 7% of global annual turnover for banned practices; up to €20M or 4% for high-risk non-compliance; lower tiers for transparency / cooperation failures. National supervisory authorities + EU AI Office oversee enforcement.
U.S. Executive Order 14110 - Safe, Secure, and Trustworthy AI (2023)	U.S. federal government operations, federal procurement, national security, critical infrastructure, and high-risk / frontier models developed or deployed in the U.S.	**Executive policy instrument** (not a statute). **Rescinded Jan 20, 2025,** but still influential as a policy blueprint.	Safety testing, red-teaming, disclosure of high-risk models, NIST standards, content provenance, equity & civil rights, critical infrastructure risk.	No direct fines in the EO itself. Enforcement is via **agency directives, procurement requirements, and regulatory follow-on** (e.g., conditions for selling to U.S. government, sectoral regulators incorporating EO principles).
NIST AI Risk Management Framework (AI RMF 1.0)	Global applicability; primarily targeted at U.S. organizations but designed for any public or private entity managing AI risk.	**Voluntary guidance,** non-regulatory. Can be referenced in contracts, policies, or future regulations.	Enterprise AI risk management: GOVERN, MAP, MEASURE, MANAGE; trustworthy AI characteristics (valid, reliable, safe, secure, explainable, privacy-enhanced, fair, accountable).	No direct penalties. Enforcement only arises when **adopted into contracts, internal policies, or sectoral regulations.** Misalignment can still create liability or audit findings if an organization has committed to NIST principles.
ISO/IEC AI Standards (22989, 23053, 23894, 42001, 38507, etc.)	International; sector-agnostic. Applicable to organizations that **choose** to align or certify. ISO/IEC 42001 introduces an AI Management System (AIMS) that can be certifiable.	**Voluntary standards,** but **42001 can be used for certification** via accredited bodies. Often cited by regulators, auditors, and customers.	Concepts & terminology; lifecycle processes; AI risk management; AI management systems; board-level governance. Strong emphasis on traceability, documentation, oversight, and alignment with existing ISO systems (27001, 9001, 31000).	No regulatory fines from ISO itself. However, **failure to meet certified requirements can lead to loss Of certification, audit issues, contract non-compliance,** and reputational damage.
OECD Principles on AI (and G20 adoption)	Adopted by >40 countries as **high-level policy principles;** intended to guide national strategies and sectoral rules.	**Non-binding soft law /** intergovernmental principles. Influence national legislation and regulatory approaches.	Inclusive growth, human-centric values, transparency, robustness, safety, security, accountability. Act as a normative baseline for "trustworthy AI."	No direct penalties. Impact is via **translation into national laws,** funding priorities, procurement rules, and regulator expectations.
Other Frameworks & Initiatives (UNESCO, G7 Hiroshima Process, Singapore Model Framework, UK AI White Paper, WEF AI Governance Alliance)	Global and regional guidance spanning ethics, policy coordination, and practical governance (e.g., UNESCO ethics, G7 alignment, Singapore's industry playbook, UK flexible regulation).	**Non-binding frameworks and guidance,** sometimes used as reference by regulators, donors, and standard-setters.	AI ethics, human rights, safety, interoperability, practical governance patterns, regulatory coordination. Singapore's framework is particularly operational for industry.	No direct sanctions; influence comes from **alignment pressure,** expectations from multinationals, donors, and cross-border cooperation. Some pieces may later be operationalized into binding law in specific countries.

Table 5.1 Regulatory Comparison

Framework	Core Risk / Governance	Key Organizational	Transparency / Documentation	Human Oversight & Rights	Cybersecurity & Technical
EU AI Act	**Risk-based, legally binding framework** with four tiers (unacceptable, high, limited, minimal). High-risk systems subject to strict lifecycle controls;	For **high-risk** systems: risk management system, quality management, data governance, robustness & accuracy, logging, monitoring, post-market	Detailed **technical documentation**, logs, model performance evidence, risk management files; CE-like marking for compliant systems;	Explicit **human oversight requirements** for high-risk AI; protection of fundamental rights; bans on social scoring, manipulative and exploitative	Requires **robust cybersecurity**, resilience against data poisoning, model manipulation, and attacks; secure lifecycle processes; alignment with state of the art in
U.S. Executive Order 14110	**Policy and standards-driven** approach emphasizing safety, national security, equity, and critical infrastructure protection. Strong focus on "frontier" / foundation models.	Directs agencies to require **safety testing, red-teaming, and reporting** for high-risk and large-scale models; integrates AI risk into federal procurement; mandates development of sector-specific guidance.	Encourages **content provenance, watermarking**, disclosures to government on high-risk models, sharing of test results with designated agencies.	Stresses **civil rights, equity, anti-discrimination** in housing, employment, credit, criminal justice; instructs agencies to guard against disparate impact and reinforce human oversight.	Emphasizes **pre-deployment testing, continuous monitoring, anomaly detection,** cyber-risk assessments in biotech and infrastructure, and alignment with NIST security standards.
NIST AI RMF (GOVERN, MAP, MEASURE, MANAGE)	**Risk management lifecycle** integrated into enterprise risk and cybersecurity programs. Focus on **tustworthy AI characteristics** rather than prescriptive rules.	Establish governance structures, roles, and policies (GOVERN); inventory and context (MAP); metrics, testing, and evaluation (MEASURE); risk treatment and	Strong emphasis on **traceability**, documentation of design choices, data lineage, evaluation methods, and risk acceptance decisions; encourages model cards, data	Promotes **human oversight, accountability, and impact assessment** for affected stakeholders; encourages alignment with civil rights and	Encourages adversarial testing, robustness assessment, monitoring for drift, secure engineering practices, privacy-enhancing technologies and
ISO/IEC AI Standards (22989, 23053, 23894, 42001, 38507)	**Standardized, certifiable management and lifecycle approach;** integrates AI into existing ISO management systems and risk frameworks.	42001 requires an **AI Management System (AIMS)**: policies, objectives, risk processes, roles, internal audit, management review, corrective actions. 23053 and 23894 define lifecycle and risk processes across design–decommission.	Require **documented processes, risk assessments, lifecycle artefacts**, technical and organizational controls, audit evidence, and continuous improvement records; supports model cards, governance logs, and change records.	38507 targets **board-level governance** and alignment of AI use with ethical principles, stakeholder expectations, and legal obligations. Human oversight and accountability are baked into decision-making structures.	Address **robustness, safety, security, privacy, and data governance,** often integrated with ISO 27001, 27701, 31000, and 27005. Emphasize secure development lifecycle monitoring, logging, incident response, and traceability.
OECD AI Principles	**High-level normative framework** focused on human rights, democracy, and sustainability. Provides a values-based north star for national policies and	Encourage organizations and states to **embed AI into broader policy, R&D, and ecosystem strategies,** invest in trustworthy AI, and build capacity; not	Call for **transparency, explainability, and traceability** at a level appropriate to context; encourage communication with users about AI Stem capabilities	Strong focus on **human-centred values, fairness, non-discrimination, accountability, and meaningful human control** over AI systems, especially in high-	Require that AI systems be **robust, secure, and safe throughout the lifecycle,** with ongoing risk identification and mitigation, but leave implementation details to
Other Frameworks (UNESCO, G7, Singapore, UK, WEF)	Blend of **ethics, policy coordination, and practical governance.** Often bridge between high-level principles (like OECD) and more operational standards (NIST/ISO).	UNESCO: ethical obligations for states and organizations. Singapore: concrete model governance practices (e.g., explainability, data governance). UK: regulator-led, context-based oversight rather than single AI law.	Strong emphasis on **disclosure, documentation, and stakeholder communication;** Singapore and UK focus on practical explainability and audit trails.	Prioritize **human rights, cultural diversity, inclusion, and accountability,** with explicit ethics language (UNESCO) and multi-stakeholder oversight mechanisms.	Provide **guidance on robustness, safety, security, and risk,** encourage testing and validation, and promote interoperability with existing cybersecurity and privacy regimes, but no direct technical mandates.

Table 5.2 Requirements, Controls, and Thematic Emphasis

Framework / Region	Legal Force	Scop & Approach	Risk Classification?	Enforcement	Primary Focus	Ideal For
EU AI Act	**Legally binding law**	Horizontal – applies across all sectors	**Yes — 4-tier (Unacceptable → Minimal risk)**	Very strict (fines up to 7% global revenue)	Safety, fundamental rights, transparency	Companies selling into EU / high-risk use cases
U.S. Executive Order L4110	**Policy directive (not law)**	Federal agencies + influence on private sector	Indirect (focus on "high-risk" systems)	Soft enforcement via procurement & security classifications	Innovation + national security + civil rights	U.S.-based firms; foundation-model providers
NIST AI RMF	**Voluntary industry framework**	Enterprise governance & risk management	No — emphasizes lifecycle controls instead	None — guidance only	Trustworthy AI (Govern / Map/ Measure / Manage)	Enterprises designing internal responsible AI programs
SO/IEC 42001 & SC42	**Certifiable global standard**	Technical + management system standard	No — lifecycle & process-based	Market-led, audit-ready	Auditability, governance, interoperability	Global enterprises pursuing formal certification
DECD AI Principles	**Soft international policy**	Ethical & societal outcomes	No	None — norms & diplomacy	Human rights, fairness, accountability	Governments & enterprises seeking high-level alignment

Table 5.3 Fitting Regulation to Company Types

    - Supports consistent communication and policy alignment across industries and sectors.
2. ISO/IEC 23053:2022—AI System Lifecycle Processes
    - Provides a structured process framework for managing AI system lifecycles.
    - Covers stages such as design, development, deployment, monitoring, and decommissioning.
3. ISO/IEC 23894:2023—Risk Management for AI
    - Establishes principles and a structured approach for identifying, assessing, and mitigating AI risks.
    - Can be integrated with ISO 31000 (risk management) and ISO/IEC 27005 (information security risk management).
4. ISO/IEC 42001:2023—AI Management System Standard (AIMS)
    - First certifiable standard for managing AI risk, governance, and trust.
    - Integrates with other ISO management system standards such as ISO 27001 and ISO 9001.
    - Requirements include governance, risk identification, human oversight, transparency, and data quality.
5. ISO/IEC 38507:2022—Governance Implications of AI
    - Offers guidance to boards and executive leadership on the implications of AI for corporate governance.
    - Aligns AI use with ethical principles and stakeholder accountability.

Trustworthiness and Risk Control Themes

- Robustness and safety
- Transparency and explainability
- Accountability and human oversight
- Security, privacy, and data governance
- Alignment with ethical and legal norms

Cybersecurity and Compliance Implications

- Integration with ISMS (ISO/IEC 27001) and privacy standards (ISO/IEC 27701)
- Emphasis on lifecycle-based risk controls and technical documentation
- Support for auditability, monitoring, and performance validation

- Reinforcement of model traceability and input/output logging
- Applicability to global compliance regimes (e.g., EU AI Act, NIST AI RMF, GDPR).

References

- ISO/IEC 22989:2022
- ISO/IEC 23053:2022
- ISO/IEC 23894:2023
- ISO/IEC 42001:2023
- ISO/IEC 38507:2022
- https://www.iso.org/committee/6794475.html (SC 42 official page)

OECD Principles on Artificial Intelligence

Adopted by over 40 countries, the OECD AI Principles provide high-level guidance for responsible AI development and deployment. They emphasize human rights, democratic values, and sustainability.

The OECD Principles on Artificial Intelligence, adopted in May 2019 by 42 countries, are the first intergovernmental AI policy standards. These principles aim to promote responsible stewardship of trustworthy AI while fostering innovation and ensuring respect for human rights and democratic values. They serve as a foundational framework for both national and global AI governance initiatives.

Five Core OECD AI Principles

1. Inclusive Growth, Sustainable Development and Well-being:
    - AI should benefit people and the planet by driving inclusive and sustainable growth, innovation, and well-being.
    - Focus on long-term impacts and societal outcomes.
2. Human-Centered Values and Fairness:
    - AI actors should respect human rights, the rule of law, democratic values, and diversity.
    - Emphasis on fairness, non-discrimination, and inclusive design.
3. Transparency and Explainability:
    - AI systems should be transparent and understandable.

   - Individuals should have meaningful insight into how AI decisions are made, especially for high-stakes use cases.
4. Robustness, Security, and Safety:
   - AI systems must be robust, secure, and safe throughout their lifecycle.
   - Risks should be continuously identified, assessed, and managed.
   - Systems must perform reliably under normal and unexpected conditions.
5. Accountability:
   - Organizations and individuals developing, deploying, or operating AI should be held accountable for its proper functioning.
   - Clear mechanisms for redress and responsibility are required.

Implementation Guidance (Policy Recommendations)

- Invest in AI research and development.
- Foster a digital ecosystem for trustworthy AI.
- Shape policy and regulatory frameworks.
- Enable international cooperation.
- Build human capacity and prepare for labor market transitions.

Cybersecurity and Compliance Implications

- Embed human oversight and explainability into AI systems.
- Conduct ongoing risk and impact assessments.
- Ensure traceability and auditability of AI decisions.
- Implement security and robustness testing at every lifecycle stage.
- Align with ISO/IEC 42001, NIST AI RMF, and EU AI Act where applicable.

References

- OECD Principles on Artificial Intelligence: https://oecd.ai/en/ai-principles
- OECD AI Policy Observatory: https://oecd.ai
- G20 AI Principles (adopted from OECD): https://www.oecd.org/going-digital/ai/principles

Other Notable AI Frameworks and Initiatives

- UNESCO AI Ethics Guidelines: First global standard-setting instrument on AI ethics.
- G7 Hiroshima AI Process: Collaborative effort to align regulatory approaches.
- Singapore's Model AI Governance Framework: A practical, industry-friendly guide.
- UK AI White Paper (2023): Emphasizes flexible, context-based regulation over horizontal laws.
- AI Governance Alliance (WEF): Multi-stakeholder initiative to align best practices globally.

Conclusion

Understanding and aligning with key AI regulations and frameworks is essential for organizations developing or deploying AI systems. As regulatory landscapes evolve, proactive governance, ethical alignment, and risk-based strategies will be critical to maintaining compliance, protecting users, and enabling sustainable innovation in the AI era.

Bibliography

European Commission. (2024). *EU Artificial Intelligence Act.*
ISO/IEC. (2023). *ISO/IEC 23894:2023 Artificial Intelligence — Risk Management.*
NIST. (2023). *AI Risk Management Framework (AI RMF) 1.0.*
OECD. (2019). *Recommendation of the Council on Artificial Intelligence.*
Singapore Personal Data Protection Commission. (2020). *Model AI Governance Framework.*
UNESCO. (2021). *Recommendation on the Ethics of Artificial Intelligence.*
White House. (2023). *Executive Order on Safe, Secure, and Trustworthy AI.*

6

COMMON THEMES IN AI REGULATION

Introduction

Artificial intelligence (AI) is transforming economies, reshaping social systems, and redefining how decisions are made across critical domains such as healthcare, finance, hiring, education, transportation, and national security. In response, governments, standards bodies, and international coalitions are rapidly developing regulatory frameworks designed to ensure that AI technologies are safe, fair, transparent, and aligned with societal values.

Despite regional variation—such as the EU's comprehensive regulatory approach, the United States' sector-specific model, and Asia's mixture of innovation-driven and tightly supervised development—there is increasing convergence around a core set of governance themes. These shared principles include **risk-based oversight, transparency, accountability, fairness, privacy, safety, security, documentation,** and **ethical guardrails**.

DOI: 10.4324/9781003682530-8

These themes create a global governance blueprint for organizations seeking to adopt or scale AI technologies responsibly. By aligning with these common principles today, enterprises can not only meet current regulatory expectations but also prepare for the evolving international AI regulatory environment.

The Risk-Based Approach to AI Governance

Regulatory Alignment

Across nearly all jurisdictions, AI governance is now grounded in a **risk-based model**, where regulatory obligations increase as the impact, sensitivity, or likelihood of harm increases. The most explicit version of this model is the **EU AI Act**, which defines four categories—unacceptable, high, limited, and minimal risk. However, similar ideas appear across the US Executive Order 14110, Canadian Algorithmic Impact Assessment (AIA), Singapore's Model AI Governance Framework, and UK's pro-innovation AI regulatory strategy.

Why It Matters

A risk-based model recognizes that not all AI is equal. AI diagnosing cancer carries fundamentally different stakes than AI recommending movies. Regulatory expectations are therefore proportionate to potential harms.

Examples of High-Risk Domains

- Biometric identification and remote surveillance
- Medical diagnostics and treatment recommendation systems
- Credit scoring and lending decisions
- Hiring, promotion, and workforce monitoring
- Education and examination scoring
- Predictive policing or justice system recommendations
- Critical infrastructure management

Common Global Themes

- **Mandatory risk assessments** for high-risk models
- **Data quality controls** for training data used in sensitive decisions

- **Human oversight requirements** (e.g., review, override capability)
- **Post-deployment monitoring** to detect drift, bias, or failures.

Implication for Organizations

AI must be **classified, assessed, and documented** before deployment—and continuously thereafter.

Ref: EU AI Act (2024), Canada AIA (2020), UK AI White Paper (2023)

Transparency and Explainability

Transparency Requirements

AI regulations consistently require organizations to disclose:

- When users are interacting with AI (e.g., chatbots, recommendation systems)
- When content is AI-generated (deepfakes, synthetic media, LLM outputs)
- What data is collected and how it is used
- Whether decisions were automated.

Explainability Expectations

Explainability is essential in high-stakes contexts—especially those involving rights, benefits, safety, or employment. Regulators emphasize:

- Plain-language explanations, accessible to non-technical users
- Rationale for automated decisions
- The ability to contest or appeal AI-driven outcomes.

Global Alignment

- **FTC (U.S.)** requires substantiated, understandable explanations.
- **EU AI Act** mandates transparency and disclosure obligations.
- **OECD Principles (2019)** stress interpretability and user awareness.
- **China's Deep Synthesis Regulations (2022)** require visible labeling of synthetic content.

Transparency is now a foundational requirement across all AI governance models.

Accountability and Human Oversight

Defining Accountability

Accountability ensures **humans—not algorithms—are ultimately responsible** for AI outcomes. This requires:

- Clearly assigned roles for oversight
- Governance structures with defined responsibilities
- Escalation mechanisms for harms or incidents.

Human Oversight Expectations

Most frameworks require:

- **Human-in-the-loop (HITL)**—humans review and approve critical decisions
- **Human-on-the-loop**—humans can monitor and intervene if needed
- **Human-in-command**—humans retain ultimate authority

Examples of Accountability Mechanisms

- Documented approval chains
- Risk ownership assignment
- AI ethics committees
- Audit committees for high-risk models

International Examples

- ISO/IEC 42001 embeds accountability into management systems.
- EU AI Act requires "appropriate human oversight" for all high-risk systems.
- Singapore's Model Framework emphasizes clear RACI assignments.

Accountability is now seen as essential for both **legal liability** and **trust worthiness**.

Data Governance and Privacy Protection

Data Is the Foundation of AI

Nearly all AI harms—bias, privacy breaches, misinformation, discrimination—stem from inadequate data governance.

Regulatory Requirements

AI-related privacy requirements build upon existing global privacy regimes:

- **GDPR (EU)**: Purpose limitation, fairness, data minimization, right to explanation
- **CPRA (California)**: Automated decision-making disclosures and opt-out mechanisms
- **PIPEDA (Canada)**: Meaningful consent for AI-driven decisions
- **China PIPL**: Strict rules around sensitive data processing

Core Data Governance Expectations

- Clearly defined data sources and lawful bases for processing
- Data quality validation and cleansing
- Documentation of data lineage and provenance
- Appropriate retention and deletion policies
- Security controls for data access and storage

Emerging Practices

- Privacy-enhancing technologies (PETs)
- Synthetic data generation
- Federated learning

Data governance is becoming the backbone of all AI regulations globally.

Fairness, Equity, and Non-Discrimination

Why Fairness Matters

AI systems that affect rights and opportunities must not discriminate against protected classes. Regulators now expect algorithmic fairness to be **measured, documented,** and **verified**.

Bias and Discrimination Controls

- Bias testing before and after deployment
- Documentation of performance across demographic groups
- Mitigation plans for identified disparities
- Ongoing fairness monitoring (e.g., drift-related bias)
- Independent third-party audits for high-stakes models

Regulatory Examples

- US EEOC guidance on AI in hiring (2023)
- New York City Local Law 144 (automated hiring tools mandate bias audits)
- EU AI Act high-risk system fairness requirements
- India's NITI Aayog Principles emphasize inclusivity and non-discrimination.

Fairness is no longer an ethical recommendation—it is a regulatory requirement.

Safety, Security, and Robustness of AI Systems

Safety Requirements

Safety includes ensuring AI performs reliably, as intended, and without causing harm through:

- System failures
- Unexpected behavior
- Model or data drift
- Operational instability.

Security Requirements

AI systems must be resilient against:

- Adversarial attacks
- Data poisoning
- Model extraction

- Prompt injection (for LLMs)
- Malicious fine-tuning or system jailbreaks.

Regulatory Frameworks Emphasizing Security

- NIST AI RMF (2023): dedicated categories for robustness, resilience, and security
- EU AI Act: mandates cybersecurity controls for high-risk systems
- China's Generative AI Measures: require mitigation of harmful outputs
- US EO 14110: emphasizes red-team testing for frontier models.

Safety and security are now inseparable components of AI reliability.

Documentation, Auditability, and Traceability

Documentation Expectations

Regulators expect organizations to generate and maintain:

- AI system descriptions
- Training data and data processing documentation
- Risk management files
- Evaluation reports, metrics, and model performance logs
- Monitoring dashboards
- Change logs and versioning histories.

Why Auditability Matters

Auditability ensures:

- Regulatory review
- Internal accountability
- Legal defense
- Trustworthiness and transparency.

Global Examples

- EU AI Act: extensive documentation requirements for high-risk systems
- ISO/IEC 42001: internal audits, management reviews, and lifecycle documentation

- NIST RMF: traceability and documentation of all design decisions
- NYC Law 144: audit logs for hiring systems.

Documentation is not optional—it's a regulatory obligation and a cornerstone of good governance.

Ethical Use and Prohibited Practices

Although regulations differ by region, many **banned or restricted AI practices** appear consistently across global regimes.

Commonly Prohibited or Restricted AI

- Manipulative or exploitative AI
- Social scoring of citizens (EU prohibition; China uses it but regulates algorithmic scoring in other contexts)
- Unconsented biometric surveillance
- Emotion recognition in workplaces or schools (restricted or banned in EU)
- Deceptive deepfakes or synthetic content without disclosure
- AI systems that undermine democratic processes.

Global Examples

- EU AI Act bans several categories of manipulative or rights-harming AI
- US FTC prohibits the deceptive use of automated systems
- China's Deep Synthesis Rules require labeling of generated content
- UNESCO guidelines emphasize ethical boundaries for AI development.

Governments are drawing clear lines to prevent harmful or abusive uses of AI.

International Convergence and Divergence

Convergence

Across regions, strong alignment exists on:

Theme	**EU AI Act (2024)**	**U.S. (Executive Orders & NIST)**	**China (CAC, 2022-2023)**	**OECD / Global Standards**
Approach	Risk-based, legally binding	Sectoral, voluntary frameworks	State-driven oversight, alignment with social goals	Principles-based
Risk Categories	Unacceptable, High, Limited, Minimal	No formal categories	Banned vs. restricted vs. permitted	Encourages risk-based
Transparency	Disclosure & explainability required	FTC requires disclosure	Labeling deepfakes required	OECD Principle 3
Accountability	Providers/operators liable	Shared responsibility; voluntary audits	Platforms directly accountable	ISO/IEC 42001
Data Protection	Tied to GDPR	Tied to sectoral laws (HIPAA, CPRA, etc.)	Data localization & security reviews	OECD privacy alignment
Fairness	Explicit anti-bias testing	EEOC guidance on hiring A1	Avoid "harmful" content to social stability	OECD fairness principle
Security	Testing & robustness mandatory	NIST AI RMF security focus	Government security testing mandatory	NIST & ISO standards
Banned Practices	Social scoring, manipulative AI	None yet federally banned	Deepfake misuse, destabilizing content	Encourages ethical guardrails

Table 6.1 International Convergence and Divergence

- Risk-based governance
- Transparency requirements
- Human oversight
- Data quality and privacy protections
- Fairness and anti-discrimination
- Safety and cybersecurity
- Documentation and auditability.

Divergence

However, there are notable differences:

- **EU**: comprehensive, binding, horizontal regulation
- **United States**: sector-specific, industry-driven, decentralization
- **China**: state-supervised, security-centered, rapid rulemaking
- **UK/Singapore**: flexible, innovation-centric, guidance-first models

Despite divergent strategies, the **core principles are converging globally**.

The Role of Standards

Standards provide the technical and operational backbone that connects diverse regulatory environments.

Key Standards

- **ISO/IEC 22989:2022**—Definitions and terminology
- **ISO/IEC 23053:2022**—AI system lifecycle processes
- **ISO/IEC 23894:2023**—Risk management for AI
- **ISO/IEC 42001:2023**—AI Management Systems certifiable
- **NIST AI RMF (2023)**—US risk management playbook
- **OECD AI Principles (2019)**—Foundational global governance norms.

Why Standards Matter

- Enable **interoperability** across jurisdictions
- Provide **structured governance methods**

- Support **audits, certification,** and **compliance assurance**
- Reduce ambiguity and accelerate internal adoption
- Help translate legal requirements into operational processes.

Standards act as the connective tissue between high-level principles and day-to-day enterprise controls.

Conclusion

Across the globe, AI regulation is coalescing around a consistent set of themes: **risk-based oversight, transparency, accountability, privacy, fairness, robustness, security, documentation, and ethical constraints**. While implementation differs across jurisdictions, these shared principles provide organizations with a stable foundation for building trustworthy AI systems.

Enterprises that proactively adopt these principles—supported by strong governance frameworks, continuous monitoring, structured risk assessment, and comprehensive documentation—will not only achieve regulatory compliance but also position themselves as leaders in responsible and trustworthy AI innovation.

AI Regulatory Compliance Checklist

As AI regulations mature across regions, organizations face increasing pressure to demonstrate that their systems are trustworthy, transparent, and compliant. Yet regulatory documents—spanning hundreds of pages across the EU AI Act, NIST frameworks, ISO/IEC standards, OECD principles, and national laws—can be difficult for practitioners to translate into concrete operational requirements.

The **AI Regulatory Compliance Checklist** simplifies this complexity by distilling the overlapping global requirements into a unified, actionable framework. It captures the essential controls that regulators, auditors, and supervisory authorities expect organizations to implement across the AI lifecycle. Whether an organization is deploying high-risk AI systems or managing lower-risk tools, this checklist provides a structured approach for assessing readiness, identifying gaps, and guiding governance improvements.

This checklist is not merely a compliance tool—it is a practical roadmap for building trustworthy AI programs that are resilient, fair, transparent, secure, and aligned with emerging global norms.

AI Regulatory Compliance Checklist

Use this checklist to evaluate whether an AI system or enterprise AI program meets the common expectations across global AI regulations and governance frameworks.

Risk Classification and Impact Assessment

- AI system inventoried and registered within enterprise AI inventory
- Risk level assigned (unacceptable, high, moderate, limited, minimal)
- Impact assessment completed (e.g., AIA, DPIA)
- Documented purpose, context, and intended use
- Stakeholder impact analysis completed
- High-risk systems documented in a regulatory risk management file
- Roles and responsibilities assigned.

Applies to: EU AI Act, NIST AI RMF, ISO 23894, Canada AIA, Singapore Model Framework

Data Governance and Privacy Controls

- Training data sources identified and documented
- Data lineage and provenance mapped
- Lawful basis for data collection established (GDPR/CPRA/etc.)
- Sensitive data minimized or properly justified
- Privacy impact assessment completed
- Data quality validation performed (accuracy, representativeness, completeness)
- PETs (anonymization, differential privacy, federated learning) implemented if needed
- Data retention and deletion policies applied.

Applies to: GDPR, CPRA, PIPL (China), EU AI Act, ISO/IEC 27701, NIST

Fairness, Equity and Non-Discrimination

- Bias/fairness testing performed on relevant protected attributes
- Disparate impact analysis completed and documented
- Remediation procedures for bias defined
- Fairness metrics continuously monitored post-deployment
- Independent or third-party audit for high-stakes systems
- Stakeholder/affected group review (as appropriate).

Applies to: EEOC, EU AI Act, NYC Local Law 144, OECD Principles, ISO 42001

Transparency and Explainability

- Users notified when interacting with AI
- AI-generated content labeled (e.g., deepfakes, synthetic media)
- Explanations provided in plain language for decisions
- Model documentation includes explanation methodology
- Content provenance/watermarking implemented where required
- User rights explained (appeal, contest, opt-out where relevant).

Applies to: EU AI Act, FTC guidance, China Deep Synthesis Regulations, EO 14110

Human Oversight and Accountability

- Human-in-the-loop or human-on-the-loop process defined
- Humans trained to oversee, intervene, and overrule AI decisions
- Governance bodies established (AI Ethics Committee, Risk Committee, etc.)
- Executive or board-level accountability assigned
- Incident escalation and override protocols in place
- Regular governance reviews and re-certification cycles.

Applies to: ISO/IEC 42001, EU AI Act, NIST AI RMF

Safety, Security, and Robustness

- Adversarial testing performed (evasion, poisoning, prompt risk)
- Red-team testing conducted pre-deployment for high-risk models
- Model robustness validated across scenarios and stress conditions
- Cybersecurity protections embedded in MLOps pipeline
- Monitoring for drift, instability, or abnormal outputs
- Incident response playbook for AI failures or attacks
- Change management and version-control applied.

Applies to: NIST AI RMF, EO 14110, EU AI Act, ISO 42001, China Security Standards

Documentation, Logging, and Traceability

- Technical documentation prepared and up to date
- Model cards, data cards, and system cards completed
- Logs maintained for inputs, outputs, decisions, and training data
- Audit-ready files maintained for regulators
- Records stored securely and follow retention requirements
- Testing and validation evidence stored

Applies to: EU AI Act, ISO/IEC 42001, NIST, Singapore, OECD

Ethical Use and Prohibited Practices

- Confirm system does not violate banned or restricted AI categories
- Emotional analysis, biometric surveillance, or manipulative AI reviewed for legality
- Social scoring prohibited
- Explicit consent obtained for biometric or sensitive uses
- Deepfake ethical requirements followed (labeling, disclosure, and safety layer).

Applies to: EU AI Act, China Deep Synthesis rules, UNESCO AI Ethics Framework

Vendor and Third-Party AI Oversight

- Third-party AI tools documented in vendor inventory
- External AI providers undergo risk and governance review
- Contractual requirements for transparency, logs, and audits
- Security and privacy controls validated
- Responsible AI commitments included in procurement.

Applies to: EU AI Act obligations for "deployers," ISO 42001, NIST, various procurement laws

Final Compliance Scorecard

You can score each section:

- **Fully compliant** (Yes)
- **Partially compliant** (In progress)
- **Non-compliant** (No)
- **Not applicable**.

This becomes the basis for executive reporting, gap analysis, and board-level governance.

Case Study: Implementing AI Governance in a Global Financial Institution

Introduction to the Case Study

To illustrate how the common themes of AI regulation translate into real-world practice, the following case study presents a detailed look at how a global financial institution operationalized responsible AI at scale. While fictionalized for confidentiality, the scenario is based on patterns observed across leading banks, insurers, and fintech organizations navigating high-stakes AI governance.

The case study follows the institution through its multi-phase journey: from building an enterprise AI inventory, to implementing rigorous data governance, to embedding fairness testing, explainability, security, and human oversight. It demonstrates how risk-based regulation, international standards, and best-practice frameworks converge into a coherent governance model.

By tracing this transformation end-to-end, the case study provides practitioners, executives, and regulators with a concrete example of what effective AI governance looks like in practice—and how organizations can use compliance not just as a defensive safeguard, but as a strategic advantage.

Background

FinSolve Bank, a multinational financial institution operating in 22 countries, deploys AI models for:

- Credit risk scoring
- Fraud detection
- Loan pricing
- Customer service chatbots
- AML transaction monitoring.

After the adoption of the EU AI Act and heightened scrutiny from US, UK, and APAC regulators, the bank recognized that its existing AI practices were fragmented and insufficient for global compliance.

Phase 1: Building the AI Inventory and Risk Classification Model

FinSolve created a centralized **AI Inventory** aligned with ISO/IEC 42001 and NIST AI RMF.

Each system was classified into risk tiers:

This classification mapped directly to the **EU AI Act's risk taxonomy** and triggered different levels of documentation, monitoring, and oversight.

Phase 2: Data Governance Overhaul

The bank discovered significant challenges:

- Training data lacked clear provenance
- Legacy historical data contained discriminatory patterns
- Different business units used inconsistent labeling practices.

AI System	Risk Category	Reason
Credit Scoring Model	**High Risk**	Impacts financial access & rights
Fraud Detection	High Risk	Security, false positives harm customers
Customer Chatbot	Limited Risk	Interaction transparency required
Loan Pricing Optimizer	High Risk	Risk of discrimination & unfair pricing
Anti–Money Laundering Model	High Risk	Regulatory enforcement environment

Table 6.2 AI Risk Classifications

Using GDPR, ISO 27701, and NIST privacy engineering guidance, FinSolve implemented:

- A unified data governance architecture
- Full data lineage mapping
- Data quality scoring
- A secure data lake for AI development
- Differential privacy for customer-sensitive models.

This improved **model accuracy**, **fairness**, and **regulatory defensibility**.

Phase 3: Bias, Fairness, and Explainability Controls

FinSolve established a **Model Fairness Office** staffed with data scientists, risk analysts, and legal advisers.

For the credit scoring model:

- Disparate impact analyses were conducted monthly
- SHAP-based explainability reports were integrated into loan decision workflows
- The bank implemented a customer-facing "Why this decision?" explanation tool
- Human credit officers reviewed edge cases flagged by the system.

Regulators later praised the bank for its "industry-leading transparency."

Phase 4: Safety, Security, and Red-Teaming

The cybersecurity team integrated AI security into the broader SOC and MLOps workflow:

- Red-teams conducted evasion and poisoning tests
- The fraud model underwent adversarial simulation (e.g., synthetic fraud patterns)
- Model monitoring flagged drift in fraud patterns during holidays
- A rollback protocol was created for model failure events.

These controls aligned with **NIST AI RMF**, **EO 14110**, and the **EU AI Act's cybersecurity requirements**.

Phase 5: Governance, Oversight, and Audit Structure

FinSolve Bank implemented ISO/IEC 42001-style governance:

- AI Ethics & Risk Committee reporting to the board
- Model approval workflow with legal, privacy, and risk sign-off
- Annual external audits for high-risk systems
- Quarterly performance, fairness, and drift reports.

This structure ensured **clear accountability**, **consistent oversight**, and **documented compliance**.

Outcome

Within 18 months, FinSolve:

- Achieved **full alignment** with the EU AI Act's high-risk system requirements
- Passed regulatory examinations in the United States and United Kingdom with strong ratings
- Reduced false positives in fraud detection by 23%
- Lowered discrimination risk in credit scoring by 31%

- Improved customer trust ratings by 18%
- Became an early adopter of ISO/IEC 42001 certification.

FinSolve now markets itself as a global leader in **trustworthy AI**, using its governance capabilities as a competitive advantage in securing customers, regulators, and partners.

Bibliography

California Privacy Rights Act. (2020). Proposition 24, Cal. Civil Code §§ 1798.100–1798.199.100. https://leginfo.legislature.ca.gov/faces/codes_displaySection.xhtml?lawCode=CIV&sectionNum=1798.100

City of New York. (2023). *Local Law 144 Regulating Automated Employment Decision Tools.*

European Parliament. (2024). *EU Artificial Intelligence Act.*

European Union. (2016). *General Data Protection Regulation.*

Federal Trade Commission. (2023). *Guidance on AI Transparency and Accountability.*

International Organization for Standardization. (2022). *ISO/IEC 22989: Artificial Intelligence Concepts and Terminology.*

International Organization for Standardization. (2023). *ISO/IEC 23894: Artificial Intelligence Risk Management.*

International Organization for Standardization. (2023). *ISO/IEC 42001: Artificial Intelligence Management System.*

National Institute of Standards and Technology. (2023). *AI Risk Management Framework.*

OECD. (2019). *Recommendation of the Council on Artificial Intelligence.*

Office of the Privacy Commissioner of Canada. (2018). *Personal Information Protection and Electronic Documents Act.*

People's Republic of China. (2021). *Personal Information Protection Law.*

Treasury Board of Canada Secretariat. (2020). *Algorithmic Impact Assessment.*

UNESCO. (2021). *Recommendation on the Ethics of Artificial Intelligence.*

U.S. Equal Employment Opportunity Commission. (2023). *Guidance on AI in Employment Decisions.*

7

CYBERSECURITY AND AI REGULATORY USE CASES

Introduction

As artificial intelligence (AI) becomes foundational to cybersecurity, digital forensics, fraud detection, identity verification, and national defense, regulators worldwide are moving quickly to define rules, expectations, and constraints around its use. AI now plays a critical role in both **defending systems** (through threat detection, anomaly monitoring, malware classification) and **attacking them** (through automated phishing, adversarial manipulation, and autonomous exploitation tools). This dual-use nature elevates AI to the center of regulatory attention.

Governments, supervisory authorities, and standards bodies—including the European Union, the United States, China, the United Kingdom, Singapore, and the OECD—are shaping a landscape where cybersecurity and AI governance are deeply intertwined. Compliance is no longer limited to data protection; organizations must demonstrate **robustness, transparency, fairness, security, explainability, human oversight, and documentation** for AI systems operating in sensitive domains.

DOI: 10.4324/9781003682530-9

This chapter explores **real-world regulatory use cases** at the intersection of cybersecurity and AI governance. These use cases illustrate how emerging global regulations—including the EU AI Act, NIST AI RMF, GDPR, NYDFS, MAS FEAT, China's cybersecurity rules, and US defense standards—shape requirements for deploying AI responsibly across security-critical applications.

Regulatory Drivers for AI and Cybersecurity Oversight

Governments are responding to several converging forces that significantly heighten regulatory scrutiny around AI in cybersecurity:

AI's Integration into Critical Infrastructure

AI is being embedded into:

- Power grid monitoring
- Water system control
- Telecom service management
- Air traffic communications
- Transportation systems (autonomous or semi-autonomous)

Regulators require that such systems demonstrate **robustness, safety under stress, fault tolerance**, and **protection against adversarial compromise**.

Growing Threat of Cyberattacks Targeting AI Models

Attackers now target AI systems directly:

- **Data poisoning** to corrupt model training
- **Model evasion** to bypass detection
- **Model extraction** to steal proprietary capabilities
- **Prompt-injection** attacks for LLM systems
- **Membership inference** to recover sensitive data.

National cybersecurity standards increasingly require explicit controls for protecting the model itself—not just the surrounding IT environment.

AI's Expanding Role in Surveillance, Profiling, and Decision-Making

Governments are concerned about:

- Facial recognition misuse
- Emotion recognition in employment or schools
- Predictive policing
- Algorithmic discrimination
- Automated offensive cyber capabilities.

These concerns lead to bans, strict limitations, or mandatory oversight in multiple jurisdictions.

Rising Expectations for AI Governance

Across jurisdictions, regulators now expect organizations to demonstrate:

- **Transparency** (informing individuals when AI is used)
- **Privacy protection** (minimization, lawful basis, secure data handling)
- **Fairness** (bias mitigation in cybersecurity decisioning)
- **Accountability** (auditable AI processes and human oversight)
- **Security** (robustness testing and adversarial evaluation).

These drivers collectively shape the regulatory use cases below.

Use Case 1: EU AI Act and Cyber Risk Classification

The **EU Artificial Intelligence Act** defines the world's most comprehensive legal framework for AI, categorizing systems by risk and imposing significant obligations on high-risk systems—many of which directly relate to cybersecurity.

Cyber-Relevant AI Systems Classified as High-Risk

Under the Act, high-risk cybersecurity systems include:

- Biometric identification and verification
- Intrusion detection and network monitoring AI

- Predictive crime analysis or behavioral profiling
- Identity fraud detection
- Security assessments affecting rights (e.g., employee monitoring)
- Critical infrastructure protection.

Compliance Requirements

Organizations must implement:

- Risk management and mitigation processes
- Human oversight and intervention capabilities
- Robustness and adversarial resistance testing
- Detailed technical documentation
- Logging, traceability, and auditability
- Post-market monitoring.

Example

An EU-based MSSP offering an AI-driven threat detection engine must:

- Demonstrate resilience to adversarial evasion
- Document training data lineage and quality
- Register the model in the EU high-risk database
- Provide logs and explanations for flagged incidents.

The EU AI Act sets the **regulatory baseline for cybersecurity AI** globally.

Use Case 2: US Executive Order on Trustworthy AI and Federal Cyber Programs

The now-rescinded but highly influential **US Executive Order 14110 (2023)** established requirements for secure AI development within the federal government and its supply chain.

Cybersecurity-Specific Requirements

Federal agencies must:

- Perform red-team testing of safety and security vulnerabilities
- Evaluate AI systems for privacy and civil-rights risks
- Implement supply chain risk management for AI components
- Conduct ongoing monitoring for misuse, drift, or instability
- Report the training, testing, and operational details of high-impact AI

AI used in national security, defense, or federal contracting must comply with **stringent robustness, transparency**, and **documentation mandates**.

Example

A federal contractor supplying AI-based malware detection tools must:

- Adopt NIST-driven cybersecurity protocols
- Validate model resistance to adversarial modifications
- Disclose vulnerabilities or incidents involving AI
- Maintain end-to-end model development documentation.

While the EO was rescinded, the **policy apparatus and regulatory expectations it created endure**.

Use Case 3: NIST AI RMF Integration with Cybersecurity Frameworks

The **NIST AI Risk Management Framework** provides a voluntary but influential structure for assessing and controlling AI risk across the lifecycle. Unlike the EU AI Act, the RMF integrates directly with cybersecurity practice.

AI RMF Function	Cybersecurity Integration
GOVERN	Security policies, oversight, roles, accountability
MAP	Threat Modelling, system definition, supply chain risk
MEASURE	Testing for robustness, drift, performance degradation
MANAGE	Incident response, continuous monitoring, patching

Table 7.1 How It Intersects with Cybersecurity

Organizations map NIST AI RMF functions to the NIST Cybersecurity Framework (CSF):

Example

A Fortune 500 company running an ML fraud analytics model performs:

- Threat modeling for model extraction
- Bias testing to avoid discriminatory fraud flagging
- Drift detection to ensure accuracy over time
- Alignment between cyber incident response and AI incident response.

NIST frameworks provide the **practical blueprint** for operationalizing AI governance in cybersecurity functions.

Use Case 4: GDPR and Automated Decision-Making

Under **GDPR Article 22**, individuals have the right **not to be subject solely to automated decisions** that significantly affect them.

This includes cybersecurity outcomes such as:

- Automated transaction blocking
- Denial of access based on risk scoring
- Fraud alert escalation
- Identity verification failures.

Compliance Expectations

Organizations must ensure:

- Human oversight for high-impact cybersecurity decisions
- Transparency regarding automated decisions
- Rights to contest and appeal
- Clear explanations (how the model reached its conclusion).

Example

A fintech firm using AI to automatically block suspicious transactions must:

- Provide customers a mechanism to challenge decisions
- Clearly disclose that algorithmic logic is being applied
- Offer meaningful human review pathways.

GDPR elevates cybersecurity AI into a domain requiring **privacy, fairness**, and **procedural due process**.

Use Case 5: Financial Sector AI Governance (NYDFS, MAS, PRA, EBA)

Financial regulators are among the most advanced in governing AI for cybersecurity because of the high stakes—fraud, insider threats, AML, identity theft, and systemic financial stability.

Key Sector Frameworks

- **NYDFS Guidance on AI and ML (US)**
- **MAS FEAT Principles (Singapore)**
- **EBA/ECB Guidelines (EU)**
- **PRA/FCA AI Supervisory Statements (UK)**.

Cybersecurity-Relevant Expectations

Financial institutions must ensure:

- Explainability for fraud, AML, and behavioral analytics AI
- Bias mitigation, especially in credit or fraud decisions
- Documentation for model validation and governance
- Monitoring of false positives and operational risk
- Secure MLOps, data privacy, and robust testing.

Example

A US bank using AI for AML monitoring under NYDFS must:

- Conduct model governance reviews
- Provide explainability for flagged transactions
- Document model changes to regulators
- Monitor operational risk created by AI-induced false positives.

Financial regulators treat cybersecurity AI as **safety-critical infrastructure**.

Use Case 6: Adversarial ML and National Security Regulations

Adversarial machine learning is now recognized as a national security threat. Governments are beginning to **mandate defenses against adversarial attacks**.

Requirements Across Jurisdictions

Agencies such as DHS, DOD, EU Cyber Agency (ENISA), and China CAC require:

- Robustness testing against evasion and poisoning
- Red-teaming of autonomous or semi-autonomous systems
- Incident reporting for AI-specific vulnerabilities
- Secure development environments
- Hardened MLOps pipelines.

Example

A defense contractor supplying AI for autonomous drones must:

- Validate the model against adversarial perturbations
- Demonstrate resistance to spoofing or sensor manipulation
- Document testing results for defense authorities.

In national security, **AI robustness is a legal requirement—not an option**.

Regulatory Use Case Table

The rapid expansion of AI into cybersecurity operations—malware detection, identity verification, anomaly monitoring, predictive analytics, and threat intelligence—has prompted regulators worldwide to establish new oversight expectations and risk controls. However, these requirements vary significantly by jurisdiction, making it challenging for organizations to understand how AI-driven cybersecurity tools are treated under different legal frameworks.

The **Regulatory Use Case Table** provides a clear, structured comparison of how leading global regulations—such as the EU AI Act, GDPR, NIST AI RMF, NYDFS, MAS FEAT, China CAC rules, and national security directives—apply to cybersecurity-related AI systems. It highlights common risk classifications, key compliance obligations, and real-world examples across regulatory environments.

By translating complex legal frameworks into practical use cases, this table offers organizations a roadmap for aligning cybersecurity AI systems with emerging laws, reducing compliance gaps, and preparing for regulatory examinations in multiple regions.

Notable Legal Cases Involving AI

The rapid adoption of AI has triggered legal disputes involving copyright, liability, explainability, and professional responsibility. These cases shape regulatory interpretation and future enforcement.

Key Themes in Legal Disputes

- **Copyright**: Conflicts over training data legality
- **Fair Use**: Courts split on whether AI training is transformative
- **Professional Responsibility**: Sanctions for relying on AI-generated false content
- **Authorship**: AI outputs frequently deemed non-copyrightable
- **Liability**: Courts exploring responsibility for AI-caused harm.

These precedents will shape the next generation of AI compliance requirements.

Table 7.2 Global Regulatory Use Cases Involving AI in Cybersecurity

Regulatory Framework	*Cybersecurity AI Use Case*	*Risk Category/Legal Trigger*	*Key Compliance Obligation*	*Example Application*
EU AI Act (2024)	Biometric access control, network intrusion detection, critical infrastructure monitoring	**High-Risk AI** (safety-critical + rights-impacting)	Risk management; robustness testing; adversarial resistance; human oversight; documentation; transparency; post-market monitoring	AI system flagging insider threat anomalies for a European bank
GDPR Article 22	Automated fraud detection, access denials, identity verification decisions	**Significant Automated Decision-Making**	Human oversight; right to contest; user notification; explainability; data minimization	AI system blocking client transactions flagged as suspicious
NIST AI RMF (2023) + NIST CSF	Malware classification, threat analytics, anomaly detection	**Lifecycle Risk Management Requirements**	Threat modeling; bias testing; drift monitoring; robustness evaluation; audit trails; secure MLOps	ML-based phishing detection integrate into SOC 2 workflows
US Executive Order 14110 (now rescinded but impactful)	AI used in national security, critical infrastructure, DHS systems	**High-Impact AI System**	Safety testing; red-teaming; model reporting; supply chain controls; evaluation of dual-use risks	AI-based malware detection tool for federal government
NYDFS AI/ ML Guidance (2024)	Fraud detection, AML, insider threat analytics	**Model Governance Requirement**	Explainability; fairness testing, validation; documentation; board oversight	XAI applied to AML transaction scoring

(Continued)

Table 7.2 (Continued)

Regulatory Framework	*Cybersecurity AI Use Case*	*Risk Category/Legal Trigger*	*Key Compliance Obligation*	*Example Application*
MAS FEAT Principles (Singapore)	Financial cybersecurity analytics, real-time transaction monitoring	**Fairness/Ethics/ Accountability/ Transparency**	Traceability; fairness monitoring; explainability; responsible use principles	Bank monitoring anomalous login behavior using AI
UK FCA/PRA AI Supervisory Statements	Cyber fraud detection, operational resilience AI models	**Model Risk Management Requirement**	Stress testing; governance; documentation; senior management accountability	Bank using AI-based behavioral biometrics
China CAC-Deep Synthesis & Generative AI Rules (2022–2023)	Deepfake detection, content filtering, security inspection AI	**Security + Content Integrity Mandates**	Content labeling; risk assessments; security reviews, and incident reporting	AI detecting manipulated media for government agencies
DOD/DHS/ National Security AI Guidelines	Autonomous systems, drone AI, surveillance AI	**Safety-Critical + National Security Restrictions**	Adversarial testing; explainability; robust training; fail-safe mechanisms; operational testing	Computer vision used in an unmanned aerial system
Sector-Specific Rules (Health, Defense, Energy)	Medical threat detection, OT network security, cyber-physical AI	**Safety + Privacy + Reliability requirements**	Validation; data governance; safety controls; continuous monitoring	AI detecting anomalies in hospital equipment networks

Cybersecurity AI Compliance Checklist

As organizations increasingly rely on AI to defend against cyber threats—ranging from phishing and malware to insider risk and critical infrastructure attacks—the regulatory expectations for responsible AI deployment have grown exponentially. Cybersecurity AI systems now operate in high-stakes environments where failures can result not only in security breaches but also in legal violations, discriminatory outcomes, and loss of public trust.

The **Cybersecurity AI Compliance Checklist** distills global regulatory requirements into a practical assessment tool that security, risk, and compliance teams can use across the AI lifecycle. It integrates the demands of the EU AI Act, NIST AI RMF, GDPR, NYDFS, MAS FEAT, ISO/IEC 42001, and national security regulations into a unified, actionable framework.

This checklist helps organizations evaluate the maturity of their cybersecurity AI controls—from data governance and adversarial robustness to human oversight, monitoring, transparency, and vendor risk management. It provides a clear path for implementing trustworthy, resilient, and legally defensible AI systems across security operations

1. **AI System Inventory and Classification**
   - All AI cybersecurity systems (IDS/IPS, ML malware detection, UEBA, fraud models, etc.) inventoried
   - Risk classification assigned (e.g., EU AI Act high-risk)
   - Security-critical systems flagged for enhanced oversight
   - Third-party AI tools included in inventory.
2. **Data Governance and Security**
   - Training datasets verified for integrity (no poisoning, tampering)
   - Data lineage documented (source, quality, labeling)
   - Sensitive data minimized (behavioral, biometric, financial)
   - Data encrypted in transit and at rest
   - Access controls applied to training, validation, and monitoring data.
3. **Robustness, Safety, and Adversarial Resistance**
   - Adversarial ML threat modeling completed
   - Evasion testing conducted (FGSM, PGD, and query-based attacks)
   - Poisoning defenses implemented (data sanitization, filtering)
   - Model extraction risk assessed and mitigated

- Stress tests done for volumetric attacks and system overload
- Fail-safe behavior implemented (safe fallback modes)

4. **Red-Teaming and Security Testing**
   - Pre-deployment red-team assessment performed
   - Prompt-injection testing for LLM-based systems
   - Penetration testing integrated into MLOps pipeline
   - Incident response simulation for AI system compromise
   - Continuous adversarial simulation (Breach-and-Attack Emulation for AI).
5. **Transparency and Explainability**
   - Explainability implemented (SHAP, LIME, counterfactuals)
   - Documented rationale for detected threats
   - Plain-language explanations available for regulators/auditors
   - User-facing transparency for automated security decisions (GDPR).
6. **Human Oversight and Decision Governance**
   - Human review required for high-impact security decisions
   - SOC analysts or security engineers trained on AI behavior
   - Override mechanisms available to humans
   - Operational playbooks define when analysts must intervene
   - Feedback loops from humans included in model updates.
7. **Monitoring, Drift Detection, and Performance Management**
   - Continuous monitoring for model drift or degradation
   - Baselines and thresholds defined for detection accuracy
   - Alerts configured for unexpected behavior or low-confidence outputs
   - Regular retraining cycle established
   - Model performance compared across demographic or behavioral groups.
8. **Compliance, Documentation, and Auditability**
   - Risk assessment conducted and documented
   - Technical documentation maintained (architecture, versioning, datasets)
   - Security logs retained (inputs, outputs, decisions)
   - Evidence repository created for regulators (EU AI Act, NYDFS, etc.)
   - Third-party audits conducted for high-stakes cybersecurity AI
   - GDPR Article 22 procedures in place for automated decisions.

9. **Ethical, Legal, and Prohibited Practice Controls**
   - o Confirm system does not deploy unauthorized biometric surveillance
   - o Deepfake detection or generation uses labeling as required
   - o AI does not profile individuals unlawfully for law enforcement purposes
   - o System complies with national restrictions on autonomous systems
   - o Review conducted for potential human rights impacts.
10. **Vendor and Supply Chain Risk Assessment**
    - o All AI cybersecurity vendors undergo risk scoring
    - o Contracts require transparency, documentation, and access to logs
    - o Supply chain includes assessment of model integrity
    - o Open-source model components reviewed for security risk
    - o Third-party penetration and red-team testing results reviewed.
11. **National Security and Critical Infrastructure Controls (If Applicable)**
    - o Compliance with DOD, DHS, NSA, or ENISA guidelines
    - o Testing for autonomous system safety
    - o Dual-use risk assessment (offensive capabilities)
    - o Security classification handling and documentation
    - o Adversarial testing across physical and cyber-physical systems.

Outcome

Completing this checklist ensures an organization's cybersecurity AI systems meet the technical, ethical, legal, and governance requirements expected across leading global regulations—significantly reducing risk, strengthening resilience, and preparing for audits or inspections.

Conclusion

Cybersecurity and AI governance are converging rapidly. AI systems used for fraud detection, access control, intrusion detection, surveillance, or national defense must now comply with a complex web of **risk management requirements, transparency obligations, privacy protections, fairness safeguards, robustness testing,** and **documentation expectations**.

Organizations that implement **structured AI governance**, grounded in international standards and regulatory best practices, will be better equipped to:

- Pass regulatory examinations
- Reduce operational and legal risk
- Defend against AI-targeted cyberattacks
- Build trust with customers, regulators, and partners.

The fusion of cybersecurity and AI regulation is not only a compliance requirement—it is a strategic imperative for modern enterprises.

Bibliography

Biden, J. R. (2023, October 30). *Executive Order 14110: Safe, Secure, and Trustworthy Development and Use of Artificial Intelligence*. Federal Register, 88(210), 75191–75226. https://www.federalregister.gov/documents/2023/11/01/2023-24283/safe-secure-and-trustworthy-development-and-use-of-artificial-intelligence

European Commission. (2024). *EU AI Act*.

Monetary Authority of Singapore. (2021). *FEAT Principles for AI and Data Analytics*.

New York State Department of Financial Services. (2024, October 16). *Industry Letter: Cybersecurity Risks Arising from Artificial Intelligence and Strategies to Combat Related Risks*. 23 NYCRR Part 500. https://www.dfs.ny.gov/industry-guidance/industry-letters/il20241016-cyber-risks-ai-and-strategies-combat-related-risks

NIST. (2023). *AI Risk Management Framework (AI RMF) 1.0*.

Regulation (EU) 2016/679 of the European Parliament and of the Council of 27 April 2016 on the protection of natural persons with regard to the processing of personal data and on the free movement of such data, and repealing Directive 95/46/EC (General Data Protection Regulation). *Official Journal of the European Union*, L 119, 1–88. https://eur-lex.europa.eu/legal-content/EN/TXT/?uri=CELEX%3A32016R0679

SECTION 3

AI AND GOVERNANCE—BALANCING INNOVATION AND REGULATION

The rapid acceleration of AI adoption has created a dual imperative for organizations: to harness AI's competitive and operational advantages while proactively managing the ethical, legal, and societal risks it introduces. AI governance has therefore emerged as the critical mechanism for achieving this balance—serving as the operational layer that translates principles and regulations into accountable, repeatable, and measurable organizational practices. Unlike external regulation, AI governance operates internally at the enterprise level, bridging strategy, risk management, compliance, and technical execution.

This section explores the evolving discipline of AI governance through four chapters:

- **Chapter 8: Key Aspects of AI Governance**—defines the foundational components of AI governance, including accountability structures, risk assessment mechanisms, transparency requirements, and ongoing oversight.

DOI: 10.4324/9781003682530-10

- **Chapter 9: AI Governance Framework Models**—analyzes leading governance models adopted by enterprises, regulators, and standards bodies, highlighting both centralized and federated approaches.
- **Chapter 10: Best Practices**—provides practical guidance on implementing governance processes across the AI lifecycle, including model development, validation, deployment, and continuous monitoring.
- **Chapter 11: The Future of AI Governance**—examines emerging trends such as governance automation, AI assurance, real-time compliance, and alignment with ESG and digital trust frameworks.

Together, these chapters provide a comprehensive understanding of how organizations can operationalize responsible AI—ensuring that innovation scales safely, ethically, and sustainably.

8

KEY ASPECTS OF AI GOVERNANCE

Approach to AI Governance

When implementing artificial intelligence (AI) systems, the objective should extend beyond immediate benefits to ensure these systems are developed and deployed in ways that are ethical, transparent, and firmly aligned with societal values and applicable regulatory standards. This is not an option; it is an ask rooted in ethics, accountability, and public trust. A robust AI governance approach balances innovation with oversight by ensuring appropriate safeguards are put in place without deterring experimentation. This balance can be maintained through clear roles, accountability structures, policies, process and controls, stakeholder engagement, supporting infrastructure, risk classification, and continuous monitoring.

Effective AI governance requires more than technical controls; it requires leadership alignment, ethical clarity, compliance readiness, and operational discipline. The governance approach must extend beyond delivering AI's immediate benefits and ensure that systems are developed, deployed, and monitored in ways that are responsible, transparent, and aligned with regulatory and societal values.

DOI: 10.4324/9781003682530-11

A strategic AI governance program includes:

- Clear principles and boundaries for AI development and deployment
- Role-based accountability across the AI lifecycle
- Policies, processes, and risk controls explicitly addressing AI
- Ongoing model monitoring, auditing, and reporting
- Cross-functional coordination across legal, IT, compliance, security, HR, and business units
- Regulatory alignment by design, not as an afterthought
- Continuous education to close AI literacy gaps at the senior leadership level.

Without foundational AI literacy at the board and executive levels, organizations risk poor oversight, technical missteps, and reputational harm. Leaders must understand the capabilities and limitations of AI, be able to question assumptions, and evaluate systemic risks.

Embedding AI literacy into governance equips leaders to make informed decisions about risk appetite, use-case prioritization, resource allocation, and compliance obligations. It elevates AI from a technical curiosity to a strategic, organization-wide capability.

Lack of literacy about AI at senior management levels is a handicap for many organizations that they must quickly overcome to ensure that AI systems can be deployed responsibly, strategically, and in alignment with organizational goals. Without foundational AI literacy at the senior management level, leaders may struggle to assess risks, evaluate opportunities, or implement effective governance frameworks. This gap can lead to poor oversight, ethical missteps, and missed chances for innovation. To overcome this, organizations must invest in executive education that demystifies AI concepts, fosters critical understanding of algorithmic decision-making, and equips leaders to ask the right questions. Embedding AI literacy into boardroom strategy not only enhances decision-making but also ensures that AI adoption is guided by informed judgment, regulatory awareness, and long-term value creation.

Defining Core AI Principles

An excellent first step for any organization to take is to articulate the core principles or the boundaries under which AI systems must operate. These

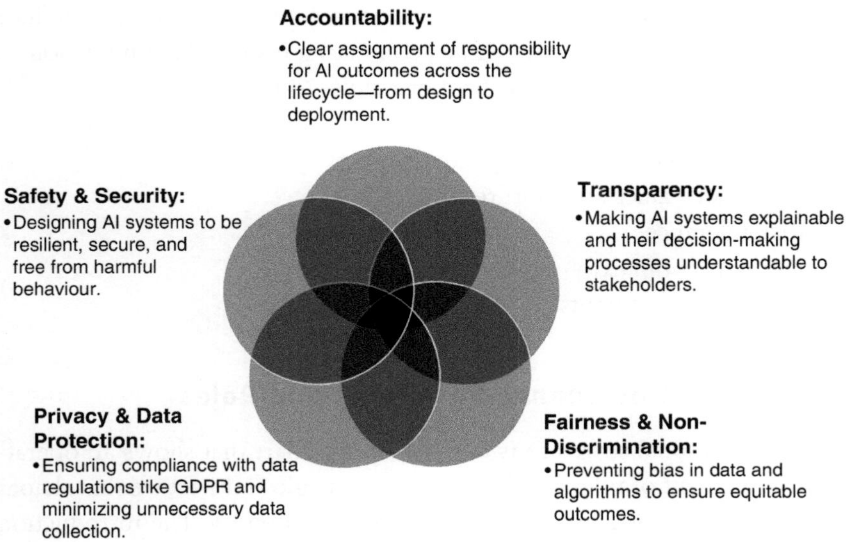

Image 8.1 Core AI Principles

core principles will serve as the ethical and operational backbone of AI governance, guiding organizations in the responsible development, deployment, and oversight of AI systems. The incentive of increased efficiency, greater competitiveness, and the promise of high financial returns might be a compelling reason to proceed with speed, however, bypassing immediate concerns and impediments that following these core principles might hamper; in the long term, they will ensure a strong governance foundation. There are at least six areas around which core principles can be formulated:

Defining core AI principles in line with the above five areas is a strong statement of intent by an organization that must be communicated to all stakeholders. Organizations can further customize principles to reflect their specific industry, risk appetite, and organizational culture. Articulating and adopting core principles for AI governance upfront can help organizations establish a clear ethical foundation, streamline decision-making, foster cross-functional alignment, and proactively mitigate risks, ultimately accelerating responsible innovation while maintaining public trust and regulatory readiness.

Defining and communicating core AI principles is not simply a compliance exercise—it is a public declaration of the organization's values and intent. When widely understood and consistently enforced, these principles help unify decision-making, streamline governance processes, and reduce friction between stakeholders while accelerating responsible innovation.

Organizations should tailor these principles to reflect:

- Industry-specific regulatory requirements
- Corporate values and culture
- Risk tolerance
- Use-case complexity
- Ethical commitments.

Governance Structures and Roles

The organizational structure is not just an org chart that shows an operating arrangement of roles and levels. It is a strategic architecture that shapes how governance principles are enacted across an entity. The introduction of AI systems in an organization has a disruptive effect on an organizations operating structure. This calls for a new definition of roles & responsibilities from board-level oversight down to operating teams as everyone should know their part in AI governance. Many organizations form dedicated committees such as an AI strategy council, ethics boards, or risk council to oversee high-impact systems.

AI governance cannot operate effectively without **formalized roles, defined responsibilities,** and **clear escalation channels**. AI introduces new kinds of risks—algorithmic bias, model drift, hallucinations, adversarial attacks—that require expertise beyond traditional technology governance.

Leading organizations are establishing new structures such as:

- **AI Governance Committees** or councils
- **Ethics review boards**
- **AI risk councils**
- **Model approval committees**
- **AI assurance or internal audit functions**.

To ensure clarity and successful oversight, organizations should:

- Form an **AI Governance Committee** with cross-functional representatives
- Define responsibilities across the AI lifecycle—from data sourcing to post-deployment monitoring

- Create **escalation paths** for high-risk use cases, security incidents, or non-compliance
- Integrate AI governance into board-level reporting and enterprise risk management.

As AI becomes central to operations, organizations will need to evolve their workforce and operating model. The following emerging roles are increasingly necessary:

AI systems could eventually lead to a complete overhaul of organization governance structure to ensure clarity, accountability, risk management, policy enforcement, compliance, and responsible innovation. As organizations embrace AI at scale, they are not just adopting new systems but are also reshaping their workforce.

Given below is a list of emerging roles that organizations need to incorporate as they progress in the large-scale deployment of AI systems:

Common emerging roles include:

- **Chief AI Officer (CAIO)**
- **AI Governance Lead / Director of Responsible AI**
- **Model Risk Manager**
- **AI Assurance or Audit Analyst**
- **Machine-Learning Safety Engineer**
- **AI Ethics and Compliance Officer**

Depending on the organization's approach—build, buy, or partner—roles may shift between engineering-heavy functions, vendor management, or governance-heavy oversight.

Role	Purpose
Chief AI Officer (CAIO)	Heads enterprise-wide AI strategy, aligning innovation with risk, ethics, and ROI.
AI Governance Lead	Ensures compliance with AI regulations and oversees model transparency and accountability.
AI Ethics Specialist	Develops frameworks to mitigate bias, ensure fairness, and uphold responsible AI.
AI Policy & Regulatory Analyst	Tracks evolving AI laws and standards, advising on compliance and risk exposure.
AI Integration Specialist	Bridges AI systems with legacy infrastructure; ensures smooth deployment across business units.
AI Training Manager	Responsible for AI skills upgradation and change management.
AI Auditor	Evaluates AI outputs for bias, accuracy, and regulatory compliance.
Data Steward for AI	Ensures data quality, lineage, and ethical sourcing for AI pipelines.

Table 8.1 Emerging Roles

In addition to the above roles, there will be requirements for technical AI specialists and AI business strategists. Organizations typically face three strategic options when adopting AI systems—build, buy, or partner. Each path has trade-offs involving control, cost, speed, and innovation alignment. Organization structure decisions too will need to be aligned with the options that they exercise.

Policies, Processes, and Controls

In any organization, policies, processes, and controls are the pillars of effective governance. These form the actionable core that ensures that high-level intent translates into measurable outcomes. AI policies together with principles are the guiding rules established by leadership to articulate the organization's stance on critical issues. They ensure that employees operate within a pre-defined remit in a manner that aligns with organizational goals and objectives. For example, an AI Usage Policy could emphasize that all algorithmic decisions affecting users must be explainable and free from bias.

AI specific policies need to be drafted covering the following:

- Data sourcing, quality, and labeling
- Model development and validation
- Fairness and bias testing requirements
- Explainability and documentation standards
- Security, privacy, and adversarial robustness
- Monitoring and drift detection
- Vendor and third-party AI usage
- Shadow AI prevention.

Processes ensure repeatability and auditability. These include:

- Algorithmic Impact Assessments (AIA)
- Risk and compliance reviews
- Conformity assessments (e.g., EU AI Act high-risk requirements)
- Continuous monitoring workflows
- Model inventory and version control
- Change management procedures.

Conducting risk and impact assessments is a key activity that must precede the implementation of AI systems. This can be done using tools like AIA or the Assessment List for Trustworthy AI (ALTAI) to evaluate ethical, legal, and societal risks. A good practice is to develop an AI asset inventory and to maintain a record of risks in a risk register to track AI systems, their purpose, and associated risks. Determining risk classification (e.g., low, medium, high) to determine oversight levels is an essential for ongoing risk management.

Another key area is that of implementing appropriate controls and ensuring risk management. Frameworks such as NIST AI RMF and ISO/IEC 42001 play a critical role in helping organizations streamline governance processes, implement robust controls, and proactively manage the spectrum of AI-related risks, from ethical implications to operational vulnerabilities. In essence, policies are the intent, processes are the implementation, and controls are the verification. Together along with the use of a framework, they build trust, resilience, and regulatory alignment in any well-governed system.

Stakeholder Engagement

Engaging all stakeholders at initial stages and involving users, regulators, and impacted communities in system design and evaluation can ensure that possible friction between organizational teams is minimized and all efforts are directed toward successful implementation. Stakeholders must be apprised of the potential harms and benefits before deploying AI systems.

AI affects employees, customers, regulators, and communities. Successful AI governance requires:

- Early engagement with stakeholders
- Clear communication of AI purpose, risks, and benefits
- Structured feedback loops during development and deployment
- Public transparency where appropriate
- Engagement with ethical or community advisory boards.

Including stakeholders throughout the lifecycle increases trust, reduces friction, and improves system accuracy and fairness.

Supporting Infrastructure

Apart from the new hardware and software requirements that form an integral part of the implementation of AI systems, new requirements in the form of model registries and related documentation are essential. This helps track AI models, their training data, and decision logic. Organizations need to look out for the use of shadow AI or unsanctioned use of AI systems.

A mature AI governance program requires robust technical and organizational infrastructure, including:

- **Model registries** to track data, training processes, risk levels, and monitoring results
- **MLOps platforms** for version control and reproducibility
- **Documentation standards** such as Model Cards and Data Sheets
- **Shadow AI detection** systems
- **Model interpretability and robustness tools**.

Strong AI infrastructure supports regulatory compliance, improves model integrity, and enables rapid response to incidents or audits.

Transparency and Explainability

To ensure transparency and explainability in AI systems, governance must integrate ethical frameworks, clear documentation, and technical tools. This includes adopting standards like the EU AI Act or ISO/IEC 42001, documenting models through tools like Model Cards, and using interpretability techniques such as SHAP or counterfactuals. SHAP (SHapley Additive exPlanations) is a powerful method for interpreting the predictions of machine-learning models by assigning each feature an importance value for a particular prediction.

Oversight mechanisms such as ethics boards and impact assessments should ensure accountability. In addition, continuous monitoring, audit trails, and user-facing explanations promote trust and clarity. Monitoring for model drift, bias, compliance, and performance degradation must become an essential feature effective governance of AI systems. Together, these mechanisms build a resilient foundation for responsible AI deployment and stakeholder confidence.

Transparency and explainability are essential for regulatory compliance and public trust. Achieving these goals requires:

- Interpretable models or post-hoc explainability (e.g., SHAP, LIME)
- Model Cards documenting training data, limitations, and performance
- User-facing explanation tools
- Governance policies requiring explanation for high-risk decisions
- Audit logs and traceability
- Regular drift monitoring and bias testing.

Explainability is both a technical and ethical requirement—especially in high-impact domains like healthcare, finance, employment, and law enforcement.

People, Skills, and Culture

When it comes to implementing AI systems on a large scale, the proverbial "elephant in the room" is the fear related to job loss. All employees who will be potentially impacted through AI systems' implementation need to be taken on board regarding the purpose and benefits that will accrue from them. Organizations can address job loss fears and skill upgradation through proactive workforce governance that blends empathy, strategy, and long-term vision. This involves embedding reskilling and upskilling into the core of AI and digital transformation policies, ensuring employees are not just informed but empowered. The following key mechanisms can help:

- Regularly share how AI or automation will impact roles, emphasizing augmentation over replacement.
- Establish internal learning platforms through partnerships with ed-tech platforms to support continuous learning.
- Create pathways for role evolution to AI oversight roles.
- Involve employees in AI deployment decisions through councils or feedback loops, fostering trust and co-ownership.
- Use tools to map current capabilities against future needs, guiding targeted training investments.

It may be necessary to look at making changes in the organization culture to accommodate AI-induced impacts. Embedding or reinforcement of values like responsibility, collaboration, and openness into organizational culture may be required in an AI-driven environment.

AI adoption cannot succeed without preparing the workforce. Organizations must proactively manage fears of job loss, skill gaps, and cultural resistance.

Key strategies include:

- Transparent communication about AI's role
- Upskilling and reskilling programs
- Partnerships with universities and ed-tech platforms
- Internal mobility pathways into AI oversight roles
- Incentivizing innovation, collaboration, and ethical thinking.

AI requires a culture shift toward adaptability, continuous learning, and responsible innovation.

Prepare for Regulatory Alignment

Maintaining regulatory compliance is a cornerstone of effective AI governance, especially in a landscape where legal frameworks are rapidly evolving. As AI becomes more deeply embedded in decision-making processes, governments across the globe are introducing new laws to address its ethical, legal, and societal implications. The EU AI Act, for instance, sets a precedent by classifying AI systems based on risk and mandating strict obligations for high-risk applications. Meanwhile, jurisdictions at both national and subnational levels, such as US states enacting their own privacy laws and are introducing nuanced requirements around data protection, algorithmic transparency, and accountability. These developments demand that organizations adopt a dynamic compliance posture: continuously monitoring regulatory trends, conducting impact assessments, and integrating compliance-by-design principles into their AI lifecycle. Failing to do so could attract legal penalties and erode public trust and organizational credibility. In this shifting regulatory terrain, agility, foresight, and cross-functional collaboration are essential to ensure that AI systems remain lawful, ethical, and resilient.

Establishing AI governance in any organization is a strategic journey that blends ethics, compliance, risk management, and innovation. Moreover, adoption faces persistent challenges such as opaque models, fragmented regulations across jurisdictions, and limited AI literacy among leadership. Cultural resistance, data quality issues, and the rapid pace of AI advancement further complicate implementation. A future-ready governance model is provided in Chapter 9 and is adaptive and scalable across technologies like quantum-AI systems, interoperable across geographies, and inclusive of stakeholder voices throughout the AI lifecycle.

Regulatory alignment is becoming a non-negotiable aspect of AI governance. With global regulations expanding—EU AI Act, GDPR, US state and federal laws, UK guidance, China's CAC rules, Singapore's MAS FEAT—organizations must adopt **compliance by design**.

A strong regulatory readiness posture includes:

- Continuous monitoring of emerging laws
- Conformity assessments and documentation
- Privacy-by-design practices
- AI risk assessments (AIA, DPIA, Model Risk Rating)
- Legal reviews of high-risk models
- Cross-functional regulatory committees.

Proactive compliance protects the organization from financial penalties, operational disruptions, and reputational damage.

AI Governance Maturity Model

As AI becomes increasingly embedded into the core operations of modern enterprises, organizations face growing pressure to implement governance structures that ensure safety, compliance, transparency, and ethical integrity. Yet the level of readiness varies dramatically across industries and institutions. Some organizations are still experimenting with AI through isolated pilots, while others have begun scaling AI across business units without fully understanding the risks. A small but rapidly growing group of leaders are building systematic, enterprise-wide governance programs aligned with global regulations such as the EU AI Act, NIST AI RMF, ISO/IEC 42001, and emerging national standards.

To navigate these differences and provide a clear pathway toward responsible, scalable AI adoption, the **AI Governance Maturity Model** offers a structured framework for assessing organizational readiness. The model outlines five levels of maturity—from ad hoc experimentation to fully optimized and transformational AI governance—and defines the characteristics, capabilities, and controls expected at each stage. It helps leaders identify gaps, prioritize strategic investments, and build a roadmap toward a comprehensive, trustworthy AI governance ecosystem.

This maturity model is not simply a diagnostic tool; it is a blueprint for aligning technical innovation with ethical responsibility, regulatory compliance, and operational resilience. By understanding where an organization stands today, stakeholders can chart an actionable path toward better risk management, improved decision quality, greater transparency, and enhanced trust with customers, regulators, and the public.

Ultimately, the AI Governance Maturity Model provides a common language for executives, technologists, risk managers, and policymakers—enabling cross-functional teams to collaborate more effectively as AI becomes a foundational capability across the enterprise.

AI Governance Maturity Model (Five Levels)

A complete enterprise framework for assessing AI governance readiness

Level 1—Ad Hoc / Awareness

"We are experimenting with AI, but have limited controls or structure."

Characteristics

- Sporadic AI usage, often by individual teams ("shadow AI")
- No formal inventory of AI systems
- Little or no understanding of AI risks
- Executives have low AI literacy
- No responsible AI principles or documented policies.

Risk Posture

- High exposure to regulatory, ethical, and operational risks
- Vulnerable to bias, privacy violations, hallucinations, and security threats.

Typical Behaviors

- Experiments with generative AI without governance
- No monitoring or documentation
- No alignment to NIST, ISO, EU AI Act, or local laws.

Level 2—Emerging / Developing

"We recognize the need for AI governance and are beginning to formalize it."

Characteristics

- Initial AI inventory created, but incomplete
- Basic AI principles drafted, not fully operationalized
- Early-stage policies (e.g., AI Acceptable Use Policy)
- Some risk assessments, but inconsistent
- Some explainability and documentation standards introduced.

Risk Posture

- Reduced but still significant risk due to uneven adoption of controls.

Typical Behaviors

- Some models reviewed by legal or IT, but not consistently
- Leadership awareness increasing; training in progress
- Pilots begin using structured tools like Model Cards or AIA templates
- Early alignment with NIST AI RMF (MAP function) or ISO 23894.

Level 3—Defined / Structured

"We have a formal AI governance program with clear roles, processes, and controls."

Characteristics

- AI Governance Committee formally established
- Defined lifecycle governance from data to deployment
- Organization-wide AI risk classification (low–medium–high)

- Formal risk assessments (AIA, DPIA, EU AI Act conformity checklists)
- Documented policies for fairness, data quality, explainability, and robustness
- Model inventory integrated into MLOps or GRC systems
- Regular monitoring for drift, bias, and model performance.

Risk Posture

- Controlled risk environment with structured oversight.

Typical Behaviors

- Cross-functional collaboration (IT, legal, compliance, security)
- Use of technical tools: SHAP, counterfactuals, drift detection
- Integration of AI governance into procurement and vendor management
- Alignment with ISO/IEC 42001 management system requirements.

Level 4—Managed / Advanced

"AI governance is operationalized, measurable, and consistently applied."

Characteristics

- Comprehensive AI risk and impact framework used across the enterprise
- Continuous monitoring and automated controls (e.g., real-time drift alerts)
- Regular independent audits (internal audit or third party)
- Red-teaming and adversarial robustness testing are standard
- Explainability requirements tied to specific use-case risk levels
- Formal human oversight workflows with documented decision trails
- AI incident response process in place with rapid mitigation procedures.

Risk Posture

- Strong governance posture; well-prepared for audits and enforcement.

Typical Behaviors

- Proactive compliance with EU AI Act high-risk obligations
- Mature documentation and traceability for all critical systems
- Bias and fairness KPIs reported to leadership
- Integrated assurance: cyber, privacy, and AI risk in unified dashboards.

Level 5—Optimized / Transformational

"AI governance is predictive, data-driven, and fully embedded in enterprise strategy."

Characteristics

- Governance fully embedded into strategy, culture, and product lifecycle
- Predictive analytics identify emerging risks before they materialize
- Real-time AI governance automation: compliance by design
- AI ethics, safety, and trust integrated into performance metrics
- Enterprise-wide literacy and accountability at all organizational levels
- Continuous regulatory horizon scanning and global coordination
- Responsible innovation embedded into R&D and product design.

Risk Posture

- Low, quantifiable, and continuously managed through automated controls.

Typical Behaviors

- Alignment with global standards: EU AI Act, ISO 42001, NIST AI RMF, OECD
- Cross-border interoperability and compliance automation
- AI assurance certifications or third-party attestations
- AI risk quantification integrated into enterprise risk modeling
- AI governance becomes a competitive differentiator and market advantage.

Level	Description	Governance Condition	Risk Exposure	Regulatory Readiness
1. Ad Hoc	Unstructured experimentation	Minimal	Very High	Non-compliant
2. Emerging	Basic structure forming	Partial	High	Low
3. Defined	Formal processes, roles, governance	Consistent	Moderate	Medium
4. Managed	Operationalized, measurable, audited	Mature	Low	High
5. Optimized	Predictive, automated, strategic	Transformational	Very Low	Very High

Table 8.2 AI Governance Maturity Model—Summary Table

AI Governance Maturity Assessment Categories

To score an organization, assess each dimension from Level 1 to 5:

1. **Leadership and Governance Structure**
2. **Risk Management and Compliance**
3. **Data Governance and Quality**
4. **Model Development Standards**
5. **Fairness, Bias and Ethics Controls**
6. **Transparency and Explainability**
7. **Security and Adversarial ML Resilience**
8. **Human Oversight and Accountability**
9. **Monitoring, Auditability and Drift Detection**
10. **Culture, Skills and Training**

We can create:

- A **weighted scoring system (0–5 per category)**
- A **heatmap showing org strengths and weaknesses**
- A **remediation roadmap to move up maturity levels.**

AI Governance Roadmap (High-Level)

1. Establish AI governance principles
2. Build AI inventory
3. Conduct risk classification
4. Implement policies and lifecycle processes

5. Integrate NIST AI RMF & ISO 42001
6. Stand up governance committees
7. Deploy monitoring and audit tools
8. Build explainability and robustness testing processes
9. Establish incident response and drift detection workflows
10. Introduce culture, literacy, and workforce transformation programs.

Bibliography

European Commission. (2023). *EU Artificial Intelligence Act.*

Future of Life Institute. (2023). *AI Governance Principles.*

ISO/ IEC. (2023). *ISO/IEC 42001: Artificial Intelligence Management System Standard.*

National Institute of Standards and Technology. (2023). *NIST AI Risk Management Framework.*

OECD. (2022). *OECD Framework for the Classification of AI Systems.*

Singapore Monetary Authority. (2018). *FEAT Principles for the Use of AI and Data Analytics.*

UK ICO. (2022). *Guidance on AI and Data Protection.*

U.S. Government Accountability Office. (2021). *Artificial Intelligence: An Accountability Framework for Federal Agencies and Other Entities.*

World Economic Forum. (2020). *Responsible Limits on Facial Recognition Technology.*

9

AI GOVERNANCE FRAMEWORK MODELS

Need and Purpose of Governance Framework Models

Organizations are increasingly optimistic about the potential of artificial intelligence (AI), not only to meet routine automation needs, but also to tackle complex challenges, enhance productivity, and fundamentally transform the way they operate. This is evident from the accelerating pace of AI integration across sectors such as healthcare, finance, manufacturing, and education. Organizations are investing heavily in AI-driven platforms to streamline operations, enhance decision-making, and unlock new revenue streams. The rise in AI-related job roles, the surge in pilot projects and proof-of-concepts, and the incorporation of AI into strategic plans reflect this growing confidence. From automated customer service and intelligent supply chains to predictive maintenance and fraud detection, AI is becoming an indispensable driver of innovation and efficiency. This optimistic outlook is also reinforced by global reports and surveys indicating that most enterprises see AI as central to their long-term competitive advantage.

DOI: 10.4324/9781003682530-12

Amidst the urgency to unlock immediate value through swift AI rollouts, organizations frequently overlook several crucial aspects of integration that warrant careful consideration and strategic foresight to ensure long-term sustainability, ethical compliance, and operational resilience. Beyond the initial performance gains, AI systems demand ongoing examination of their data integrity, algorithmic fairness, and alignment with organizational values. Overlooking these dimensions can result in unintended bias, regulatory breaches, or system failures, risks that are magnified in high-stakes environments like finance, healthcare, and critical infrastructure. Strategic planning, stakeholder consultation, strong governance mechanisms, and continuous monitoring must be woven into the AI integration process to prevent short-sighted decisions from undermining trust and long-term value. This is where AI governance framework models can help organizations harness AI's benefits while managing its risks responsibly and ethically, ensuring sustainable and trustworthy AI adoption worldwide.

The very thought of integrating yet another governance model into an already complex enterprise governance framework often acts as a deterrence to organizations who are either considering or already deploying AI solutions. True, organizations may already have governance models for IT, data, risk, or compliance, but AI introduces fundamentally new dimensions that traditional frameworks are not equipped to handle on their own.

Why Do Existing Governance Models Fall Short for AI?

As far as systems go, AI systems differ from conventional software in several critical ways. Many AI models, especially deep learning systems, operate as "black boxes," making it hard to figure out how outputs are created. Unlike static systems, AI models are designed to evolve over time for maximum effectiveness, which introduces risks like model drift and unintended behavior. AI can also amplify societal biases embedded in training data, which is something traditional IT governance rarely addresses. Increasingly, AI systems are being trained to act independently in critical environments such as healthcare and finance, where this could give rise to questions about liability and accountability. Furthermore, as AI touches legal, ethical, technical, and societal domains, a multidisciplinary governance approach becomes essential.

Managing AI systems with traditional governance systems is akin to managing air traffic control for modern-day autonomous drones by using traffic rules for cars. Autonomous drone technology is built on the foundation of AI, which requires new protocols, oversight mechanisms, and ethical guardrails because the technology behaves differently, operates at scale, and impacts society in entirely new ways. The basic purpose of AI governance frameworks is to provide sets of guidelines, policies, and organizational structures designed to ensure responsible AI development and deployment.

The adoption of an AI-specific framework ensures that not only technical and ethical imperatives are addressed, but also pathways to interoperability with sector-specific governance models in finance, healthcare, or cybersecurity are established. Proactively adopting AI governance frameworks is not just a compliance checkbox; it functions as a strategic accelerator in the following ways:

- Identification and management of biases, security vulnerabilities, and compliance risks
- Enhancing user and stakeholder confidence through explainable AI decisions

Objective	Purpose
Embed ethical principles	To establish AI systems that consistently embody principles of fairness, transparency, and accountability throughout their lifecycle
Ensure explainability	Make AI decisions understandable for regulators, users, and affected groups
Mitigate systemic risks	Address potential harms like bias, hallucinations, or privacy violations
Ensure Privacy & Security	Prevent privacy violations and misuse of personal data Address security vulnerabilities in autonomous systems
Align with regulations	Comply with global frameworks and stay ahead of legal requirements
Enable responsible innovation	Encourage innovation without compromising safety or ethics
Establish accountability	Define who is responsible for AI outcomes across the lifecycle
Promote stakeholder trust	Build and maintain public and institutional confidence in AI systems
Ensure lifecycle oversight	Monitor AI from design to deployment and post-deployment

Table 9.1 Why Are Specific AI Governance Models Needed?

- Establishing mechanisms to verify that AI systems consistently deliver reliable, impartial results and fulfill their designed objectives
- Clarifying roles and responsibilities across technical, legal, and executive teams
- Keeping organizational systems aligned with regulatory mandates
- Supporting auditability and traceability, which are increasingly required by regulators.

Although AI governance frameworks offer substantial benefits and value, it is equally crucial to recognize the complexities and hurdles involved in their implementation. Adding another layer of governance and integrating it with existing governance systems is not only resource intensive but can overwhelm teams already managing data, IT, and cybersecurity governance. Integration with older systems that could lack the flexibility to accommodate AI-specific controls like model monitoring or explainability can be a major obstacle. Excessive controls at an early stage of AI adoption could kill innovation and experimentation defeating expected transformational changes even before they have begun to take effect. Organizations are already beginning to feel the burden of regulatory compliance leading to governance fatigue and increased overheads.

It is important to understand that the benefits of governance such as trust, fairness, and risk mitigation are often intangible and hard to measure. To harness the long-term benefits of AI systems, it is essential to establish an overarching framework that guides policymaking, provides operational clarity, and ensures both compliance and risk mitigation, capabilities that only a proven and well-tested governance model can deliver. Moreover, stakeholders may question the value of investing in governance if it does not yield immediate financial returns.

Integrating a new governance framework in today's dynamic environment characterized by rapid technological evolution, regulatory uncertainty, and cross-sector complexity demands not just technical rigor but unwavering commitment from leadership. Firm resolve ensures continuity despite institutional reluctance or resistance to change, while strong management support secures the resources, alignment, and cultural shift necessary for successful implementation. Without top-down endorsement, even the most technically sound frameworks risk stalling at the deployment stage.

Global AI Governance Models

For building a new organizational edifice built of the backbone of AI, a scaffolding for a future where AI is safe, inclusive, and beneficial across borders is required. Global AI governance frameworks provide the required structural support to ensure that AI becomes deeply embedded in critical sectors and societal functions.

Implementing AI governance frameworks has significant strategic value, most notably, in bridging high-level ethical principles with operational execution. Global frameworks play a pivotal role in harmonizing regulations, thereby easing compliance efforts for multinational AI developers. As the pace of AI innovation accelerates, governance approaches must remain agile and adaptive, incorporating feedback-based refinements and real-world validation to remain effective. In recent times, multiple AI governance frameworks have emerged around the world, which have received acceptance in the respective constituencies as shown in the image:

With multiple frameworks available, how do organizations choose what is best for them? Organizations typically evaluate AI frameworks based on a mix of the following technical, strategic, and operational factors:

Image 9.1 Global AI Governance Models: Overview

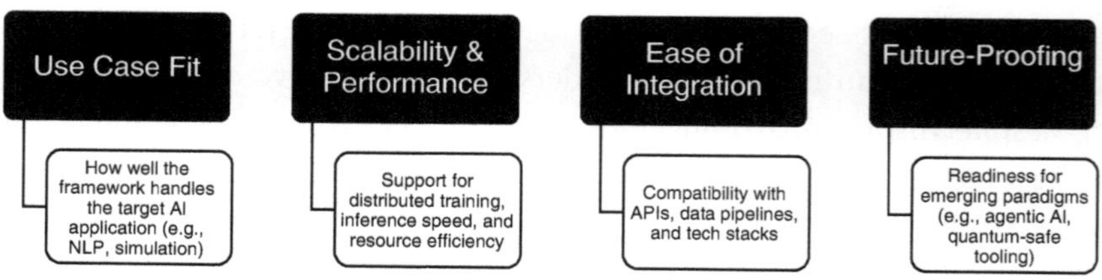

Image 9.2 Prominent Global AI Governance Frameworks

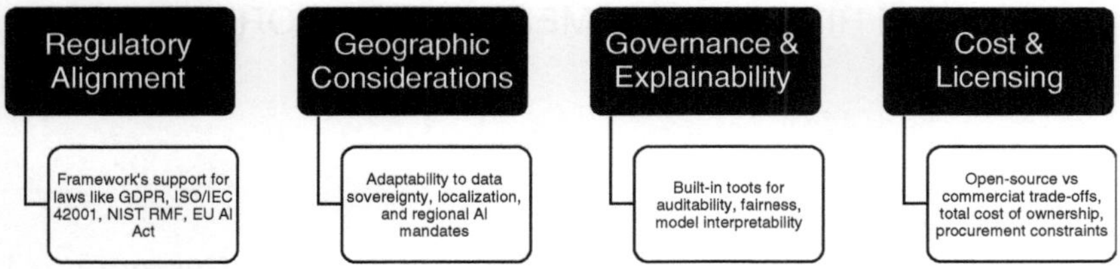

Image 9.3 Technical Criteria

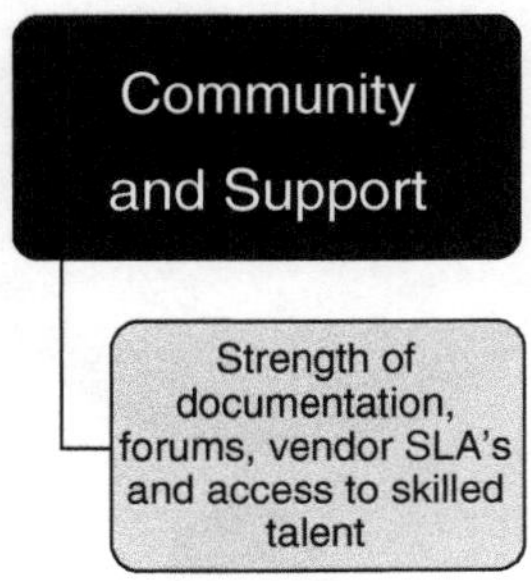

Image 9.4 Strategic Criteria

Technical Criteria—These include considerations that relate directly to system capabilities, architecture, and AI framework functionality.

Strategic Criteria—These support long-term goals like regulatory compliance, international deployment, and innovation.

Operational Criteria—These shape day-to-day implementation, maintenance, and scalability of AI initiatives.

While most AI frameworks broadly align on foundational principles and guidance, many also introduce distinct concepts and specialized approaches that set them apart in practice. Let us examine four leading AI governance frameworks to better understand what each has to offer.

NIST AI Risk Management Framework (AI RMF 1.0)

The NIST AI RMF 1.0 provides a foundation for organizations aiming to build trustworthy, responsible, and risk-aware AI systems. It offers a voluntary, flexible, and use-case agnostic framework that enables organizations to identify, assess, manage, and monitor AI risks across the lifecycle.

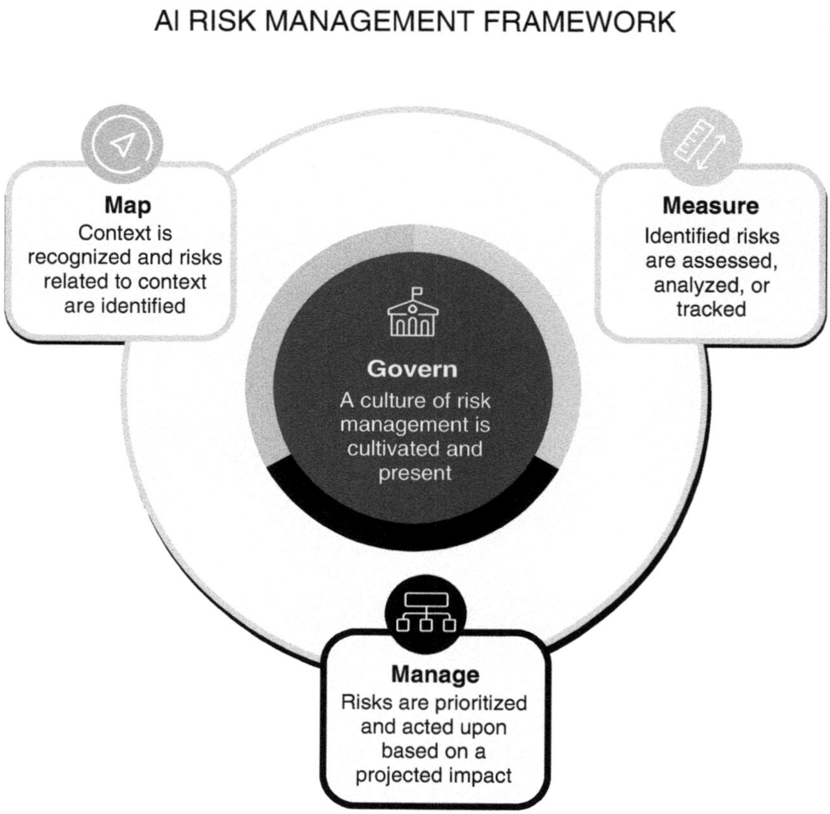

Image 9.5 Operational Criteria

In addition, it emphasizes trustworthiness of AI systems by incorporating values like fairness, transparency, and accountability.

Core functions of NIST RMF 1.0 are as follows:

Govern

The Govern function ensures that AI risk management is not an afterthought but a core organizational priority. It focuses on embedding risk awareness into policies, culture, and leadership accountability across the AI lifecycle. It also sets the tone and structure that guide how risks are identified, assessed, and mitigated throughout the AI lifecycle.

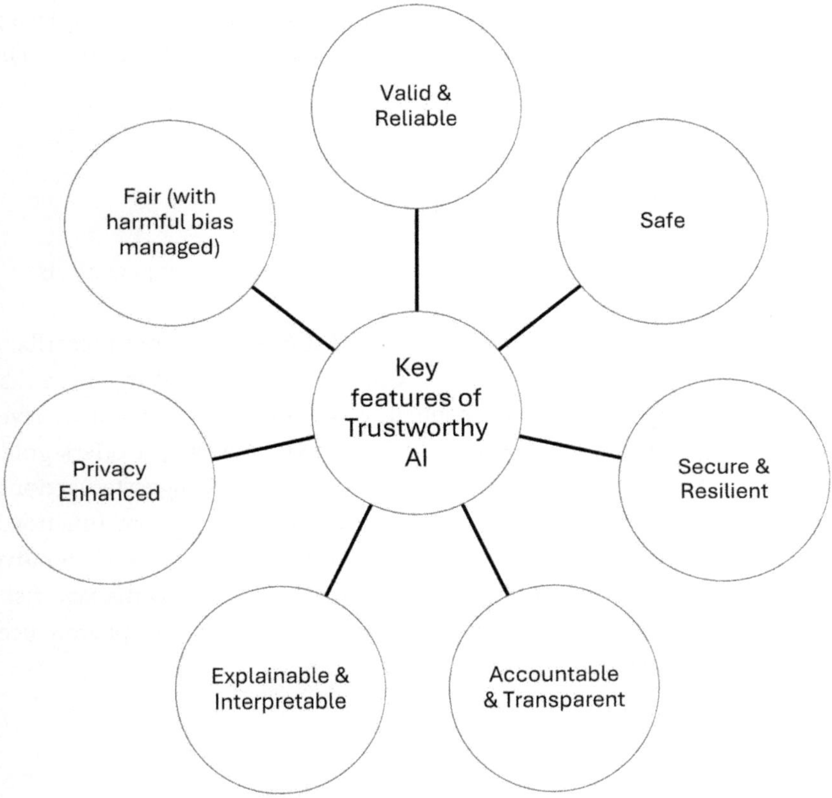

Image 9.6 AI Risk Management Framework

Source: https://airc.nist.gov/airmf-resources/airmf/5-sec-core/

Map

This function contextualizes AI systems by identifying intended use, stakeholders, and potential impacts. This is the diagnostic phase that helps develop an understanding of what the AI system is, what it is meant to do, and what could go wrong across its lifecycle.

Measure

The Measure function ensures that organizations identify, apply, and refine metrics to assess how well their AI systems align with risk tolerance, ethical principles, and performance expectations. It is the evidence-gathering mechanism that supports informed governance and risk mitigation. The Measure function also enables:

- Evidence-based decision-making
- Continuous improvement
- Transparency and accountability
- Alignment with organizational values and regulatory expectations.

The NIST AI Risk Management Framework (AI RMF) does not prescribe a fixed set of controls, but it offers a flexible, outcomes-based structure that organizations can tailor to their context, risk tolerance, and maturity level (AI Risk Management Framework | NIST, 2025). However, it offers guidance in the form of the AI RMF Playbook that outlines suggested actions, references, and implementation tips for each of the four core functions: Govern, Map, Measure, and Manage. In addition, there is the Generative AI Profile (NIST AI 600–1) that proposes specific actions to manage risks unique to generative AI, including governance, content provenance, pre-deployment testing, and incident disclosure.

Manage

The goal of the Manage function is to ensure that AI risks are actively prioritized, mitigated, and communicated throughout the system's lifecycle. It is about turning insights into action and not just identifying risks but managing them in real-world conditions.

Although frameworks like NIST AI Risk Management Framework (AI RMF) offers great value, implementing it presents a range of challenges, particularly when integrating it with existing risk policies, legacy compliance structures, and organizational governance models. Organizations often struggle with the technical complexity of AI itself. Apart from basic resistance to change, there is a need for interdisciplinary expertise to properly understand, measure, and mitigate AI-related risks. To address this, special organization-wide training efforts are essential. Another significant hurdle lies in data quality and governance, as ensuring the availability of high-quality, unbiased, and traceable data remains a persistent issue. For many teams, especially in smaller or resource-constrained settings, there is also the practical difficulty of allocating skilled personnel, time, and budget to implement the framework effectively.

Furthermore, the global regulatory landscape is highly fragmented and still evolving, requiring organizations to navigate overlapping standards like GDPR, the EU AI Act, ISO 42001, and local laws, which complicates compliance efforts. Internal challenges are equally important such as getting the buy-in from diverse stakeholders across technical, legal, and leadership teams, particularly when the risks of AI appear abstract or distant. Finally, many organizations are still maturing their AI governance structures, which means they may lack the foundational policies and controls necessary to operationalize the AI RMF effectively across use cases.

EU AI Act Compliance Framework

The European Union has been at the forefront of AI regulatory frameworks to ensure that AI systems meet safety, transparency, and human oversight requirements. EU regulations, including the EU Artificial Intelligence Act (AI Act), play a pivotal role in shaping how technology is developed, deployed, and governed across Europe and beyond. Apart from EU countries, their frameworks influence many organizations to align with EU regulations.

From a risk management perspective, the EU AI Act Compliance Framework classifies AI-related risks into four categories:

- Category 1 comprises what is termed as Unacceptable Risk, which includes social scoring, manipulative AI, and real-time biometric ID in public spaces. This type of risk is prohibited outright by regulators.
- Category 2 is High Risk, which is related to the use of AI in critical infrastructure, education, employment, law enforcement; Here there are strict obligations for risk management, conformity assessment, human oversight.
- Category 3 is Limited Risk, which comes from chatbots and deepfakes. The approach to be adopted here is to keep users informed that they are interacting with AI.
- Category 4 refers to Minimal Risk, which emanates from spam filters, AI in video games. Here there are no specific obligations now.

The purpose of risk categorization under the EU AI Act is to ensure that regulatory obligations are proportionate to the potential harm an AI system might cause. It forms the basis for the Act's risk-based approach, which aims to balance innovation with the protection of fundamental rights, safety, and democratic values.

The framework further emphasizes the following seven key attributes of trustworthy AI:

The EU Artificial Intelligence Act (AI Act) framework aligns with other standards like ISO/IEC 42001 and OECD AI Principles. It has extraterritorial reach, applying not only to AI systems developed or deployed within the European Union, but also to those used outside the EU if their outputs affect individuals within the EU (Article 2: Scope | EU Artificial Intelligence Act, n.d.). Non-compliance can result in significant penalties, including (Article 99: Penalties | EU Artificial Intelligence Act, n.d.):

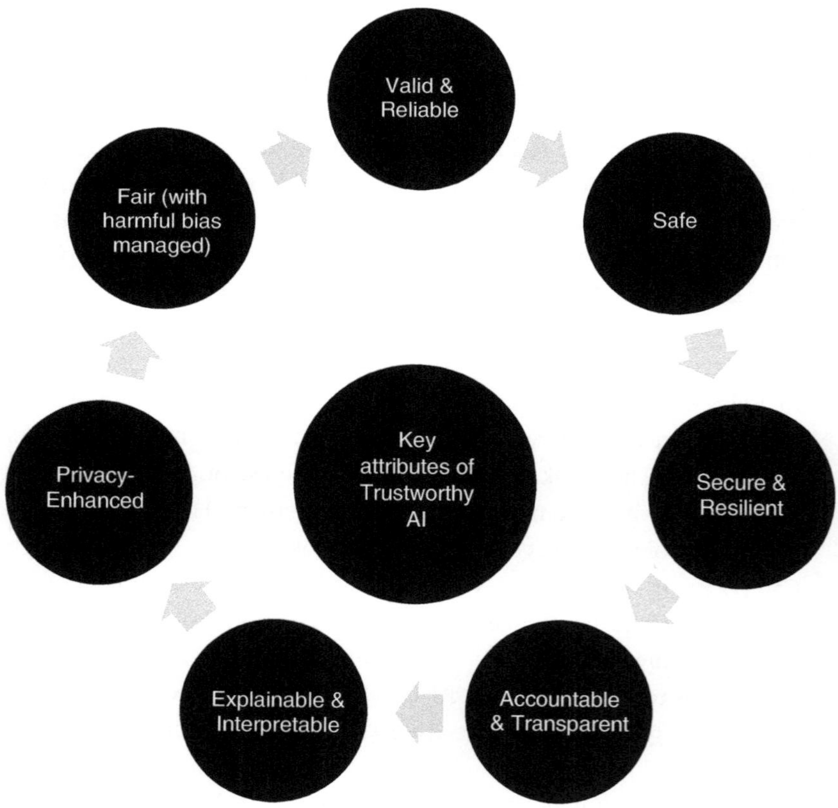

Image 9.7 Key Attributes of Trustworthy AI

1. Up to €35 million or 7% of global annual turnover for prohibited AI practices (whichever is higher).
   - This applies to **prohibited AI practices** under **Article 5** of the Act. These are considered the most serious violations and include:
   - **Subliminal manipulation** that distorts behavior in a harmful way.
   - **Exploitation of vulnerabilities** (e.g., age, disability) to materially distort behavior.
   - **Social scoring** by public authorities that leads to unjustified or disproportionate treatment.
   - **Real-time remote biometric identification** in public spaces without legal authorization.
   - **AI systems that manipulate human behavior to circumvent free will or safety**.

   These are deemed **unacceptable risk** systems and are outright banned in the EU.
2. Up to €15 million or 3% of global annual turnover for other regulatory violations.
   - This applies to **other regulatory violations**, such as:
   - **Non-compliance with obligations for High-Risk AI Systems**, including:
     - Failing to conduct conformity assessments
     - Inadequate risk management or data governance
     - Lack of transparency or human oversight
   - **Failure to register high-risk systems** in the EU database
   - **Improper documentation or record-keeping**
   - **Violations by providers, importers, distributors, or users** of AI systems who do not meet the required standards.

     These are serious but not outright banned but are typically tied to **high-risk systems** that require strict controls.

The EU AI Act requires compliance with the following requirements for High-Risk AI Systems detailed in Chapter III, Section 2 of the regulation. If an AI system is embedded in or constitutes a regulated product that must undergo independent safety evaluation, it is automatically classified as high-risk under the EU AI Act (The AI Act Explorer | EU Artificial Intelligence Act, n.d.) This ensures that AI used in critical applications such as autonomous vehicles or surgical robots meet stringent safety and compliance standards (Article 6: Classification Rules for High-Risk AI Systems | EU Artificial Intelligence Act, n.d.). These include obligations related to:

- Risk management systems across the AI lifecycle (Article 9)
- Data and data governance—representative, relevant, and error-minimized datasets
  (Article 10)
- Technical documentation and Record-Keeping (Article 11)
- Record-keeping (Article 12)
- Transparency and provision of information to deployers (Article 13)
- Human oversight mechanisms (Article 14)
- Accuracy, robustness, and cybersecurity standards (Article 15).

Under the EU Artificial Intelligence Act**,** General-Purpose AI (GPAI), the following obligations apply to providers of GPAI models, irrespective of whether

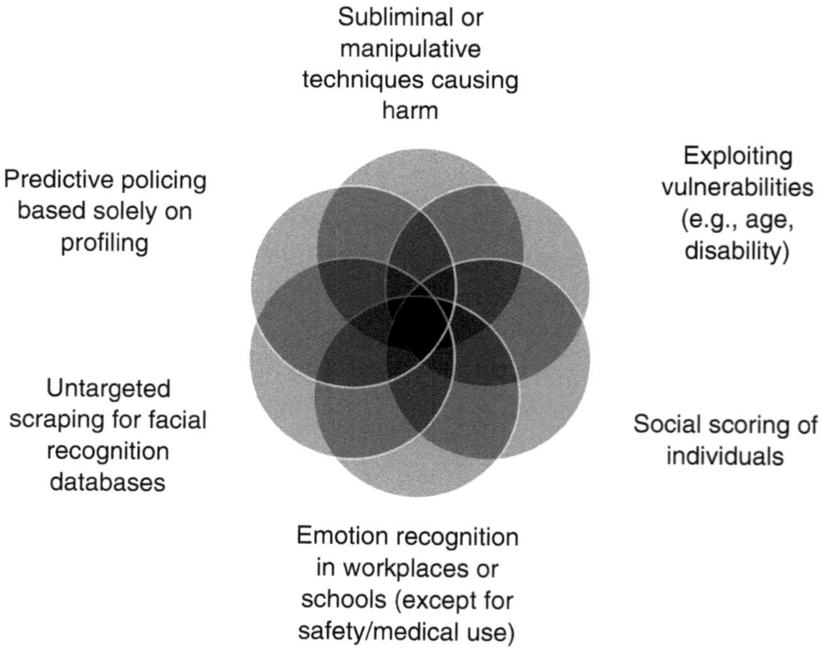

Image 9.8 Prohibited Areas under EU Act

they are based inside or outside the EU. All GPAI providers are required to publish summaries of training data, comply with the EU Copyright Directive, and provide technical documentation and usage instructions. They must also conduct model evaluations and adversarial testing, track/report serious incidents, and implement cybersecurity safeguards.

The EU AI Act prohibits certain AI practices under Article 5 (Article 5: Prohibited AI Practices | EU Artificial Intelligence Act, n.d.). This article outlines AI systems that are considered to pose an unacceptable risk to fundamental rights, safety, and democratic values, and are therefore banned outright from being placed on the market, put into service, or used in the EU. The prohibited areas listed in the article are shown in the following image.

The EU AI Act officially came into force in August 2024 with an implementation deadline of 2027. Nonetheless, the CEOs of prominent firms such as Philips, Siemens, and Mistral have called on the European Commission to introduce a two-year deferral of critical obligations outlined in the AI Act. The argument put forth by the business leaders for postponing the AI Act's obligations include the need to prioritize regulatory quality over speed and the fact that the Code of Practice on General-Purpose AI (GPAI), which is a voluntary framework designed to guide providers of foundational models like ChatGPT and Gemini in aligning with the EU AI Act, is still under development (Kroet, 2025).

ISO/IEC 42001:2023

The ISO/IEC 42001:2023 is the primary ISO standard for AI. It establishes a formal Artificial Intelligence Management System. The standard is still in its early adoption stage globally. Major technology firms (like Microsoft) have already begun aligning their AI governance practices with ISO/IEC 42001 and pursuing certification.

Regulatory requirements from privacy legislations from across the world are providing momentum and accelerating interest in ISO 42001 as a compliance-ready framework. Any organization that builds, offers, or uses AI products or services can apply this framework, no matter its size or industry. It follows the Plan-Do-Check-Act cycle, which is also used in other ISO standards to support continuous improvement in AI governance. The overall objective of the framework is to help manage AI-related risks and opportunities while ensuring ethical, transparent, and accountable AI practices. The four core functions of ISO/IEC 42001 are shown in the image as follows:

The framework provides a structured path for compliance, trust-building, and innovation for organizations deploying AI. Adoption is growing in sectors with high AI exposure such as finance, healthcare, and cloud services since trust, transparency, and accountability are critical for them.

The domains (clauses) and controls of ISO 420001 (Annex A) are as follows (CyberZoni, 2025):[9]

Core Domains (Clauses 4–10)—These clauses define the structure of the AI Management System:

Annex A Controls (A.2–A.10)—These are grouped into ten control domains, each with specific objectives and controls:

Each domain includes multiple controls. For example, **A.6** includes controls for responsible design, documentation, and lifecycle criteria.

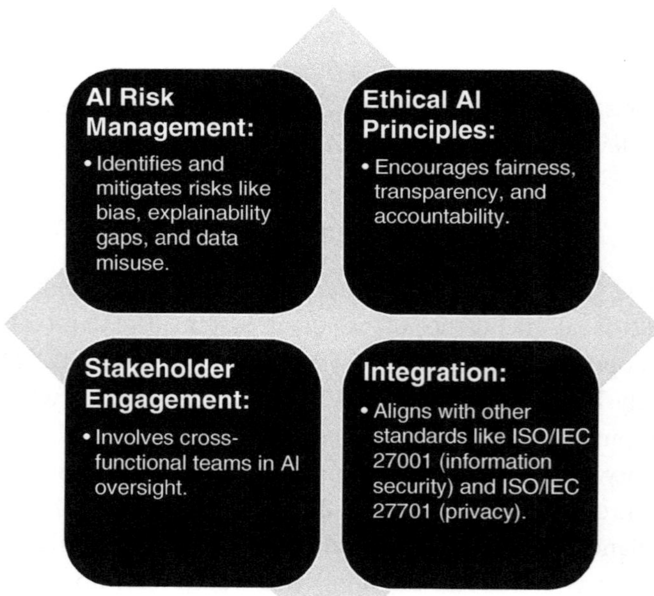

Image 9.9 Core Functions ISO 42001

Domain	Objective
A.2 Policies	Provide direction and support for AI aligned with business needs
A.3 Internal Organization	Establish accountability and governance for AI systems
A.4 Resources	Identify and manage AI system components and assets
A.5 Impact Assessment	Evaluate AI's effects on individuals, groups, and society
A.6 AI Lifecycle	Govern design, development, deployment, and decommissioning
A.7 Data	Ensure data quality, integrity, and relevance across the AI lifecycle
A.8 Information for Stakeholders	Communicate AI risks and impacts transparently
A.9 Use of AI	Ensure responsible and policy-aligned AI usage
A.10 Third Parties	Manage risks from suppliers and external AI systems

Table 9.2 ISO42001 Core Domains

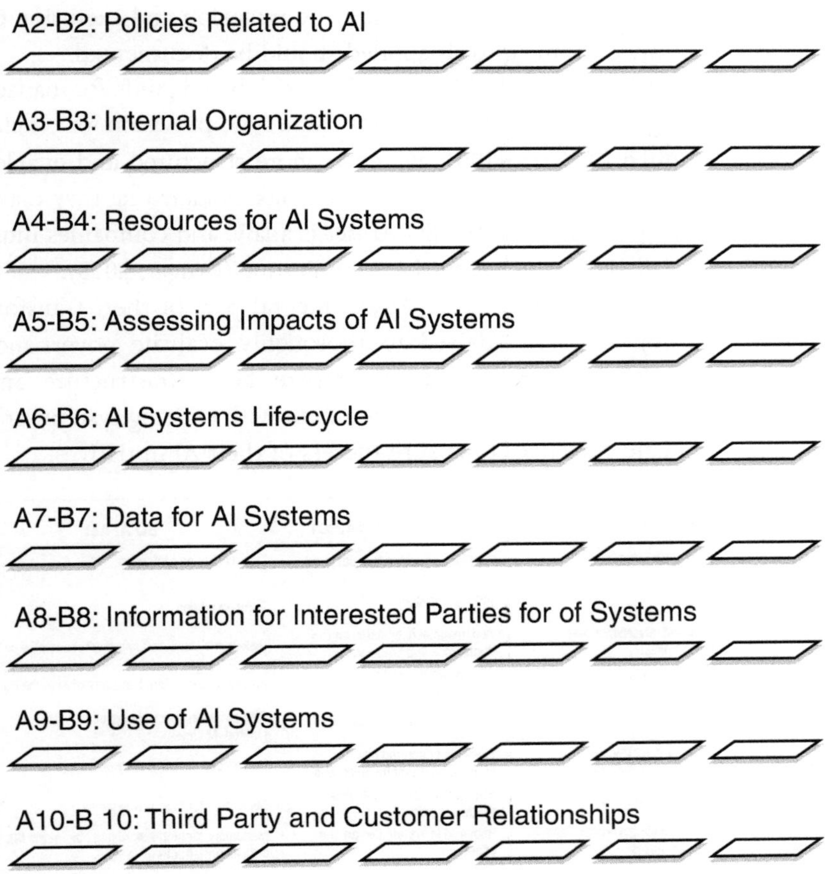

Image 9.10 Control Domains

Contextual Guidance

Annex C: Helps identify AI-related objectives and risk sources (e.g., bias, explainability, autonomy).

Annex D: Shows how ISO 42001 integrates with other standards like ISO/IEC 27001, ISO 9001, and GDPR.

Like other ISO standards, organizations are not required to implement all Annex A controls. However, they are required to conduct an AI risk assessment (Clause 6.1.2), determine applicable controls based on identified risks and opportunities, and consider organizational objectives and stakeholder expectations. A statement of applicability must be prepared not only listing the controls deployed but also justifying inclusion and exclusion of every control. Any custom controls applied should be documented.

To summarize, The NIST AI RMF is a flexible, risk-based guide for managing AI, and using it is completely voluntary. There is no provision for official certification unlike ISO/IEC 42001, which is more structured and enables organizations to get certified and to show their stakeholders that they manage AI responsibly. In contrast, the EU AI Act is a law, and companies must follow it, especially if they use high-risk AI in Europe (Kruger, 2025):

Organizations planning to make AI an integral part of their transformational journey are well advised to thoroughly evaluate governance frameworks, budget for implementation, prepare their infrastructure, and invest in workforce training, ensuring alignment with existing systems and long-term strategic objectives to ensure success of their AI initiatives.

Dimension	NIST AI RMF	ISO/IEC 42001	EU AI Act
Type	Voluntary framework	Certifiable international standard	Legally binding regulation
Origin	U.S. (NIST)	ISO / IEC (Global)	European Union
Primary Focus	Risk-based governance and trustworthiness	AI management systems and continuous improvement	Risk-tiered regulation and market compliance
Applicability	All sectors and AI use cases	All organizations using or developing AI	Providers, users, and importers of AI in the EU
Core Structure	Govern, Map, Measure, Manage	Plan, Do, Check, Act (PDCA)	Risk classification: Unacceptable, High, Limited, Minimal
Ethical Principles	Embedded in trustworthiness traits (e.g., fairness, transparency)	Explicitly integrated into Management system objectives	Referenced but not deeply operationalized
Risk Management	Central to all functions	Structured assessments and treatment plans	Mandatory for high-risk systems
Human Oversight	Encouraged via governance and lifecycle controls	Required in system design and operation	Mandatory for high-risk AI (e.g., biometric ID), critical infrastructure)
Certification	Not certifiable	Certifiable via accredited bodies	Compliance enforced by national regulators
Interoperability	Aligns with ISO/IEC 42001 and OECD AI Principles	Dsigned to integrate with ISO 27001, 27701, 23894	May require mapping for global compliance alignment

Table 9.3 NIST AI RMF vs. ISO/IEC 42001 vs. EU AI Act—A Comparison

In addition to the above three most prominent AI governance frameworks, there are several others that merit consideration. These fall under the following categories:

Global and Intergovernmental Frameworks

Prioritize ethical, human rights–centered governance frameworks that extend beyond national jurisdictions.

- OECD AI Principles (2019, updated 2024)
- UNESCO Recommendation on the Ethics of AI
- Council of Europe Convention on AI (CAI)
- Global Partnership on AI (GPAI)

These are mainly non-binding (except CAI), value-based, emphasize inclusivity, transparency, and human rights.

National and Regional Regulatory Frameworks

Legal and policy frameworks developed by individual countries or regions.

- EU AI Act (tiered risk-based regulation across the EU)
- China's Algorithmic Regulation Framework
- Singapore's Model AI Governance Framework
- Canada's Directive on Automated Decision-Making (DADM)
- US Executive Orders & AI Bill of Rights.

These have varying degrees of enforceability, reflect distinct policy priorities (e.g., innovation vs. control).

Industry-Led/Corporate Governance Models

Voluntary frameworks developed by major firms to manage AI risk at scale.
PwC Responsible AI Framework

- IBM AI Governance Framework
- Microsoft Responsible AI Standard
- Google AI Principles and Model Cards
- Meta's Responsible AI Approach.

These frameworks emphasize responsible innovation, often aligned with ISO/NIST, include tools like impact assessments and model governance boards.

Such a wide variety of AI governance frameworks make the job of choosing one that is the best fit for an organization a difficult one. However, there are three important criteria that must be prioritized to make a choice.

1. Purpose Alignment and Scope—Evaluate whether the framework matches your organization's AI use cases, industry context, and strategic goals.
2. Jurisdictional and Sectoral Applicability—Does the framework apply within your operating region or industry? Is it recognized by national regulators or clients? Are there sector-specific extensions?
3. Integrability and Interoperability—Ensure that the framework can integrate with your existing management systems, risk models, and audit workflows.

Bibliography

AIRisk Management Framework | NIST. (2025, May 5). NIST. https://www.nist.gov/itl/ai-risk-management-framework

Article2: Scope | EU Artificial Intelligence Act. (n.d.). https://artificialintelligenceact.eu/article/2/

Article5: Prohibited AI Practices | EU Artificial Intelligence Act. (n.d.). https://artificialintelligenceact.eu/article/5/

Article6: Classification Rules for High-Risk AI Systems | EU Artificial Intelligence Act. (n.d.). https://artificialintelligenceact.eu/article/6/

Article99: Penalties | EU Artificial Intelligence Act. (n.d.). https://artificialintelligenceact.eu/article/99/

CyberZoni. (2025, March 1). ISO 42001 explained | Full list of clauses and controls. *CyberZoni.com*. https://cyberzoni.com/standards/iso-42001/

Kroet, C. (2025, July 3). Europe's top CEOs call for Commission to slow down on AI Act. *Euronews*. https://www.euronews.com/next/2025/07/03/europes-top-ceos-call-for-commission-to-slow-down-on-ai-act

Kruger, N. (2025, January 21). Managing AI Governance in the future: An overview of the EU AI Act, ISO/IEC 42001, and NIST AI RMF. CertPro LLC. https://certpro.com/ai-governance-eu-iso-nist-overview/

The AI Act Explorer | EU Artificial Intelligence Act. (n.d.). https://artificialintelligenceact.eu/ai-act-explorer/

U.S. Department of Commerce, Raimondo, G. M., Locascio, L. E., Autio, C., Dunietz, J., Hall, P., Jain, S., Roberts, K., Schwartz, R., Stanley, M., & Tabassi, E. (2024). Artificial Intelligence Risk Management Framework: Generative Artificial Intelligence Profile. In NIST Trustworthy and Responsible AI. National Institute of Standards and Technology. https://nvlpubs.nist.gov/nistpubs/ai/NIST.AI.600-1.pdf

10

BEST PRACTICES IN AI GOVERNANCE

Best practices in AI governance are not abstract ideals—they are the small, repeatable habits that keep innovation safe, compliant, and trusted. Organizations that embed these habits early build resilience; those that delay find themselves forever chasing fixes. This chapter brings together the lessons that matter most: how to set up clear processes, bake in privacy and security, make risk decisions quickly, and keep humans—both the builders and the impacted—at the center.

Building Practical Foundations

Every effective AI program starts with visibility. Create a single entry point for every AI initiative so that nothing slips under the radar. A simple intake form—covering what the model does, what data it uses, who owns it, and who might be affected—can replace dozens of scattered conversations. Once logged, each use case is triaged by risk: some will be routine and low impact, others will warrant deeper review. The goal isn't to slow

DOI: 10.4324/9781003682530-13

progress but to make it traceable. When people know where to go and what's expected, compliance becomes second nature.

Anchoring to a Reference Model

Frameworks bring consistency. The NIST AI Risk Management Framework is a flexible way to manage risk across the lifecycle, while ISO/IEC 42001 offers a certifiable management-system approach. For organizations operating in the European Union, the EU AI Act is the mandatory reference point. Each serves a different purpose—NIST helps you think in outcomes, ISO ensures process discipline, and the EU Act enforces accountability. Choose one as your base, then adapt it to your culture and structure rather than adopting it verbatim.

Privacy and Security by Design

The strongest AI programs build privacy and security from the start. Data protection isn't a compliance layer—it's a design principle. Before development begins, teams should challenge their assumptions: Is the data necessary? Is its use lawful and proportionate? Could the same result be achieved with less?

The goal is to reduce exposure and build confidence at every stage. Keep the amount of sensitive data to the minimum required, control who can access it, and ensure strong encryption in transit and at rest. Align data retention with purpose—delete what's no longer needed—and continuously monitor for drift or misuse.

Privacy threat-modeling tools such as LINDDUN help teams identify weak points early and guide secure design choices. When these practices are built in, they don't slow down innovation; they remove friction later. Teams move faster because their systems are already safe, explainable, and ready to earn trust.

Making Risk Reviews Work in Practice

Formal risk reviews often fail because they feel bureaucratic. Keep them short, focused, and scaled to impact. A low-risk use case may only need quick self-assessment and manager sign-off. Higher-risk projects—those touching people's rights, safety, or finances—deserve a deeper look with privacy, security, and legal teams at the table. The key is predictability: everyone should know what triggers a full review and how long it will take. Risk-based gates give leadership confidence without choking momentum.

Documenting with Purpose

Documentation builds trust when it's concise and useful. Every AI model should travel with a few essential artifacts: a model card explaining what it does and where it works best; a data sheet describing where the data came from; and an evaluation summary showing accuracy, fairness, and safety results. Together these serve as the memory of the system—what decisions were made, who made them, and why.

Testing, Red-Teaming, and Continuous Monitoring

Good AI governance doesn't end at launch. Regular testing and adversarial "red teaming" expose blind spots before they reach customers. Continuous monitoring ensures models stay within safe and ethical bounds as conditions change. Tracking model drift, bias shifts, and data quality degradation can be automated with alerts that prompt human review. The principle is simple: test before you trust and keep testing after you deploy.

Keeping Humans in the Loop

Human oversight must be more than a tick box exercise. Design systems so that people can understand, question, and override automated outputs when needed. Clear explanations, escalation paths, and user controls reinforce accountability. In high-impact domains like credit, employment, or health, the ability for a person to step in is not optional; it's what earns and maintains legitimacy.

Managing Vendors and the AI Supply Chain

Most organizations will rely on third-party models, APIs, or cloud services. Each of these relationships carries its own risks. Conduct due diligence that looks beyond price and performance to include data sourcing, bias testing, and security commitments. Contracts should reflect privacy and ethical standards: no unapproved secondary use of data, clear incident-reporting expectations, and transparency around model updates. Treat vendors as part of your governance ecosystem, not as outsiders.

Measuring What Matters

Metrics give leaders clarity without overwhelming teams. Track how many AI projects flow through the intake system, how long reviews take, and how often risks are mitigated on schedule. Add measures for fairness, privacy, and transparency—such as bias stability across groups or the rate of user requests for explanations or data deletion. These indicators tell a story about both operational efficiency and ethical maturity.

Culture, Communication, and Continuous Learning

Policies and frameworks succeed only when people understand them. Communicate governance in plain language: "Here's how we build AI safely," not "Here's our compliance matrix." Hold short, regular learning sessions to share lessons from audits or incidents. Recognize teams that spot and fix issues early; reward transparency over perfection. Culture grows through repetition and example, not mandates.

Being Incident-Ready

No program is flawless, but preparedness minimizes harm. Build and rehearse joint playbooks for privacy, security, and AI incidents. Simulate model malfunctions, data leaks, or unfair outcomes. Practice escalation, notification, and remediation together. After every drill or real event, update controls and share learnings widely. The measure of maturity is not the absence of incidents, but the speed and honesty of your response.

Continuous Improvement

AI governance is a moving target. Technologies evolve; regulations tighten, and social expectations shift. Review your program quarterly: refresh the risk register, update metrics, and retire outdated tools. Keep a simple maturity roadmap that shows progress. When people see improvement, they stay engaged. When leadership sees progress, they stay invested.

AI Governance Policy

An **AI Governance Policy** is a formal organizational document that outlines how artificial intelligence (AI) technologies are developed, used, and managed in a safe, ethical, and compliant manner.

Purpose of an AI Governance Policy

It serves as a **blueprint** for ensuring that AI systems:

- Operate within legal and regulatory boundaries
- Align with ethical principles like fairness, accountability, and transparency
- Protect data privacy and security
- Support responsible innovation across all teams.

Key Components of an AI Governance Policy

Here's what's typically included:

1. **Purpose and Scope**
   - Defines the intent of the policy (e.g., safe deployment of AI)
   - Identifies the types of AI systems and stakeholders covered (internal models, third-party AI services, etc.).
2. **Roles and Responsibilities**
   - Assigns accountability (e.g., AI Ethics Committee, Data Governance Officer, legal, engineering)
   - Outlines the duties of model developers, reviewers, auditors, and business owners.
3. **Governance Framework**
   - Refers to frameworks like:
     - NIST AI RMF (Risk Management)
     - ISO/IEC 42001 (AI management systems)
     - EU AI Act (legal compliance).
4. **Use Case Intake and Approval**
   - Describes how new AI use cases must be submitted, risk-assessed, and approved before development or deployment.
5. **Risk Classification and Assessment**
   - Defines how AI systems are classified by impact/risk (e.g., low, medium, high).

- o Triggers enhanced review for systems affecting privacy, safety, or human rights.

6. **Data Governance and Privacy**
   - o Mandates:
     - – Lawful basis for data use
     - – Data minimization and retention
     - – Privacy-by-design and consent mechanisms.
7. **Bias and Fairness Evaluation**
   - o Requires ongoing testing for demographic fairness
   - o Sets policies for redress or retraining if bias is found.
8. **Explainability and Transparency**
   - o Encourages documentation (e.g., model cards, data sheets)
   - o Requires human-readable explanations for high-stakes decisions.
9. **Human Oversight**
   - o Ensures the ability to override AI decisions where appropriate (e.g., credit, healthcare)
   - o Defines clear escalation and appeal processes.
10. **Monitoring and Incident Response**
    - o Sets up real-time monitoring for model drift, security threats, and ethical risks
    - o Requires playbooks for AI failures or harmful outcomes.
11. **Third-Party and Vendor Management**
    - o Applies governance to outsourced or third-party AI
    - o Requires contractual clauses covering transparency, retraining, and incident response.
12. **Training and Culture**
    - o Promotes awareness and training programs on AI ethics and governance
    - o Encourages a speak-up culture around questionable AI use.

Why It Matters

A good AI governance policy:

- Protects your **organization** from legal, reputational, and financial risk
- Builds **trust** with customers, regulators, and the public
- Promotes **responsible innovation** by embedding ethics into AI from design through deployment.

Bibliography

Brundage, M., Avin, S., Wang, J., Belfield, H., Krueger, G., Hadfield, G., Khlaaf, H., Yang, J., Toner, H., Fong, R., & Maharaj, T. (2020). Toward trustworthy AI development: Mechanisms for supporting verifiable claims. *arXiv preprint* arXiv:2004.07213.

European Commission. (2023). *The EU Artificial Intelligence Act*. https://artificialintelligenceact.eu

Goodman, B., & Flaxman, S. (2017). European Union regulations on algorithmic decision-making and a "right to explanation". *AI Magazine*, 38(3), 50–57.

International Organization for Standardization. (2023). *ISO/IEC 42001: Artificial Intelligence – Management System Standard*.

National Institute of Standards and Technology. (2023). *AI Risk Management Framework*. https://www.nist.gov/itl/ai-risk-management-framework

Raji, I. D., & Buolamwini, J. (2019). Actionable auditing: Investigating the impact of publicly naming biased performance results of commercial AI products. *Proceedings of the 2019 AAAI/ACM Conference on AI, Ethics, and Society (AIES '19)*, 429–435. https://doi.org/10.1145/3306618.3314244

Veale, M., & Edwards, L. (2018). Clarity, surprises, and further questions in the Article 29 Working Party draft guidance on automated decision-making and profiling. *Computer Law & Security Review*, 34(2), 398–404.

Appendix

Artificial Intelligence ("AI")

Governance Policy

Used with Permission from RISKQ

September 2025

Table of Contents

Purpose

This policy establishes general guidelines and best practices for the responsible and ethical use of AI within RISKQ and each of its subsidiaries (the "Company"). It aims to mitigate the risk of adverse consumer outcomes and ensure that our employees are using AI systems and platforms in a manner that aligns with the company's values, adheres to legal and regulatory standards, and promotes the safety and well-being of our clients and stakeholders.

Any individual subsidiary or business unit within the Company may adopt additional policies and procedures that are more tailored to that subsidiary or business unit's specific and actual use of an AI product or service; provided, however, that any specific policies and procedures are consistent with the general guidelines and best practices set forth herein.

Scope of Applicability

What Does This Policy Apply To?

This policy covers the development or use of Company-approved AI tools and systems that enable authorized users to explore their capabilities to improve decision-making, enhance productivity, automate tasks, or otherwise help the Company achieve its business objectives.

The following types of AI are covered by this policy and are further defined in Section 3:

- Traditional Machine Learning
- Deep learning (i.e., neural networks)
- Natural Language Processing
- Generative AI (e.g., ChatGPT)
- Robotic Process Automation (RPA)

This policy covers the life cycle for the Company's AI products including product planning and analysis, development, design, implementation, testing and integration, and maintenance. It applies to certain components of implementation including marketing, underwriting, rating, and pricing, case management, withdrawal and claims administration and payment, and fraud detection.

To Whom Does This Policy Apply?

This policy governs the actions and decisions of all employees, contractors, consultants, and temporary employees who have authorized access to the Company's data and/or Information Technology ("IT") systems, including, but not limited to, networks, computers, tablets, mobile devices, databases, storage facilities, applications, and internet resources, in connection with the use or development of AI.

All users of AI are responsible for reading this policy and abiding by its terms and conditions, as well as any other policies and procedures adopted by specific Company subsidiaries or business units.

Definitions

The application of this policy depends on a shared understanding of the meaning of specific terms and phrases. The table below includes such terms.

Table 10.1 Definitions

Term/Phrase	*Abbreviation*	*Definition*
Artificial Intelligence	AI	Artificial intelligence applies advanced analysis and logic-based techniques, including machine learning, to interpret events, support and automate decisions, and take action.
Bias		Bias is the inappropriate valuation or deprecation of information in favor of or against people, things, or ideas.
Deep Learning		A type of AI that uses artificial neural networks that simulate the actions of the brain to learn more complex patterns and relationships within data.
Explainability		In the context of AI, explainability refers to the ability of humans to discover how the tool or service arrived at the output generated based on the prompts (input data) and the dataset underpinning the model.
External AI		Publicly accessible AI tools and systems (e.g., ChatGPT) that are not structured or designed to comply with the Company's policies or needs, or for which the inputs and outputs are not contained within the Company's environment.
Foundation Models	FM	Foundation models are large-parameter models that are trained on a broad gamut of datasets in a self-supervised manner. They are mostly based on transformer or diffusion deep neural network architectures, addressing conversational needs and a wide range of generative tasks including text, image, audio, and code generation.

(Continued)

Table 10.1 (Continued)

Term/Phrase	*Abbreviation*	*Definition*
Generative Artificial Intelligence		Generative AI refers to AI techniques that use data representations to learn about and generate brand-new, unique artifacts that resemble but do not necessarily repeat original data. These artifacts can serve both benign and nefarious purposes. Generative AI can produce novel content (including text, images, videos, audios, computer code, synthetic data, and models of physical objects).
High-Risk AI		Models that materially influence decisions for employment, education, financial matters, healthcare, government services, housing, legal services, and insurance.
Internal AI		AI tools and systems developed or licensed for use by the organization. This includes external or third-party AI tools for which the inputs and outputs are maintained within the Company's environment.
Large Language Model	LLM	A large language model (LLM) is a specialized type of AI that has been trained on vast amounts of text to understand existing content and generate original content.
Machine Learning	ML	Advanced machine learning algorithms are composed of many technologies (under the categories of statistical learning, algorithmic machine learning, and deep learning, etc.) The algorithms are trained with data using, supervised, unsupervised and/or reinforcement learning techniques to create useful models.

(Continued)

Table 10.1 (Continued)

Term/Phrase	*Abbreviation*	*Definition*
Must		Any action that *must* occur is mandatory and non-negotiable.
Natural Language Processing	NLP	Processes that allow computers to recognize and generate human-like speech and text, and to engage in related communications.
Protected Health Information	PHI	An individual's health, treatment, and payment information, and any further information maintained in the same designated record set that could identify the individual or be used with other information in the record set to identify the individual.
Personal Identifiable Information	PII	Any information that directly or indirectly identifies, or assists in the identifiability of, a natural person.
Prompt		A prompt is the information provided to a GenAI model to produce content desired by the creator of the prompt. The information in a prompt is structured to be interpreted and used an LLM or an SLM (Small Language Model) and supporting technologies (e.g., agents).
Prompt Engineering		Prompt engineering is an emerging skill and profession focused on the development of highly effective prompts to optimize GenAI performance.
Robotic Process Automation	RBA	The use of software to automate processes to perform repetitive functions in a manner that emulates human-driven activities.

(Continued)

Table 10.1 (Continued)

Term/Phrase	*Abbreviation*	*Definition*
Sensitive Data		Specific personal data with additional sensitivity as defined in applicable laws/regulations. For example, data revealing racial or ethnic origin, political opinions, religious or philosophical beliefs, trade union membership, genetic data, biometric data, data concerning a person's health, sex life or sexual orientation.
Software as a Service	SaaS	Software as a service (SaaS) is software that is owned, delivered, and managed remotely by one or more providers. The provider delivers software based on one set of common code and data definitions that is consumed in a one-to-many model by all contracted customers at any time on a pay-for-use basis or as a subscription based on usage metrics.
Should		Any action that should occur is recommended but is not mandatory.

Roles and Responsibilities

AI Governance Committee: Maintains oversight of AI usage and the administration of this policy. The committee will perform the following functions:

- Ensure that all AI projects use and comply with this policy.
- Review the risks of approved AI projects.
- Ensure the AI Product Counsel (AIPOC) is properly executing its functions.
- Define and propose modifications to improve this policy.

The Committee will consist of the following representatives or their designees:

- Chief Compliance Officer
- Chief Information & Digital Officer
- Chief Information Security & Privacy Officer
- Chief Technology Officer
- General Counsel
- Head of Artificial Intelligence
- Head of Audit and Risk Management

RISKQ Leadership Team

Consists of the Chief Information & Digital Officer, Chief Technology Officer, Chief Information Security & Privacy Officer, the Senior Vice President of Application Development, and the Senior Executive Vice President & Assistant to the CEO. The RISKQ leadership team will perform the following functions:

- Implement and administer AI tools and systems; monitor usage, performance, and ensure compliance with this policy.
- Establish the AI strategy for the company with approval from the AI Governance Committee.
- Oversee the execution and implementation of the AI strategy, tools and services.

AIPOC

The AIPOC will serve as the front-line authority for the review and approval of AI usage for the Company. The AIPOC will be responsible for the following functions:

- Review, approve, and prioritize AI projects and usage.
- Communicate approval decisions and exceptions to the policy to the AI Governance Committee and advise them on a project's risks.
- Maintain a list of all designated owners of AI tools and systems.
- Maintain an inventory of approved AI projects and projects reviewed but not approved, as described in Section 5 of this policy.

Users

Employees, temporary employees, contractors, and consultants who are granted access to Company AI tools or who are authorized to use.

Inventory

For each AI application that is governed by the program, the following details about the application must be documented and maintained by the AIPOC prior to the application's delivery to users:

- its purpose.
- the problem it is intended to solve.
- the owner of the product.
- the inputs and outputs.
- the data used to train it.
- whether it is an internal or external application.
- the anticipated benefits to the Company and its customers.
- potential risks (and risk rating if deemed appropriate).
- who may potentially be harmed if anyone.
- whether the model involves automated decision-making or human oversight.
- any necessary safeguards.
- who is responsible for the successful deployment of the AI application.

Risk Management and Compliance

AI use and development guidelines, and risk management processes shall be based on the NIST AI Risk Management Framework (RMF), when applicable, as well as any current or future laws or regulations to which the Company is subject.

AI Risks

The risks associated with AI are unique and inherent in the processing of inputs and outputs and how those outputs are used. The material AI risks include, but are not limited to, the following:

- Sensitive data may be leaked through the inputs or outputs of the AI model.
- Company data may be stored in unsecured third-party environments.
- AI models may produce incorrect, misleading, or copyrighted results unbeknownst to the user.
- The Company's use of AI may violate certain federal and state laws.
- AI algorithms and results may be discriminatory or biased toward people or groups of people based on their race, gender, ethnicity, sex, religion, gender, national origin, disability, or any other class protected by law. This can be attributed to poor model design, biased training data, or lack of diversity on the development team.

Risk Mitigation

To reduce these risks, an AI Governance Committee will be established to oversee and monitor the design, development, validation, implementation, use, ongoing monitoring, updating, and retirement of AI tools by authorized users in accordance with this policy. The AIPOC shall advise the Committee on the statistics that will be compiled and the process by which each AI system will be monitored. The AI Governance Committee will determine the frequency required to receive updates for each system.

Algorithmic Discrimination Risk Mitigation

Reasonable care to protect against AI discrimination must be taken including, but not limited to, the following:

- Completing an impact assessment of the AI system, where applicable.
- Annually reviewing the deployment of each AI system is used to ensure that it is not causing algorithmic discrimination.
- Disclosing information about the AI system; that may be a substantial factor in making a consequential decision concerning the consumer, where applicable.
- Providing a consumer with an opportunity to correct any incorrect personal data that an AI system processed in making a consequential decision, where applicable.
- Providing a consumer with an opportunity to appeal, via human review if technically feasible, an adverse consequential decision concerning the consumer arising from the deployment of an AI system, where applicable.

- Making a publicly available statement summarizing the types of AI systems being developed or substantially modified and how the developer manages any known or reasonably foreseeable risks of discrimination, where applicable.

Risk Mitigation for External AI

Information for external AI systems that are owned by a vendor or third party, and which are licensed to the company, shall be obtained through responses to a company-administered AI survey that each vendor must complete. Use of external AI will be risk-based and consider the following factors, among others:

- The expected inputs of outputs of the model and how such elements are protected.
- The vendor's use of other third parties for the AI.
- The vendor's AI Governance Program and an Employee AI Code of Conduct, if any.
- Statistics to validate the accuracy of the model, where applicable.
- Compliance with applicable laws.
- Tier 1 vendors who provide AI systems or services to the Company shall be required to review and update their responses to the survey at least annually or as deemed appropriate by the Company's AI Governance Committee.

Information Security and Privacy Management of AIs

The Information Security and Privacy Department is responsible for expanding existing cybersecurity and privacy controls and practices to support this policy. This includes defining, designing, deploying, and maintaining policy compliance monitoring and enforcement tools, systems, and processes in support of all elements of this policy, including, but not limited to:

- Identity and access management for Company-controlled environments.
- AI user activity monitoring and control.
- Assurance of model data provenance.
- Use and handling of PII and other sensitive information, including the ability to opt-out of processing PII for AI decisions where applicable.
- Data movement and storage.

- AI deployment.
- AI modification.
- AI retirement.
- AI output monitoring (i.e., compliance with content guidelines).
- AI performance integrity (e.g., model drift).
- Installation and attempted installation of AI applications.
- Vulnerability management of AI.
- Response management of AI policy violations.

The Information Security and Privacy Department will perform a review of the security and privacy risks identified from AI usage and provide the results of the assessment to the Committee.

For internal AI involving LLMs, the review will follow, at a minimum, the OWASP Top 10 for LLM Applications framework:

1. Prompt Injections
2. Insecure Output Handling
3. Training Data Poisoning
4. Denial of Service
5. Supply Chain
6. Permission Issues
7. Data Leakage
8. Excessive Agency
9. Overreliance
10. Insecure Plugins

AI Requirements for Capital Management and Securities LLC Personnel

Ensure that with respect to any AI systems used in connection with Capital Management's investment advisory business (e.g., portfolio management, trading) and Securities LLC's broker-dealer business (e.g., rendering of investment advice), each of these subsidiaries: (i) complies with applicable SEC and other regulatory requirements and (ii) adopts, implements and maintains written policies and procedures (or revises existing written policies and procedures), as necessary to comply with such applicable regulatory requirements.

Policy Statements

Application Security

AI tools and systems must comply with all existing policies, architectures, and standards governing the development, use, maintenance, monitoring, security, modification, updating and retirement of applications, including SaaS.

Data Security

All data use associated with AI tools or systems must comply with existing policies, architectures, and standards governing data creation, transportation, monitoring, security, modification, updating and destruction.

Identity and Access Management

Access to AI tools or systems must comply with all existing policies, architectures, and standards governing identity and access management.

Acceptable Use of AI

This Acceptable Use Policy applies to all employees, temporary employees, contractors, and consultants who develop or use AI systems for Company business.

Things You Must DO

- Understand that all AI systems may be useful, but they are not a substitute for human judgment.
- Understand that AI systems are prone to "hallucinations," false answers or information that is stale, and therefore a human must carefully verify responses.
- Treat all information you provide to AI systems as if it will go viral on the Internet, be attributed to you or the Company, regardless of the settings you have selected within the tool, or the assurances made by its administrators.
- Ensure that only the authorized Company-managed AI systems are used for business purposes.

- Verify that any response from AI systems that you intend to rely on, or use is accurate, appropriate, and unbiased.
- Ensure that responses from AI systems are not a violation of another individual's or entity's intellectual property or privacy rights and are consistent with all Company policies and applicable laws. If you are unsure, consult with RISKQ management.
- Ensure the use of AI complies with the Electronic Communications Policy and the acceptable use of electronic media.
- Ensure that any documents containing AI system output are labeled as "Contains AI output from [*AI application name*]." Such labeling can be incorporated into a document footnote. In cases where no document is generated or prepared, e.g., a chat bot, disclosure of the use of AI shall be made on the webpage where the chat bot is accessed.
- Only use AI systems for lawful, ethical, and authorized purposes.
- Monitor the performance and output of the AI system and report unexpected or inappropriate AI behaviors to RISKQ management and the AI system owner.

Things You Must NOT DO:

- DO NOT use AI systems to make or help you make employment decisions about applicants or employees, including recruitment, hiring, retention, promotions, transfers, performance monitoring, discipline, demotion, or terminations.
- DO NOT use AI systems to provide advice, guidance, or recommendations to clients.
- DO NOT use Personal Identifiable Information (PII), such as names combined with social security numbers, dates of birth, username and password combinations, or financial account information, as inputs to AI systems, unless such information is properly processed by the AI system pipeline and will not expose PII to unauthorized persons or entities.
- DO NOT share inputs and outputs from AI systems with unauthorized individuals or third parties.
- DO NOT purchase, integrate, download, or install any AI application or software that was not previously approved by the AIPOC with or on internal Company systems. This prohibition applies to the downloading of modules or add-ons for authorized AI systems unless such add-ons are approved by RISKQ management.

- DO NOT use any version or implementation of an approved AI system for business purposes other than the Company's approved version(s). Doing so may result in the termination of your AI privileges or other disciplinary action.
- DO NOT provide or attempt to provide AI systems or tools to clients that permit direct client input unless the AI tools are expressly approved for such use by RISKQ management.
- DO NOT use AI systems in an unethical or unlawful manner including, but not limited to, fraudulent, abusive, obscene, defamatory, offensive, or otherwise harmful activities.
- DO NOT use recordings of meetings as inputs to AI systems unless the recording of the meeting was approved by Information Security in advance or the use of recordings was approved by the AIPOC as part of the AI system approval process, and all meeting attendees agree to the use of their voice, content, likeness, and image.
- DO NOT use AI systems to breach any contractual or fiduciary obligation.
- DO NOT use as inputs files or data that you are not authorized to view. DO NOT download data from unknown or untrusted sources on the public Internet to use as inputs.
- DO NOT use AI systems to interfere with or disrupt the operation or security of any network, system, or service, or to gain unauthorized access or control over any such network, system, or service.
- DO NOT use AI systems to generate or transmit malicious code, such as viruses, worms, trojans, or ransomware.
- DO NOT use AI systems to impersonate or misrepresent any person or entity, or to deceive or mislead anyone.

Exceptions

Exceptions may be granted by the AIPOC on a case-by-case basis. The product owner must submit, in writing, an exception request to the AIPOC that includes, at a minimum, the following information:

- Date of request
- Name of person making the request and name of product owner if they are different
- Name of project or AI tool, if applicable
- Type or description of the exception being requested
- Justification for the exception.

The AIPOC will review the request and render a decision based on the facts and circumstances at the time of the review and the risks and opportunities presented by the exception.

The AIPOC will present each approved exception to the AI Governance Committee.

Internal AI Development

All processes, tools, infrastructure, and data used in the development, modification or refinement of AI must comply with all applicable policies, standards and processes for application development, deployment, monitoring, security, and maintenance.

All data used in the development of AI must be, as applicable, created, collected, and secured in compliance with existing policies governing the use of data in application development and testing processes.

New applications must conform to the Company's project approval process and the Software

Development Life Cycle requirements and documentation.

Prior to and following AI deployment, all AI output must be monitored for degradation of accuracy and quality.

AI Ownership

AI tools or services used within the Company must have designated owners. For each AI, the owner is responsible, as applicable for each use case, for:

- Establishing and documenting the minimum acceptable quality and performance standards used to evaluate the acceptability for, and appropriateness of, the AI's use, and assuring that such standards are met.
- Establishing and documenting the required training associated with each AI for developers, owners, and users.
- Assuring that the development, implementation, functionality, and use of the AI system complies with this policy.
- Assuring that data used with or produced by the AI complies with this and other policies and regulations governing data management and data security.

- Working with the AIPOC to perform an impact assessment of the AI product.
- Assuring that security controls are reviewed and approved by Information Security throughout the AI product lifecycle and in accordance with security policies and procedures.
- Reviewing the AI outputs and ensuring that such outputs are accurate and free from bias.
- Reviewing proposals for modifying or retiring the AI and forwarding the approved changes to the AI Governance Committee for consideration.
- Investigating reports of inappropriate or aberrant AI behaviors and leading efforts to remediate them.

AI Proposals

All AI owners must submit a business case for the development or use of AI (internal or external) to the AIPOC. The AI business case must include, at a minimum, answers to the following questions, as applicable for each use case:

- Is this a proposal to develop a new AI or modify an existing AI?
- Is this a proposal to use a vendor-supplied and licensed AI?
- Is this a proposal to use a publicly accessible AI?
- Who is the proposed owner of this AI?
- What functions will this AI provide?
- Which business processes (if extant) will be augmented by this AI?
- Which new business processes will be supported by the AI?
- What data will be used in the development or use of this AI?
- What data will be produced by this AI?
- How will the performance of the AI-supported processes be measured over time?
- How will use of the AI be monitored and managed?
- How will the use of data consumed or produced by this AI be monitored and managed?
- How much labor (in FTEs) is the development, adoption, implementation, and maintenance of the AI expected to consume?
- What threats to trust and/or security are produced or increased by the AI?
- What risks to corporate performance and value are produced or increased by the AI?

Change Management

Material changes to previously approved AI products, such as a modification to the use case or changes to the AI algorithm, must be brought to the AIPOC for review and approval. The term "material" shall mean any change that creates additional risk for the Company. The materiality of a change will be determined by the AIPOC and any decision to approve a material change will be reviewed with the AI Governance Committee.

Approved changes that require modifications to Company IT resources may require an additional review and approval by the TCAB, as determined by the AIPOC.

Training and Support

- For each AI, the AI owner shall design and document an appropriate training program specific to:
    - AI developers
    - business owners
    - users
    - testers
- The training must address the legal, operational, and reputational risks of the AI in addition to how to use the AI and comply with this policy.
- Business owners of the data shall be trained on the data that will be used by the AI and what the expected outputs will be.
- The AI owner and the Artificial Intelligence team within RISKQ will provide support to AI users.

Performance Monitoring and Evaluation

The criteria for performance monitoring and evaluation will be determined by each AI owner; however, the following criteria may be considered, among others:

- **Abandonment rate:** The percentage of sessions ended before users find answers.
- **Accuracy range:** A baseline expectation for accuracy.
- **Adoption rate:** The percentage of active users over the lifetime of a campaign or project divided by the total intended audience.

- **Bias indicators:** The percentage of responses that favor one protected class or group over another.
- **Data relevance:** The degree to which all the data is necessary and unbiased.
- **Error rate:** The percentage of AI responses that are incorrect or invalid.
- **Frequency of use:** The number of times queries are sent per user on a daily, weekly, or monthly basis.
- **Integration and backward compatibility:** The upstream and downstream APIs available to integrate directly with the AI.
- **Latency:** The time delay between when a query is submitted to the AI and when it returns the response.
- **Queries per session:** The number of queries users submit per session.
- **Safety Score:** The number of harmful categories and topics that may be considered sensitive for the business.
- **Session length:** The average duration of continuous interactions.
- **Throughput:** The volume of information the AI can handle in a specific period.
- **User satisfaction:** Surveys assessing user experience or other customer satisfaction metrics, Performance criteria and the results for each AI shall be documented and provided to the AI.

Governance Committee by the AIPOC following approval of the AI and at least annually thereafter.

Policy Reviews and Maintenance

This plan will be reviewed and updated at least annually or whenever deemed appropriate. Revisions may be made to reflect material changes in:

1. advancements in AI and the introduction of new AI technologies.
2. the Company's operating, financial, and legal environments.
3. the regulatory environment.
4. other internal controls or processes.

The Company expressly reserves the right to change, modify, or delete the provisions of this Policy without notice.

RISKQ, in consultation with the Law Division, is responsible for the administration of this policy. If you have any questions regarding this policy, please contact Ariel Evans, Chief Information Security and Privacy Officer.

Consequences of Noncompliance

Violating this policy may result in disciplinary action, up to and including termination, and could result in legal action as well as legal exposure for the Company. If you are concerned that someone has violated this policy, report this behavior to your supervisor or any member of the Information Security team as soon as possible.

Appendix: Sample AI Governance Implementation Example

To illustrate practical implementation of an AI governance policy, consider the following example from a mid-sized healthcare technology firm deploying a machine learning-based diagnostic support system.

1. Intake and Registration:
   - All new AI projects must be submitted through a standardized intake form.
   - Intake includes details such as model type, training data, intended users, affected stakeholders, and regulatory touchpoints (e.g., HIPAA, EU AI Act).
2. Risk Classification:
   - Models are scored based on likelihood and impact (aligned with NIST AI RMF and ISO/IEC 42001).
   - This diagnostic system is flagged as "high risk" due to direct patient impact.
3. Privacy and Security Controls:
   - Data minimization strategies are enforced during model training.
   - Encryption (AES-256) is applied to training and inference data.
   - Audit trails are maintained for all model updates and predictions.
4. Human Oversight and Testing:
   - Clinical experts are integrated into model output review.
   - All predictions must be approved by a licensed physician.
   - The system is red-teamed quarterly to test robustness against drift, bias, and malicious inputs.

5. Documentation and Vendor Accountability:
   - A model card, data sheet, and impact assessment summary accompany the deployment.
   - The vendor contract includes data use restrictions, transparency clauses, and obligations for breach notification.
6. Metrics and Continuous Improvement:
   - Monthly bias audits are conducted across demographics.
   - Patient satisfaction and override rates are tracked to refine explainability features.

This structured, documented approach ensures compliance, transparency, and patient trust in sensitive AI deployments.

11

THE FUTURE OF AI GOVERNANCE

AI Outpaces Governance in the Race for Control

Determining the future of artificial intelligence (AI) governance requires a multidimensional lens, one that balances innovation, ethics, geopolitics, and operational realities. Top-down efforts in AI governance at both global and national levels have proliferated in recent years, but many have struggled to deliver meaningful impact due to fragmentation, lack of enforcement, and geopolitical divergence. It is not due to lack of initiative that governance issues have either been resisted or taken a back seat even as AI is rapidly becoming an infrastructural force reshaping economies, institutions, and social norms at an unprecedented pace.

Currently, apart from lack of global consensus on AI governance, there are deep structural tensions between innovation and regulation, techno-optimism and ethical caution, and centralized control versus distributed accountability. In many cases, governments and industries launched initiatives with genuine intent, but lacked the institutional dexterity, stakeholder alignment, or enforceable frameworks to keep up with AI's velocity and

DOI: 10.4324/9781003682530-14

Year(s)	Initiative	Objective
2019	OECD AI Principles	First intergovernmental framework emphasizing human-centric, trustworthy AI
2021	UNESCO Ethics Recommendation on AI	Adopted by 193 member states; non-binding guidance promoting ethical AI
2020–ongoing	GPAI (Global Partnership on AI)	Multistakeholder forum fostering responsible and inclusive AI development
2023	G7 Hiroshima Process	Code of conduct for advanced AI systems with democratic values and safeguards
2024	Council of Europe's AI Convention	First legally binding treaty on AI & human rights; focused on rule-of-law alignment
2023	UN High-Level Advisory Body on AI	UN-appointed experts tasked with shaping global governance frameworks
2023–2025	China's Global AI Governance Initiative	Proposes Shanghai-based platform to democratize AI access and promote shared benefits

Table 11.1 Major AI Governance Initiatives

complexity. AI is surging forward as a generational transformer, while governance mechanisms remain fragmented, reactive, and ill-equipped to deal with its systemic impact. Hence, what is unfolding is not a failure of interest, but a failure of integration. Some of the major AI governance initiatives listed below, though well meaning have not produced desired outcomes.

Major AI Governance Initiatives

It is more than likely that these early initiatives will need to be revisited and revised as AI technology evolves further, and regulatory needs are better understood. It is important to understand two of the most important governance initiatives that are being actively observed across the world for their acceptance and effectiveness.

The first is President Biden's 2023 Executive Order on AI, which was aimed at establishing a comprehensive, government-wide framework for the safe, secure, and trustworthy development and use of AI. It emphasized eight core principles, including robust safety testing, protection of civil rights, consumer safeguards, privacy preservation, and support for American workers. The order further directed over fifty federal agencies to undertake more than a hundred specific actions, such as creating AI safety standards, evaluating national security risks, and promoting equity in AI deployment. It also called for transparency in AI-generated content and sought to mitigate risks from dual-use foundation models and large-scale computing clusters. This order was considered quite comprehensive in its scope, spanning safety standards, rights protections, labor impact, and national security. However, it was found to be complex too due to the multidimensional nature of AI itself. The order sought to balance innovation with regulation, global competitiveness with domestic accountability, and technical specificity with sector-wide applicability. The Trump administration was of the view that too many safeguards stifled innovation and competitiveness of US companies and under the 2025 AI Action Plan reversed many of these initiatives, framing AI as a geopolitical race that the US must win through deregulation, infrastructure expansion, and global tech exports. Trump's plan was focused on speed, competitiveness, and minimal regulatory interference, reflecting a fundamental shift in thinking about how AI should be governed.

Across the Atlantic, the EU Artificial Intelligence Act (AI Act) that came into force on August 1, 2024 provided a phased implementation model. Despite its significance as the world's first comprehensive AI regulation, the Act has met resistance across several fronts. Industry leaders, including organizations like Airbus and ASML, have voiced concerns over regulatory complexity, fearing it may stifle innovation and hinder Europe's digital competitiveness. Even member states such as France, Germany, and Italy opposed strict oversight on foundation models, warning this could deepen Europe's technological lag behind global rivals. Big tech companies too found the act to be burdensome and vague. Warnings were also raised that the Act would increase compliance costs, create uncertainty, and hamper Europe's strategic edge in AI innovation.

This brings us to the question as to why all these AI governance initiatives have not yielded the expected results. It could be argued that many AI governance initiatives have faltered because they were predominantly top-down in design, lacking a deep understanding of ground-level realities such as operational constraints, institutional readiness, and cultural contexts. Furthermore, they often emphasize abstract principles without clear pathways for implementation, especially in resource-constrained or rapidly evolving environments.

Challenge	Global Level	National Level
Enforcement	Mostly voluntary, non-binding	Weak legal frameworks, slow rollout
Coordination	Fragmented regime complex	Inter-ministerial silos
Representation	Global South underrepresented	Marginalized communities excluded
Technical Capacity	Limited institutional expertise	Lack of AI literacy and tooling
Geopolitical Tensions	U.S.–China–EU divergence	Export controls and techno-nationalism
Public Trust	Opaque systems, limited accountability	Bias, surveillance concerns

Table 11.2 Why Has Top-Down Governance Been Ineffective?

Causes	Organizational Level	Sectoral Level
Governance treated as reactive	Compliance-driven, not strategic	Principles without enforcement
Siloed structures	Legal, IT, and product misalignment	Regulator–industry disconnect
Lack of tooling	Legacy systems, poor model visibility	Few sector-specific audit frameworks
Ethical blind spots	No board-level AI ethics integration	Limited public engagement
Capacity gaps	Low AI literacy across teams	Regulators lack technical expertise

Table 11.3 Why Do These Failures Persist?

Why Top-Down Governance Has Been Ineffective

At the organizational level, governance has often been looked at as a compliance checkbox or even a showstopper rather than a strategic enabler. Policies have been put in place, but they are rarely embedded into business processes, monitored post-deployment, or aligned with business outcomes. Sectorally, regulators have issued broad guidelines, but few have developed domain-specific guidelines that reflect the nuanced risks of AI in healthcare, finance, or education. Another issue that needs to be highlighted in the context of AI governance concerns how small firms and startups can cope with regulatory diktats. These organizations though small are nimble and are increasingly deploying powerful models without the capacity, processes tooling, or awareness to operationalize governance, creating systemic vulnerabilities. The following image shows why governance initiatives have failed at the organizational and sectoral level.

Why Do These Failures Persist?

In short, AI governance has often been aspirational rather than operational. To move forward, future efforts must be co-designed with practitioners, context-aware, and iteratively tested and not just imposed from above.

The future of AI governance depends on how well the lessons learned from past initiatives are used to design a new regime that can achieve the right balance between innovation and regulation. It must be shaped by a confluence of complex, rapidly evolving factors that reflect both technological dynamism and societal nuances. The accelerating advancement of agentic AI, multimodal models, and autonomous systems calls for governance frameworks that are not static but adaptive responsive to emergent behaviors, explainability challenges, and rising compute intensity.

Ethics and societal impact are equally important when it comes to safeguarding against algorithmic bias, privacy violations, and human rights infringements. This is critical to maintaining public trust, especially in culturally sensitive areas like health, policing, and education.

Geopolitical tensions add another layer of complexity. Even as countries strive to emerge winners in the global AI race, a broad consensus on key matters related to AI governance must evolve. Here big tech too has an important role to play as they influence law making as well as enforcement and compliance. Issues like digital sovereignty with regard to AI export controls must not hamper multilateral cooperation through institutions like the UN. Many governments and organizations need to develop technical depth, interdisciplinary capabilities, and agility required for meaningful oversight. Building capacity through literacy programs and dynamic regulatory bodies is a strategic imperative.

The future of AI governance will rely heavily on a shift from rigid, prescriptive regulation to more agile and layered approaches. What is required is the use of soft law instruments like standards, certifications, and voluntary codes of conduct. These mechanisms, such as ISO/IEC 42001 and the NIST AI Risk Management Framework, are emerging as practical building blocks for operationalizing responsible AI across diverse sectors and jurisdictions. In this evolving landscape, governance must embed principles of transparency and accountability at its core, ensuring that AI systems, especially those with opaque or black-box architectures are auditable, traceable, and supported by strong human oversight. Open-source development and explainable AI techniques will continue to play a critical role in fostering trust and enabling scrutiny.

Equally vital is the recognition that AI is not just a technical challenge but a socioeconomic force. The future governance paradigm must directly address the effects of automation on jobs, livelihoods, and social equity. This includes mechanisms for reskilling displaced workers, promoting inclusive digital participation, and evaluating the environmental footprint of large-scale AI compute operations. Lastly, governance must be participatory by design. It should actively engage stakeholders from civil society, academia, industry, and underrepresented communities to ensure that power is not concentrated in a few hands, and that diverse voices help shape the rules of AI governance.

Governance in the Age of Autonomous AI Systems

The future of AI governance demands a fundamental shift toward anticipatory and adaptive frameworks that can keep pace with transformative technologies like agentic AI, quantum-powered systems, and fully autonomous applications. As AI systems evolve to make decisions independently, governance must incorporate agent operations management, rules for multi-agent coordination, and robust human-in-the-loop safeguards. In addition, continuous monitoring for goal alignment and behavior drift will be essential to prevent unintended consequences.

At another level, the convergence of quantum computing and AI necessitates new standards in post-quantum cryptography, ethical frameworks tailored to quantum-AI capabilities, and inclusive access models that prevent infrastructure dominance by a few players. Global coordination and anticipatory regulation must precede mass commercialization. For fully autonomous technologies, whether in mobility, infrastructure, or strategic systems, governance must embed real-time policy enforcement, emergency shutdown mechanisms, and fail-safes that support human override and social values. This future-ready governance model must evolve from static compliance regimes to dynamic, trust-based systems that are participatory, distributed, and context-aware. Only then can it responsibly realize the immense potential and effectively navigate risks of next-generation AI.

System Type	Risk Tier	Oversight Mechanism	Ethical Imperatives	Governance Tools
Autonomous Vehicles	High	Regulatory approval, real-time monitoring	Safety prioritization, liability attribution	Digital twins, behavioural modelling
Drones (civilian)	Medium-High	Airspace rules, operator licensing	Privacy, surveillance limits	Geofencing, mission logs
Carebots & Medbots	High	Healthcare compliance, consent protocols	Dignity, data security, informed consent	Explainable AI, scenario testing
Industrial Robotics	Medium	Factory safety audits, operational logs	Labor displacement, safety assurance	Predictive maintenance, value drift monitoring
Financial Agents	High	Algorithmic audits, fail-safe mechanisms	Transparency, bias mitigation	XAI models, audit trails
Defence Autonomy	Critical	Human-in-command rules, red-line constraints	Lethal decision ethics, proportionality	Sandbox simulations, chain-of-command verification
Social AI Agents	Medium	UX testing, feedback loops	Manipulation risks, cognitive	Sentiment tracking, intent auditing

Table 11.4 AI Governance for Autonomous Systems

Governing autonomous systems is one of the most complex challenges in AI governance. This is due to the fact that these systems evolve from reactive tools to agentic entities capable of independent decision-making. The following image shows risks, oversight mechanisms, ethical imperatives, and available governance tools for different types of autonomous systems.

AI Governance for Autonomous Systems

The rapid proliferation of autonomous AI systems not only raises questions about their safe use and governance but also points us in the direction of using AI systems for their own governance. AI can enable self-monitoring agents that not only enforce regulatory frameworks but also monitor their compliance. Furthermore, AI-driven governance systems can audit other models for bias, drift, and regulatory compliance in complex, federated environments. AI-driven model registries and lineage tracking foster transparency by cataloging models, their data provenance, and context of use.

We are already witnessing the use of multi-agent governance architectures and agent-to-agent protocols that are unlocking real-time collaboration among autonomous entities, with standards like the Model Context Protocol, ensuring secure and interpretable interactions. In addition, centralized governance gateways oversee ethical operations, cost efficiency, and performance across networks of agents.

In future, AI governance will be embedded to work across the lifecycle from build to deploy to scale. It will be integrated into every layer: designing modular components with compliance safeguards, orchestrating deployment pipelines with role-based access control and auditing. Furthermore, Kubernetes-native platforms can integrate governance directly into scalability protocols.

AI governance is entering a recursive era where intelligent systems could govern their own kind, continuously auditing and optimizing each other in a self-sustaining loop. As autonomy scales, the human role evolves from hands-on supervision to meta-governance. This involves curating the frameworks, constraints, and ethical structures that AI agents operationalize. This shift marks a profound transformation in digital oversight, one where trust is embedded not only in outcomes but in the very architecture of intelligent collaboration.

Bibliography

Binns, R. (2018). Fairness in machine learning: Lessons from political philosophy. *Proceedings of the 2020 Conference on Fairness, Accountability, and Transparency*. (*FAT* 2018*), *Proceedings of Machine Learning Research*, 81, 149–159. PMLR. https://proceedings.mlr.press/v81/binns18a.html

Cath, C. (2018). Governing artificial intelligence: Ethical, legal and technical opportunities and challenges. *Philosophical Transactions of the Royal Society A*.

European Commission. (2021). *Proposal for a Regulation Laying Down Harmonized Rules on Artificial Intelligence (Artificial Intelligence Act)*.

Floridi, L., & Cowls, J. (2019). A unified framework of five principles for AI in society. *Harvard Data Science Review*.

ISO/ IEC. (2023). *ISO/IEC 42001: Artificial Intelligence Management System Standard*.

National Institute of Standards and Technology. (2023). *NIST AI Risk Management Framework (AI RMF 1.0)*.

OECD. (2019). *Recommendation of the Council on Artificial Intelligence*. OECD Legal Instruments.

U.S. White House. (2023). *Executive Order on the Safe, Secure, and Trustworthy Development and Use of Artificial Intelligence*.

SECTION 4

AI AND CYBER CONTROLS—STRENGTHENING SECURITY AND MITIGATING THREATS

The convergence of artificial intelligence and cybersecurity has created both unprecedented defensive capabilities and profoundly sophisticated new attack vectors. AI is now actively weaponized by threat actors—enabling large-scale automated attacks, deepfake-driven social engineering, and adaptive malware that constantly evolves to evade detection. At the same time, AI has become an essential component of modern cyber defense, powering threat intelligence, autonomous response, and predictive risk detection. This dual-edged nature of AI has made security and control frameworks not optional—but foundational to responsible AI adoption.

This section examines AI's role in cybersecurity from both the threat and protection perspectives across seven chapters:

- **Chapter 12: Real-World Incidents of AI-Enhanced Cyberattacks**—analyzes documented cases where AI has been leveraged to accelerate or amplify cybercrime.

DOI: 10.4324/9781003682530-15

- **Chapter 13: AI in Cybersecurity**—explores how AI is augmenting defensive capabilities across detection, response, fraud prevention, and resilience.
- **Chapter 14: Cyber Risks Posed by AI**—identifies inherent risks introduced by AI systems themselves, including model poisoning, adversarial inputs, and data exploitation.
- **Chapter 15: Cybersecurity Controls for AI**—provides tactical control strategies to secure AI systems throughout their lifecycle.
- **Chapter 16: Control Frameworks for AI**—reviews emerging industry and regulatory frameworks (e.g., NIST AI RMF, ISO/IEC 27001 extensions, EU AI Act security obligations).
- **Chapter 17. AI Risk Assessment Framework**—identifies, quantifies, prioritizes, mitigates, and monitors risks across the AI lifecycle. Objectives include improving reliability, supporting compliance, and providing assurance that AI systems are safe, secure, and trustworthy.
- **Chapter 18: Applications and Platforms—Copilot and Beyond**—evaluates enterprise AI assistants such as Microsoft Copilot and their unique security governance challenges.
- **Chapter 19: The Future of AI Cybersecurity**—forecasts how AI-driven threat landscapes and defense architectures will evolve in the coming decade.

This section equips readers with both strategic and technical understanding of how to secure AI—and how AI is simultaneously reshaping the future of cybersecurity itself.

12

AI AND CYBERCRIME

Traditional vs. AI-Enabled Cybercrime

Cybercrime has evolved from petty cybercrimes to isolated acts of digital damage and basic online fraud into a sophisticated, enterprise-scale ecosystem. In its early stages, attackers relied on basic tools such as phishing emails, brute-force attacks, and malware payloads to exploit technical vulnerabilities and human error. These were opportunistic, targeting individuals and small businesses with limited defenses.

As connectivity expanded and digital infrastructure improved, cybercrime became professionalized. The rise of ransomware, botnets, and exploit kits marked a shift toward monetization and scalability. State-sponsored cyber espionage emerged, targeting critical infrastructure, intellectual property, and geopolitical assets.

Today, cyber adversaries operate like agile enterprises, leveraging AI, automation, and social engineering to breach even the most fortified systems. Machine-learning algorithms analyze system configurations and user behavior to identify obscure vulnerabilities. AI-generated malware can

DOI: 10.4324/9781003682530-16

Category	Traditional Cybercrime	AI-Enabled Cybercrime
Impersonation	Phishing emails with generic content	Deepfakes & voice cloning for CEO fraud and social engineering
Malware	Static malware with known signatures	Adaptive, polymorphic malware that evolves to evade detection
Phishing	Mass phishing with poor grammar	Hyper-personalized spear phishing using AI-generated content
Hacking	Manual vulnerability scanning	Autonomous AI agents exploiting zero-days at scale
Disinformation	Manual fake news campaigns	AI-generated fake news, bots amplifying narratives
Identity Theft	Stolen credentials from breaches	Synthetic identities created using AI to bypass KYC
Dark Web Operations	Human-operated marketplaces	AI chatbots offering 24/7 support for illicit services
Ransomware	Manual encryption and negotiation	AI-optimized targeting and automated ransom negotiation

Table 12.1 AI-Enabled Cybercrime

morph into thousands of variants in seconds, bypassing signature-based defenses. Bots and large language models (LLMs) now generate convincing fake news, manipulate social media trends, and influence elections, weaponizing information at scale. Given below is a visual matrix that compares traditional cybercrime with AI-enabled cybercrime to highlight how threat vectors are evolving:

This matrix illustrates how AI is not just enhancing existing threats. It is redefining the speed, scale, and sophistication of cyberattacks. At the same time, AI tools themselves are becoming targets of cyberattacks, with the most common forms being poisoning, inference, extraction, and evasion. These types of attacks are aimed at manipulating or compromising AI systems. In response, cybersecurity professionals are also turning to AI-driven solutions to enhance threat detection and accelerate incident response, recognizing AI as both a risk and a critical defense asset in the evolving digital landscape.

AI Reshaping the Cybercrime Landscape

In early 2024, a high-stakes cybercrime unfolded like something right out of a thriller novel. Arup, the British multinational design and engineering firm, renowned for iconic structures like the Sydney Opera House, found itself at the center of a massive US$25 million fraud. Cybercriminals used deepfake technology so convincingly that one of Arup's Hong Kong employees believed they were in a legitimate video call with senior executives. By creating a digitally manipulated impression of the company's CFO and key staff members, the fraudsters successfully deceived an employee to remit the money in 15 wire transfers across multiple bank accounts (Wesen 2025).

The fraudsters, leveraging AI-generated likenesses and voices, manipulated the employee into transferring HK$200 million to their account. This incident, now considered the most significant AI-leveraged cybercrime to date, exposed the chilling power of synthetic media, and marked a turning point in global cybersecurity awareness.

In recent times, deepfake threats represent one of the most dramatic increases in any cybercrime category. There were 19% more deepfake incidents in the first months of 2025 than there were in all of 2024, and deepfakes are now responsible for 6.5% of all fraud attacks, a 2,137% increase from 2022 (Martin 2025)[2].

AI-powered phishing attacks too have experienced explosive growth in terms of frequency and enhanced sophistication. Cybercriminals are now wielding AI to sharpen their tactics with alarming precision. Instead of just relying on chatbots to write malware, the real disruption is happening earlier in the cyber kill chain, especially during reconnaissance and initial weaponization. Attackers are using AI to craft highly personalized phishing emails, mimic voices for social engineering, and automate the gathering of target-specific data. By using machine learning to analyze public information and behavioral patterns, they can contextualize and hyper-personalize their attacks, dramatically boosting the odds of a successful breach. The game has shifted from broad attacks to surgical strikes. AI is the scalpel. It is not surprising that senior executives are targeted with great precision with a success rate of one in four falling victims to AI-driven, personalized attacks. Modern AI-powered phishing uses sophisticated techniques, including Natural Language Processing (NLP) creates flawless, believable emails and adaptive phishing kits change tactics based on victim responses in real-time.

While precise figures vary, industry estimates suggest that AI-leveraged cybercrime could account for up to 20%–30% of the projected US$15.63 trillion global cybercrime cost by 2029. This includes AI-enhanced phishing, deepfake fraud, automated reconnaissance, and adaptive malware threats that are rapidly scaling due to the accessibility and sophistication of generative AI tools (SentinelOne 2025).

AI is fundamentally transforming the cybercrime landscape, making attacks more sophisticated, personalized, and difficult to detect, while significantly increasing both the frequency and financial impact of cyber incidents. It is reshaping the cybercrime landscape in ways both subtle and staggering. Let us examine some of the most dangerous attack vectors that are rapidly evolving by leveraging AI.

1. Deepfake Fraud and Impersonation

   There are an increasing number of sources to access sophisticated "deepfake generation on demand," voice and video impersonation software. This new service model will democratize deepfakes further and will enable fraudsters to run more complex social engineering campaigns, like impersonating high-level executives or family members in real-time to manipulate targets. No wonder that AI-generated videos or voice clones impersonate CEOs, politicians, or family members are flourishing on the internet. Deepfake deception covers the entire spectrum of cybercrime, from Business Email Compromise, where synthetic voices and videos impersonate executives to authorize fraudulent transactions, to large-scale disinformation campaigns that destabilize public trust, manipulate elections, and incite social unrest. These AI-generated forgeries blur the line between reality and fabrication, enabling attackers to exploit human psychology, institutional protocols, and digital ecosystems with unprecedented precision and scale. As deepfakes become even more accessible and convincing, they pose a systemic threat across financial, political, and social domains.
2. AI-Powered Phishing and Social Engineering

   Hackers are increasingly leveraging AI tools like ChatGPT to craft more convincing phishing emails, making it harder for individuals and organizations to detect malicious intent. Cybercriminals have also begun using AI-generated deepfakes and voice clones to execute sophisticated identity theft scams, exploiting the realism and accessibility of generative technologies. WormGPT is a malicious AI tool promoted on the dark web as a rogue counterpart to ChatGPT. It can generate highly convincing phishing emails tailored to specific targets using scraped LinkedIn and social media data. In early 2025, cybersecurity analysts uncovered a Phishing-as-a-Service operation on the dark web, powered by WormGPT, a jailbroken AI model designed for malicious use. The service offered subscription-based access to AI-generated phishing kits, deepfake voice scripts, and real-time social engineering prompts.

   Studies show that today 82.6% of phishing emails use AI technology in some form. There is also an increase in success rates for attackers as 78% of people open AI-generated phishing emails and 21% click on malicious content inside. Furthermore, generative AI tools and automation help hackers compose phishing emails up to 40% faster.

Attackers are increasingly shifting toward precision-targeted and automated strategies with AI becoming central to their attack strategy both from an evolution and escalation point of view (Fox 2025).

3. AI-Generated Malware

While AI capabilities like AI-enhanced phishing, voice cloning and deep fake have been on the forefront, there are other ways in which cybercriminals have learned to launch cyber threats. AI enables the use of targeted AI Logic, which activates only when specific conditions are met, such as recognizing a target's face or voice. Another variant is adaptive malware that learns from its environment and modifies its behavior to evade detection. This means that the AI-powered malware can change its code structure to bypass antivirus filters. A high-powered version of this is polymorphic malware that uses AI to generate thousands of unique variants, making signature-based detection ineffective. Malware-as-a-Service offerings available on the dark web now include AI-powered hacking tools.

4. Precision Targeting and Scalability

Cybercriminals are increasingly harnessing machine-learning algorithms to dissect system configurations and analyze user behavior, allowing them to uncover and exploit obscure vulnerabilities with remarkable precision. This capability extends to targeting zero-day flaws and misconfigurations, often with surgical accuracy that bypasses conventional defenses. Compounding the threat, automated malware frameworks now enable the rapid generation of thousands of polymorphic variants within seconds, effectively overwhelming even the most robust security systems and rendering traditional detection methods insufficient.

5. AI-Powered Ransomware

Ransomware is said to be the defining cyber threat of the decade. A UK study called ransomware a scourge on society, citing harm to individuals, national security, and public trust. In 2023 alone, ransomware attacks cost businesses over a billion US dollars globally, with escalating ransom demands and recovery costs. Critical sectors like healthcare, education, and manufacturing have been repeatedly crippled, leading to operational shutdowns and data loss. Now, AI adds a new dimension to this ransomware adding new capabilities such as precision targeting, real-time code adaptation, automated attack life cycle, hyper-personalized phishing at scale, and deepfakes and other synthetic media used to impersonate trusted individuals. AI possesses the ability to identify high-value targets and encrypt critical files. To top it all, some ransomwares even leverage AI to negotiate ransoms autonomously.

6. Autonomous Hacking Agents

   AI agents can act autonomously, scan for vulnerabilities, exploit them, and launch attacks without human input. Experts predict that autonomous systems also known as 'AI Agents' trained to perform tasks are set to evolve quickly. These autonomous agents can launch browsers, retrieve passwords, and scanning entire networks with minimal human intervention. Soon, a single adversary could orchestrate dozens of AI-powered agents simultaneously—each performing distinct phases of the cyber kill chain with speed, precision, and scale that far surpasses even the most coordinated human hacking teams. Further down the road, Swarm intelligence where AI agents collaborate autonomously will enhance the attackers' powers exponentially. However, imagining AI agents within botnets actively discovering CVEs is an alarming possibility.

7. Automated Attack Lifecycle

   AI can used to completely automate an attack lifecycle, including reconnaissance, vulnerability scanning, payload delivery, and encryption. This reduces human intervention, enabling faster and more scalable attacks that have the potential to disrupt critical infrastructure like water or energy systems. Furthermore, it can enable follow-on attacks with greater impact and precision.

8. Synthetic Identity and Credential Abuse

   AI can create fake identities by combining real personal data. AI-driven identity synthesis is emerging as a potent tool for fraudsters; by combining fragments of real personal data, malicious actors can fabricate convincing synthetic identities. Fraudsters could use these to open fraudulent bank accounts, apply for jobs, or bypass KYC checks posing a significant risk to financial institutions and digital trust frameworks.

9. AI-Driven Disinformation and Fake News

   AI-driven bots and LLMs are rapidly transforming the information warfare landscape. These systems can autonomously generate hyper-realistic fake news articles, deepfake interviews, and fabricated expert analyses that mimic credible sources with alarming accuracy.

When deployed at scale, they can manipulate social media trends, amplify divisive narratives, and distort public discourse, often without detection. This capability is already being weaponized by malicious actors to influence electoral outcomes, destabilize democratic institutions, and erode trust in journalism and governance.

In financial markets, cybercriminals use coordinated botnets and AI-generated sentiment manipulation to trigger artificial volatility, sway investor behavior, and execute pump-and-dump schemes. These tactics exploit algorithmic trading systems and sentiment-driven analytics, creating systemic risks that ripple across global markets. The convergence of generative AI with real-time data feeds and social engineering tactics has made it possible to conduct market-moving events with minimal human oversight.

From political propaganda to economic sabotage, the misuse of AI in information operations demands urgent regulatory, technological, and ethical countermeasures. Without robust provenance frameworks, watermarking standards, and AI-safe governance protocols, the line between truth and fabrication will continue to undermine digital trust, democratic resilience, and financial stability.

10. Threats to National Security

    The NSA, CISA, and FBI have also drawn attention to other threats to AI systems that could potentially compromise national security. These and other allied agencies have released new guidance on AI data security. The federal guidance breaks the threat into the following distinct attack vectors:

    - Exploitation of Data Supply Chain Weakness—If AI is trained on data from unverified or unsafe sources, it can be corrupted before anyone even notices.
    - Poisoned Data—Malicious or misleading information can be slipped into training sets, causing AI to make bad calls in mission critical systems, from defense logistics to infrastructure planning, leading to undesirable consequences.

Investigation of AI-Aided Cybercrimes

Even as cybercriminals have taken their strategies to another level by embedding AI into their attack vectors, investigators too are relying on

AI-enhanced digital forensics that include both AI-powered detection tools, and seamless legal-technical coordination. This multifaceted approach has evolved to address the growing complexity and scale of AI-enhanced criminal activities.

At the core of modern digital forensics, artificial intelligence can function as both investigator and analyst. Machine-learning models now can instantly sift through massive datasets, including logs, emails, and metadata to detect subtle anomalies or malicious behavior patterns that would be impossible for human investigators to identify manually.

Specialized AI tools are being used to undertake deepfake detection, analyze facial micro-expressions, voice inconsistencies, and pixel-level artifacts to expose synthetic media with increasing accuracy. NLP technologies play a crucial role in analyzing phishing emails, chat logs, and dark web conversations, helping investigators decode intent and identify deception cues that might otherwise go unnoticed.

Another important aspect of cybercrime investigation is threat attribution. Today, behavioral analysis has been revolutionized through AI-driven approaches that correlate attack signatures, IP behavior patterns, and malware characteristics to identify specific threat actors. Behavioral biometrics technology has significantly evolved to track typing rhythms, mouse movement patterns, and login behaviors to detect synthetic identities or insider threats, creating unique digital fingerprints that are difficult to replicate or spoof.

AI-assisted cybercrime prevention systems have given defenders the ability to deal with adaptive threat mitigation. Real-time response systems powered by artificial intelligence can autonomously isolate compromised systems, block malicious traffic, and trigger appropriate alerts without human intervention. Multi-Factor Authentication systems have also been enhanced with AI capabilities to detect spoofed credentials or behavioral anomalies, adding layers of security that adapt to emerging threats. These safeguards also help investigators in mapping trajectories of cyberattacks.

Despite these advances, significant challenges persist in the investigation of AI-aided cybercrimes. Encrypted data and sophisticated obfuscation techniques continue to slow investigations, even with AI assistance. The issues of bias and transparency in AI tools require constant attention, as these systems must be regularly audited to avoid false positives or discriminatory profiling that could compromise investigations or violate people's rights. Most challenging is the jurisdictional complexity that arises when

AI crimes span multiple borders, complicating questions of legal authority and evidence sharing between different legal systems and enforcement agencies.

Looking ahead, cybercrime will likely converge with emerging technologies such as quantum computing, autonomous agents, and decentralized infrastructures. Quantum threats could render current encryption obsolete, while AI-powered autonomous malware may self-propagate, adapt, and execute complex missions without human oversight. Supply chain attacks, deepfake-driven fraud, and geopolitical cyber conflicts will intensify.

Bibliography

Fox, J. (2025, April 14). Top cybersecurity statistics for 2025. Top-cybersecurity-statistics-2025. https://www.cobalt.io/blog/top-cybersecurity-statistics-2025

Martin, K. (2025, May 27). AI cyber attack statistics 2025: Phishing, deepfakes & cybercrime trends. *Tech Advisors*. https://tech-adv.com/blog/ai-cyber-attack-statistics/

SentinelOne. (2025, July 30). Key Cyber security Statistics for 2025. *SentinelOne*. https://www.sentinelone.com/cybersecurity-101/cybersecurity/cyber-security-statistics/

Wesen, R. (2025, April 8). Beyond phishing: Exploring the rise of AI-enabled cybercrime. *CLTC*. https://cltc.berkeley.edu/2025/01/16/beyond-phishing-exploring-the-rise-of-ai-enabled-cybercrime/

13

AI IN CYBERSECURITY

Why AI Is Transforming Cyber Defense

The digital threat landscape has grown rapidly in both scale and complexity. Attackers now employ automation, polymorphic malware, and AI-generated phishing, which are more designed to bypass legacy defenses. Traditional cybersecurity approaches, rooted in rule-based engines and static detection models monitored by human analysts, can no longer keep pace with the speed and sophistication of modern threats.

AI-driven cybersecurity tools offer a significant edge. Instead of relying on predefined signatures, AI systems learn from data, log streams, user behavior, network traffic patterns, and identify anomalies that may indicate malicious activity. This ability to detect unknown zero-day threats gives organizations a strategic advantage. By integrating telemetry across systems, AI helps detect threats in real-time and reduce the risk of advanced persistent threats.

More importantly, AI enhances scalability and repeatability. Human analysts are developing alert fatigue while processing terabytes of logs or

DOI: 10.4324/9781003682530-17

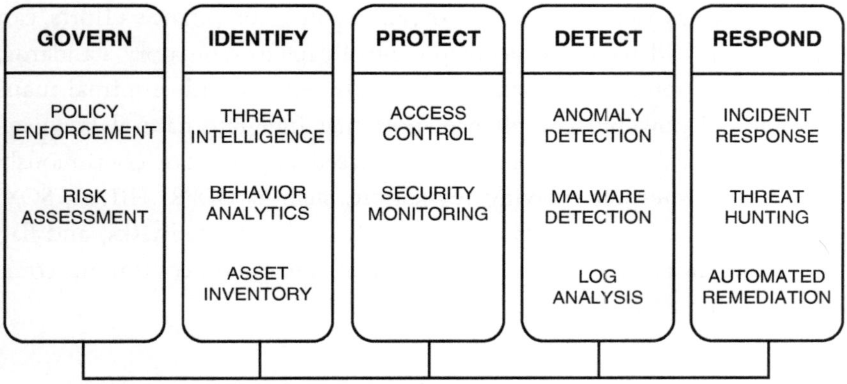

Image 13.1 AI Use Cases Aligned with NIST CSF 2.0 Functions

correlating thousands of alerts across tools and systems. AI augments their capacity, processes all the data much faster, eliminates noise, and highlights only what matters most.

Core Applications of AI in Cybersecurity

The deployment of AI spans nearly every layer of the cybersecurity stack. The following figure illustrates how AI capabilities map to the core functions of the National Institute of Standards and Technology's Cyber Security Framework (NIST CSF 2.0):

While the figure highlights AI's alignment with the leading cybersecurity framework, the next sections focus on its practical applications, starting with risk management and compliance.

AI in Risk Management and Compliance

Risk quantification is becoming a standard practice in cyber risk management, as it enables the translation of cybersecurity threats into measurable financial impact. This allows organizations to make informed decisions and better prioritize their security investments. Beyond detection, AI is increasingly helping to quantify risks with greater accuracy by modeling likely attack scenarios and estimating their potential financial, operational, and reputational impact. This allows CISOs to develop more precise and proactive cybersecurity strategies.

As regulatory scrutiny grows, organizations' compliance efforts can now rely on AI-driven tools to map control gaps to regulatory standards, identify deviations, and generate audit-ready reports with minimal manual input. AI-powered compliance tools that integrate natural language processing, machine learning, and rule-based engines can continuously monitor and interpret evolving regulations such as GDPR, HIPAA, SOX, and DORA. These systems track changes, assess associated risks, and flag non-compliant behavior, helping organizations maintain continuous compliance with readiness.

Anomaly and Behavior-Based Detection

AI-powered User and Entity Behavior Analytics models, trained on user activity logs, logins, access patterns, file movements, and application usage, create a baseline of normal activity for users, devices, and networks. When deviations from this baseline occur, such as a user accessing sensitive data at an unusual hour, a device communicating with a known malicious site, or a sudden increase in downloads, the system flags them for review. These models continuously adapt as behavioral patterns evolve, refining their baselines over time. This detection capability is especially valuable for protecting intellectual property and sensitive client data, and for identifying low and slow attacks or insider threats, which traditional rule-based systems often miss or flag with high volumes of false positives.

AI-Driven Threat Forecasting, Hunting, and Monitoring

Effective threat intelligence is critical for timely identification and mitigation of cyber risks. AI-driven platforms now play a pivotal role in this by enabling organizations to anticipate future attacks, uncover hidden threats, and continuously monitor digital environments.

AI empowers cybersecurity teams with the ability to forecast likely attack vectors by analyzing historical threat data, emerging tactics, and behavioral patterns of known threat actors. This predictive intelligence enables timely countermeasures, such as targeted patching, fine-tuning firewall policies, or launching risk-specific awareness campaigns aligned with the current threat of landscape. As these models mature, their output is being integrated into cyber risk management engines and proactive defense planning tools.

In parallel, AI enhances threat hunting accuracy by identifying subtle anomalies such as misuse of administrative tools, lateral movement, or low and slow behaviors that may indicate the presence of an adversary. AI-enabled threat hunting tools reduce manual effort by highlighting potential leads, assisting analysts in drafting detection queries across large datasets, and providing situational explanations. These capabilities enable analysts to uncover previously undetectable threats while accelerating the pace of investigation.

Beyond prediction and hunting, AI excels at real-time threat monitoring. By ingesting, correlating, and contextualizing telemetry from across the enterprise, AI systems can match emerging activity against known Tactics, Techniques, and Procedures, drawing on frameworks like MITRE ATT&CK. They proactively identify indicators of compromise (IOCs) relevant to the organization's industry, geography, and threat profile, enabling faster detection and response.

Together, these AI-driven capabilities form a shield against cyber threats by detecting the unknown, anticipating the likely, and surveilling the ongoing. They help defenders stay ahead in a threat landscape that rewards speed, foresight, and adaptability.

Vulnerability Prioritization

Modern vulnerability scanners may identify tens of thousands of issues in large enterprises. AI prioritization engines analyze these results with context, considering the probability of an exploit to affect organization's systems, the sensitivity of possible affected systems, historical exploitation trends, and correlations to industry-specific threats. AI can also simulate attack paths to determine which vulnerabilities are most likely to be exploited, allowing prioritization decisions to be both risk-aware and threat-informed.

Malware Detection

Polymorphic malware that is more evasive, persistent, and capable of launching targeted attacks, is posing significant challenges to traditional cybersecurity tools. AI-based malware detection leverages static, dynamic, and behavioral analysis to deliver faster and more accurate threat identification across endpoints, networks, and cloud environments. It is effective against both known and unknown threats. Deep learning algorithms, trained on large datasets of malicious and benign files, can recognize subtle IOCs by evaluating hundreds of features such as opcode sequences, API calls, and runtime behavior to identify malicious intent. These techniques complement traditional antivirus solutions and can be deployed across multiple layers, including endpoints, email gateways, and cloud storage. Additionally, AI can assist in reverse engineering compromised binaries, helping analysts identify malware variants more rapidly.

Adaptive Security Awareness Training

Security awareness training effectiveness is improved by AI. AI-aided training tools enable the delivery of timely and relevant phishing simulations, targeted awareness modules, and tailored reinforcement schedules by personalizing content based on individual risk profiles and behavioral insights. Behavioral signals such as click rates, response times, and training completion rates are continuously fed into AI models, which then determine the most effective next training action. Over time, this adaptive approach reduces user fatigue, improves knowledge of retention, and strengthens the human firewall.

AI in Zero Trust Architecture

The Zero Trust framework is gaining widespread adoption as it helps reduce the risk of lateral movement and insider threats in today's perimeter-less, cloud-based environments. Zero Trust relies on dynamic, context-aware access decisions. AI-driven tools make those decisions by analyzing the live signals, such as user behavior, device risk posture, access patterns, and geolocation, and adjusting authentication or authorization decisions accordingly. AI-driven policy engines facilitate continuous verification and implement risk-based access controls without disrupting user workflows. These engines can also create micro-segmentation by dynamically redefining trust boundaries.

AI-Augmented Security Operations

As the heart of operational cybersecurity, the efficiency of security operations centers (SOCs) is critical to organizational resilience. Today, SOCs are inundated with a high volume of alerts from a growing number of security tools, At the same time, they are also facing pressure from an expanding threat landscape and a shortage of skilled cybersecurity professionals. In this environment, Large Language Model (LLM)-powered agents assist as co-pilots to analysts, assist with investigation of workflows, summarizing case data, generating response suggestions, and translating technical indicators into plain language. These tools improve SOC productivity and serve as mentoring aids for less-experienced analysts, helping to shorten the learning curve. As agentic AI evolves, it is becoming increasingly capable of handling delegated tasks, executing response playbooks autonomously, and escalating only those issues that require human oversight.

Security analytics platforms are evolving from static dashboards into dynamic AI-driven insights engines. These platforms aggregate and process vast amounts of telemetry, including endpoint logs, network traffic, DNS queries, and user behavior. AI identifies anomalies, detects attack chains, and assigns risk scores. This enables security teams to focus on the most critical events and make better informed decisions. Some advanced tools also incorporate reinforcement learning to continuously improve alerting strategies based on feedback and outcomes.

Automated Incident Response

With the rise in both the volume and sophistication of cyberattacks, no defense can guarantee complete protection. Beyond preventive controls, organizations must also prioritize the speed, consistency, and effectiveness of their incident response processes to ensure faster containment, minimized impact, and quicker restoration of normal operations. Automation, powered by AI, helps to achieve these objectives by enabling faster, smarter, and more coordinated actions.

Security orchestration, automation, and response (SOAR) platforms increasingly depend on AI to integrate security tools across the organization, correlate threat indicators, process high volumes of alerts, detect incidents, and assign severity. These systems can also recommend or automatically execute predefined response playbooks. For example, an AI-driven SOAR platform can isolate a compromised endpoint, revoke access credentials, or block malicious IP addresses without manual intervention. In addition, AI can generate incident reports, allowing analysts to focus on investigation and decision-making.

Economic and Workforce Benefits

By automating manual repetitive tasks and highlighting critical insights, AI allows security teams to shift focus to strategic issues. It improves job satisfaction, reduces burnout, and shortens onboarding time for new analysts, amplifying overall cybersecurity effectiveness. From an economic standpoint, AI adoption correlates with lower incident costs, enhanced operational efficiency with fewer false positives and SLA violations, and improved risk management and regulatory compliance. Collectively, these benefits demonstrate the return on investment that AI can bring to cybersecurity programs.

Measuring the Benefits of AI in Cybersecurity

To justify AI investments and guide strategy, organizations must quantify outcomes across risk, efficiency, and culture. Measuring the benefits of AI in cybersecurity requires a combination of quantitative and qualitative metrics showing risk reduction, operational efficiency, and business resilience. Key approaches include:

Risk Reduction Metrics

- Shorter Mean Time to Detect and Mean Time to Respond (MTTR)
- Fewer false positives and missed threats
- Decline in successful phishing or malware incidents
- Reduced manual errors due to automation

Operational Efficiency Metrics

- Higher volume of alerts triaged or resolved autonomously
- Considerable time savings on repetitive tasks such as alert correlation and log analysis
- Reduced analyst fatigue and response bottlenecks
- Greater ability to reassign staff to more strategic, value-added work

Financial Impact Metrics

- Cost avoidance from reduced breach frequency and minimized downtime
- Lower expenditures on outsourced SOC support or incident response services

- Higher return on investment from AI tools compared with traditional technologies

Strategic and Compliance Gains Metrics

- Better audit readiness and increased accuracy of compliance reporting
- Quicker alignment with frameworks such as NIST and ISO 27001
- Improved enterprise security ratings through risk engines and third-party assessments.

User and Culture Impact Metrics

- Higher engagement with AI-personalized security awareness training
- Measurable reduction in risky behaviors through adaptive user interventions
- Increased job satisfaction and productivity across security teams.

Risks, Limitations, and Governance

Despite its transformative promise, AI is not a silver bullet. Poorly governed AI systems can generate false positives, miss nuanced threats, or make wrong decisions that erode trust. Common risks include model bias, data drift, adversarial inputs, and the lack of explainability, particularly problematic in regulated industries where outputs must be transparent, auditable, and defensible.

Generative AI models present additional complexities. From leaking sensitive data in prompts to hallucinating incorrect conclusions, these systems require thoughtful design, strong access controls, and continuous validation. Over-reliance on AI is also a risk; human oversight must remain central to critical security functions.

To address these challenges, organizations must formalize AI governance frameworks. These define acceptable use cases, approval of workflows, retraining schedules, accountability models, and escalation paths. Ethical principles, fairness, privacy, and transparency should guide both model development and deployment. Increasingly, board-level oversight on AI usage is becoming standard. For example, a multinational energy company includes an 'AI Governance Update' in its quarterly Risk and Audit

Committee meetings. This update outlines all enterprise AI deployments tagged by risk level and includes a 'Model Change Log' to ensure traceability. This structured, risk-aligned oversight is emerging as best practice across sectors.

Conclusion

AI is no longer a futuristic concept in cybersecurity. It is already helping us to detect threats, respond to incidents, and build more resilient defenses. Its strength lies in speed, scalability, and the ability to detect patterns that human teams alone may miss.

Still, the value of AI depends on how it is implemented and governed. Without thoughtful design and oversight, AI can introduce new risks, make incorrect decisions, or erode trust. The goal is not to replace human judgment, but to enhance it by combining machine precision with human intuition.

The path forward will be shaped by the decisions we make today. With the right safeguards, clear accountability, and a commitment to responsible innovation, AI can tip the balance in favor of defenders. As the next chapter explores how adversaries are beginning to exploit the same technologies, one thing remains clear: staying ahead will require not only better tools, but wiser choices.

Bibliography

Data & Trust Alliance. (2022). *Algorithmic Safety: AI Governance for Responsible Deployment.* https://dataandtrustalliance.org

European Commission. (2024). *Digital Operational Resilience Act (DORA).* https://finance.ec.europa.eu/regulation-and-supervision/financial-services-legislation/implementing-and-delegated-acts/digital-operational-resilience-regulation_en

European Union Agency for Cybersecurity (ENISA). (2023). *AI Cybersecurity Challenges – Threat Landscape for Artificial Intelligence.* https://www.enisa.europa.eu/publications/artificial-intelligence-cybersecurity-challenges

Forrester Research. (2023). *The Total Economic Impact of AI-Driven Security Platforms.* https://www.forrester.com

Gartner. (2023). *Emerging Technologies: AI Use Cases in Cybersecurity.* Retrieved from https://www.gartner.com

Google Cloud. (2023). *AI for SOC: Enhancing Incident Detection and Response with Gemini-Powered Security Tools.* https://cloud.google.com

Gradient Cyber. (2024). *MXDR: AI-Driven Monitoring for Maritime Environments*. https://www.gradientcyber.com

Microsoft. (2024). *Security Copilot: Generative AI for Cybersecurity*. https://www.microsoft.com/en-us/security/blog

MITRE Corporation. (2023). *MITRE ATT&CK® Framework*. https://attack.mitre.org

National Cyber Security Centre (UK). (2022). *Zero Trust Architecture Design Principles*. https://www.ncsc.gov.uk/collection/zero-trust-architecture

National Institute of Standards and Technology. (2024). *Cybersecurity Framework 2.0*. https://www.nist.gov/cyberframework

OpenAI. (2024). *GPT-4 System Card*. https://cdn.openai.com/papers/gpt-4-system-card.pdf

Palo Alto Networks. (2024). *Cortex XSIAM: Autonomous Security Operations*. https://www.paloaltonetworks.com

Ponemon Institute. (2023). *Cost of a Data Breach Report 2023*. IBM Security. https://www.ibm.com/reports/data-breach

SANS Institute. (2023). *Measuring the Effectiveness of AI-Enabled Security Awareness Training*. https://www.sans.org

World Economic Forum. (2023). *Global Cybersecurity Outlook 2023*. https://www.weforum.org/reports/global-cybersecurity-outlook-2023

14

CYBER RISKS POSED BY AI

Introduction: The Double-Edged Sword of Artificial Intelligence

Artificial Intelligence (AI) is rapidly transforming the cybersecurity battlefield. On one side, defenders are leveraging machine learning to detect anomalies, automate responses, and orchestrate defenses. On the other hand, adversaries are using AI to craft realistic phishing emails, generate polymorphic malware, and bypass traditional detection mechanisms. This arms race is further complicated by the reality that AI systems themselves—especially complex models like LLMs—introduce new vulnerabilities. The dual-use nature of AI demands a shift in how cybersecurity professionals think about both protection and risk. Understanding AI not just as a tool, but also as a potential target and threat vector, is foundational to modern cyber resilience.

This chapter builds on that duality, examining both how AI can be misused by cyber criminals and how AI systems themselves may become vulnerable. Each section describes a distinct category of threat, spanning social

DOI: 10.4324/9781003682530-18

engineering, zero-day acceleration, adversarial manipulation, and emergent model behavior, to offer a comprehensive picture of the evolving AI threat landscape.

Malicious Uses of AI in Cyberattacks

AI is no longer a luxury or theoretical capability in cybercrime; it is an active and integral tool in the hands of attackers. With AI, threat actors can mimic human communication, automate discovery, and optimize their attack strategies across multiple vectors. The following sections explore the key offensive use cases.

AI-Enhanced Phishing and Social Engineering

Traditionally, phishing relied on generic messages and guesswork. AI changes that. Using LLMs, attackers can craft highly personalized, fluent, and convincing messages that reflect the target role, company, recent events, and even internal lingo. These messages may reference real meetings, quote familiar phrases, or mimic trusted senders convincingly.

AI also automates reconnaissance. Tools can scrape LinkedIn, company websites, past breaches, and other social media to create detailed profiles of individuals and organizations. The result is spear-phishing campaigns that feel eerily authentic and are more likely to succeed, especially when combined with timing and urgency cues that exploit human psychology.

Organizations are reporting phishing emails that bypass spam filters not because they are cleverly disguised, but because they are authentically written. The democratization of such capabilities through freely available AI tools means that even low-skill attackers can achieve high-impact results.

Organizations can protect against AI-enhanced phishing by training employees to spot realistic, personalized scams, using advanced email security tools, and monitoring unusual communication patterns across channels.

Deepfakes and Synthetic Media

Deepfakes represent the convergence of visual deception and AI-driven manipulation. What was once considered sci-fi is now accessible to mid-level criminals with access to generative media tools. Videos and audio clips can now be generated using AI, impersonating voices, facial movements, and gestures with stunning accuracy.

In corporate environments, deepfake videos or voice calls have already led to financial fraud. In one case in Hong Kong, fraudsters used a deepfake video call to impersonate a CFO, tricking an employee into transferring US$25 million (Reuters 2024). Unlike email scams, these attacks happen to live and pressure the victim into complying.

In another case, malicious actors used AI-generated text and voice impersonating US Secretary of State Marco Rubio to contact high-level officials. Recipients included at least three foreign ministers, a US governor, and a member of Congress, via Signal and voicemail messages.

The impact is not limited to fraud. Deepfakes can be used in corporate sabotage, regulatory manipulation, political disinformation, and reputational damage campaigns. Their psychological effect and the challenge they pose to verification protocols make them a top concern.

Organizations can reduce the risk of deepfakes and synthetic media by verifying the source of audio and video communications, using biometric or multi-factor authentication for sensitive actions, and training staff to question unexpected or high-pressure requests.

AI-Generated Polymorphic Malware

Just as AI helps defenders automate malware detection, it empowers attackers to write, mutate, and evolve malware at scale. AI can generate executable payloads, obfuscate code, and test against known signatures to ensure evasiveness. This leads to polymorphic malware that evolves with each delivery attempt.

This type of malware can mimic user behavior, hide system processes, and adjust to different environments. Some variants even incorporate feedback loops, learning from failed attempts and modifying tactics in near real time.

Malware as a Service platform is now embedding these AI capabilities, giving rise to plug-and-play offensive tools with machine learning baked in.

Organizations can defend against AI-generated polymorphic malware by using behavior-based detection tools, maintaining up-to-date endpoint protection, and continuously monitoring unusual patterns across systems.

AI-Accelerated Zero-Day Exploits

Zero-day vulnerabilities have traditionally been the purview of only elite hackers. AI is shifting that dynamic. Machine learning can now assist in identifying flaws in code, reverse-engineering patches, and proposing exploit pathways.

Tools built on LLMs can parse vulnerability disclosures, correlate them with known systems, and generate working exploit code. In some reported cases, time-to-exploit has dropped from weeks to mere hours. This significantly shortens defenders' patch windows and puts immense strain on traditional incident response timelines.

Moreover, a growing market for AI-assisted "Zero-Day-as-a-Service" has emerged on the dark web. Here, newly discovered vulnerabilities are packaged, documented, and sold before security teams have time to respond.

Organizations can mitigate AI-accelerated zero-day exploits by applying virtual patching, adopting threat intelligence feeds, and reducing exposure through network segmentation and timely system updates.

Disinformation and Influence Operations

In (mis)information warfare, AI greatly increases the power and impact of attacks. LLMs can mass-generate text that appears credible, coherent, and persuasive. Bots can flood social platforms, comment sections, and media outlets with tailored narratives designed to shift public opinion or sow confusion.

These campaigns often combine AI-generated text, deepfake images, voice clips, and synthetic videos. The goal is not always creating belief but doubt, making it difficult to determine what is real, thereby eroding trust.

Such attacks target elections, financial markets, geopolitical events, and corporate reputations. Defenders must now consider not only network intrusions but also narrative manipulation as part of their threat landscape. They should combat disinformation and influence operations by monitoring social and digital channels for coordinated narratives, verifying the authenticity of content before acting on it.

Vulnerabilities within AI Systems

AI technology is not only being used by attackers as a weapon. The AI systems used in business operations and cybersecurity can also introduce new cyber risks that are often overlooked. These vulnerabilities come not just from the model code or training process, but also from the data it uses, the interfaces it connects to, and the environment in which it operates. As AI becomes more central to decision-making, communication and automation, the risk of it being breached becomes a serious cybersecurity concern.

Adversarial Attacks

Adversarial attacks are deliberate attempts to breach an AI system by subtly altering input data in ways that cause the model to produce incorrect or unexpected results, even though the changes are not easily noticeable to humans. For example, an AI-powered image recognition model might mistake a stop sign for a speed limit sign if just a few pixels are changed. In cybersecurity, this could mean that the attacker modifies the malware slightly so that the AI-based detection system misclassifies it safely. Since these manipulations often go undetected by traditional alerts, they require rigorous testing and validation to identify any manipulation and incorporating model hardening techniques such as adversarial training.

Data Poisoning

AI models are only as good as the data they are trained on. When attackers infiltrate training datasets, either by compromising data pipelines or injecting false data through open-source contributions, they can poison the model. This may lead to models that behave maliciously under certain triggers (backdoors), exhibit biased decisions, or degrade in accuracy over time. The decentralized and dynamic nature of data collection, especially in open or federated systems, increases this risk significantly.

Data poisoning can be prevented by controlling and validating training data sources, monitoring anomalies during model training, and applying robust data hygiene practices throughout the AI development lifecycle.

Model Inversion and Membership Inference

Attackers can reverse-engineer models to reveal aspects of their training data. In sensitive contexts such as healthcare or finance, this may result in the exposure of personal data, violating privacy laws and regulations.

Membership inference attacks can even determine whether a specific individual's data was used during training, a grave concern under GDPR and similar data protection regimes.

The risk of model inversion and membership inference attacks can be reduced by limiting access to model outputs, applying differential privacy techniques during training, and avoiding the exposure of sensitive or identifiable training data.

Prompt Injection

Prompt injection is a threat specific to LLMs and natural language systems. Attackers embed malicious instructions into user input or external content to manipulate the model's behavior. For example, a customer support chatbot connected to internal tools could be tricked into revealing private account details or performing unauthorized actions. This type of risk is especially serious in enterprise settings where LLMs interact with sensitive data or business systems.

Organizations can reduce the risk of prompt injections by keeping user input separate from system instructions, cleaning and checking inputs, limiting what the model can do, and watching for unusual behavior.

Jailbreaking

Jailbreaking refers to the act of manipulating an LLM into ignoring its built-in safety rules or usage restrictions. This is typically done through prompts that are designed to confuse, mislead, or reframe from the model context. Attackers often use role-play scenarios, disguised instructions, or chains of commands to gradually steer the model toward generating prohibited content. To help prevent jailbreaking, organizations should regularly test their models for known jailbreak techniques, limit exposure to sensitive functions, and use strong content filtering to block harmful or unauthorized outputs.

Hallucination

A hallucination refers to a known limitation of LLMs, where the system generates information that is factually incorrect, unverifiable, or entirely made up, often delivered in a way that appears fluent and authoritative.

This creates a serious risk in professional and enterprise settings, where users might rely on these responses to make decisions involving contracts, compliance, technical guidance, or customer communication. For example, an AI-generated legal summary might misinterpret a clause, or a chatbot might provide inaccurate advice to clients based on flawed output.

Because hallucinated responses often sound confident and well-structured, they are easy to accept at face value. These can lead to misinformed decisions, operational failures, reputational harm, or breaches of regulatory requirements. Preventing harm from hallucination requires human oversight, output validation, and clear policies for how and when AI-generated content should be trusted or used in decision-making.

Emergent Behavior and Model Drift

As AI models continue to evolve through updates, fine-tuning, or scaling, they may begin to display behaviors that were not present in earlier versions. These changes are not always predictable and can affect how the model responds in familiar situations. For instance, a chatbot that used to summarize company policies correctly might begin to misinterpret certain clauses after an update, even if no one deliberately changed its instructions.

This kind of drift poses a challenge for governance and reliability. Because large models learn from vast and often complex datasets, even a minor change in training inputs or system context can lead to unexpected outputs. It becomes difficult to trace how and why the model's behavior has changed over time.

In enterprise environments, this unpredictability can impact customer experience, legal compliance, or business decisions. A model used for HR queries, for example, might start providing outdated or inconsistent information, creating confusion or even risk. To manage this, organizations need to monitor AI behavior regularly, document version changes carefully, and build feedback loops to catch and correct unexpected shifts early.

Model Extraction and Intellectual Property Theft

AI models are not just tools. They represent valuable intellectual property, built through significant investment in research, data collection, and training. If attackers gain repeated access to a model, especially through public interfaces, they can begin to copy it by studying how it responds to carefully crafted inputs. Over time, they may be able to reconstruct the model's logic, behavior, and even parts of the data it was trained on.

The copied model can be used for harmful purposes. Attackers may test it offline to find weaknesses, use it to impersonate trusted systems or build tools that bypass detection. In some cases, they may even resell the stolen model as their own. This puts years of work and competitive advantages at risk.

The threat is especially high for AI services offered through open APIs, where models respond to large numbers of user queries. Without the right safeguards in place, organizations may not realize that their model is being copied. Preventing this requires strong access controls, usage monitoring, response watermarking, and limits on how much of the model's behavior can be exposed to any single user.

Inadvertent Data Leakage from Employees Using Public LLMs

This growing risk arises not from malicious actors, but from well-meaning employees. When staff use public LLMs like ChatGPT to summarize emails, generate code, or translate documents, they may inadvertently paste confidential or proprietary data into the tool. Since most commercial LLM providers retain user inputs for training unless explicitly disabled, this creates a risk of data exfiltration.

For example, in 2023, engineers at Samsung leaked sensitive source code by using ChatGPT to assist with debugging. Though not a cyberattack, the outcome—exposure of intellectual property—was the same. Organizations must now treat public AI usage with the same scrutiny as other shadow IT practices.

AI Supply Chain Risks

AI systems rarely exist in isolation. They rely on open-source frameworks, third-party APIs, cloud hosting environments, and pretrained models from external providers. Each of these dependencies introduces a supply chain risk.

One major concern is compromised pretrained models from external providers that contain hidden behaviors or backdoors. After integration, these models might perform normally until triggered by a specific input.

Similarly, poisoned datasets sourced from public repositories can subtly degrade performance or embed malicious correlations.

Moreover, during model transfer or storage, weights can be tampered with, especially in environments lacking cryptographic integrity checks. AI deployment pipelines must now be treated as sensitive infrastructure, with controls mirroring those used for traditional software supply chains.

Organizations should manage AI supply chain risks by verifying the integrity of pretrained models and datasets, using trusted sources, applying cryptographic checks, and maintaining a clear record of all third-party components used in model development and deployment.

Future-Forward Risks

Looking ahead, the evolution of AI presents a class of risks that are still speculative but potentially catastrophic. These include both technological advancements and socio-political developments.

Autonomous Agents

AI agents can plan and carry out a sequence of actions to achieve a goal, often without constant human guidance. These agents use LLMs combined with tools like memory, APIs, or search engines to decide what to do next, carry it out, then move on to the next step, effectively linking multiple tasks together. While useful in automation, if misaligned or manipulated, such agents could consume excessive resources, alter configurations, or perform harmful actions, all without direct human oversight.

Risks from task-chaining AI agents can be reduced by restricting their access to sensitive systems, setting clear operational boundaries, and closely monitoring their actions through audit logs and human oversight.

AI Arms Race

States and corporations around the world are investing heavily in AI systems designed for both defensive and offensive purposes. This includes AI-driven cyberattack tools, autonomous drone swarms, large-scale surveillance platforms, and systems that make real-time decisions with limited human input. As these technologies become more capable and more autonomous, the potential for misuse or miscalculation increases significantly.

The lack of clear international agreements, ethical guidelines, or oversight mechanisms adds to the danger. Without shared standards or accountability, the global development of military and intelligence-focused AI may accelerate in unpredictable ways. Competing interests, national security concerns, and rapid innovation can create an unstable environment, where one side's advancement triggers another's response.

This growing arms race raises the risk of unintended escalation or conflict, not through direct intent but through algorithmic misunderstanding, faulty data, or misaligned objectives. In such high-stake situations, even a minor technical error could lead to significant consequences. The need for global cooperation, transparency, and guardrails in AI development is becoming urgent, not just for safety but for the long-term stability of international relations.

Proto-AGI Threats

While true artificial general intelligence, or AGI, is still considered a long-term goal, today's most advanced models already show early signs of general intelligence capability. Many of these systems can reason, plan, and apply knowledge across different domains without task-specific training. This growing flexibility brings forward one of the most critical challenges in AI safety, the alignment problem.

The alignment problem refers to the difficulty of ensuring that advanced AI systems consistently act in ways that match human goals, values, and expectations. As models become more autonomous, even small misalignments between intended objectives and how the system interprets them can lead to harmful or unpredictable outcomes. This risk becomes more serious when such systems have access to tools, data, or infrastructure that allows them to act independently in the real world.

A misaligned AI does not need to be malicious to cause damage. It could follow a poorly framed instruction too literally, prioritize unintended outcomes, or optimize the wrong metric, all while operating with a level of efficiency and scale that makes mistakes harder to catch in time. As models continue to advance, ensuring safe design, transparent reasoning, and effective oversight will be essential to preventing unintended consequences.

As these AI threats grow in complexity and impact, proactive defense strategies must evolve accordingly.

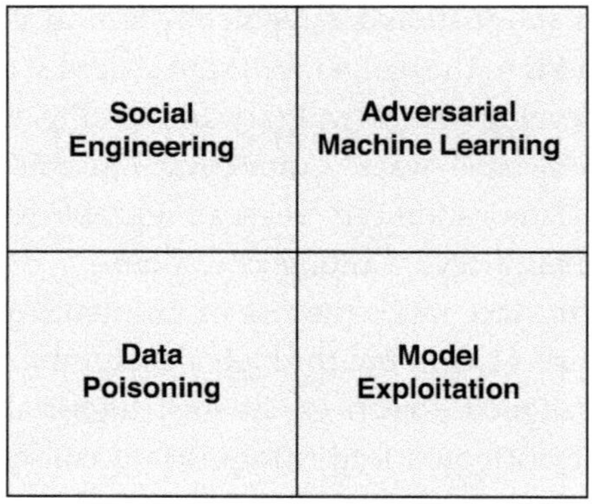

Image 14.1 AI Threat Landscape

Defense and Mitigation Strategies

As AI becomes more embedded in critical systems, defending against AI-related threats requires more than just traditional security controls. It demands a broader strategy that combines secure design, testing, governance, and awareness.

A strong starting point is regular AI red teaming. Security teams should simulate real-world attacks on deployed models using techniques such as prompt injection, data poisoning, jailbreak prompts, and model inversion. These exercises help expose hidden vulnerabilities that may not surface during routine testing.

Security must also be built into the AI development process. This means modeling threats early, vetting data sources, testing models in controlled environments, and monitoring their behavior once deployed. Developers can strengthen model defenses using adversarial training, reinforcement learning with human feedback, and input–output validation to ensure that the system responds reliably under different conditions.

Some threats are more advanced and harder to detect. Polymorphic malware generated by AI can change form with every attempt, making it difficult for signature-based tools to catch. In these cases, organizations should use behavior-based detection, stay connected to threat intelligence feeds, and apply virtual patching to protect systems while permanent fixes are developed.

AI also introduces new privacy risks. Attackers may attempt to extract information about the model's training data through model inversion or

Traditional	AI-Driven
Social engineering Generic low-customization	Highly personalized, tailored
Malware Static signature-reliant	Polymorphic, adaptive
Machine Learning manipulation	Adversarial attacks
Training data issues	Data poisoning risk

Image 14.2 Comparison of Traditional vs. AI-Driven Cyber Threats

membership inference attacks. Techniques such as differential privacy, along with careful control of what the model reveals, can help reduce this risk.

For AI services exposed through public or commercial interfaces, protections against model theft are essential. Rate limiting, usage monitoring, and watermarking of outputs can help detect and prevent model extraction. Organizations should also track the full history of how models are trained, updated, and used to ensure nothing has been tampered with.

As task-chaining agents become more capable, the risks they pose also increase. These agents can independently carry out multi-step actions using tools, APIs, or other systems. To reduce risk, organizations should define clear boundaries, restrict access to sensitive functions, and log all agent activity for review.

Governance is the foundation that supports everything else. Organizations should follow established frameworks such as the NIST AI Risk Management Framework and the OWASP Top Ten for LLMs. Preparing for future regulations, including the EU AI Act, is also important. Good governance includes documentation, traceability, and accountability.

Finally, security depends on people. Employees must be trained to recognize AI-generated phishing, deepfakes, and misinformation. They should understand the risks of pasting sensitive data into public AI tools and be encouraged to use enterprise-grade solutions that protect data and comply with policy.

Recommendations for CISOs, Policymakers, and Developers

CISOs should begin by auditing how AI is currently used across the organization. This includes identifying critical dependencies, assessing risk exposure, and integrating AI-specific threats into the broader enterprise cyber risk framework. Monitoring, detection, and governance must be embedded across departments, not siloed within IT or security teams.

Policymakers should promote transparency and accountability in AI systems by supporting independent audits, encouraging the sharing of threat intelligence, and mandating clear documentation of model behavior and limitations. Building and aligning global standards will be essential to maintaining trust and reducing fragmentation across regulatory environments.

Developers must follow secure design principles at every stage of the AI lifecycle. This includes limiting permissions, enforcing access control, sanitizing inputs, logging interactions, and regularly retraining models. Security and privacy protections should be implemented from the data layer upward and maintained throughout deployment.

Only through close collaboration between security teams, business leaders, developers, and regulators can the complex risks posed by AI be addressed effectively and at scale.

Real-World Corporate Impact

The cyber risks introduced and amplified by AI are no longer hypothetical, experimental, or confined to research labs. Across industries—hospitality, finance, healthcare, aviation, technology, and critical infrastructure—organizations are already experiencing material financial loss, legal liability, operational disruption, and regulatory exposure directly attributable to AI-enabled attacks and AI system failures. These incidents demonstrate that AI has fundamentally changed the threat model: attackers now automate persuasion, reconnaissance, malware evolution, and exploitation at machine speed, while enterprises are simultaneously exposed to new internal risks such as hallucination liability, supply chain poisoning, model theft, and prompt-level data exfiltration. The following real-world corporate cases illustrate how AI-driven cyber risks are manifesting today—and why AI governance, security architecture, and continuous monitoring are now essential components of enterprise resilience.

1. **MGM Resorts—Social Engineering + AI Reconnaissance (2023)**

Risk Type: AI-augmented social engineering, identity impersonation
What Happened:
Scattered Spider used LinkedIn scraping, voice impersonation, and AI-assisted reconnaissance to convincingly impersonate MGM employees and trick the IT helpdesk into resetting MFA credentials.
Impact:

- 10-day operational outage
- Slot machines, hotel systems, and payments disrupted
- **>US$100 million direct financial loss**

Why It Matters:
Demonstrates how AI-assisted profiling and voice impersonation can fully bypass MFA.

2. **Caesars Entertainment—AI-Optimized Phishing and Data Extortion (2023)**

Risk Type: AI-enhanced spear phishing, data exfiltration
What Happened:
Attackers used AI-assisted reconnaissance to craft internal communications and trick employees into credential disclosure.
Impact:

- Loyalty program data of millions exposed
- Caesars paid US**$15 million ransom**

Why It Matters:
AI makes reconnaissance and persuasion scale exponentially.

3. **Air Canada—LLM Hallucination Legal Exposure (2024)**

Risk Type: LLM hallucination, compliance failure

What Happened:

Air Canada's chatbot fabricated a refund policy. A court ruled Air Canada legally bound by the hallucinated output.

Impact:

- Legal liability
- Brand trust erosion

Why It Matters:

Hallucination becomes **legal and financial risk**, not just accuracy risk.

4. **Okta—AI-Driven Supply Chain Compromise (2023)**

Risk Type: AI-enabled supply chain attack

What Happened:

Threat actors used AI-generated tooling to pivot from a support vendor into Okta's internal systems.

Impact:

- Customer tenants exposed
- Regulatory scrutiny

Why It Matters:

Shows AI-accelerated lateral movement inside SaaS supply chains.

5. **WormGPT / FraudGPT Campaigns (2023–2024)**

Risk Type: AI-generated polymorphic malware and phishing at scale

What Happened:

Criminal AI models were released on darknet markets designed specifically for phishing, malware generation, and BEC fraud.

Impact:

- Industrialized phishing and malware production
- Spike in BEC losses globally

Why It Matters:

Marks the **productization of cybercrime AI**.

6. **Microsoft Azure OpenAI—Prompt Injection and Data Exfiltration (2023)**

Risk Type: Prompt injection, tool abuse
What Happened:
Researchers demonstrated that system-connected copilots could be tricked into leaking private corporate data using indirect prompt injection.
Impact:

- Demonstrated systemic enterprise AI exposure

Why It Matters:
Shows LLM copilots can become **enterprise data exfiltration channels**.

7. **Hugging Face—Poisoned Model Backdoors (2024)**

Risk Type: AI supply chain poisoning
What Happened:
Backdoored AI models were found uploaded to public repositories.
Impact:

- Compromised ML pipelines
- Hidden triggers embedded in models

Why It Matters:
AI supply chains now mirror SolarWinds-level risk.

8. **Tesla / Waymo—Adversarial Vision Attacks**

Risk Type: Adversarial input manipulation
What Happened:
Researchers demonstrated that small visual perturbations caused autonomous driving systems to misinterpret traffic signs and lane markings.
Impact:

- Safety and liability risk
- Regulatory scrutiny

Why It Matters:

Shows how adversarial attacks move from cyber risk into **physical-world harm**.

9. **IBM Watson Health—Training Data Bias and Model Drift**

Risk Type: Model drift, training bias, regulatory failure

What Happened:

IBM Watson Health systems were withdrawn after models produced unsafe and inaccurate medical recommendations.

Impact:

- Multi-billion dollar write-down
- Program canceled

Why It Matters:

Governance failure destroyed an entire AI product line.

10. **Robinhood—Automated AI Bot Manipulation (2021–2024)**

Risk Type: AI-driven disinformation and bot trading manipulation

What Happened:

Automated bots amplified false narratives, triggering market volatility and regulatory review.

Impact:

- Market integrity concerns
- SEC scrutiny

Why It Matters:

AI influences **financial market stability**.

Conclusion

AI is not just another wave of innovation; it marks a fundamental shift in how technology operates, learns, and makes decisions. As cyber threats become increasingly AI-driven, traditional defenses will fall short. Our response must evolve just as quickly, guided by foresight, technical rigor, and governance that keeps pace with innovation.

Cybersecurity professionals can no longer rely on reactive measures alone. They must understand how AI systems function, where they are deployed, and how they might fail or be exploited. This includes recognizing not just the external threats that use AI, but also the internal risks that emerge from how AI is built, trained, and connected to business operations.

In a landscape where machines learn and adapt in real time, the margin for error continues to shrink. The ability to respond quickly, correct intelligently, and govern transparently will determine whether AI becomes a source of resilience or risk.

Ultimately, navigating this era of intelligent systems will require more than technical tools. It will demand vigilance, cross-functional collaboration, and a culture of continuous learning. The organizations that invest in these capabilities now will be the ones best equipped to thrive in a future shaped by AI.

Bibliography

Bloomberg. (2023). *Samsung Bans ChatGPT after Data Leak*. Retrieved from https://www.bloomberg.com

European Commission. (2024). *EU Artificial Intelligence Act*. Retrieved from https://artificialintelligenceact.eu

GoogleBrain. (2022). *Privacy Risks in Model Inversion*. Retrieved from https://research.google

Hugging Face. (2024). *Security Advisory on Compromised Models*. Retrieved from https://huggingface.co

MITCSAIL. (2023). *Adversarial Attacks in Medical AI*. Retrieved from https://www.csail.mit.edu

OWASP Foundation. (2024). *OWASP Top 10 for LLMs*. Retrieved from https://owasp.org

NIST. (2023). *AI Risk Management Framework*. Retrieved from https://www.nist.gov/itl/ai-risk-management-framework

Reuters. (2024). *Deepfake Scam in Hong Kong*. Retrieved from https://www.reuters.com

Tencent Keen Labs. (2023). *Adversarial Examples in Autonomous Driving*. Retrieved from https://keenlab.tencent.com

WithSecure. (2023). *Generative AI in Phishing Attacks*. Retrieved from https://www.withsecure.com

15

CYBER SECURITY CONTROLS FOR AI

Introduction

Artificial Intelligence (AI) is undeniably one of the most captivating and transformative phenomena to emerge in the IT landscape in recent years. It has revolutionized countless processes, enhanced operational efficiency, and redefined the boundaries of innovation. Yet, as with any groundbreaking technology, its ascent is accompanied by potential risks and unintended consequences.

While AI continues to evolve at an unprecedented pace, it is imperative that we establish and enforce robust controls to govern its development and deployment. The immense power of AI to achieve complex objectives demands a heightened sense of responsibility and ethical stewardship. As the adage goes—repeated countless times—with great power comes great responsibility.

Concerns surrounding the misuse of AI, its manipulation to disseminate misinformation, and the fear of its unpredictable evolution are increasingly prevalent. These issues underscore the need for a deeper understanding of AI's underlying mechanisms, its intended purpose, and the frameworks required to manage and regulate its influence.

DOI: 10.4324/9781003682530-19

As we venture further into the realm of intelligent systems, it becomes essential to approach AI not just as a tool, but as a force that must be harnessed with foresight, discipline, and accountability. In this chapter, we will explore key strategies and governance models that can help organizations responsibly develop, consume, and leverage AI technologies.

Potential Risks

The myriad variants of AI currently available can be perplexing. This technological expanse is both beneficial and hazardous. The key benefit is the emergence of specialized AI models, which perform with exceptional aptitude in their areas of focus, alongside versatile, general-purpose models. The associated risk profiles and necessary mitigation controls will subsequently differ across this spectrum.

It is paramount that you gain clarity on the specific AI model you employ, scrutinizing its competencies, constraints, and functionalities. This diligence will fortify your ability to establish effective oversight before adverse events materialize.

Unintentional Data Compromise

The possibility of unintentional data leakage is acute. Insufficient vigilance when supplying data for model training can inadvertently unmask private or sensitive data to unauthorized parties. You must critically evaluate the nature of the data you are feeding the model: does it include confidential records, health information, or financial particulars? What are the ramifications of exposure?

The Threat of Malice

We have witnessed various lapses, such as AI models delivering inappropriate material on consumer platforms. While some instances are likely technical hiccups, threat actors will leverage these vulnerabilities with malicious intent. They will strive to compromise and subvert your AI models for their own illicit purposes. Like all networked systems, your AI deployment is a potential target for cyber-attacks. For a detailed exposition on common AI attack methodologies, reference the MITRE ATLAS Matrix.

Erosion of Trust

Misinformation, which can occur even without malicious motivation, results when a suboptimally trained AI model produces erroneous or low-quality information. This outcome serves to alienate customers and clients, leading them to reject any proposed AI initiatives.

Due Diligence and Mandates

If you rely on a third-party commercial AI model, you must ensure that contractual agreements preclude the vendor from using your data to further train their proprietary model. A final consideration is the complexity of regulatory adherence. If your organization operates under specific legal mandates, you are obligated to verify that your AI systems maintain unwavering compliance with all applicable regulations.

Mitigations

Effective AI security demands a cross-functional alliance among key organizational stakeholders—including SecOps, DevOps, legal counsel, and governance, risk, and compliance teams. Rather than hastily deploying AI solutions, organizations should adopt a deliberate and strategic approach, engaging leadership, legal advisers, and IT experts to ensure alignment with operational, ethical, and regulatory standards. A meticulously planned rollout will invariably yield more sustainable and secure outcomes than a rushed implementation.

Continuous Monitoring and Behavioral Oversight

As with any security apparatus, AI systems require vigilant monitoring to detect anomalies, erratic behavior, or signs of misuse. Encourage end-users to promptly report suspicious activity and implement mechanisms to identify and restrict unusual API usage patterns that may indicate abuse or exploitation.

Data Sanitization and Minimization

During model training, prioritize data sanitization and anonymization wherever feasible. Reducing the volume of training data not only enhances privacy but also mitigates the risk of inadvertently embedding sensitive information into AI models. Thoughtful data curation is a cornerstone of responsible AI development.

SaaS vs. Self-hosted AI Models

Organizations now have the flexibility to choose between cloud-based (SaaS) and self-hosted (on-premises) AI deployments. Each option offers distinct advantages: while localized models afford greater control and data sovereignty, they often entail higher operational costs. If your primary concern is safeguarding sensitive or proprietary data, an on-premises solution may be more appropriate.

Access Control: RBAC and Zero Trust

Robust access control is non-negotiable in minimizing cyber risks associated with AI. Employ role-based access control (RBAC) and embrace the principles of least privilege and zero trust to ensure that only authorized personnel can interact with critical AI components.

Integrating AI into Cyber Governance

Governance is the linchpin of a resilient cybersecurity program. AI must be woven into your broader governance framework through structured policies, oversight mechanisms, and documentation. Reference established frameworks such as MITRE ATLAS and NIST's AI Risk Management Framework (AI RMF) to guide your strategy and ensure compliance.

Incident Response: AI-Ready Protocols

Update your incident response (IR) protocols to reflect the unique risks posed by AI systems. Whether by integrating AI into existing IR plans or developing dedicated AI-specific playbooks, preparedness is essential to mitigate potential breaches and ensure swift recovery.

Looking Ahead

As we navigate the ongoing transformation ushered in by AI, government and regulatory bodies are increasingly taking notice. The General

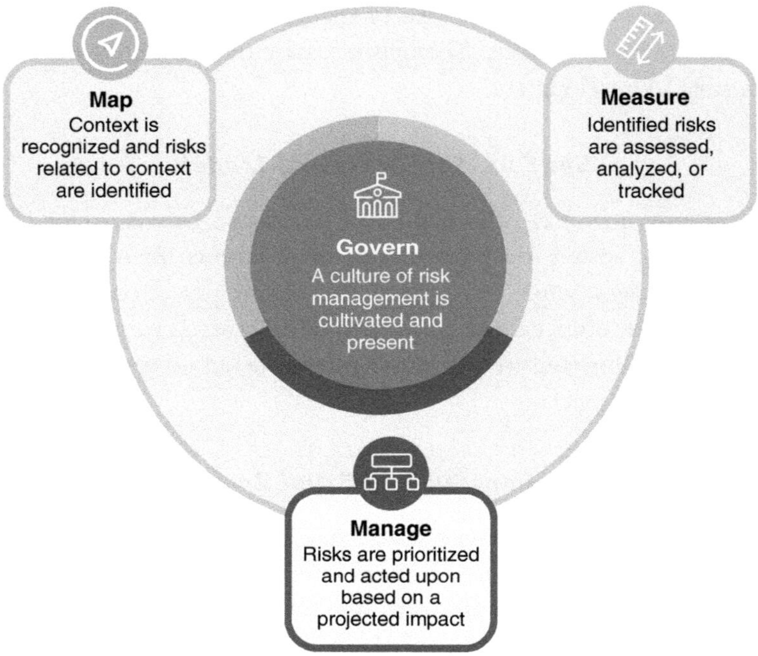

Image 15.1 AI Risk Management Activities (NIST AI RMF)

Data Protection Regulation (GDPR) recognizes that AI models trained on anonymized data may fall outside its scope; however, large language models that potentially contain personally identifiable information (PII) remain subject to GDPR provisions.

In the European Union, the landmark Artificial Intelligence Act has been enacted to establish a comprehensive regulatory framework for AI technologies. Meanwhile, in the United States, California lawmakers have amended the California Consumer Privacy Act to clarify that AI-generated data may be classified and treated as personal data.

Secure Model Development Lifecycle (MDLC)

Integrating security into the AI model development lifecycle ensures that threats are addressed from ideation through deployment. Key practices include:

- Secure coding standards for machine-learning pipelines
- Threat modeling during architecture planning

- Vulnerability scanning of training environments and ML libraries
- Continuous integration with secure testing gates
- Segregation of development, test, and production environments

Adversarial Robustness and Poisoning Defenses

AI systems are susceptible to attacks like adversarial examples and data poisoning. Mitigation techniques include:

- Adversarial training using perturbation-based examples
- Data provenance and integrity checks during ingestion
- Input validation and anomaly detection at inference time
- Using certified robust models in high-risk applications

Model Governance and Logging

Logging and traceability are vital for monitoring model behavior, especially during post-deployment. Governance controls should include:

- Logging model inputs/outputs with appropriate redaction
- Tracking changes in training datasets and hyperparameters
- Versioning models and configuration files
- Audit trails for access, updates, and retraining events

Integration with Zero Trust Architectures

As AI models interface with various systems and APIs, Zero Trust principles provide strong baseline security:

- Enforce least privilege access to models and data
- Apply continuous authentication for users and endpoints
- Monitor and verify all interactions between model services
- Isolate AI components into segmented zones with strict controls

Cybersecurity Controls for Generative AI Systems

Generative AI introduces unique cybersecurity risks, including model inversion, prompt injection, and hallucination of sensitive data. Effective controls must address both model behavior and the platforms enabling generation.

- Prompt Filtering and Output Guardrails: Implement input sanitization and output moderation to prevent misuse and avoid generation of harmful or toxic content. This includes using automated detection layers for hate speech, misinformation, and data leakage.
- Red Teaming of Generative Models: Regular adversarial testing should assess how generative models respond to coercive prompts, jailbreaks, and malicious queries.
- Training Data Scrubbing: Scrutinize training datasets for inclusion of PII, copyrighted material, or sensitive internal documents, and apply automated data classification tools during ingestion.
- Audit Trails for Generation Events: Log all prompts and outputs in a tamper-evident system to ensure traceability and forensic readiness.
- Fine-Tuning Restrictions: Enforce strict controls over who can fine-tune or retrain generative models, using RBAC and requiring business justification.

Federated Learning Security Considerations

Federated learning distributes model training across edge devices, reducing the need to centralize sensitive data. However, it introduces new attack surfaces.

- Secure Aggregation Protocols: Use cryptographic aggregation to ensure that no individual client update can be intercepted or reverse-engineered.
- Differential Privacy in Client Updates: Apply differential privacy techniques to reduce leakage of sensitive training information from edge devices.
- Model Poisoning Defenses: Detect anomalous client updates that may skew the global model or introduce backdoors.
- Device Authentication and Update Signing: Require mutual authentication between server and edge nodes, and sign model updates to prevent tampering in transit.

- Resilience to System Heterogeneity: Monitor training consistency across devices with varying data quality, connectivity, and hardware security.

Edge AI Cybersecurity Controls

AI deployed at the edge—such as on IoT devices, autonomous vehicles, or wearables—operates with minimal oversight and is highly vulnerable to physical and remote attacks.

- Runtime Integrity Monitoring: Ensure model binaries and runtime environments are validated at startup and periodically checked using secure boot and remote attestation.
- Encrypted Model Storage and Execution: Models stored on edge devices should be encrypted with keys bound to hardware and executed in secure enclaves when possible.
- Minimal Attack Surface Design: Eliminate unnecessary services, ports, and admin interfaces from edge AI devices to reduce the potential for exploitation.
- Over-the-Air (OTA) Security Patching: Establish automated, signed, and authenticated OTA update channels for firmware and AI models.
- Localized Fail-Safes and Kill Switches: For high-risk environments (e.g., robotics, industrial systems), implement local controls that can override or shut down AI operations during anomalies.

Visual Aids and Mapping Tables

Architecture Diagrams

The following diagrams illustrate the cybersecurity architecture for securing AI across various environments:

- Diagram 1: Secure Development and Deployment Flow for AI/ML Pipelines
- Diagram 2: AI Inference Security in Edge Devices
- Diagram 3: Zero Trust Architecture with AI Integration

Control Area	NIST RMF Core
Model Input Validation	MAP
Adversarial Robustness Testing	MEASURE
Logging & Monitoring of AI Inference	GOVERN
Role-based Access Control for AI Assets	GOVERN
Secure API Gateway for AI Models	MANAGE

Image 15.2 Mapping AI Cybersecurity Controls to NIST AI RMF

Each diagram includes components such as data pipelines, encryption layers, access controls, audit logging, anomaly detection, and model validation checkpoints.

Control Mapping Tables

Below are examples of how key AI cybersecurity controls map to popular frameworks:

- NIST AI RMF 1.0
- ISO/IEC 42001
- EU AI Act

More detailed tables can be developed to support compliance documentation, internal audits, and risk assessments.

Conclusion

It is essential to recognize that AI systems are fundamentally built upon traditional IT infrastructure. Consequently, many foundational principles from frameworks such as the CIS Controls and NIST 800-53 remain highly relevant and applicable to securing AI environments.

An organization's AI adoption journey encompasses multiple critical components, beginning with the use of high-quality training data that is both minimized and sanitized to reduce risk and preserve privacy. The underlying IT architecture supporting AI must be fortified with robust security measures, including RBAC and other industry-standard safeguards.

Configuration details should be meticulously documented, and system behavior must be continuously monitored to detect anomalies and ensure operational integrity. Furthermore, it is imperative that AI systems comply with applicable local regulations and are fully integrated into the organization's IR protocols.

Bibliography

CIS Critical Controls. https://www.cisecurity.org/controls/v8-1

Google's Secure AI Framework (SAIF). https://safety.google/cybersecurity-advancements/saif/

MITRE ATLAS Matrix. https://atlas.mitre.org/matrices/ATLAS

NIST AI Risk Management Framework (AI RMF). https://www.nist.gov/itl/ai-risk-management-framework

NIST Security and Privacy Controls for Information Systems and Organizations. https://csrc.nist.gov/pubs/sp/800/53/r5/upd1/final

The EU Artificial Intelligence Act. https://artificialintelligenceact.eu/

16

CONTROL FRAMEWORKS FOR AI

Introduction

Artificial Intelligence (AI) is no longer a futuristic concept; it is a present-day force shaping how governments operate, how businesses compete, and how society functions. From process automation and real-time data analysis to decision support and content generation, AI offers transformative opportunities. However, with that opportunity comes risk. Poorly designed or poorly governed AI systems can introduce serious consequences: unreliable outputs, security vulnerabilities, privacy breaches, and decisions that are difficult or impossible to explain. In this environment, control frameworks are not optional; they have become essential (NIST, 2023b).

Control frameworks provide structure, language, and accountability for managing AI risk across the full lifecycle of a system, from design and development to deployment and monitoring. They help organizations operationalize principles such as safety, transparency, and fairness in ways that are repeatable and measurable (U.S. Department of Commerce, 2023). More importantly, control frameworks foster trust: between developers and

DOI: 10.4324/9781003682530-20

users, between the public and institutions, and across ecosystems where AI decisions affect real people in real-time (NIST, 2024f).

At the center of this effort is the National Institute of Standards and Technology (NIST). As a non-regulatory agency under the US Department of Commerce, NIST plays a unique role in bridging innovation and oversight (NIST, 2024a). Its AI risk-management efforts are grounded in measurement science, cybersecurity, and decades of experience crafting voluntary, consensus-driven standards. Unlike more prescriptive approaches, such as the European Union (EU) AI Act (European Union, 2024), NIST's frameworks are descriptive, providing organizations the flexibility and scalability to tailor them to their specific needs. Throughout this chapter, NIST's frameworks, including the AI Risk Management Framework (AI RMF 1.0) (NIST, 2023b), the Generative AI Profile (AI 600-1) (NIST, 2024f), and the Secure Software Development Framework (SP 800-218A) (Booth et al., 2024), will serve as the foundation for understanding how structured AI risk management is evolving in practice.

That said, NIST is not alone. AI is both a global challenge and a global opportunity, and its governance reflects that reality. Across the world, international bodies, national governments, industry coalitions, and ethics organizations have developed their own standards, principles, and models (ISO/IEC, 2023). From ISO/IEC 42001 to the EU AI Act, and from the Organization for Economic Co-operation and Development (OECD) AI Principles (OECD, 2019) to the Singapore Model AI Governance Framework (IMDA, 2020), the ecosystem is rich with guidance, some complementary and some contrasting. For example, while NIST's AI RMF emphasizes voluntary adoption, ISO/IEC 42001 provides a structured management system for AI, and the OECD AI Principles focus on high-level ethical guidance (OECD, 2023). Rather than viewing these frameworks as competing, this chapter takes the position that they are mutually reinforcing, offering organizations a toolkit to address AI risks comprehensively.

What follows is a structured overview of today's most influential AI control frameworks. NIST remains the central focus, with detailed coverage of its tools, priorities, and implementation strategies. Alongside that, we explore international standards, industry-specific guidance, and ethical frameworks, together with emerging trends that point to where this space is heading next. The goal is not to catalog frameworks, but to provide a practical roadmap for how organizations can align them in a way that supports responsible innovation, regulatory readiness, and sustained public trust (NIST, 2024c).

NIST AI Research and Frameworks

Overview of NIST's Role in AI Risk Management

AI is revolutionizing industries, unlocking unprecedented opportunities in logistics, healthcare, defense, and public services. Yet, alongside these advancements come significant risks: unpredictable outputs, embedded bias, adversarial manipulation, and a lack of transparency, all of which demand urgent attention. As AI systems become more pervasive, the challenge of governing them in a way that ensures safety, security, and trustworthiness has shifted from theoretical debate to real-world necessity.

The NIST plays a leading role in addressing these challenges. As a non-regulatory agency under the US Department of Commerce, NIST has earned global recognition for developing voluntary, consensus-driven frameworks that guide innovation without stifling it. Its contributions to cybersecurity, privacy, cryptography, and digital trust have made it a foundational partner to both government agencies and private-sector organizations. NIST's influence extends beyond US borders through collaboration with international organizations such as ISO and the OECD, helping to harmonize AI standards and foster global trust in AI systems (NIST, 2023d).

In the context of AI, NIST's mission is to promote safety, security, privacy, and fairness, not as abstract ideals, but as measurable attributes that can be embedded across the AI lifecycle. What sets NIST apart is its commitment to descriptive guidance rather than prescriptive regulation. For example, while the EU AI Act imposes strict legal requirements on high-risk AI systems, NIST's frameworks allow organizations the flexibility to tailor risk-management practices to their specific operational, regulatory, and ethical contexts (NIST, 2023a).

NIST's approach is grounded in three core objectives:

1. Delivering actionable guidance through technically sound, implementation-ready tools and resources.
2. Providing global leadership in AI standards development and risk management frameworks.
3. Anticipating and addressing emerging risks associated with advanced and generative AI technologies.

These objectives are realized through a suite of frameworks and resources designed to help organizations manage AI risks effectively. This section introduces NIST's evolving role in AI governance and highlights the key tools that support its mission. These include the AI Risk Management Framework (AI RMF 1.0), the Generative AI Profile (AI 600-1), the Secure Software Development Framework for AI Systems (SP 800-218A), and the Trustworthy and Responsible AI Resource Center. Together, these initiatives form a comprehensive foundation for AI risk management across both public and private sectors, serving as the focal point for this chapter.

Understanding NIST: Origins, Mission, and Modern Mandate

Building on NIST's current mission and objectives, it is important to understand the agency's historical roots and how its evolution has positioned it to address the challenges of AI governance today. The NIST is one of the most influential scientific and technical agencies in the federal government, yet it often operates behind the scenes. Established in 1901 as the National Bureau of Standards, NIST was created at a time when the United States faced a growing industrial challenge: inconsistent measurements and incompatible standards were undermining the country's ability to compete globally. The agency's original mission was straightforward but ambitious: to bring coherence, reliability, and scientific rigor to the standards underpinning American commerce and industry (NIST, 2023d).

In 1988, the organization was renamed the NIST and placed under the US Department of Commerce. This transition expanded NIST's role beyond physical measurement to include digital infrastructure, cybersecurity, and emerging technologies. Today, NIST operates as a non-regulatory agency, meaning it does not impose or enforce laws, but instead provides voluntary, consensus-based guidance that shapes both public policy and private-sector practice. This unique position allows NIST to act as a bridge between innovation and oversight, fostering trust in rapidly evolving technologies without stifling progress.

NIST's current mission is to "promote U.S. innovation and industrial competitiveness by advancing measurement science, standards, and technology in ways that enhance economic security and improve our quality of life" (NIST, 2023a). This mission places NIST at the intersection of science, policy, and industry. It empowers the agency to address the complexities of emerging technologies such as AI. By developing frameworks, benchmarks, reference materials, and collaborative models, NIST equips organizations with the tools needed to navigate both the risks and the opportunities of AI adoption across diverse sectors, including government, healthcare, manufacturing, energy, and finance.

Over the past two decades, NIST has become a cornerstone in the fields of cybersecurity and digital trust, best known for its Cybersecurity Framework (CSF), its Special Publication 800-series, and its contributions to cryptographic standards and privacy engineering. These efforts have laid the groundwork for NIST's growing leadership in AI governance, where its science-based approach ensures that safety, fairness, and accountability remain at the forefront of innovation (NIST, 2023b).

Why AI Risk Management?

AI is no longer confined to research labs or niche applications. It is actively shaping how we live, work, and innovate. In government and business operations alike, AI supports everything from Level 1 to Level 2 service desk support to predictive maintenance and fraud detection. In creative fields, generative AI tools are being used to produce visual media, compose music, and even write scripts or marketing copy, blurring the line between human- and machine-generated content.

Technology's reach continues to expand across sectors, including healthcare, finance, defense, logistics, and education, underscoring its transformative potential. Yet, like any disruptive force, AI introduces new and amplified risks: technical, operational, ethical, and societal. Managing these risks is no longer optional; it is essential to ensure AI systems are deployed responsibly and with long-term resilience in mind.

This transformative potential also amplifies risks; technical, operational, ethical, and societal:

- Security vulnerabilities, including adversarial attacks and model manipulation.
- Bias and fairness concerns, where system outputs may reinforce discrimination or inequity.
- Cloudiness, where model-driven decisions are difficult to trace, understand, or explain.
- Privacy concerns, especially when models are trained on sensitive or proprietary data.

- Loss of trust, as users question the reliability, intent, or safety of AI-enabled systems.
- Greater threat from bad actors: amateur hackers are becoming master hackers via AI.

Recognizing this dual reality, NIST identified the need for a structured, multidisciplinary approach to AI risk management, one that supports innovation while protecting individuals, organizations, and society. This recognition led to the release of the NIST AI Risk Management Framework (AI RMF 1.0) in January 2023 (NIST, 2023c). The AI RMF is a voluntary, resource-rich framework designed to help organizations identify, assess, manage, and monitor AI risks throughout the system lifecycle (NIST, 2023b).

Unlike rigid regulatory checklists, the AI RMF emphasizes trustworthiness as a design and operational priority. According to NIST, trustworthy AI systems should demonstrate characteristics such as:

- Validity and reliability
- Safety and security resilience
- Accountability and explainability
- Privacy enhancement and fairness.

These attributes are not isolated benchmarks; they are interconnected and context-dependent, requiring both technical safeguards and organizational alignment (NIST, 2023b).

To support the AI RMF, NIST has developed a suite of complementary resources, including:

- Generative AI Profile (NIST AI 600-1): July 2024 release offering 200+ actions to mitigate risks in generative models like LLMs and diffusion systems (NIST, 2024g).
- Secure Software Development Framework for AI (SP 800-218A): Extends secure-by-design principles to foundation models and dual-use AI systems (NIST, 2024j).
- AI Safety Institute (AISI-US): Established in 2023 to lead AI safety science, benchmarking, and global collaboration on standards (White House, 2023).

Through these initiatives, NIST positions AI risk management as an enabler of responsible innovation, creating shared vocabularies and methods that foster trust, security, and resilience.

At the core of this effort is the AI Risk Management Framework (AI RMF 1.0), a comprehensive tool for governing AI risk throughout its lifecycle.

AI Risk Management Framework (AI RMF 1.0)

The NIST AI Risk Management Framework (AI RMF 1.0) is a foundational resource designed to help organizations manage complex and evolving risks associated with AI. Released in January 2023, the framework offers a voluntary, flexible, and sector-agnostic approach to promoting trustworthy AI. Its design reflects a growing recognition that effective risk management must be embedded throughout the AI lifecycle, shaped by organizational mission, stakeholder context, and the dynamic nature of digital value creation.

Purpose and Audience

The AI RMF was developed to address a core challenge: how to responsibly integrate AI systems into environments where innovation and risk coexist. Rather than imposing rigid compliance mandates, the framework offers descriptive guidance that organizations can tailor to their unique operating models, objectives, and levels of AI maturity. It supports a proactive, continuous improvement approach enabling teams to align strategy, risk, and operational decision-making across functions (NIST, 2023b).

The intended audience is broad. Policymakers, system developers, risk professionals, program managers, and executive leadership can each use the framework to inform decisions, assess vulnerabilities, and foster collaboration around AI deployment. Whether in a startup experimenting with generative models or a federal agency scaling AI for mission-critical services, the AI RMF provides a common structure to drive value while minimizing harm (NIST, 2023b).

The Four Core Functions

At the heart of the AI RMF are four interdependent functions: *Govern*, *Map*, *Measure*, and *Manage*. These pillars support a systems-oriented approach to AI risk management that is repeatable, scalable, and grounded in both technical and organizational realities.

Govern: The Govern function establishes the institutional foundation for responsible AI use. It focuses on leadership, accountability, policy alignment, and organizational culture.

Activities include, but are not limited to:

- Define roles and responsibilities across AI governance, operations, and oversight
- Promote a risk-aware culture that anticipates downstream impacts on individuals and systems
- Embed AI-specific principles into governance charters, data management policies, and procurement guidelines
- Ensure alignment with ethical frameworks, regulatory expectations, and organizational values

Example: A healthcare system creates an AI governance board that includes clinicians, privacy officers, and technologists to guide the deployment of decision-support algorithms.

Map: The Map function focuses on understanding the context in which an AI system operates. This includes its intended purpose, stakeholders, data sources, and potential risk exposure throughout its lifecycle.

Activities include, but are not limited to:

- Conduct use-case scoping and risk characterization exercises
- Identify data dependencies, performance assumptions, and societal impacts
- Map stakeholders and examine how system outcomes affect different communities or business units
- Incorporate feedback mechanisms that allow for realignment as new risks or use cases emerge.

Example: A financial services firm uses mapping exercises to assess the impact of an AI-based fraud detection tool on customer experience and compliance obligations.

Measure: Measurement involves developing and applying metrics, testing protocols, and evaluation tools to assess how well AI systems are meeting defined objectives, and where gaps or trade-offs exist.

Activities include, but are not limited to:

- Monitor AI system performance for reliability, accuracy, fairness, and robustness
- Test for vulnerabilities such as bias, adversarial behavior, or concept drift
- Integrate both technical measures and qualitative assessments, such as stakeholder trust or explainability
- Align metrics with evolving industry standards and mission-specific benchmarks.

Example: A transportation company regularly tests its AI routing engine for accuracy across geographies to avoid reinforcing inequities in service access.

Manage: Management involves applying controls, processes, and remediation strategies to reduce identified risks and enhance AI system resilience over time.

Activities include, but are not limited to:

- Implement mitigation controls such as adversarial defenses, human-in-the-loop safeguards, and data quality reviews
- Establish escalation paths for AI system failures or anomalous behavior
- Use findings from monitoring and stakeholder feedback to improve design and operations
- Ensure change management processes keep pace with evolving business needs and regulatory expectations.

Example: A media platform uses periodic retraining and model explainability testing to reduce bias in its content recommendation engine.

Practical Applications and Benefits

Organizations that adopt the AI RMF can expect several benefits, including improved alignment between technical teams and leadership, enhanced transparency for regulators and users, and more efficient adaptation to shifting regulatory landscapes.

Industry Examples:

- *Healthcare*: Ensuring AI diagnostic tools comply with HIPAA while maintaining clinical trust
- *Finance*: Minimizing algorithmic bias in credit scoring and loan underwriting systems
- *Defense*: Securing mission-critical systems against adversarial exploitation and cascading failure risks.

Strategic Value:

- Builds public trust by demonstrating accountability and ethical design
- Strengthens resilience by embedding AI risk management into enterprise risk portfolios
- Positions organizations for long-term compliance with global standards such as ISO/IEC 42001 and the EU AI Act (NIST, 2023b, 2024f).

Integration and Alignment

The AI RMF is not intended to operate in isolation. It complements other frameworks such as:

- NIST CSF for broader digital risk alignment
- NIST SP 800-53 Rev. 5 for integrating AI-specific controls into privacy and security programs
- Secure Software Development Framework (SSDF) to enhance secure-by-design principles in AI development (NIST, 2023j).

These crosswalks support enterprise-wide integration, enabling a more holistic and agile approach to managing risk and delivering value across digital systems.

Final Thoughts

The AI RMF is not a checklist by any stretch; it is a dynamic toolset that empowers organizations to balance opportunity and risk across the AI lifecycle. By embedding governance, contextual awareness, measurement, and iterative management into their AI strategies, organizations can ensure their systems are not only compliant, but also trusted, responsible, and sustainable. As future technologies emerge, frameworks like the AI RMF provide the foundation for long-term digital resilience and measurable assurance of trustworthy AI (NIST, 2023b).

Generative AI Profile (NIST AI 600-1)

Generative AI Overview

If the NIST AI Risk Management Framework (AI RMF 1.0) is the "what" of compliance and governance requirements for AI, the Generative AI Profile (AI 600-1) is the "how" (NIST, 2023b). Released in July 2024, this Profile extends the AI RMF by providing targeted, practical guidance for one of the fastest growing and riskiest areas of AI: generative models (NIST, 2024g). These include Large Language Models (LLMs), diffusion models, and other systems capable of creating text, images, code, and synthetic media.

The transformative potential of generative AI is immense, automating workflows, accelerating creativity, and enhancing decision-making across industries. Yet, this potential is matched by distinctive risks. Outputs may be biased, inaccurate, or manipulated in ways that undermine trust (NIST, 2024g). Systems may leak sensitive data, generate offensive or misleading content, or are repurposed for harmful applications. The Generative AI Profile addresses these challenges by providing over 200 recommended actions organized across twelve key risk categories (NIST, 2024g).

In essence, the Generative AI Profile acts as a "playbook" or Standard Operating Procedure for organizations seeking to deploy generative AI systems responsibly. Where the AI RMF establishes high-level principles, the Profile delivers actionable guidance that organizations can adapt to their missions, maturity levels, and regulatory environments (NIST, 2023b, 2024g).

Expanded Focus Areas

Generative AI doesn't just inherit risks from traditional AI, it significantly magnifies them. Since these systems create new content, decisions, or code that can resemble human output, they bring enormous potential for innovation while also opening the door to new vulnerabilities (NIST, 2024g).

The Generative AI Profile identifies where these risks are most pronounced and organizes them into practical focus areas. These domains highlight the ways generative AI can fail, be exploited, or undermine trust if unmanaged, while also giving organizations a roadmap to embed safeguards that build resilience and confidence (NIST, 2024g).

The Generative AI Profile consists of several domains where risks may be amplified in generative systems:

- *Security & Privacy*: Preventing attacks such as prompt injection, data leakage, and malicious manipulation of models (NIST, 2024g).
- *Bias & Fairness*: Identifying and mitigating harmful stereotypes or biases embedded in training data (NIST, 2024g).
- *Robustness & Resilience*: Ensuring AI systems continue to perform reliably under stress, including adversarial or unexpected inputs (NIST, 2024g).
- *Explainability*: Enabling outputs that can be understood, audited, and justified, which is critical in high-stakes domains like healthcare or finance (NIST, 2024g).
- *Operational Sustainability*: Recognizing the resource intensity of training and deploying models, including environmental and financial costs (NIST, 2024g).
- *Actionable Guidance*: Offering over 200 concrete recommendations across the twelve structured risk categories (NIST, 2024g).

These focus areas reflect a broader philosophy: true value from AI comes not just from innovation, but from embedding safeguards that protect integrity, accountability, and resilience.

There actually is a NIST AI RMF Playbook available on the NIST website for download: https://airc.nist.gov/airmf-resources/playbook/

NIST AI RMF Playbook

The Generative AI Profile is not a stand-alone framework, but a companion overlay to the AI RMF. The two are designed to work in tandem. While the AI RMF identifies outcomes and functions, such as Governance, Mapping, Measuring, and Managing, the AI Profile and its supporting AI

RMF Playbook provide practical suggestions on how to achieve those outcomes (NIST, 2023).

This approach is descriptive rather than prescriptive. The Playbook does not impose a rigid checklist; instead, it provides a menu of adaptable practices that organizations can tailor to their context. Whether a team chooses to adopt a few recommended actions or implement the full suite, the guidance is flexible enough to scale across industries and organizational sizes.

This distinction is critical. Prescriptive compliance often drives organizations to meet the minimum requirements. The Generative AI Profile, by contrast, "enables" assurance of a higher level of confidence that systems are trustworthy, resilient, and aligned to mission outcomes (NIST, 2023b, 2024g).

The Twelve Risk Categories

The Generative AI Profile moves from broad principles to specific, real-world risks. NIST identifies twelve categories where generative systems are most likely to create harm if left unmanaged, ranging from security flaws and data leakage to bias, misinformation, and resource intensity (NIST, 2023b, 2024g).

These categories cut across technical, ethical, and operational domains, helping organizations translate abstract risks into concrete challenges they can govern, measure, and mitigate. Each category is aligned with the four functions of the AI RMF: Govern, Map, Measure, and Manage (as mentioned above) ensuring risks are not just identified, but systematically addressed across the AI lifecycle (NIST, 2024g). These defined risk categories include:

1. **Hallucination:** Generative models can produce outputs that sound convincing but are factually wrong, creating risks when relied on for decisions in healthcare, finance, or legal communication.
2. **Prompt Manipulation:** Attackers can craft inputs that exploit weaknesses in the model, bypassing filters or tricking the system into revealing sensitive or harmful information.
3. **Sensitive Data Leakage:** Models may inadvertently expose proprietary or regulated data used in training, creating privacy, compliance, and reputational risks.
4. **Misinformation/Disinformation:** Generative AI can be weaponized to amplify misleading narratives, deepfakes, or propaganda, threatening trust in media, elections, and public institutions.

5. **Intellectual Property Violations:** Outputs may replicate copyrighted text, images, or code, raising legal and ethical challenges around ownership and originality.
6. **Bias and Fairness:** Generative models can reinforce stereotypes or biases embedded in their training data, resulting in discriminatory or unfair outcomes.
7. **Security Vulnerabilities:** Flaws in model design or deployment may allow adversaries to compromise systems or use them to generate malicious content like phishing emails.
8. **Synthetic Identity Fraud:** AI can generate realistic false personas that are used to commit fraud, manipulate systems, or deceive individuals online.
9. **Opacity/Lack of Traceability:** Generative systems often operate as "black boxes," making it difficult to explain or audit why certain outputs were produced, which limits accountability.
10. **Dual-Use Misuse:** Models designed for beneficial purposes may be repurposed for harmful applications, such as creating biological simulations or cyberattack tools.
11. **Content Moderation Failures:** Despite safeguards, models can produce offensive, unsafe, or toxic outputs that damage organizational reputation or harm users.
12. **Resource Intensity:** Training and deploying large generative systems can consume vast amounts of energy and financial resources, raising sustainability and cost concerns.

Each category maps back to the AI RMF's four functions, ensuring that risks are identified (Map), assessed (Measure), governed (Govern), and mitigated (Manage).

Practical Applications Across Sectors

The Generative AI Profile is designed to be modular and adaptable, allowing organizations in government, industry, and civil society to apply its safeguards to their specific missions. By grounding risk management in practical examples, the Profile ensures that guidance is not abstract but tied to the challenges organizations face in real operations (NIST, 2024g).

Government Services: Government agencies must balance public trust with operational resilience. Generative AI used in citizen-facing systems, such as multilingual service portals or AI-supported regulatory drafting, must deliver reliable outcomes in secure environments while also being resilient against adversarial misuse or manipulation. The Profile provides the structure to ensure transparency, equity, and assurance, so that services remain both trusted and resilient under scrutiny or threat.

Healthcare: In healthcare, the risks of generative AI are amplified: diagnostic tools, clinical documentation, or patient communications must function reliably and with clear, defensible reasoning, even when faced with incomplete, adversarial, or unexpected inputs. The Profile supports governance and assurance by embedding safeguards that protect patient safety and privacy while reinforcing resilience in contested digital environments, such as ransomware-driven disruption or adversarial tampering.

Finance: Financial institutions depend on trustworthy outputs in areas like fraud detection, credit scoring, and investment analysis. The Profile helps organizations implement controls that minimize hallucinations, mitigate embedded bias, and strengthen oversight of model-driven decisions. This approach aligns with regulatory expectations while reducing reputational and material risk.

Defense and National Security: Mission-critical AI must be designed for assurance; that is resilient in contested environments where adversarial manipulation is expected, and trustworthy in secure environments where continuity and confidence are essential. The Profile offers a structured path to reinforce both resilience and reliability, reducing risks of dual-use misuse and hostile exploitation.

Education and Media: Schools, universities, and publishers must manage risks tied to content authenticity, plagiarism, and reputational harm. The Profile provides practical safeguards to ensure AI-generated material can be attributed, explained, and aligned with institutional values. This protects both academic integrity and public trust.

By adopting the Profile, organizations create a shared risk vocabulary that bridges technical staff, policymakers, and mission owners. This common language enables collaboration across functions and strengthens both innovation and trust.

Strategic Benefits

The adoption of the Generative AI Profile (NIST AI 600-1) is about reducing risk and creating enduring advantages for organizations that depend on AI to deliver value. By embedding safeguards into workflows, the Profile shifts the focus from reactive compliance to proactive assurance. This approach allows organizations to demonstrate resilience, transparency, and accountability while continuing to innovate. In practice, the Profile equips leaders to balance opportunity and risk in a way that builds confidence with stakeholders, regulators, and the public (NIST, 2024g).

Builds Resilience: The Profile enables organizations to anticipate emergent threats such as prompt manipulation, model drift, or adversarial use. By embedding layered safeguards and continuous monitoring, organizations can maintain operational continuity and recover quickly when disruptions occur.

Fosters Trust: Transparent practices—such as explainability, bias testing, and content traceability—allow organizations to demonstrate fairness and accountability. This builds confidence with customers, partners, and regulators, which is essential in high-stakes domains like healthcare and finance.

Enhances Compliance Readiness: By aligning practices with evolving global standards such as ISO/IEC 42001 and the EU AI Act (ISO/IEC, 2023; European Union, 2023), the Profile prepares organizations for regulatory scrutiny while preserving flexibility. This proactive stance reduces the risk of penalties or reputational harm and positions organizations as leaders in responsible AI.

Institutionalizes Continuous Improvement: Generative AI systems evolve rapidly, and risks can change just as quickly. The Profile encourages feedback loops, scenario testing, and cross-functional governance to ensure systems remain aligned with mission outcomes, even as technology and operating environments shift.

Taken together, these benefits represent a shift away from compliance-driven minimums toward assurance-driven governance. Compliance may prove that an organization meets the baseline, but assurance builds confidence that AI systems are resilient, trustworthy, and aligned with mission outcomes (ISO/IEC, 2023; European Union, 2023).

Conclusion and Transition

The Generative AI Profile (NIST AI 600-1) serves as a practical playbook that translates broad principles of responsible AI into safeguards that can be embedded across missions, industries, and government functions. By addressing risks such as bias, security vulnerabilities, and opacity with concrete, actionable steps, the Profile empowers organizations to mitigate harm and to build trust and resilience into the very fabric of their AI systems (NIST, 2024g).

This shift from abstract principles to structured, measurable actions represent an important inflection point. Generative AI is no longer experimental; it is fully operational, and its governance must be equally operational. By adopting the Profile, organizations can move from reactive compliance toward proactive assurance, aligning innovation with accountability.

Plan for Global Engagement on AI Standards (NIST AI 100-5).

Setting the Table: The Four Layers of AI Control Frameworks

To understand how NIST and its partners are building a global system of trustworthy AI, it helps to view their collective work as a four-layer framework (NIST, 2024b). Each layer builds upon the previous one, translating high-level principles into practical, secure, and verifiable implementation. Together, they form a cohesive structure moving from strategy to execution, and ultimately to assurance at scale.

This layered model serves as the connective thread for the remainder of the chapter.

From Global Strategy to Institutional Assurance, these interconnected layers form a continuous system of assurance, where governance intent, technical practice, and institutional oversight operate in harmony to sustain trustworthy AI (NIST, 2024b).

- Section 16.4 covers the *Global Strategy* in defining and developing standards for AI.

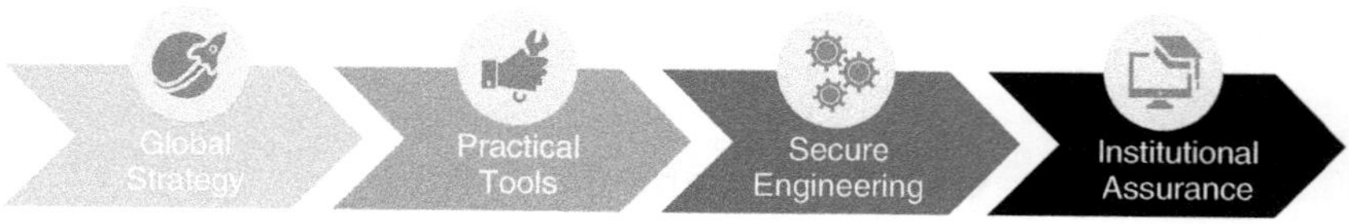

Image 16.1 The Four Layers of AI Control Frameworks

- Section 16.5 explores the *Practical Tools* that help organizations operationalize AI trustworthiness.
- Section 16.6 focuses on *Secure Engineering*, embedding those practices within technical development.
- Section 16.7 culminates in *Institutional Assurance*, where collaboration and policy ensure trust at scale.

Together, these layers reflect a holistic approach consistent with best practices and the approach or creating, protecting, and delivering digital business value, where digital value is governed, secured, and continuously assured (NIST, 2024b).

Global Strategy

The United States is taking a leading role in establishing global standards for AI (NIST, 2024b). Driven by the October 2023 Executive Order on Safe, Secure, and Trustworthy AI (EO 14110) (White House, 2023) and directed by the US Department of Commerce (DOC), the NIST has been tasked with setting the foundation for US engagement in international AI governance.

The publication of NIST AI 100-5: *A Plan for Global Engagement on AI Standards* outlines a roadmap to ensure that AI technologies are safe, secure, trustworthy, and interoperable worldwide. Technical standards are the bridge between high-level AI principles, such as the Organization for Economic Co-operation and Development (OECD) AI Principles (OECD, 2019) and the G7 Hiroshima Process on AI Governance (G7, 2023), and the practical implementation and security controls that governments and industries need to operate responsibly.

At its core, NIST's Publication *AI 100-5* seeks to drive outcomes in a scientifically sound, inclusive, and consensus-driven way (NIST, 2024b). These outcomes include, but are not limited to:

- *Scientifically Sound Standards* grounded in research, clear, implementable, and globally accessible
- *Diverse & Inclusive Participation* incorporating input from governments, industry, academia, and civil society worldwide, including low- and middle-income nations

- *Consensus-Driven Processes* developed through open, transparent, voluntary, and market-driven collaboration
- *Stronger International Relationships* building trust and co-operation across borders through shared standards.

Tiered Priorities for Standards Development

NIST AI 100-5 takes a tiered approach to identify which standards require immediate attention, which need more research, and which remain long-term challenges (NIST, 2024b). This prioritization ensures that the most urgent issues are addressed quickly, while building momentum toward broader global adoption.

Tier 1: Urgent and Ready for Action

These are the areas where standards can be developed now and have the greatest immediate impact (NIST, 2024b; OECD, 2019):

- **Terminology and Taxonomy**: Establishing a shared global language for AI
- **Testing and Evaluation (TEVV)**: Defining methods to measure reliability, safety, and trustworthiness
- **Provenance of Digital Content**: Standards to authenticate synthetic media and counter misinformation
- **Risk-Based Management**: Leveraging frameworks like ISO/IEC 23894 and the NIST AI RMF 1.0 to align risk management practices (NIST, 2023b; ISO/IEC, 2023)
- **Security and Privacy**: Safeguarding systems against data leakage, adversarial attacks, and misuse
- **Transparency Among AI Actors**: Setting expectations for openness across developers, deployers, and regulators
- **Training Data Practices**: Ensuring datasets are properly documented, representative, and traceable
- **Incident Response and Recovery**: Creating playbooks for handling AI-related failures or malicious exploitation.

Why it matters: These standards address the front line of AI risks, such as misinformation, safety, privacy, and systemic trust. They are also the most achievable in the near term, thanks to ongoing international momentum.

Tier 2: Areas Needing More Work

These priorities are essential but require more research and coordination (NIST, 2024b):

- **Energy and Resource Measurement**: Standards to measure the environmental and financial costs of AI training and deployment.
- **Conformity Assessment**: Establishing processes for certifying and auditing AI systems against standards.
- **Evaluation Datasets**: Developing benchmark datasets that can be used consistently across industries and geographies.

Why it matters: These areas are critical for sustainability and accountability but remain technically challenging and politically complex.

Tier 3: Foundational Work Still Needed

These areas represent future-facing challenges where foundational science is still maturing:

- **Interpretability and Explainability**: Building methods for understanding how AI systems reach decisions.
- **Human–AI Teaming**: Defining effective collaboration and oversight between people and machines.
- **AI Hardware Performance Metrics**: Establishing measures for efficiency, capability, and resource consumption of AI hardware.

Why it matters: While less urgent, these issues are essential for long-term trust and resilience. Advancing them requires deeper R&D before consensus standards can emerge.

The Big Picture

By structuring global AI standards into three tiers, NIST has provided a clear roadmap for international collaboration. Tier 1 delivers *immediate* safeguards; Tier 2 builds the infrastructure for *sustainable* adoption; and Tier 3 points to the horizon of scientific and technical *challenges*.

Taken together, AI 100-5 represents not just US leadership in AI governance but a practical and inclusive strategy for shaping the future of AI worldwide as well (NIST, 2024b; OECD, 2019).

The next sections illustrate how NIST and its global partners have developed a multi-layered approach to AI assurance. These layers move from strategy to execution, from setting international standards, to developing practical tools, to embedding secure engineering, and finally institutionalizing safety and accountability through global collaboration. Together, they form a complete system of assurance that enables organizations to create, protect, and deliver digital value with confidence.

Trustworthy and Responsible AI Resource Center

The Trustworthy and Responsible AI Resource Center is NIST's implementation hub for translating the principles of trustworthy AI into practical, repeatable, and measurable actions. While frameworks such as the AI Risk Management Framework (AI RMF 1.0) (NIST, 2023b) and the Generative AI Profile (NIST AI 600-1) (NIST, 2024f) define the structure for responsible AI, the Resource Center functions as the operational toolkit that enables organizations to apply these concepts in practice. Its purpose is straightforward but ambitious: to make the responsible adoption of AI achievable, measurable, and sustainable across industries and borders (NIST, 2024k).

Core Purpose and Value

At its core, the Resource Center focuses on translation and accessibility. NIST recognizes that frameworks only create value when they can be implemented, adapted, and maintained by organizations of varying size, sector, and maturity. The Center provides this bridge through a curated, evolving collection of tools, crosswalks, and learning resources that integrate AI governance into daily operations.

Key Capabilities include:

- **Crosswalks to Global Standards** (ISO/IEC, 2019, 2023):
  Mappings between the AI RMF 1.0 and major international frameworks such as ISO/IEC 42001 (AI Management Systems), the OECD AI Principles, and regulatory frameworks like the GDPR and CCPA. These

crosswalks help organizations demonstrate interoperability and provide traceable evidence of compliance and assurance.

- **Sector-Specific Guidance** (NIST, 2024k):
  Tailored resources for high-impact industries such as healthcare, finance, and defense, where risk tolerance, regulatory expectations, and ethical considerations differ. This ensures that the principles of trustworthy AI are contextualized within each domain's operational and cultural environment.
- **Implementation Tools and Templates** (NIST, 2024k):
  Practical aids such as self-assessment checklists, governance models, and policy templates that allow organizations to operationalize the AI RMF without reinventing foundational processes.
- **AI RMF Roadmap** (NIST, 2023b, 2024k):
  A step-by-step adoption guide from scoping and stakeholder engagement through continuous monitoring and lifecycle management.
- **Training and Community Engagement** (NIST, 2024k):
  A platform for workshops, webinars, and collaborative events where industry, academia, and government partners co-develop and refine responsible AI best practices.

By combining these elements, the Resource Center enables both compliance and assurance while instilling confidence that AI systems are not only lawful but also resilient, transparent, and aligned with organizational and societal values.

Strategic Context and Policy Alignment

The Resource Center underpins the US strategy for safe, secure, and trustworthy AI established under Executive Order 14110 (2023). It operates in concert with NIST's AI Safety Institute and serves as the connective link between technical research, policy implementation, and global collaboration. Through participation in international bodies such as ISO/IEC JTC 1/SC 42 and the OECD, NIST ensures that the guidance emerging from the Resource Center reflects a harmonized, science-based approach to governance and interoperability (OECD, 2019).

This alignment positions the Resource Center as a domestic implementation portal and a strategic bridge between nations. It provides a mechanism for promoting shared trust frameworks and advancing the principles of responsible innovation across borders.

Governance and Assurance Integration

Beyond enabling compliance, the Resource Center strengthens the concept of governance through assurance. Its self-assessment tools, maturity models, and cross-framework mappings provide the foundation for a verifiable system of assurance, ensuring that digital value is created, protected, and delivered in a manner consistent with both organizational intent and public interest (DVMS Institute, 2024).

Organizations that adopt these tools evolve from simply checking compliance boxes to demonstrating evidence-based confidence in the performance, fairness, and reliability of their AI systems. This marks a fundamental cultural shift toward continuous validation and measurable trust, echoing the broader philosophy underpinning the create–protect–deliver approach.

Practical Application—Defense Sector Example

A defense contractor developing AI-enabled logistics and mission-planning systems can leverage the Resource Center to align with AI RMF 1.0 while ensuring compliance with CMMC, NIST SP 800-171, and SP 800-218A requirements (NIST, 2024i). Using crosswalks to ISO/IEC 42001 and the OECD AI Principles, the contractor can demonstrate interoperability vital to coalition operations.

The AI RMF Roadmap helps program managers structure assurance activities, from initial risk assessments to continuous model monitoring, while template resources support documentation, red-team testing, and incident response. Together, these tools build measurable assurance and sustained trust with DoD stakeholders.

Looking Ahead

As AI technologies evolve, NIST's Resource Center will continue to expand with sector-specific playbooks, implementation case studies, and integrations with future NIST guidance such as SP 800-218A (Secure Software

Development for AI Systems) and SP 800-161r1 (Cyber Supply Chain Risk Management). These extensions will connect high-level governance principles to detailed engineering practices ensuring that trustworthy AI remains verifiable, auditable, and adaptive over time (NIST, 2024i).

Secure Software Development Practices for AI Systems (SP 800-218A)

Published in July 2024, NIST SP 800-218A builds on the Secure Software Development Framework (SSDF v1.1) (NIST, 2022) by embedding AI-specific practices, tasks, and recommendations throughout the software lifecycle. Mandated by Executive Order 14110 (2023), it complements rather than replaces the baseline SSDF, guiding model producers, integrators, and acquirers in developing AI systems that are secure, resilient, and trustworthy (Booth et al., 2024; NIST, 2024h).

By incorporating SP 800-218A into our chapter, we bridge the gap between AI risk management frameworks and concrete engineering practices. This section shows how NIST integrates governance with assurance through engineering controls (NIST, 2023b).

Background and Relationship to SSDF and AI RMF

The SSDF v1.1 (SP 800-218) outlines foundational secure software practices: preparing the organization, protecting software, producing well-secured software, and responding to vulnerabilities (NIST, 2022). The SP 800-218A builds on these by layering AI-specific tasks and considerations, especially for generative models and dual-use applications (ITI, 2024).

Where the SSDF focuses on traditional software assurance, SP 800-218A extends those principles into the data-centric and probabilistic world of AI. It operationalizes AI RMF **Measure** and **Manage** functions by formalizing the engineering pathways that sustain trustworthy AI (Booth et al., 2024; NIST, 2023b).

In the AI RMF structure, SP 800-218A primarily supports the Measure and Manage functions. It offers controls for assessing and mitigating AI-specific threats and ensures continuous validation and adaptation over time. It also reinforces the Govern and Map functions, by formalizing development practices tied to governance policies and system scoping.

Core Focus Areas and Enhanced Practices

NIST SP 800-218A introduces targeted enhancements to the SSDF that directly address AI-specific risks (Booth et al., 2024). These extend traditional concepts, such as code integrity, vulnerability management, and configuration control, into data-driven learning systems (Pivot Point Security, n.d.; Black Duck Software, n.d.). The approach focuses on building security and assurance into every stage of the AI lifecycle, from training data acquisition to deployment and monitoring, enabling organizations to identify vulnerabilities and maintain transparency throughout system evolution (Booth et al., 2024; DVMS Institute, 2024).

Secure Development Lifecycle for AI Models

Building AI securely starts long before deployment; it starts with how models are conceived, trained, and integrated. The secure development lifecycle introduced in SP 800-218A embeds protection throughout every phase, from data sourcing to model release (Booth et al., 2024).

Key practices include, but are not limited to:

- **Integrate Security Early**: Embed threat assessments, access control, and documentation from initial model design (NIST, 2022; Booth et al., 2024).
- **Verify Training Data**: Ensure dataset origin and guard against manipulation or poisoning (NIST, 2022).
- **Version and Track Models**: Maintain model versioning, metadata, and transparency to support traceability and reproducibility (Booth et al., 2024; Pivot Point Security, n.d.).
- **Secure Pipeline Architecture**: Embedding security checks in pipelines, enforcing access controls, supply chain verification, and isolation between training environments (Booth et al., 2024; NIST, 2024e).

These practices ensure that risk is managed from the earliest stages of design, rather than treated as an afterthought. This lifecycle focuses on security and assurance. Each stage generates verifiable evidence (logs, versioning, audit trails) that demonstrates trustworthy AI engineering in action.

Threat Modeling and Secure Training

AI introduces threat vectors far beyond traditional software risks (Booth et al., 2024). SP 800-218A expands classic threat modeling to account for adversarial manipulation, data bias, and misuse of generative systems. It also incorporates emerging Adversarial Machine Learning (AML) techniques, recognizing that models themselves can become attack surfaces through manipulated inputs, data poisoning, or prompt injection.

Key practices include, but are not limited to:

- **Develop AI-Specific Threat Models**: Identify risks such as prompt injection, model inversion, data exfiltration, and adversarial perturbations designed to deceive or mislead models (Booth et al., 2024).
- **Apply Secure Training Protocols**: Use isolation techniques, AML-driven testing, and human oversight checkpoints to detect weaknesses before release (Booth et al., 2024; ITI, 2024).
- **Integrate Red-Team and Misuse Testing**: Evaluate systems for both intentional attacks and unintentional misuse scenarios, leveraging adversarial testing frameworks to validate robustness (Booth et al., 2024; Pivot Point Security, n.d.).

Through these steps, developers shift from theoretical risk consideration to actionable mitigation strategies, embedding assurance directly into the AI model lifecycle (Booth et al., 2024; NIST, 2023b).

Monitoring, Detection, and Resilience

Deploying AI resilience is built through continuous oversight. Security in AI does not end at deployment but evolves with the system. Continuous monitoring and resilience practices ensure the AI remains trustworthy over time (Booth et al., 2024; NIST, 2023b; DVMS Institute, 2024).

Key practices include, but are not limited to:

- **Detect Model Drift**: Track deviations in model performance or data context that may signal degradation.
- **Monitor for Adversarial Behavior**: Use runtime anomaly detection, explainability tools, and behavioral baselines.

- **Respond and Recover**: Implement rollback, retraining, and post-incident reviews to restore integrity and assurance.
- **Dashboards and Assurance Logs**: Real-time operational visibility to support audit, governance, and assurance reviews.

These controls institutionalize continuous AIOps where monitoring, validation, and retraining cycles are automated to sustain assurance over time (NIST, 2022, 2023b, 2024e; DVMS Institute, 2024; ISO/IEC, 2023).

Framework Alignment and Crosswalks

SP 800-218A doesn't exist in isolation; it's part of a growing ecosystem of NIST and international frameworks that reinforce trustworthy AI governance. Its alignment with the AI Risk Management Framework (NIST, 2023b), the SSDF, and global standards like ISO/IEC 42001 allows organizations to unify technical controls with strategic risk and assurance objectives, creating a consistent model for secure AI adoption.

SP 800-218A integrates smoothly into the broader AI control architecture:

- **AI RMF Integration**: Maps to the *Measure* and *Manage* functions of the NIST AI Risk Management Framework, linking engineering metrics to organizational risk governance.
- **SSDF Alignment**: Builds on the SSDF core practices: *Prepare, Protect, Produce, Respond,* so organizations can extend existing DevSecOps pipelines to AI without reinvention.
- **Supply Chain Risk Management (SP 800-161r1):** Reinforces cybersecurity supply chain integrity by embedding SP 800-218A practices within the broader **Cyber Supply Chain Risk Management (C-SCRM)** framework. This alignment helps organizations manage dependencies on third-party AI components, data providers, and cloud services across the full model lifecycle.
- **Crosswalks and Global Standards:** Mappings are emerging between SP 800-218A, SP 800-53 Rev. 5, ISO/IEC 42001 (AI Management Systems), and other international control sets. These crosswalks create a common language for embedding AI security into existing compliance ecosystems across defense, finance, and healthcare sectors.

Together, these integrations support the broader concept of a system of assurance, where technical controls and governance mechanisms operate in tandem to validate that digital value is created, protected, and delivered with confidence.

Sources: NIST SP 800-218A; NIST SP 800-161r1 Cyber Supply Chain Risk Management; NIST AI RMF 1.0; NIST Computer Security Resource Center (CSRC), 2024.

Use Cases and Application Scenarios

The strength of NIST SP 800-218A lies not only in its technical precision but in its ability to translate security principles into measurable assurance across diverse industries. By embedding its practices into daily operations, organizations move beyond compliance toward resilience, demonstrating accountability and trust in how AI-enabled systems are built, tested, and maintained. The following examples illustrate how SP 800-218A serves as both a governance and engineering bridge, linking strategy to execution across defense, finance, and transportation. Each use case reflects how secure development practices, when integrated early and continuously, create the conditions for trustworthy, auditable, and mission-ready AI. These real-world examples show how organizations translate SP 800-218A's guidance into measurable assurance (ITI, 2024; Pivot Point Security, n.d.).

Defense Contractor—Achieving Mission Assurance in Contested Environments

A Department of War (DoW) contractor developing an AI-enabled situational awareness system applies SP 800-218A to ensure operational reliability and mission assurance under hostile conditions. Using the framework's guidance, the contractor validates sensor fusion algorithms, integrates adversarial testing to detect spoofed or manipulated data inputs, and implements version-controlled model repositories to maintain traceability across the system lifecycle. Continuous model drift monitoring and rollback protocols enable rapid recovery from unexpected performance degradation or tampering attempts. Through these practices, the organization demonstrates compliance with defense cybersecurity standards while achieving measurable assurance, ensuring that AI-driven decision systems remain trustworthy, resilient, and ready for deployment in contested environments.

Financial Services Startup—Application Development

A Financial-Tech startup developing an AI-driven stock trading application applies SP 800-218A to embed security and trustworthiness from the outset; critical to earning investor confidence and passing due diligence reviews. The team incorporates secure data ingestion practices to verify the integrity of market feeds and user financial data, establishes model version control for auditability, and implements adversarial testing to identify potential manipulation of trading algorithms. Continuous drift monitoring ensures that market conditions do not erode model reliability, while explainability tools provide transparency to both regulators and investors. By aligning early with SP 800-218A and the AI RMF, the startup demonstrates not only regulatory readiness but a culture of assurance, turning cybersecurity and responsible AI engineering into a competitive advantage during funding rounds.

Automotive Manufacturer—Ensuring Passenger Safety and System Resilience

An automaker applies SP 800-218A throughout the development of its autonomous driving systems to ensure that safety-critical AI functions remain secure and reliable. The company conducts adversarial robustness testing against manipulated sensor inputs (e.g., modified traffic signs or spoofed GPS data), establishes continuous drift monitoring to maintain perception model accuracy, and incorporates rollback and recovery procedures for failed updates. By embedding these practices into its DevSecOps pipeline, the automaker demonstrates not only regulatory compliance and technical safety, but also operational assurance, building public trust in autonomous vehicle technology.

Each scenario illustrates how SP 800-218A turns governance goals into engineering practice and how organizations can generate audit-ready evidence of assurance.

Challenges, Trade-Offs, and Future Directions

Even the most comprehensive framework faces real-world limitations. Implementing SP 800-218A requires balancing speed with security, innovation with governance, and assurance with agility. Understanding these trade-offs prepares organizations to evolve their practices as AI threats mature, tools advance, and new assurance mechanisms emerge (ITI, 2024; Pivot Point Security, n.d.).

- **Balancing Security and Performance**: Hardening models (e.g., adversarial training) may incur computational or latency costs.
- **Legacy Integration**: Retrofitting pipelines with AI security require investment and change management.
- **Threat Evolution**: As AI threats evolve, the Profile must be updated, which is a good incentive for the Community Profile model.
- **Tooling Maturity**: As AI security tools mature from explainability analyzers to adversarial testing suites, integration into established DevSecOps pipelines will demand new automation standards and shared assurance metrics.

SP 800-218A is designed to evolve with feedback and real-world experience (public comment period and industry engagement were part of its development).

Closing and Framework Connection

In NIST's AI control architecture, SP 800-218A serves as the technical anchor, where policy intent becomes engineering practice. Its principles transform compliance into assurance, and assurance into trust. By embedding secure AI design, adversarial resilience, and continuous monitoring into every stage of the model lifecycle, SP 800-218A enables organizations to operationalize trustworthy AI with measurable evidence of assurance.

In the next section, we'll move from this technical layer of assurance, where frameworks like SP 800-218A define how to secure AI systems, to the governance layer, where global standards, safety institutes, and policy collaborations ensure those systems remain trustworthy, interoperable, and accountable at scale (Booth et al., 2024; NIST, 2023b; DVMS Institute, 2024).

AI Safety Institute (AISI-US) and International Collaboration

As we progress from the technical layer of assurance into the realm of governance, the AI Safety Institute (AISI-US) and its international counterparts emerge as the institutional backbone for building trust and accountability in AI. Where NIST SP 800-218A embeds secure engineering practices within organizations, AISI-US establishes the frameworks and partnerships that ensure those practices are recognized, validated, and harmonized across borders.

Mandate, Structure, and Strategic Purpose

The AISI-US was created to advance the scientific foundations of AI safety, develop standardized measurement methodologies, and coordinate research and evaluation across government, industry, and academia (NIST, 2024l). Operating under the NIST, the Institute leads the AI Safety Institute Consortium (AISIC), a collaborative body of more than 280 partners (NIST, 2024d). This consortium develops testing environments, benchmark datasets, and measurement protocols for assessing AI risks and safety performance.

Unlike a regulatory agency, AISI-US serves as a governance enabler, bridging policy and practice. It convenes experts, sets evidence-based safety benchmarks, and performs independent evaluations that help organizations demonstrate compliance and assurance. Established under the direction of Executive Order 14110, the Institute supports the US government's broader objective of ensuring that AI systems are safe, secure, and trustworthy (Executive Order 14110, 2023).

Integration with the AI Risk Management Framework

AISI-US is deeply aligned with the AI Risk Management Framework (AI RMF 1.0), particularly the Govern, Measure, and Manage functions (NIST, 2023b):

- **Govern**: AISI-US operationalizes governance by defining accountability models, assurance mechanisms, and certification criteria for safety validation.
- **Measure**: It develops reproducible safety metrics, evaluation protocols, and standardized testing practices that organizations can adopt to benchmark AI performance.

- **Manage**: Through continuous evaluation and feedback loops, it supports post-deployment monitoring and adaptive risk management for evolving AI systems.

Together, these activities close the assurance loop between policy intent and technical execution, creating the foundation for measurable, verifiable trust in AI.

Key International Partnerships and Initiatives

Because AI systems transcend national boundaries, AISI-US is building a network of international collaborations that amplify safety, consistency, and transparency (U.S. Department of Commerce & NIST, 2024):

- **UK–US Partnership**: The AISI-US and AISI-UK collaborate on model evaluation, red-team testing, and incident-response coordination, enabling cross-recognition of assurance results and reducing redundant testing (U.K. Department for Science, Innovation and Technology & U.S. Department of Commerce, 2024).
- **G7 Hiroshima AI Process**: This initiative, launched under the 2023 G7 Summit, promotes a Comprehensive Policy Framework and International Code of Conduct for advanced AI systems, harmonizing principles of governance, safety, and transparency among member nations (OECD & G7 Governments, 2024).
- **EU–US Trade & Technology Council (TTC)**: Through this forum, the US and EU are aligning technical standards and regulatory approaches, ensuring interoperability between NIST frameworks, ISO/IEC 42001, and the EU AI Act (European Commission & U.S. Department of Commerce, 2024).
- **International Network of AI Safety Institutes**: Launched in 2024 by the US Departments of Commerce and State, this network links research institutes worldwide to coordinate model testing, data transparency, and AI risk assessment (U.S. Departments of Commerce and State, 2024).

These partnerships transform AISI-US from a national research hub into a cornerstone of global AI assurance infrastructure.

Functional Roles and Systemic Impact

The AISI-US plays a central role in strengthening assurance across the AI ecosystem:

- **Benchmark & Testbed Provider**: Develops reference models, standardized test scenarios, and safety evaluation suites for both commercial and public-sector use.
- **Cross-Recognition Enabler**: Establishes evaluation standards recognized across allied nations, accelerating cross-border AI certification and reducing duplicative audits.
- **Standards Feedback Loop**: Translates empirical research and field data into updates for NIST's AI RMF, SP 800-218A, and international standards such as ISO/IEC 42001 (ISO/IEC, 2023).
- **Frontier Risk Assessment**: Focuses on high-risk, dual-use, or generative AI models, identifying misuse vectors, adversarial manipulation patterns, and systemic dependencies (DVMS Institute, 2024).

These activities ensure that AI safety remains measurable, comparable, and auditable across domains, laying the groundwork for a global system of assurance.

Use Case: Joint Safety Evaluation of a Frontier Model

A multinational AI developer submits a generative model for joint evaluation under the US–UK safety collaboration. AISI-US and AISI-UK jointly define test conditions covering prompt injection, data leakage, and model drift scenarios, and execute parallel assessments in secure environments. Results are cross-analyzed, discrepancies reconciled, and a joint assurance report issued to regulatory bodies. The mutual recognition of this report allows both governments to rely on shared evidence, reducing redundancy, and accelerating responsible AI deployment across markets.

Challenges, Risks, and Governance Trade-Offs

As AISI-US and its partners scale their influence, several challenges remain:

- **Sovereignty vs Harmonization**: National regulations and political priorities may hinder full alignment of international safety protocols.

- **Legitimacy and Independence**: Maintaining scientific integrity and neutrality is essential to preserve credibility.
- **Pace of Innovation**: AI evolves faster than institutional frameworks, requiring constant adaptation and agile governance.
- **Balancing Innovation and Precaution**: Overly restrictive safety criteria may stifle progress; insufficient oversight may expose systemic risks.

AISI-US navigates these tensions by anchoring its work in transparency, scientific evidence, and multi-stakeholder engagement.

The Emerging AI Risk Governance Ecosystem

As AI systems scale across sectors and borders, the global community is converging around a federated model of AI risk governance, one that blends technical standards, organizational practices, and policy coordination into a unified system of trust. No single framework stands alone; rather, a collection of interlocking efforts from NIST, ISO, OECD, and the AI Safety Institute (AISI-US) defines the current landscape of AI assurance (NIST, 2023b, 2024d, 2024i; Executive Order 14110, 2023).

At the technical level, NIST's suite of frameworks, including the AI Risk Management Framework (AI RMF 1.0) and SSDF (SP 800-218A), establishes the engineering foundation for secure and trustworthy AI (NIST, 2024i). In parallel, ISO/IEC 42001 and related international standards codify management system requirements that operationalize these principles globally (NIST, 2024d). These give organizations a structured way to demonstrate compliance and assurance across jurisdictions.

At the organizational and societal level, the OECD AI Principles anchor the ethical and transparency commitments underpinning responsible AI (Executive Order 14110, 2023), while the AI Safety Institute (AISI-US) leads collaborative research and alignment among national safety institutes (NIST, 2023b). These efforts form a networked ecosystem where safety, accountability, and interoperability are continuously reinforced through shared metrics, red-teaming methodologies, and cross-standard mappings.

Together, these initiatives represent a Risk Governance Ecosystem; a distributed architecture that connects policy to practice and strategy to assurance. It is through this ecosystem that the global community is beginning to achieve institutional assurance; the highest layer of the AI control framework where governance is written into policy and evidenced through secure engineering and measurable outcomes (NIST, 2023b, 2024d, 2024i; Executive Order 14110, 2023).

Closing and Transition

In many ways, AISI-US represents the evolution of NIST's role from developing frameworks to validating AI safety through global collaboration. It transforms national standards into international assurance mechanisms, ensuring that AI systems are technically secure and governed with accountability and shared trust.

In the next section, we will synthesize these frameworks into a comprehensive model for AI governance and cybersecurity, examining how technical controls and institutional collaboration together define the future of responsible AI.

Summary and Transition: The Integrated AI Control Ecosystem

The frameworks and institutions discussed throughout this chapter form a layered system of AI control, one that links global policy, practical engineering, and institutional assurance into a single ecosystem of trust. From NIST's technical foundations to international collaborations led by AISI-US, OECD, and ISO, this ecosystem provides both the structure and the adaptability needed to manage AI risk across sectors, supply chains, and jurisdictions.

Each layer serves a distinct yet interconnected role. Governance frameworks establish principles and policy coordination; assurance institutes advance safety testing, validation, and model evaluation; engineering frameworks such as SP 800-218A operationalize secure development; and implementation frameworks such as the AI RMF 1.0 translate these goals into ongoing risk management and accountability practices. Together, these layers create a continuous feedback loop where strategy, execution, and assurance reinforce one another.

This convergence reflects the growing maturity of the global AI ecosystem, a recognition that no single nation, standard, or organization can manage AI risk alone. Instead, interoperability across NIST, ISO, OECD,

Layer	Framework / Institution	Primary Objective	Example Implementation
Governance	NIST AI 100-5, OECD AI Principles	Global cooperation and harmonized AI governance	G7 Hiroshima AI Process
Assurance	AI Safety Institute (AISI-US)	Testing, evaluation, and certification of AI systems	Frontier model red-teaming, safety benchmarks
Engineering	NIST SP 800-218A	Secure software development practices	Adversarial testing, model versionmg, configuration control
Implementation	NIST AI RMF 1.0	Operational AI risk management	Continuous monitoring and governance lifecycle mapping

Table 16.1 Layers of the AI Risk Governance Ecosystem

and AISI ensures alignment of safety principles, technical standards, and policy outcomes. Initiatives such as the G7 Hiroshima AI Process, EU–US TTC, and UK–US AI Safety Partnership exemplify this alignment in action, advancing shared accountability, and trustworthy AI development at scale.

Transition: The Future of AI Cybersecurity

The frameworks described here provide the foundation for AI assurance but in the coming years, AI will also become central to cybersecurity itself. As organizations implement these control systems, the same technologies used to safeguard AI models will be leveraged to detect, defend, and anticipate threats in cyberspace. Chapter 17 explores this evolution from AI risk management to AI-enabled cyber defense, examining how intelligent automation, red-teaming, and predictive analytics are reshaping the future of cybersecurity.

Acronyms

Acronym	*Full Term / Definition*
AI	Artificial Intelligence
AI RMF	Artificial Intelligence Risk Management Framework
AISI-US	AI Safety Institute—United States
AISIC	AI Safety Institute Consortium
AML	Adversarial Machine Learning
C-SCRM	Cyber Supply Chain Risk Management
CCPA	California Consumer Privacy Act

(*Continued*)

Acronym	*Full Term / Definition*
CMMC	Cybersecurity Maturity Model Certification
CSF	Cybersecurity Framework
DOC	US Department of Commerce
DVMS	Digital Value Management System
EO 14110	Executive Order 14110—Safe, Secure, and Trustworthy Development and Use of AI
EU	European Union
GDPR	General Data Protection Regulation
G7 TTC	G7 Trade and Technology Council
IMDA	Infocomm Media Development Authority (Singapore)
ISO	International Organization for Standardization
IEC	International Electrotechnical Commission
LLM	Large Language Model
NIST	National Institute of Standards and Technology
NIST AI 100-5	*Plan for Global Engagement on AI Standards*
NIST AI 600-1	*Generative AI Profile*
NIST SP 800-218A	*Secure Software Development Practices for Generative AI and Dual-Use Foundation Models*
OECD	Organisation for Economic Co-operation and Development
SP 800-161r1	*Cyber Supply Chain Risk Management (Revision 1)*
SP 800-218	*Secure Software Development Framework (SSDF v1.1)*
TEVV	Testing, Evaluation, Verification, and Validation
UK	United Kingdom
US	United States
US DOC	US Department of Commerce

Bibliography

Black Duck Software. (n.d.). *Implementing NIST SSDF: Best Practices for Secure Software Development*. Retrieved October 2025, from https://www.blackduck.com/blog/nist-ssdf-secure-software-development.html

Booth, H., Souppaya, M., Vassilev, A., Ogata, M., Stanley, M., & Scarfone, K. (2024). *Secure Software Development Practices for Generative AI and Dual-Use Foundation Models (NIST SP 800-218A)*. National Institute of Standards and Technology. https://doi.org/10.6028/NIST.SP.800-218A

DVMS Institute. (2024). *Create–Protect–Deliver Model for Digital Value Management*. DVMS Institute Publication.

European Commission & U.S. Department of Commerce. (2024). *EU–U.S. Trade and Technology Council Joint Statement on AI Interoperability*.

European Union. (2023). *EU Artificial Intelligence Act*. https://artificialintelligenceact.eu/

European Union. (2024). *Regulation (EU) 2024/1689 of the European Parliament and of the Council on Artificial Intelligence (AI Act)*. Official Journal of the European Union. https://eur-lex.europa.eu

Executive Order No. 14110, 88 Fed. Reg. 75191 (Oct. 30, 2023). *Safe, Secure, and Trustworthy Development and Use of Artificial Intelligence*. Federal Register 88(75191).

G7. (2023). *Hiroshima AI Process on Governance*. Group of Seven Leaders Communiqué.

Infocomm Media Development Authority (IMDA). (2020). *Singapore Model AI Governance Framework (2nd Edition)*. Government of Singapore. https://www.imda.gov.sg

Information Technology Industry Council (ITI). (2024, May 31). *Feedback to NIST SP 800-218A Secure Software Development Practices for Generative AI and Dual-Use Foundation Models*. https://www.itic.org/documents/artificial-intelligence/2024-5-31_ITICommentsonSSDF-GenAIProfile_Final.pdf

International Organization for Standardization (ISO) & International Electrotechnical Commission (IEC). (2023). *ISO/IEC 23894: Artificial Intelligence – Risk Management*. International Organization for Standardization.

ISO/IEC (2023). *ISO/IEC 42001: Artificial Intelligence — Management System Standard*. ISO Publications. https://www.iso.org/standard/81230.html

National Institute of Standards and Technology (NIST). (2022). *Secure Software Development Framework (SSDF) Version 1.1: Recommendations for Mitigating the Risk of Software Vulnerabilities (NIST SP 800-218)*. https://doi.org/10.6028/NIST.SP.800-218

NIST. (2023a). *About NIST*. Retrieved from https://www.nist.gov/about-nist

NIST. (2023b). *Artificial Intelligence Risk Management Framework (AI RMF 1.0): Managing AI Risk for Trustworthy and Responsible AI*. National Institute of Standards and Technology. https://www.nist.gov/itl/ai-risk-management-framework

NIST. (2023c). *AI Safety Institute (AISI-US) Launch Announcement*. NIST / U.S. Department of Commerce.

NIST. (2023d). *NBS/NIST: Foundations for Progress*. Retrieved from https://www.nist.gov

NIST. (2023e). *Research Directions for Trustworthy AI Standards*. NIST Internal Report (NISTIR 8467).

NIST. (2024a). *About NIST: Mission and Role*. U.S. Department of Commerce. https://www.nist.gov

NIST. (2024b). *AI 100-5: Plan for Global Engagement on AI Standards*. National Institute of Standards and Technology. https://nvlpubs.nist.gov/nistpubs/ai/NIST.AI.100-5.pdf

NIST. (2024c). *A plan for global engagement on AI standards (NIST AI 100-5)*. U.S. Department of Commerce. https://doi.org/10.6028/NIST.AI.100-5e2025

NIST. (2024d). *Artificial Intelligence Safety Institute Consortium (AISIC)*. https://www.nist.gov/artificial-intelligence/artificial-intelligence-safety-institute-consortium-aisic

NIST. (2024e). *Cyber Supply Chain Risk Management (C-SCRM): NIST SP 800-161 Revision 1*. https://doi.org/10.6028/NIST.SP.800-161r1

NIST. (2024f). *Generative AI Profile (AI 600–1): A Profile of the AI RMF*. National Institute of Standards and Technology. https://doi.org/10.6028/NIST.AI.600-1

NIST. (2024g). *NIST AI 600–1: Generative AI Profile*. National Institute of Standards and Technology. https://nvlpubs.nist.gov/nistpubs/ai/NIST.AI.600-1.pdf

NIST. (2024h). *NIST Publishes SP 800-218A* [News release]. NIST Computer Security Resource Center. https://csrc.nist.gov/news/2024/nist-publishes-sp-800-218a

NIST. (2024i). *Secure Software Development Practices for Generative AI and Dual-Use Foundation Models (NIST SP 800-218A)*. https://doi.org/10.6028/NIST.SP.800-218A

NIST. (2024j). *SP 800-218A: Secure Software Development Practices for Generative AI*. National Institute of Standards and Technology. https://csrc.nist.gov

NIST. (2024k). *Trustworthy and Responsible AI Resource Center*. https://airc.nist.gov

NIST. (2024l). *U.S. AI Safety Institute (AISI-US)*. NIST AI Safety Initiative. https://www.nist.gov/caisi

Organisation for Economic Co-operation and Development (OECD). (2019). *OECD Principles on Artificial Intelligence*. OECD Legal Instruments. https://legalinstruments.oecd.org/en/instruments/OECD-LEGAL-0449

OECD. (2023). *State of Implementation of the OECD AI Principles*. OECD Publishing.

OECD & G7 Governments. (2024). *G7 Hiroshima AI Process: International Code of Conduct for Advanced AI Systems*.

Pivot Point Security. (n.d.). *NIST SP 800-218 (SSDF) Consulting Services*. Retrieved October 2025, from https://www.pivotpointsecurity.com/services/nist-sp-800-218-ssdf-consulting-services/

U.K. Department for Science, Innovation and Technology & U.S. Department of Commerce. (2024). *Joint AI Safety Testing Framework Statement*.

U.S. Department of Commerce. (2023). *Safe, Secure, and Trustworthy Development and Use of Artificial Intelligence: Executive Order 14110*. Federal Register Vol. 88, No. 210. https://www.federalregister.gov/documents/2023/10/30

U.S. Department of Commerce & NIST. (2024). *International Collaboration on AI Safety*. https://www.nist.gov/news-events

U.S. Departments of Commerce and State. (2024). *Launch of the International Network of AI Safety Institutes*.

White House. (2023). *Executive Order 14110 – Safe, Secure, and Trustworthy Development and Use of Artificial Intelligence*. Retrieved from https://www.whitehouse.gov

17

AI RISK ASSESSMENT FRAMEWORK

Introduction

Artificial Intelligence (AI) systems introduce a unique risk surface that blends cybersecurity, data governance, regulatory exposure, operational resilience, and ethical considerations. Unlike static software, AI models evolve, adapt, and behave probabilistically, making risk assessment a continuous lifecycle activity rather than a single event. This chapter outlines a comprehensive AI Risk Assessment Framework aligned with NIST AI RMF, ISO/IEC 42001, the EU AI Act, and global best practices.

Scope and Objectives

An AI risk assessment seeks to identify, quantify, prioritize, mitigate, and monitor risks across the AI lifecycle. Objectives include improving reliability, supporting compliance, and providing assurance that AI systems are safe, secure, and trustworthy.

DOI: 10.4324/9781003682530-21

Categories of AI Risk

- Data Risks
- Model Risks
- Cybersecurity and Adversarial Risks
- Operational and Reliability Risks
- Ethical and Societal Risks
- Compliance and Regulatory Risks

AI Risk Assessment Process

Executive Summary: AI Risk Assessment Process

The AI Risk Assessment Process provides a disciplined, end-to-end methodology for evaluating and governing AI systems across their entire lifecycle. It ensures that AI deployments are **safe, secure, fair, transparent, compliant,** and **aligned with enterprise risk appetite**. The process integrates technical testing, governance reviews, regulatory requirements, and operational safeguards. It is structured into six core stages:

1. **AI Inventory**

The assessment begins with a full understanding of the AI system's purpose, architecture, data flows, regulatory classification, and inventory completeness. This includes validating system diagrams, verifying data lineage, confirming model metadata, and applying the EU AI Act decision tree to determine risk category.

Outcome: A complete, accurate AI inventory, with defensible description of the AI system, supported by evidence such as architecture diagrams, lineage logs, and classification records.

2. **Risk Identification**

Next, risks are identified across data quality, bias, adversarial threats, privacy exposure, operational failure modes, and potential harm to individuals or processes. Activities include bias analysis, sensitivity scanning for PII/PHI, MITRE ATLAS threat modeling, privacy impact reviews, and safety scenario evaluation.

Outcome: A comprehensive risk profile and documented harm scenarios with no unidentified or unexamined risk categories.

3. **Risk Quantification**

Identified risks are then quantified by evaluating likelihood, impact, and potential residual exposure. Quantification includes statistical reliability testing, uncertainty analysis, hallucination benchmarking, financial exposure modeling, and scenario simulations.

Outcome: Evidence-based, traceable risk scores that can be used for executive governance, risk committees, regulatory documentation, and insurer evaluations.

4. **Control Mapping and Mitigation**

Controls are mapped to each identified risk and tested for effectiveness. This includes evaluating bias mitigation techniques, explainability tools (e.g., SHAP/LIME), adversarial robustness, privacy safeguards, and human-in-the-loop oversight checkpoints. Results are documented to demonstrate risk reduction.

Outcome: Improved robustness, fairness, transparency, and privacy protection, validated through before/after comparisons and aligned with recognized frameworks (NIST AI RMF, ISO 42001, EU AI Act).

5. **Residual Risk Evaluation**

After mitigation, remaining risks are assessed against enterprise risk appetite, regulatory expectations, and governance thresholds. This includes compliance verification, benchmarking against internal standards, and alignment with board-approved tolerance levels.

Outcome: A clear and defensible deployment decision—approve, approve with conditions, or require additional mitigation—with documented justification.

6. **Continuous Monitoring**

Finally, the system is placed under continuous monitoring for model drift, performance degradation, security threats, fairness impacts, hallucination changes, and audit logging integrity. Monitoring pipelines ensure that risks remain controlled as the model, data, and operating context evolve.

Outcome: Ongoing operational assurance and readiness for audits, regulatory inquiries, and incident response.

Integrated Value of the Process

Together, these six stages form a **holistic, auditable,** and **regulator-aligned AI risk lifecycle**. They allow organizations to:

- Ensure transparency, traceability, and defensibility of AI system components
- Reduce the likelihood of operational failures, harms, or regulatory violations
- Strengthening cybersecurity and privacy safeguards
- Demonstrate compliance with global standards and laws
- Provide assurance to executives, auditors, boards, and insurers
- Maintain trust across customers, stakeholders, and regulators.

This structured process transforms AI governance from ad hoc reviews into a reproducible, evidence-driven discipline embedded in enterprise risk management.

Details of Each Category and Testing Activities

1. **AI Inventory**

   Goal: Validate the AI system's purpose, inputs, components, architecture, integrations, and regulatory classification.

Testing Activities

- Inventory
  - Confirm system component, data flows, and classifications.
- **Architecture Validation Test**
  - Confirm system diagrams match deployed environment.
  - Verify API interactions, dependencies, and third-party components.

- **Data Lineage Verification**
  - Check provenance of training data.
  - Validate documentation of data transformations.
- **Regulatory Classification Test**
  - Apply EU AI Act decision tree.
  - Validate risk category (Minimal, Limited, High, Prohibited).
- **Model Inventory Completeness Test**
  - Ensure model is listed in enterprise AI inventory.
  - Validate metadata completeness.

Evidence Collected

- System inventory
- System diagrams
- Data lineage logs
- Model registry entries
- EU AI Act classification sheet.

Acceptance Criteria

- All documentation complete
- Accurate and verifiable architecture
- Risk classification defensible.

2. **Risk Identification**

   Goal: Identify all risks across data, model, security, ethics, privacy, and operations.

Testing Activities

- Bias Identification Test
  - Run statistical disparity analysis across protected groups.
- Data Sensitivity Screening
  - Detect PII/PHI/PCI using automated scanners.
- Threat Modeling (MITRE ATLAS)
  - Identify adversarial techniques relevant to the model.
- Privacy Impact Analysis
  - Validate compliance with GDPR/CCPA.

- Use Case Safety Review
  - Validate no potential for undue harm (e.g., medical misclassification).

Evidence Collected

- Bias detection reports
- Security threats matrix
- Data classification results
- PIA/DSA reports.

Acceptance Criteria

- All material risks identified
- No "unknown risks" categories left blank
- Potential harm scenarios documented.

3. **Risk Quantification**
   Goal: Quantify risk likelihood, impact, and residual exposure.

Testing Activities

- **Likelihood Scoring Test**
  - Validate scoring methodology (Low–Critical).
  - Verify evidence for likelihood ratings.
- **Impact Modeling Test**
  - Run financial risk quantification scenarios.
  - Stress test safety impacts.
- **Statistical Reliability Testing**
  - Conduct confidence interval analysis.
  - Quantify uncertainty.
- **Hallucination Rate Testing**
  - Benchmark hallucination frequency and severity.

Evidence Collected

- Risk scores
- Exposure models

- Statistical reliability results
- Scenario analysis logs.

Acceptance Criteria

- Likelihood and impact are justified.
- Quantitative values are traceable to evidence.
- Residual risk shows downward trend after mitigation.

4. **Control Mapping and Mitigation**

   Goal: Validate effectiveness of proposed controls and map them to frameworks.

Testing Activities

- Bias Mitigation Effectiveness Test
  - Re-test bias after mitigation and compare reduction percentage.
- Explainability Test
  - Validate SHAP/LIME results generate stable explanations.
- Adversarial Robustness Testing
  - Run adversarial test cases (perturbation, prompt injection).
- Privacy Control Validation
  - Test differential privacy or anonymization effectiveness.
- Human Oversight Simulation
  - Validate approval workflows and human-in-the-loop checkpoints.

Evidence Collected

- Before/after mitigation reports
- Explainability visualizations
- Adversarial attack logs
- Privacy test results
- Oversight simulation logs.

Acceptance Criteria

- Controls lower risk scores
- Adversarial robustness improved
- Model explainability meets policy thresholds.

5. **Residual Risk Evaluation**
   Goal: Validate remaining risks are acceptable and within enterprise risk appetite.

Testing Activities

- **Residual Risk Impact Test**
  - Recompute risk after mitigation.
- **Comparative Risk Benchmarking**
  - Compare system to enterprise AI risk benchmarks.
- **Legal and Regulatory Alignment Test**
  - Ensure compliance with mandatory obligations.
- **Board Risk Appetite Alignment Test**
  - Validate risk scores align with documented appetite.

Evidence Collected

- Residual risk matrix
- Benchmarking tables
- Compliance validation results.

Acceptance Criteria

- Residual risk must fall within thresholds
- Any remaining high-risk items require exception approval.

6. **Continuous Monitoring**
   Goal: Verify monitoring plan is complete, effective, and configured.

Testing Activities

- **Drift Detection Test**
  - Simulate data distribution drift.
- **Model Performance Stability Test**
  - Evaluate stability over time and across updates.
- **Security Monitoring Test**
  - Validate alerts for model extraction, poisoning, or prompt attacks.
- **Fairness Monitoring Simulation**
  - Stress test disproportionate outcomes over time.

- **Audit Logging Test**
  - Validate audit logs are complete and immutable.

Evidence Collected

- Drift detection logs
- Performance monitoring dashboards
- Security alert test logs
- Fairness monitoring snapshots
- Audit trail samples.

Acceptance Criteria

- Alerts are triggered correctly
- Monitoring pipelines capture anomalies
- Audit logs trusted and exportable.

Required Documentation

Artifacts include AI inventory, model cards, data sheets, bias testing reports, security testing, explainability results, governance approvals, audit logs, and regulatory classifications.

Comprehensive documentation is essential for demonstrating transparency, traceability, compliance, and governance readiness throughout the AI lifecycle. The following artifacts must be created, maintained, and updated as part of the AI Risk Assessment Process. These documents serve as evidence for audits, regulatory inquiries, internal governance reviews, and insurance underwriting.

Core Technical and Model Documentation

- **AI Inventory**

  System components used in the model, including data sources, AI tools, servers, and virtual machines.
- **Model Cards**

  Describe the AI system's intended purpose, architecture, training methodology, performance metrics, and known limitations.

  Include: input/output definitions, dataset summary, KPIs, reliability constraints.

- **Data Sheets / Data Documentation Records**
  Detail training, validation, and production data sources, collection methods, transformations, data quality checks, consent basis, retention, and lineage.
  Must include adherence to privacy regulations (GDPR/CCPA) and data minimization principles.
- **Bias and Fairness Testing Reports**
  Summaries of statistical disparity analyses, fairness testing results, mitigations applied, and longitudinal bias monitoring outputs.
  Should incorporate protected classes defined by law or ethics policy.
- **Model Explainability and Transparency Reports**
  Outputs from SHAP, LIME, feature attribution, rule-based explanations, and model interpretability tools.
  Document stability tests and explanations provided to end users.

Security and Adversarial Documentation

- **Security Testing Artifacts**
  Penetration testing, adversarial robustness results (MITRE ATLAS-aligned), red-team evaluations, prompt injection tests, model extraction assessments, and infrastructure security controls.
- **Threat Models**
  Documented adversarial scenarios, assets at risk, threat actor profiles, and model attack surfaces.
  Include MITRE ATLAS mappings where relevant.
- **Incident Response Playbooks (AI-Specific)**
  Define detection, response, containment, and recovery procedures for AI-related events such as drift, data poisoning, or misuse.

Compliance, Legal, and Regulatory Documentation

- **Regulatory Classification Records**
  Evidence of EU AI Act risk classification (Minimal, Limited, High, Prohibited), conformity assessment steps, harmonized standards, and technical documentation requirements.
- **Privacy Impact Assessments (PIA) / Data Protection Impact Assessments (DPIA)**

Evaluation of privacy risk, lawful basis for processing, data retention, anonymization/pseudonymization methods, and cross-border transfer safeguards.

- **Governance Approvals and Review Logs**
  Ethics committee reviews, AI oversight board approvals, risk acceptance logs, and exception handling documentation.

Operational and Monitoring Documentation

- **Continuous Monitoring Dashboards and Reports**
  Drift detection logs, performance degradation alerts, fairness monitoring snapshots, and anomaly detection outputs.
- **Audit Logs (Immutable)**
  Record model inputs/outputs, training data access, model versioning, change history, monitoring events, and human review actions.
  Must meet standards for integrity and retention.
- **Change Management Documentation**
  Includes risk assessments for updates, retraining events, hyperparameter changes, dependency modifications, and deployment approvals.

Enterprise Integration and Assurance Documentation

- **Enterprise Risk Assessments and Quantification Outputs**
  Likelihood/impact scoring, financial exposure modeling, scenario analysis, and residual risk summaries.
- **Vendor or Third-Party AI Assurance Documentation**
  For external or API-based AI systems, include vendor attestations, shared responsibility models, SLAs, and compliance certificates.
- **Insurance Underwriting Evidence Package (Optional)**
  Documentation prepared for cyber/AI risk insurers: exposure quantification, model safety controls, adversarial robustness results, governance structure, and monitoring evidence.

Integration with Enterprise Governance

AI risk assessment must integrate with cybersecurity, privacy, compliance, operational resilience, and enterprise risk management for holistic governance.

AI risk assessment cannot exist as a standalone function—it must be integrated into the organization's broader governance, risk, and compliance ecosystem. Effective AI governance requires alignment across cybersecurity, privacy, legal, compliance, operational resilience, enterprise risk management (ERM), and business leadership. This ensures that AI systems are safe, secure, ethical, and compliant throughout their lifecycle and that risks are continuously monitored and acted upon.

Below is a comprehensive expansion across all enterprise governance dimensions:

Cybersecurity Governance Integration

AI systems introduce new security challenges: adversarial attacks, model inversion, data poisoning, model theft, and prompt manipulation. These must be tightly integrated into the enterprise cybersecurity framework.

Required Cybersecurity Integrations

- **Secure ML pipelines** aligned to zero-trust principles
- **Model supply chain security**, including validation of datasets, training code, and model packages
- **Adversarial threat modeling** using MITRE ATLAS
- **Continuous vulnerability and patch management** for AI infrastructure
- **Monitoring for AI-specific attacks** (prompt injection, jailbreaks, inference attacks)
- **Integration with SIEM/SOAR** for AI incident detection and automated response.

Outcomes

- AI becomes part of enterprise threat intelligence
- The CISO gains visibility into AI-specific risk vectors
- AI systems follow the same security rigor as critical applications.

Privacy Governance Integration

AI systems often rely on sensitive personal data, making privacy risks more acute. AI governance must tightly align with enterprise privacy programs.

Key Privacy Integrations

- **Data minimization** and strict purpose limitation
- **Privacy Impact Assessments (PIA/DPIA)** for AI deployments
- **Consent, legal basis, retention, and deletion policies** mapped to training data
- **Automated detection of PII** within model inputs and datasets
- **Assessment of re-identification risk** for model outputs
- **Cross-border transfer assessments** for training and inference data.

Outcomes

- Compliance with GDPR, CCPA, HIPAA, GLBA, and sector privacy rules
- Reduced risk of privacy claims related to biased or unsafe outputs
- Evidence for regulators and auditors demonstrating responsible data use.

Compliance and Legal Governance Integration

AI introduces significant regulatory obligations. Governance must integrate with legal, compliance, and regulatory affairs to track evolving laws.

Required Compliance Integrations

- **EU AI Act alignment**: Risk classification, conformity assessment, documentation
- **ISO/IEC 42001 AI Management System**
- **NIST AI RMF governance controls**
- **Industry-specific obligations** (e.g., FCA/FINRA in finance, HIPAA in healthcare)
- **Automated regulatory mapping** for new AI laws
- **Legal review of AI system transparency, rights, and consumer disclosures.**

Outcomes

- Reduced exposure to sanctions and regulatory failures
- Clear defensibility during audits, legal reviews, and investigations
- Proactive compliance posture for AI deployments.

Operational Resilience Integration

AI systems can amplify operational failures (e.g., outages, misclassifications, automation failures). AI governance must fold into resilience frameworks.

Key Resilience Integrations

- AI business continuity planning (BCP)
- AI disaster recovery scenarios, including corrupted training data or model drift
- Fallback controls and human-in-the-loop procedures
- Stress testing AI systems during peak load or anomalous conditions
- Fail-safe modes that prevent unsafe or unethical decisions.

Outcomes

- AI systems remain functional and safe during disruptions
- Reduced downtime, incident impact, and reputational damage
- Regulator-ready resilience documentation.

ERM Integration

AI introduces financial, reputational, operational, compliance, and strategic risks. These must be measured, quantified, and governed at the enterprise level.

Required ERM Integrations

- **Risk quantification** for financial exposure, aligned with enterprise scoring models
- **Integration into ERM risk register** with inherent and residual scoring
- **Scenario-based stress testing** (e.g., systemic model bias, widespread hallucinations)
- **Risk appetite alignment**, ensuring systems do not exceed board-approved thresholds
- **AI risk dashboards** feeding into CRO/board reporting
- **Insurance underwriting alignment**, including cyber and AI liability coverage.

Outcomes

- Enterprise-wide visibility into AI risk exposure
- Clear risk ownership between business, IT, and governance teams
- Better insurance pricing and loss prevention outcomes.

Business Governance and Strategy Integration

AI risk is ultimately a business risk. AI governance must integrate with strategic planning, product development, and leadership oversight.

Strategic Integrations

- **Board-level AI oversight** (ethics, risk, technology committees)
- **AI investment governance**: Approval gates for high-risk systems
- **Product lifecycle integration**: AI risk checks at design, build, deploy, and retire stages
- **Vendor and third-party AI governance** with due diligence and assurance assessments
- Alignment with DEI, ESG, and corporate ethics frameworks.

Outcomes

- AI systems advance business goals without unintended harm.
- Leadership has clear visibility into AI's strategic value and risk.
- AI systems help make informed investment, deployment, and risk acceptance decisions.

Cybersecurity	Protects models, data, access, and pipelines
Privacy	Ensures lawful and ethical data use
Compliance & Legal	Ensures alignment with global AI regulations
Operational Resilience	Ensures AI reliability during failure events
ERM (Enterprise Risk Management)	Aggregates and quantifies AI risk enterprise-wide
Business Leadership	Guides strategy, ethics, and decision-making

Table 17.1 Integrated Governance Summary

Effective AI governance requires coordinated oversight across the organization.

Together, these functions form the foundation of a **holistic, defensible, enterprise-wide AI governance program.**

Conclusion

AI risk assessment is a regulatory expectation, market requirement, and business imperative. Organizations that operationalize structured risk frameworks reduce exposure and enable responsible innovation. For an automated AI Risk Assessment vendors like RiskQ provide a comprehensive solution. See risk-q.com.

Bibliography

Government and Standards Bodies

European Commission. (2024). *EU Artificial Intelligence Act (AI Act). Final Text.*

ISO/IEC 23894:2023. (2023). *Artificial Intelligence Risk Management.* ISO/IEC.

ISO/IEC 42001:2023. (2023). *Artificial Intelligence Management System (AIMS).* International Organization for Standardization.

ISO/IEC TR 24028:2020. (2020). *Trustworthiness in Artificial Intelligence.* ISO/IEC JTC 1/SC 42.

NIST *Artificial Intelligence Risk Management Framework (AI RMF 1.0).* (2023). National Institute of Standards and Technology.

NIST *Special Publication 1270: Towards a Standard for Identifying and Managing Bias in AI.* (2022). NIST.

OECD Council on Artificial Intelligence. (2019). *OECD AI Principles. Organisation for Economic Co-operation and Development.*

Singapore Infocomm Media Development Authority (IMDA). *Model AI Governance Framework, 2019–2022 Editions.*

The White House (2023). *US Executive Order on Safe, Secure, and Trustworthy AI.*

UK Department for Science, Innovation and Technology (DSIT). (2023). *AI Regulation Framework.*

Security and Adversarial ML

Biggio, B., & Roli, F. (2018). Wild patterns: Ten years after the rise of adversarial machine learning. *Pattern Recognition*, 84, 317–331. https://doi.org/10.1016/j.patcog.2018.07.023.

Carlini, N., & Wagner, D. (2017). *Towards Evaluating the Robustness of Neural Networks.* IEEE S&P.

Goodfellow, I., Shlens, J., & Szegedy, C. (2014). Explaining and harnessing adversarial examples. *arXiv:1412.6572*.
MITRE Corporation (2021–2024). *MITRE ATLAS (Adversarial Threat Landscape for Artificial-Intelligence Systems)*.
Papernot, N. et al. (2017). *Practical Black-Box Attacks against Machine Learning*. ACM Asia CCS.

AI Documentation Standards (Model Cards, Datasheets, etc.)

Gebru, T. et al. (2021). *Datasheets for Datasets*. Communications of the ACM.
Google Responsible AI Practices. (2020–2024). *Guidance for Model Cards*.
Holland, S., Hosny, A., Newman, S., Joseph, J., & Chmielinski, K. (2020). The dataset nutrition label: A framework to drive higher data quality standards. In D. Hallinan, R. Leenes, S. Gutwirth, & P. De Hert (Eds.), *Data protection and privacy: Data protection and democracy* (pp. 1–26). Hart Publishing. https://doi.org/10.5040/9781509932771.ch-001.
Meta AI. (2023). *Responsible AI Transparency Guide*.
Mitchell, M. et al. (2019). *Model Cards for Model Reporting*. *ACM FAT**.

Explainability, Transparency and Fairness

Barocas, S., Hardt, M., & Narayanan, A. (2019). *Fairness and Machine Learning*.
IBM Research. (2018–2024). *AI Fairness 360 Toolkit Documentation*.
Lundberg, S., & Lee, S. (2017). *A Unified Approach to Interpreting Model Predictions (SHAP)*. NIPS.
Ribeiro, M.T., Singh, S., & Guestrin, C. (2016). *"Why Should I Trust You?" Explaining the Predictions of Any Classifier (LIME)*. KDD.
Selbst, A.D. et al. (2019). *Fairness and Abstraction in Sociotechnical Systems*. FAT.

Model Robustness, Drift, Monitoring and Operations

AWS.(2022–2024). *Machine Learning Drift Monitoring and Model Governance*.
Breck, E. et al. (2017). *The ML Test Score: A Rubric for ML Production Readiness*. Google Research.
Google Cloud. (2023). *Continuous Evaluation and ML Monitoring Guidelines*.
Microsoft.(2023). Responsible AI Standards.
Sculley, D. et al. (2015). *Hidden Technical Debt in Machine Learning Systems*. NIPS, 2015.

AI Governance, Ethics and Organizational Controls

Accenture.(2022). *Responsible AI: From Principles to Practice*.
Deloitte.(2023). *AI Governance & Model Risk Management*.
Floridi, L., & Cowls, J. (2019). A unified framework of five principles for AI in society. *Harvard Data Science Review*.
IEEE.(2019). *Ethically Aligned Design (EAD) Framework*. IEEE Standards Association.
World Economic Forum. (2023). *Global AI Governance Framework*.

AI Risk Management and Quantification

DARPA.(2016–2022). *XAI (Explainable s) Program Documentation.*
Gartner.(2023–2024). *AI TRiSM: AI Trust, Risk and Security Management.*
Google Cloud. (2023). *Risk Management in Responsible AI.*
McKinsey & Company. (2022). *AI Risk: Mitigation Strategies for Enterprise Deployment.*
PwC.(2023). *AI Governance and Risk Frameworks for Regulated Industries.*
RiskQ AI Assessment. (2025). *Risk Management Framework.*

Insurance, Liability, and Regulatory Enforcement

EBA (European Banking Authority). (2021). *Use of Machine Learning in Credit Risk.*
FINRA.(2020). *Artificial Intelligence in the Securities Industry.*
Lloyd's of London. (2023). *AI Risk and Emerging Technology Insurance Insights.*
NAIC.(2020). *Insurance Regulator Principles for AI.*
U.S. FTC. (2023). *Using AI and Algorithms: Guidance for Businesses.*

18

AI APPLICATIONS IN BUSINESS—FROM CHATGPT TO COPILOT

CYBERSECURITY CONCERNS

AI Platforms and Their Cybersecurity Concerns

While copilots represent a specific application of generative AI, organizations are also adopting **general-purpose AI platforms**. These large language model (LLM) systems are powerful because they can be adapted to multiple tasks—from drafting reports to writing code to providing customer support. However, each platform comes with unique cybersecurity, compliance, and governance challenges.

The following is a dissection of the currently available platforms and their cybersecurity concerns.

ChatGPT (OpenAI / Microsoft Azure)

Use Cases:

- Text generation, summarization, and brainstorming
- Integrated with Microsoft Copilot products
- Extensible via plugins and APIs.

DOI: 10.4324/9781003682530-22

Cybersecurity Concerns:

- **Data Leakage**: Users pasting proprietary data into prompts (especially in free or non-enterprise tiers).
- **Hallucinations**: Plausible but false answers leading to regulatory missteps.
- **Third-Party Integrations**: Plugins may access sensitive information with unclear boundaries.
- **Model Supply Chain Risk**: Reliance on OpenAI/Microsoft cloud infrastructure concentrates risk in a few providers.

Claude (Anthropic)

Use Cases:

- Enterprise-friendly AI with long context windows (summarizing long documents, handling compliance reports).
- Marketed as "constitutional AI" with stronger guardrails.

Cybersecurity Concerns:

- **Prompt Injection Still Possible**: Guardrails reduce but do not eliminate manipulation risks.
- **Context Overload**: Long prompts may inadvertently expose sensitive documents.
- **Data Residency**: Enterprises need to verify where Claude-hosted data is processed and stored.

Gemini (Google DeepMind)

Use Cases:

- Multimodal AI (text, image, video, code).
- Integrated into Google Workspace (Docs, Sheets, Gmail, Meet).

Cybersecurity Concerns:

- **Phishing Amplification**: AI-generated spear-phishing emails in Gmail contexts.

- **Cross-Domain Leakage**: Sensitive enterprise data from Google Drive or Gmail may unintentionally inform Gemini outputs.
- **Model Bias and Transparency**: Enterprise users lack visibility into Gemini's training data and red-teaming processes.

Copilot (Microsoft)

Use Cases:

- Embedded into Office apps and GitHub (coding, documents, spreadsheets, emails).

Cybersecurity Concerns:

- **Code Vulnerabilities**: AI-suggested insecure functions or dependencies.
- **Enterprise Data Exposure**: Risk of cross-pollination between corporate tenants if governance isn't enforced.
- **Compliance Gaps**: Drafting contracts, HR documents, or board reports without legal validation risks errors with regulatory impacts.

LLaMA (Meta) and Open-Source LLMs

Use Cases:

- Custom deployment of open-source models (fine-tuned for specific industries).
- Popular in research, startups, and regulated industries that need **on-premise AI**.

Cybersecurity Concerns:

- **Model Poisoning**: Open-source weights can be tampered with, introducing backdoors.
- **Lack of Guardrails**: Few built-in safety checks; responsibility shifts to enterprise teams.
- **Patch Management**: Frequent updates; failure to patch leaves exploitable vulnerabilities.

Sector-Specific AI Platforms

- **Healthcare AI (IBM Watson Health, MedPaLM, etc.)**
  - Concern: Patient data privacy (HIPAA/GDPR compliance).
- **Finance AI (BloombergGPT, FinGPT)**
  - Concern: Accuracy in trading/credit decisions; high risk of financial loss.
- **Legal AI (Harvey, Casetext CoCounsel)**
  - Concern: Unauthorized reproduction of client-sensitive case law.

Cross-Platform Cyber Risks

Regardless of vendor, enterprises face shared concerns:

1. **Data Governance Gaps**: AI models are only as secure as the data pipelines feed them.
2. **Supply Chain Concentration**: Over-reliance on a few cloud/AI providers creates systemic risk.
3. **Shadow AI Use**: Employees using unauthorized platforms outside corporate controls.
4. **Regulatory Uncertainty**: Lack of consistent global standards for AI security and accountability.

Introduction to CoPilot

Artificial Intelligence (AI) is no longer confined to research labs or experimental pilots. It is now embedded in the daily workflows of employees across industries. Among the most transformative advances are *"copilot" systems*—AI-powered assistants that augment human capabilities in real-time. Unlike earlier automation tools, copilots do not merely execute preprogrammed instructions; they *collaborate* with humans, providing contextual recommendations, drafting content, writing code, and even shaping business decisions.

The proliferation of copilots marks a fundamental shift in how organizations operate. Yet, this shift is not without consequence. AI copilots introduce new categories of **cyber risk**, **governance challenges**, and **ethical dilemmas**. Business leaders must weigh the productivity gains against data security risks, intellectual property disputes, and regulatory exposure.

This chapter explores AI applications in the enterprise, focusing on copilots, their benefits, and the cybersecurity issues that must be addressed to use them responsibly.

Quadrants:

- **Data Security and Leakage** → Shadow data, sensitive input risks
- **Adversarial Attacks** → Prompt injection, model manipulation
- **Intellectual Property and Legal Risks** → Copyright, unclear ownership
- **Bias and Compliance** → Hallucinations, regulatory violations.

The Emergence of Copilot Systems

The term *copilot* was popularized by Microsoft's integration of generative AI into its Office suite, but the concept now extends broadly across industries. Copilots act as *intelligent partners*—sitting alongside the human operator rather than replacing them.

Defining Copilot Systems

- **Natural Language Interface**: Accept commands or prompts in plain English (or other natural languages).
- **Context-Aware Assistance**: Interpret the user's intent and provide tailored responses.

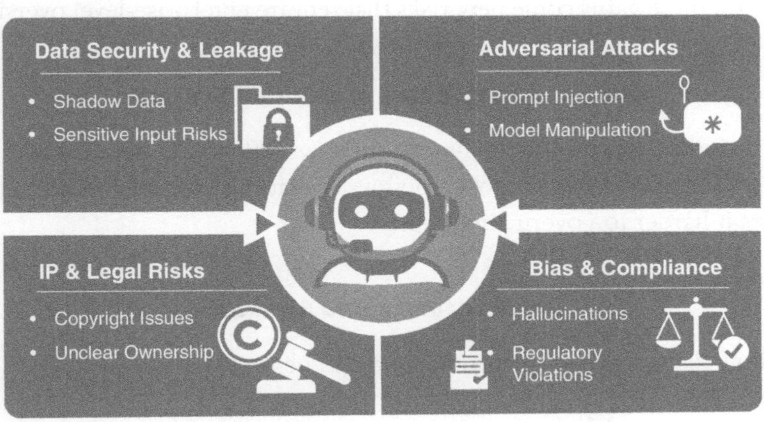

Image 18.1 Copilot Risk Landscape

- **Generative Capabilities**: Create new content (text, code, images, analysis) rather than merely retrieving information.
- **Learning in Context**: Adapt recommendations based on organizational data and workflows.

Examples of Copilot Applications

- **Software Engineering**: GitHub Copilot, Amazon CodeWhisperer
- **Enterprise Productivity**: Microsoft Copilot in Word, Excel, PowerPoint, Outlook, and Teams
- **Customer Experience**: AI copilots embedded in call centers to suggest answers, detect sentiment, and reduce handling time.
- **Risk and Compliance**: Generating draft audit reports, mapping evidence to frameworks like ISO 27001 or NIST CSF, and pre-populating regulatory forms.

Why Copilots Matter

For executives, copilots represent:

- **Efficiency Gains**: Reduced manual effort and faster turnaround.
- **Talent Augmentation**: Extending expertise to less experienced staff.
- **Scalability**: Enabling teams to handle more volume without proportional headcount growth.

But with these gains come new risks that require enterprise-level oversight.

Cybersecurity Risks of Copilot Systems

The introduction of copilots into sensitive workflows changes the risk calculus. Unlike traditional tools, copilots operate in *open-ended* ways, which makes it harder to govern and secure.

Data Security and Leakage

Copilots require access to corporate data to be useful. Risks include:

- **Inadvertent Disclosure**: Employees pasting confidential information (source code, financials, patient data) into prompts.

- **Cross-Tenant Risks**: Cloud-based copilots potentially storing or reusing data across organizations.
- **Shadow IT Concerns**: Employees using consumer copilots without IT oversight.

Prompt Injection Attacks

Prompt injection is a novel attack vector where adversaries craft malicious prompts to manipulate an AI's behavior. For example:

- Embedding instructions in a web page, which, when summarized by a copilot, exfiltrates sensitive data
- Instructing AI to ignore safety rules and generate disallowed outputs.

A process-flow diagram showing how attackers manipulate copilots.

Steps:

- **User Prompt** (benign request).
- **Injected Prompt** (hidden in external content, e.g., website or email).
- **AI Copilot Processing** (executes malicious instructions).
- **Output Manipulation** (exfiltrates data, generates vulnerabilities).
- **Attacker Receives Data** (or exploits the system).

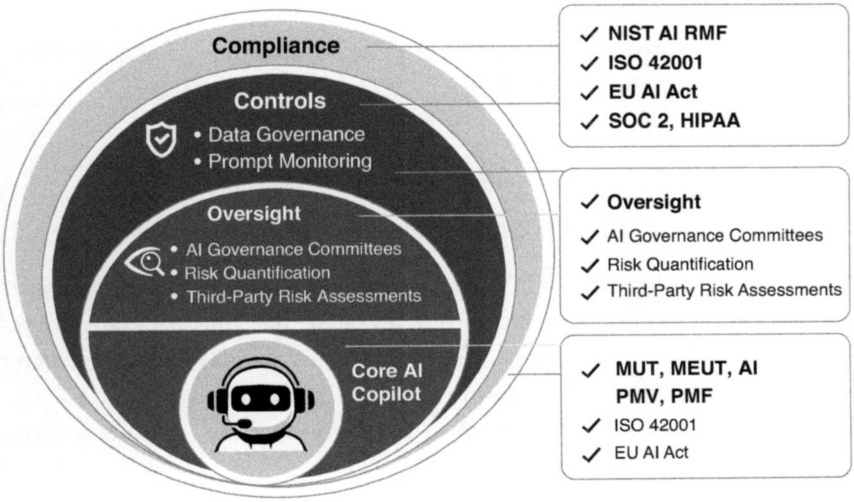

Image 18.2 Prompt Injection Attack Flow

Intellectual Property (IP) and Ownership

Copilots may output text or code that resembles training data. This creates risk in:

- **Copyright Infringement** claims from rights holders
- **Unclear IP Ownership** of AI-assisted work (Who owns the AI-generated code: the developer, the employer, or the AI provider?)

Hallucinations, Bias, and Compliance

- **Hallucination Risk**: AI producing plausible but false information (e.g., citing non-existent regulation).
- **Bias Amplification**: Copilots may reinforce systemic biases in hiring, lending, or law enforcement contexts.
- **Regulatory Non-Compliance**: Inaccuracy in financial reporting, privacy notices, or legal filings could lead to fines or lawsuits.

Attack Surface Expansion

Copilots can be exploited as entry points:

- Malicious actors target APIs used by copilots.
- Adversaries reverse-engineer copilot outputs to glean sensitive training data.
- Phishing campaigns leverage trust in AI outputs (e.g., "the copilot recommended I click this link").

Case Studies

Case 1: Software Development

A global bank adopted GitHub Copilot for coding. While developer productivity increased, a penetration test revealed that auto-generated functions failed to follow the company's secure coding standards. Attackers later exploited an insecure API, resulting in a data breach.

Lesson: Copilot-assisted code must undergo the same rigorous security review as human-written code.

Case 2: Legal and Compliance

A multinational law firm used Microsoft Copilot to draft contracts. AI trained firm documents; inadvertently reproduced confidential clauses from a private client agreement in an unrelated draft.

Lesson: Confidentiality boundaries must be enforced to prevent cross-use of sensitive data.

Case 3: Healthcare

A hospital tested an AI copilot to summarize patient records. While it improved efficiency, mis-summarization led to an incorrect medication order.

Lesson: Human-in-the-loop validation is mandatory in life-critical contexts.

Governance and Risk Management

Organizations must embed copilots within a **structured governance framework**.

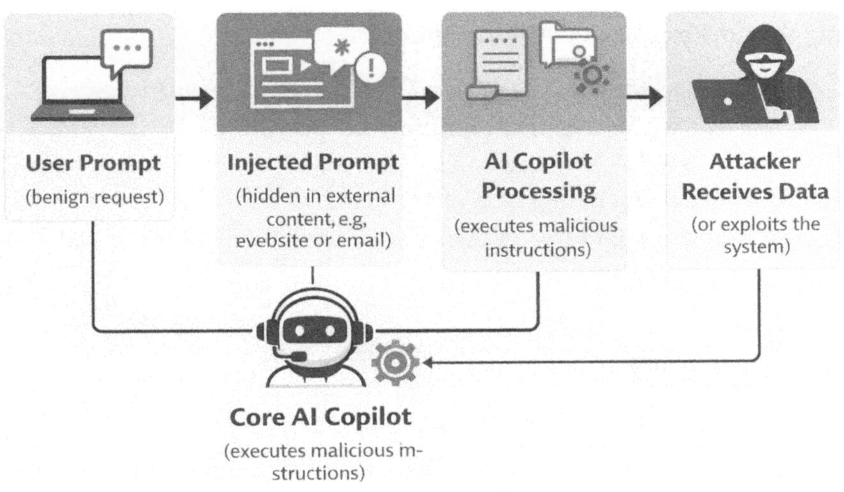

Image 18.3 Copilot Governance Framework

Layers (Inner to Outer):

1. **Core AI Copilot** (the system itself).
2. **Controls**: Data governance, prompt monitoring, audit trails, validation workflows.
3. **Oversight**: AI governance committees, risk quantification, third-party risk assessments.
4. **Compliance**: Alignment with NIST AI RMF, ISO 42001, EU AI Act, SOC 2, HIPAA.

Data Governance

- Limit data accessible to copilots.
- Apply classification rules (e.g., restrict "confidential" data from prompts).
- Establish *data loss prevention* monitoring for AI use.

Secure Design and Use

- Implement **prompt sanitization** to reduce injection risks.
- Require **output validation of** workflows.
- Deploy copilots in **sandboxed environments** where feasible.

Legal and Regulatory Alignment

- Copilot adoption must be mapped to frameworks such as:
- **NIST AI Risk Management Framework (AI RMF)**.
- **ISO/IEC 42001** (AI management systems).
- **EU AI Act** (risk classification of AI systems).
- **US Executive Orders on AI** (governance, transparency, and red-teaming requirements).

Training and Awareness

Employees must be trained to:

- Avoid entering sensitive information into copilots.
- Validate outputs against trusted sources.
- Recognize signs of AI manipulation.

Incident Response

Update playbooks to include:

- AI-specific threats (e.g., adversarial attacks).
- Escalation paths for copilot-related incidents.
- Forensic logging of AI prompts and outputs.

Broader AI Applications Beyond Copilot

Copilots are part of a larger AI ecosystem reshaping industries:

- **Cyber Defense**: AI-driven threat detection, anomaly spotting, and SOC automation.
- **Fraud Detection**: Identifying suspicious patterns in real-time transactions.
- **Supply Chain Risk**: Predicting vendor vulnerabilities and geopolitical disruptions.
- **Healthcare**: Diagnostics, drug discovery, and personalized treatments.
- **Education**: Adaptive learning platforms providing individualized coaching.

Each domain carries its own cyber issues, but the copilot discussion offers a blueprint for responsible AI adoption.

The Road Ahead

AI copilots will become more powerful, moving from assistants to **autonomous agents** capable of decision-making. This evolution magnifies both the opportunities and risks:

- **Opportunity**: Unlocking productivity, accelerating innovation, and democratizing expertise.
- **Risk**: Ceding too much decision authority to AI, creating systemic vulnerabilities if copilots are compromised.

Enterprises must prepare today by embedding **cyber risk quantification**, **AI governance structures**, and **board-level oversight** into their AI strategies.

Conclusion

AI copilots embody both the promise and peril of digital transformation. They allow businesses to operate faster and smarter, but they also expose organizations to novel forms of cyber risk.

The key insight for leaders: **AI copilots are not plug-and-play productivity tools—they are enterprise assets requiring governance, monitoring,** and **security controls**. Organizations that adopt copilots responsibly will gain competitive advantage. Those that fail may find that copilots accelerate not just innovation, but also the scale and speed of cyber incidents.

Bibliography

Bai, Y., Jones, A., Ndousse, K., Askell, A., Chen, A., DasSarma, N., Drain, D., Fort, S., Ganguli, D., Henighan, T., Joseph, N., Kadavath, S., Kernion, J., Conerly, T., El-Showk, S., Elhage, N., Hatfield-Dodds, Z., Hernandez, D., Hume, T., … Kaplan, J. (2022). *Constitutional AI: Harmlessness from AI feedback*. Anthropic. https://arxiv.org/abs/2212.08073

Biden, J. R. (2023, October 30). *Executive Order 14110: Safe, secure, and trustworthy development and use of artificial intelligence*. Federal Register, 88(210), 75191–75226. https://www.federalregister.gov/documents/2023/11/01/2023-24283/safe-secure-and-trustworthy-development-and-use-of-artificial-intelligence

European Commission. (2024). *EU Artificial Intelligence Act*. https://artificialintelligenceact.eu

Google DeepMind. (2023). *Gemini Multimodal AI Overview*. https://deepmind.google/technologies/gemini/

ISO/IEC 42001. (2023). *Artificial Intelligence Management System Standard*. International Organization for Standardization.

Meta. (2023). *LLaMA: Open Foundation Models*. https://ai.meta.com/llama/

Microsoft. (2023). *Copilot in Microsoft 365*. https://www.microsoft.com/en-us/microsoft-365/copilot

NIST. (2023). *Artificial Intelligence Risk Management Framework (AI RMF 1.0)*. National Institute of Standards and Technology. https://doi.org/10.6028/NIST.AI.100-1

OECD. (2019). *Recommendation of the Council on Artificial Intelligence*. https://legalinstruments.oecd.org/en/instruments/OECD-LEGAL-0449

Open AI. (2023). *GPT-4 Technical Report*. https://openai.com/research/gpt-4

The White House. (2023). *Executive Order on the Safe, Secure, and Trustworthy Development and Use of Artificial Intelligence*. https://www.whitehouse.gov/briefing-room/presidential-actions/2023/10/30/executive-order-on-safe-secure-and-trustworthy-artificial-intelligence/

19

THE FUTURE OF AI CYBERSECURITY

Introduction

The role of artificial intelligence (AI) in cybersecurity is both compelling and complex. AI possesses the capacity to serve as a formidable guardian of digital infrastructure, while simultaneously presenting itself as a sophisticated instrument for malicious actors. As any seasoned professional will attest, cybersecurity is never mundane—it is a relentless contest to safeguard valuable assets from adversaries, both domestic and international.

Gone are the days of rudimentary viruses and trivial nuisances. With the exponential growth in computing power, cybercriminals have escalated their tactics, leveraging cutting-edge technologies to orchestrate increasingly intricate attacks. Innovations once conceived with benevolent intent—automation, machine learning, and AI—are now being repurposed for nefarious ends. Threat actors are exploiting these advancements to launch assaults at unprecedented scale, amplifying the urgency for robust mitigation strategies.

DOI: 10.4324/9781003682530-23

The threat landscape has evolved dramatically. Today, one can effectively "invest" in cybercrime without possessing any technical expertise, thanks to the accessibility of AI-driven tools. Among the most prevalent AI-enabled threats are phishing campaigns. These attacks now feature impeccably written, highly persuasive emails that can deceive even the most vigilant recipients. Moreover, AI has been weaponized to disseminate political propaganda across social media platforms, further complicating the digital battlefield.

While phishing and propaganda are among the more recognizable threats, the full spectrum of AI-based attack vectors remains difficult to anticipate. As with any domain of risk, preparedness and resilience are paramount. This chapter will delve deeper into the mechanics of AI-driven threats and explore strategic approaches to fortify defenses.

Harnessing the power of AI for protection is not just advantageous—it is imperative. A growing concern shared by many is that the proliferation of AI will catalyze a surge in cyberattacks and malware. In the past, crafting malicious software required advanced coding skills; today, even individuals with minimal technical knowledge can potentially generate malware simply by prompting an AI system to do the heavy lifting.

How Does AI Empower You?

Although not strictly AI, many vendors have introduced autonomous capabilities that can be triggered based on predefined conditions. These innovations are immensely beneficial, especially as cybersecurity teams grapple with an overwhelming volume of alerts and notifications generated daily. Managing this deluge manually is simply untenable.

This is precisely where AI can be transformative—capable of sifting through thousands, even millions, of events to identify credible threats and actionable insights. AI possesses the technical acumen to elevate cybersecurity operations to new heights. As advancements continue, numerous security vendors are integrating AI into their product portfolios to enhance threat detection and accelerate response mechanisms. When meticulously calibrated and tailored to the nuances of a specific environment, these tools can deliver remarkable outcomes.

However, it is essential to remember a fundamental truth: tools, no matter how advanced, are not inherently magical. The true efficacy lies in human expertise—through thoughtful configuration, continuous tuning, and strategic deployment. Even the most sophisticated solution will falter if poorly implemented.

We must also acknowledge a sobering reality: AI is here, and it will inevitably be exploited for malicious purposes. This underscores the urgency of equipping ourselves with the right arsenal to confront the evolving threat landscape. What sets AI-driven automation apart from its predecessors is its capacity to learn. This learning capability not only improves detection accuracy but also significantly reduces false positives—a persistent challenge in cybersecurity, often exacerbated by misconfigurations.

By assimilating behavioral patterns within an environment, AI-based security systems can establish baselines and autonomously alert teams or initiate protective actions when anomalies arise. At this juncture, it is clear that traditional security stacks are no longer sufficient.

Industries such as finance and healthcare are already capitalizing on AI's potential. Financial institutions employ AI to detect fraudulent activity by analyzing vast volumes of transactions, while healthcare providers leverage it to identify and prevent the inadvertent exposure of sensitive PHI/PII data. As AI continues to evolve, its adoption will inevitably permeate a broader array of sectors.

When evaluating your next generation of security tools, consider the following strategic inquiries:

1. *Workflow Optimization*: Identify a labor-intensive or repetitive process within your current operations. Ask your vendor how their AI solution can streamline or automate this scenario.
2. *Live Demonstration*: Request a product demo. Seeing the tool in action will help assess its practical value and alignment with your organizational needs.
3. *Trial Engagement*: If a trial is available, seize the opportunity. While it may require an upfront investment of time, the long-term insights gained can be invaluable.
4. *Ecosystem Integration*: Recognize that your environment likely includes tools from multiple vendors. Ask about interoperability and how the AI solution enhances visibility across platforms.
5. *Data Privacy*: Inquire whether your data will be used to train the vendor's AI models. Understanding how your information is handled is critical to maintaining trust and compliance.

How Is AI Being Used to Launch Attacks?

Some prevalent attack vectors targeting AI systems include prompt injection, data extraction, data poisoning, and model corruption. As discussed earlier, malicious actors are increasingly leveraging the power of AI to orchestrate highly sophisticated phishing campaigns and conduct reconnaissance operations with unprecedented speed and precision.

Traditional security frameworks often prove inadequate in detecting AI-driven threats. With the aid of AI, adversaries can execute complex and nuanced attacks that evade conventional detection mechanisms. While identifying and anticipating such threats presents a formidable challenge, organizations equipped with the right skill sets, strategic foresight, and a robust arsenal of tools will be better positioned to defend against them.

It is imperative to recognize that AI-enabled attacks diverge significantly from conventional cyber threats, which typically aim to disrupt operations, deploy ransomware, or exfiltrate sensitive data. For instance, a self-driving vehicle could be deceived into running a red light by manipulating its visual input to interpret red as green. This scenario underscores the inherent difficulty in forecasting the full spectrum of AI-based threats. Here, one autonomous system is exploited to misinterpret its environment, leading to potentially catastrophic outcomes.

As AI continues to permeate critical systems, the complexity and unpredictability of its vulnerabilities demand a proactive and adaptive security posture. Understanding these emerging risks is essential to safeguarding the future of intelligent technologies.

How Can You Protect Your Organization from AI-Driven Attacks?

As previously noted, AI tools can be immensely powerful when properly configured and tailored to their operational environment. However, misconfigurations not only heighten the risk to the AI system itself but may also lead to inadvertent data leakage. Such incidents, while preventable, can significantly hinder the broader adoption of AI technologies.

To deepen your understanding of adversarial tactics targeting AI systems, I strongly recommend reviewing the MITRE ATLAS Matrix—a comprehensive framework that outlines known techniques and threat vectors specific to AI.

One of the most foundational security controls is access minimization. In cybersecurity, minimalism is a virtue. Implement Role-Based Access Control (RBAC) for your AI systems, and ensure they are fed only a curated, controlled dataset. This approach limits exposure and mitigates potential damage. Additionally, establish rigorous auditing and monitoring protocols to detect anomalous behavior in real time.

It is essential to recognize that AI systems themselves can become prime targets for cyberattacks. Therefore, robust protective measures must be in place. Collaborate closely with your technology vendors, study their recommended best practices, and implement those guidelines diligently. Equip your teams with the necessary training, and continuously update and refine your AI models to address emerging vulnerabilities and optimize performance.

To safeguard AI infrastructure, organizations should adopt comprehensive security practices, including routine assessments, stringent access controls, and continuous surveillance. Incorporating adversarial training—where models are exposed to deceptive inputs—can further enhance resilience against sophisticated attacks.

Consider implementing network traffic filtering as an additional layer of defense. Much like RBAC, controlling inbound and outbound traffic to and from AI systems can thwart unauthorized access and reinforce your existing access control policies.

Finally, be vigilant about the rise of "Shadow AI," akin to the challenges posed by "Shadow IT." Unregulated AI deployments can introduce significant risk. Strong governance, coupled with active collaboration across business units, is essential to maintaining oversight. Above all, foster a culture where cybersecurity is viewed as a shared responsibility—one that extends beyond IT and security teams to every individual within the organization.

Conclusion

It is imperative that we begin augmenting human analysts with advanced AI tools. Adversaries are evolving at a pace that often outstrips our defensive planning, necessitating a proactive approach to training and upskilling

AI-integrated security teams capable of confronting both current and emerging cyber threats.

AI systems can significantly bolster an organization's security posture; however, we must remain vigilant about the inherent vulnerabilities they may introduce. Employing AI models with built-in explainability is essential—these models empower security professionals to understand the rationale behind AI-driven decisions. Blind trust in AI, particularly within critical infrastructure, is neither prudent nor sustainable.

Combating sophisticated threat actors requires a united front—collaboration across academia, technology vendors, cybersecurity experts, and business leaders is vital. Time-tested principles of auditing and monitoring remain relevant and must be thoughtfully extended into the domain of AI. As we embrace AI autonomy, it is crucial to carefully define its scope, assess its impact, and establish contingency plans, all while adhering to applicable regulatory frameworks.

On a practical note, let us not overlook the often-undervalued discipline of documentation. Though rarely celebrated, comprehensive documentation is indispensable for AI systems. This includes configuration details, network connectivity, access mechanisms, data sources, and more. I cannot overstate its importance—many prolonged troubleshooting efforts could have been resolved in mere hours had proper documentation been in place.

In essence, the shift from reactive, human-led defense to autonomous, AI-enhanced security is inevitable. Yet, as we embrace this transformation, governance and explainability must stand shoulder to shoulder with technical innovation to ensure resilience, accountability, and trust.

Bibliography

CIS Critical Controls. https://www.cisecurity.org/controls/v8-1

Cloud Security Alliance – AI Controls Matrix. https://cloudsecurityalliance.org/artifacts/ai-controls-matrix

Google's Secure AI Framework (SAIF). https://safety.google/cybersecurity-advancements/saif/

Microsoft AI Security Risk Management. https://github.com/Azure/AI-Security-Risk-Assessment

MITRE. (2024). ATLAS: Adversarial threat landscape for artificial-intelligence systems. https://atlas.mitre.org

NIST AI Framework. https://www.nist.gov/itl/ai-risk-management-framework

SECTION 5

AI AND EXPLAINABILITY—UNDERSTANDING THE BLACK BOX

As AI systems grow more complex—particularly with the rise of deep learning and large language models—their internal decision-making processes are increasingly opaque. This "black box" nature presents significant challenges for trust, accountability, compliance, and adoption. Explainability (also referred to as XAI—explainable AI) has therefore become a critical requirement, not only for technical interpretability, but also for meeting legal obligations, enabling human oversight, and ensuring fairness and ethical use of AI in high-impact domains.

This section explores the necessity, methods, and future direction of AI explainability through six chapters:

- **Chapter 20: Why Explainability Matters**—examines the role of explainability in trust, accountability, ethical governance, and regulatory compliance.
- **Chapter 21: Types of AI Explainability**—distinguishes between global vs. local explainability, intrinsic vs. post-hoc, and technical vs. business interpretability.

DOI: 10.4324/9781003682530-24

- **Chapter 22: Challenges in Explainability**—explores limitations such as model complexity, tradeoffs with performance, bias interpretation, and human comprehension barriers.
- **Chapter 23: Explainability Methods and Tools**—analyzes leading techniques, including SHAP, LIME, counterfactuals, saliency maps, surrogate modeling, and model cards.
- **Chapter 24: Regulations and Explainability Standards**—maps how frameworks such as the EU AI Act, NIST AI RMF, GDPR, and ISO standards are formalizing explainability expectations.
- **Chapter 25: The Future of AI Explainability**—forecasts the evolution toward proactive, real-time, and user-tailored explainability aligned with adaptive AI ecosystems.

This section provides both the conceptual foundation and practical understanding required to move beyond "black box AI" toward transparent, trusted, and accountable intelligent systems.

20

WHY EXPLAINABILITY MATTERS IN AI

Artificial intelligence is often described as a "black box"—systems that make decisions without human users fully understanding how those decisions are made. While this may be acceptable for low-stakes tasks like recommending a movie, it is deeply problematic in business, healthcare, finance, or security contexts, where decisions can have **legal, ethical, and financial consequences**.

Explainability, sometimes called *interpretability* or *transparency*, is the practice of making AI systems understandable to humans. It ensures that stakeholders—from executives and regulators to customers and auditors—can trust, verify, and hold AI accountable.

The Business Case for Explainability

- **Trust and Adoption:** Users and executives are more likely to adopt AI solutions they understand. Without transparency, skepticism can derail implementation.

DOI: 10.4324/9781003682530-25

- **Risk Reduction:** Explainability helps identify model errors, biases, and vulnerabilities before they cause harm.
- **Accountability:** In regulated industries, organizations must be able to justify decisions made with AI, especially if outcomes are challenged in court.
- **Competitive Advantage:** Companies that can explain their AI can build customer trust, brand credibility, and regulatory goodwill.

Regulatory Drivers of Explainability

Global regulatory frameworks increasingly mandate AI transparency:

- **EU Artificial Intelligence Act (2024)**: Requires transparency and risk assessments for "high-risk" AI systems.
- **GDPR (General Data Protection Regulation):** Grants individuals the right to know how automated decisions affect them.
- **US Federal Trade Commission:** Warns that businesses must provide clear explanations for AI-driven consumer outcomes.
- **ISO/IEC 42001:2023:** Introduces governance requirements for AI management systems, including explainability controls.

Failing to meet these standards exposes organizations to fines, reputational damage, and legal liability.

Ethical Imperatives

Explainability is not just a compliance issue—it is a moral one. AI systems affect lives and livelihoods. Without transparency, organizations risk:

- **Bias and Discrimination:** Hidden algorithms may treat individuals unfairly based on gender, race, or socioeconomic status.
- **Erosion of Autonomy:** If people do not understand AI decisions, they cannot meaningfully challenge or consent to them.
- **Loss of Accountability:** Blaming "the algorithm" does not absolve an organization of responsibility for harmful outcomes.

Technical Dimensions of Explainability

Explainability techniques can be grouped into two categories:

- **Intrinsic Explainability:** Using simpler, inherently interpretable models (e.g., decision trees, linear regression).
- **Post-Hoc Explainability:** Applying tools to interpret complex models (e.g., neural networks) after training. Common methods include:
  - **LIME (Local Interpretable Model-Agnostic Explanations):** Explains individual predictions by approximating models locally.
  - **SHAP (SHapley Additive exPlanations):** Uses game theory to assign feature importance values.
  - **Saliency Maps:** Visual tools to show which parts of an image influence a computer vision model.

Project managers, CISOs, and compliance officers must ensure that whichever approach is used, it aligns with business needs and regulatory requirements.

Challenges in Achieving Explainability

- **Complexity vs. Accuracy:** Highly accurate models (e.g., deep learning) are often harder to explain.
- **Audience Diversity:** What is "explainable" to a data scientist may be meaningless to a regulator or board member.
- **Dynamic Systems:** AI models evolve as they are retrained on new data, making explanations a moving target.
- **Trade Secrets:** Companies may resist sharing model details to protect intellectual property, creating tension with transparency needs.

Best Practices for Organizations

- **Adopt Explainability by Design:** Build interpretability into the AI lifecycle from the start.
- **Tailor Explanations to Stakeholders:** Executives need business impact explanations; regulators need compliance clarity; end users need understandable reasoning.
- **Document Decision Paths:** Maintain clear audit trails for all AI-driven decisions.
- **Integrate with Governance Frameworks:** Link explainability efforts to existing IT governance, data governance, and risk management programs.

- **Test for Bias Regularly:** Use explainability tools to surface hidden discrimination.

The Strategic Advantage

Explainability transforms AI from a risky "black box" into a **trusted business asset**. Organizations that can confidently explain their AI decisions not only avoid regulatory penalties but also foster trust among customers, partners, and employees. In a market where trust is scarce, explainability becomes a differentiator.

Conclusion

AI can only be safe, ethical, and valuable if it is explainable. Without transparency, businesses risk regulatory violations, ethical failures, and loss of trust. By making explainability a core requirement—embedded in project management, governance, and compliance—organizations can harness AI responsibly and sustainably.

Bibliography

Doshi-Velez, F., & Kim, B. (2017). Towards a rigorous science of interpretable machine learning. *arXiv*.

European Commission. (2024). *Artificial Intelligence Act*.

Goodman, B., & Flaxman, S. (2017). European Union regulations on algorithmic decision-making and a "right to explanation." *AI Magazine*.

ISO/IEC 42001:2023. *Artificial Intelligence Management System Standard*.

Lundberg, S., & Lee, S. (2017). *A Unified Approach to Interpreting Model Predictions (SHAP)*. Advances in Neural Information Processing Systems.

Project Management Institute (PMI). (2023). *AI Governance and Risk Management*.

21

TYPES OF AI EXPLAINABILITY

Artificial intelligence is powerful, but without explainability, it risks becoming a "black box." Organizations need to understand how and why AI systems make decisions—especially in regulated or high-stakes environments. Explainability can be approached in different ways, depending on the **purpose, audience,** and **complexity** of the AI system.

This chapter explores the **types of AI explainability**, highlighting how each contributes to transparency, accountability, and trust.

1. **Global vs. Local Explainability**
   - **Global Explainability:**
     Focuses on understanding how the entire model works across all predictions.
     - *Example:* A credit scoring model where decision-makers want to know the top five factors that influence loan approvals overall.
     - *Use Cases:* Regulators, executives, and auditors.
   - **Local Explainability:**
     Explains why the AI made a specific decision in a particular case.

DOI: 10.4324/9781003682530-26

- *Example:* Why one customer was denied a loan despite having a high income.
- *Use Cases:* Customer service, compliance, fairness reviews.

2. **Intrinsic vs. Post-Hoc Explainability**
   - **Intrinsic Explainability:**
     Achieved by using simpler, interpretable models where the decision process is transparent by design.
     - *Techniques:* Decision trees, linear regression, rule-based systems.
     - *Trade-Off:* Easier to interpret but may lack accuracy in complex problems.
   - **Post-Hoc Explainability:**
     Applied after training complex models (e.g., deep neural networks) to interpret their outputs.
     - *Techniques:*
       - **LIME (Local Interpretable Model-Agnostic Explanations)**
       - **SHAP (SHapley Additive exPlanations)**
       - **Counterfactual Explanations** (e.g., "If your income had been $5,000 higher, your loan would have been approved.")
     - *Trade-Off:* Retains model accuracy but requires specialized tools for interpretation.
3. **Feature Importance vs. Example-Based Explainability**
   - Feature Importance:
     Shows which input features had the most influence on the model's decision.
     - *Example:* Identifying that age and income together account for 70% of a loan approval decision.
   - Example-Based Explainability:
     Explains predictions by referencing similar past cases.
     - *Example:* "This loan was denied because it closely resembles past applications that were denied."
4. **Model-Specific vs. Model-Agnostic Explainability**
   - **Model-Specific Methods:**
     Techniques tailored to specific algorithms.
     - *Example:* Visualization of decision trees, attention weights in neural networks.
   - **Model-Agnostic Methods:**
     Work with any model, regardless of its internal structure.

– *Example:* LIME or SHAP applied to both linear models and deep learning systems.

5. **Human-Centered Explainability**

   Explainability must also consider the **audience**:
   - **Technical Explainability:** For data scientists and engineers to debug and validate models.
   - **Business Explainability:** For executives and decision-makers to understand business impact.
   - **User Explainability:** For end-users to comprehend decisions that affect them (e.g., loan rejections, medical diagnoses).

6. **Visual vs. Narrative Explainability**
   - **Visual Explainability:** Uses heatmaps, saliency maps, or decision-path visualizations.
     – *Example:* In medical imaging, a heatmap shows that part of an X-ray influenced a cancer diagnosis.
   - **Narrative Explainability:** Provides textual or verbal explanations.
     – *Example:* "Your claim was flagged because it contained unusual spending patterns compared to your history."

7. **Comparative Explainability**

   Some approaches explain decisions by comparing **what happened vs. what could have happened**:
   - **Counterfactuals:** "If your credit history were one year longer, the model would have approved your loan."
   - **What-If Analysis:** Allows stakeholders to test scenarios and understand model sensitivity.

Conclusion

AI explainability is not one-size-fits-all. Organizations must adopt the type—or combination—of explainability approaches that best suit their **risk profile, industry regulations,** and **stakeholder needs**. Whether through global or local explanations, intrinsic or post-hoc methods, or human-centered communication, the goal is the same: **to build AI systems that are trustworthy, transparent, and accountable.**

Bibliography

Doshi-Velez, F., & Kim, B. (2017). Towards a rigorous science of interpretable machine learning. *arXiv*.

European Commission. (2024). *Artificial Intelligence Act.*
ISO/IEC 42001:2023. (2023). *AI Management System Standard.*
Lundberg, S., & Lee, S. (2017). *A Unified Approach to Interpreting Model Predictions (SHAP).* NeurIPS.
Ribeiro, M. et al. (2016). *"Why Should I Trust You?" Explaining the Predictions of Any Classifier* (LIME). KDD.

22

CHALLENGES IN EXPLAINABILITY

As artificial intelligence (AI) becomes increasingly woven into the fabric of modern society—powering everything from healthcare diagnostics to loan approvals and predictive policing—its decision-making processes remain frustratingly opaque. This chapter explores the multifaceted and evolving challenge of explainability in AI, offering both technical and societal context. Through vivid examples and reflections from regulatory and industry trends, we examine why explainability is so difficult to achieve, and why it is nonetheless critical for trust, governance, and ethical oversight.

Introduction

Explainability—the ability to understand, interpret, and trust the outputs of an AI system—has become a critical requirement for responsible AI adoption. As AI systems grow in scale and complexity (especially deep-learning models and large language models), explaining how and why these models

DOI: 10.4324/9781003682530-27

make decisions becomes increasingly difficult. This chapter explores technical, operational, regulatory, psychological, and organizational challenges that complicate the pursuit of explainability in AI systems.

Technical Complexity of Black-Box Models

Modern AI systems—particularly deep neural networks and transformer-based architectures—are often considered **black boxes**. With billions or trillions of parameters, models like GPT-4 lack transparent reasoning pathways. For instance, a financial institution using a deep-learning model to assess loan risk may find it impossible to justify a declined application to regulators or applicants.

Example: In 2023, a major European bank faced backlash after an AI model rejected thousands of loan applications with no human-understandable rationale. Regulators demanded interpretability reports, but none existed.

The Trade-Off Between Model Accuracy and Interpretability

There is often a trade-off between model performance and interpretability. Simpler models (e.g., decision trees, linear regression) are easy to explain but underperform in complex tasks. Meanwhile, high-performance models (e.g., transformers) are harder to interpret.

Example: In a healthcare diagnostics scenario, a hospital opted for a more transparent but less accurate model over a high-performing deep-learning model after patient advocacy groups raised concerns about accountability.

Opportunity: Research into Explainable AI (XAI) methods—such as SHAP (SHapley Additive exPlanations) or LIME (Local Interpretable Model-Agnostic Explanations)—is helping close this gap.

Contextual Explainability Challenges

Explainability needs differ by stakeholder:

- Data Scientists want feature importance metrics.
- Regulators seek compliance documentation.
- Executives need business context.
- End users want clear, intuitive justifications.

Example: An HR system flagged an internal promotion candidate as **unsuitable**. The internal audit team required traceability, the manager wanted business rationale, and the candidate demanded their rights under GDPR. A single model output had to be translated into three distinct explanations.

Regulatory and Compliance Pressures

Explainability is no longer optional—especially under regulations like:

- EU AI Act: Demands transparency for high-risk AI.
- GDPR: Grants individuals the **right to explanation** (Article 22).
- US Executive Order on AI (2023): Emphasizes trustworthy AI as a national priority.

Example: A US fintech company paused deployment of its credit scoring AI when the Consumer Financial Protection Bureau raised concerns about explainability and potential discrimination.

Risks of Misleading or False Explainability

AI models can **hallucinate**—confidently providing false or misleading explanations. This is known as rationalization, where the system retroactively generates an explanation not tied to its actual internal reasoning.

Example: A generative AI used in legal research produced confident citations to court cases that didn't exist. Lawyers relying on the output unknowingly submitted fictitious cases in court—leading to sanctions.

Implication: False explainability can cause more damage than no explanation at all.

Organizational and Human Factors

Explainability also faces organizational hurdles:

- Lack of cross-functional collaboration between data science, legal, compliance, and product teams.

- Low explainability literacy among executives and board members.
- AI developers may lack incentives to prioritize interpretability.

Solution: Create AI Governance Committees that include cross-disciplinary roles responsible for overseeing explainability metrics and validation.

Evolving Toward Lifecycle Explainability

Explainability must be embedded across the AI lifecycle:

Data Collection—Verify data source legality, consent, and bias
Model Training—Review licensing/IP rights of training data
Model Evaluation—Assess discrimination risk and fairness metrics
Deployment—Ensure explanations meet end-user expectations
Post-Deployment—Monitor for drift, bias, and compliance violations.

Recommended Training for Stakeholders

Stakeholder—Training Needs

Developers—XAI techniques (SHAP, LIME), bias detection, documentation
Compliance Teams—Regulatory frameworks (EU AI Act, GDPR), audit trails, ethical AI
Executives—Business impact of explainability, board-level AI risk communication
Product Owners—Model transparency requirements, UX design for explainability
HR & Legal—Interpretability and discrimination case law, rights-based AI design

Conclusion

Explainability is a cornerstone of responsible AI, but its implementation remains fragmented. The technical opacity of black-box models, regulatory demands, stakeholder misalignment, and false explainability risks form a complex web of challenges. The future lies in moving beyond post-hoc explanations to embedding explainability throughout the AI lifecycle—from design to retirement—with governance, training, and cross-functional collaboration at its core.

Real-World Case Studies in Explainability

CASE STUDY

COMPAS RECIDIVISM RISK TOOL

In the United States, the Correctional Offender Management Profiling for Alternative Sanctions (COMPAS) tool has been widely used to assess the likelihood of a criminal defendant reoffending. While designed to aid in parole and sentencing decisions, investigations revealed that the model exhibited racial bias—predicting higher recidivism rates for Black defendants compared with white defendants with similar profiles. The proprietary nature of the algorithm made it difficult for defendants to challenge its fairness or accuracy. This case underscored the importance of transparency, explainability, and auditability in criminal justice applications of AI.

CASE STUDY

APPLE CARD GENDER DISCRIMINATION ALLEGATIONS

In 2019, Apple and Goldman Sachs faced allegations of gender discrimination in credit limit assignments by their joint Apple Card. Users, including high-profile tech executives, reported that women received significantly lower credit limits than their male counterparts despite similar financial backgrounds. The opaque nature of the underwriting algorithm made it difficult to understand or contest the decisions. This controversy sparked regulatory scrutiny and prompted calls for greater explainability and accountability in financial AI systems.

CASE STUDY

AMSTERDAM'S 'SYRI' WELFARE FRAUD DETECTION SYSTEM

The Dutch government deployed an AI system known as System Risk Indication (SyRI) to detect welfare fraud by cross-referencing data from multiple sources. The system was criticized for targeting low-income and immigrant communities, raising concerns about discrimination and lack of transparency. In 2020, a Dutch court ruled that the system violated human rights due to its lack of explainability and accountability, leading to its suspension. This case highlights the legal risks of opaque AI in public sector use.

Bibliography

Brundage, M., et al. (2022). Towards trustworthy AI development: Mechanisms for supporting verifiable claims. *arXiv*:2004.07213.

Doshi-Velez, F., & Kim, B. (2017). Towards a rigorous science of interpretable machine learning. *arXiv preprint arXiv*:1702.08608.

European Commission. (2024). *EU Artificial Intelligence Act*.

European Union. (2016). *General Data Protection Regulation (GDPR), Article* 22.

Goodman, B., & Flaxman, S. (2017). European Union regulations on algorithmic decision-making and a 'right to explanation'. *AI Magazine*, 38(3), 50–57.

MIT CSAIL. (2023). *Adversarial Attacks in Medical AI*.

NIST. (2023). *AI Risk Management Framework (AI RMF 1.0)*.

OECD. (2019). *OECD Principles on Artificial Intelligence*.

OpenAI. (2024). *GPT-4 Technical Report*.

Selbst, A. D., & Barocas, S. (2018). The intuitive appeal of explainable machines. *Fordham Law Review*, *87*, 1085.

Wachter, S., Mittelstadt, B., & Russell, C. (2018). Counterfactual explanations without opening the black box: Automated decisions and the GDPR. *Harvard Journal of Law & Technology*, *31*(2), 841–887.

23

EXPLAINABILITY METHODS AND TOOLS

Artificial Intelligence can generate extraordinary insights, but without explainability, it risks undermining trust and accountability. To overcome this challenge, organizations rely on **methods and tools** that make AI models more transparent. These techniques translate complex computations into human-understandable insights, enabling regulators, executives, and end users to interpret outcomes.

This chapter explores the main methods and tools for AI explainability, their use cases, and best practices for implementation.

Feature Importance Methods

Feature importance identifies which input variables had the greatest impact on a model's decision.

- **Permutation Importance:** Measures how prediction accuracy changes when a feature's values are randomly shuffled.

DOI: 10.4324/9781003682530-28

- **Gini Importance (Decision Trees):** Evaluates how much each feature reduces impurity when splitting data.
- **SHAP (SHapley Additive exPlanations):** Uses cooperative game theory to assign each feature a contribution value for predictions.

Strengths: Clear ranking of influential factors, easy to communicate with business leaders.

Limitations: May oversimplify relationships in highly nonlinear models.

Local Explanation Methods

Local methods explain individual predictions rather than the model as a whole.

- **LIME (Local Interpretable Model-Agnostic Explanations):** Creates simpler local models (e.g., linear) around a single prediction to explain it.
- **SHAP (local use):** Breaks down an individual prediction into feature contributions.
- **Counterfactual Explanations:** Show how slight changes to inputs could alter the decision (e.g., "If your income had been $5,000 higher, your loan would have been approved").

Strengths: Useful for customer-facing scenarios or appeals.

Limitations: May not scale well across millions of predictions.

Visualization Methods

Visual tools are especially powerful for AI systems working with images, text, or complex structures.

- **Saliency Maps (Computer Vision):** Highlight in which parts of an image influenced the model's decision.
- **Attention Maps (NLP):** Show which words in a sentence are most important for a model's output.
- **Partial Dependence Plots:** Show how a single feature affects predictions while holding others constantly.
- **ICE (Individual Conditional Expectation) Plots:** Extend PDPs to show variability across individual cases.

Strengths: Intuitive, visually compelling, valuable in healthcare and security contexts.

Limitations: Can be misleading if users over-interpret the visuals.

Example-Based Methods

Instead of explaining abstract features, these methods rely on comparisons with other examples.

- **Case-Based Reasoning:** The system explains decisions by pointing to similar past cases.
- **Prototype and Criticism Models:** Highlight "representative examples" (prototypes) and unusual cases (criticisms) from the dataset.

Strengths: Highly intuitive for end users, especially in medical and legal domains.

Limitations: Quality depends on the representativeness of stored examples.

Model-Specific Tools

Certain algorithms come with built-in explainability:

- **Decision Trees:** Show explicit decision paths.
- **Rule-Based Models:** Provide human-readable rules ("IF income > $50,000 THEN approve loan").
- **Linear Models:** Directly show coefficients for each feature.

Strengths: Transparent by design, easy to explain.

Limitations: Less accurate for extraordinarily complex tasks.

Software Frameworks and Platforms

Numerous open-source and commercial tools support explainability:

- **SHAP:** Python library implementing Shapley values for global and local explanations.
- **LIME:** Widely used Python package for local interpretability.
- **InterpretML (Microsoft):** Combines glass-box models and black-box explainers.

- **AI Explainability 360 (IBM):** Open-source toolkit offering multiple methods.
- **Google What-If Tool:** Visualizes model performance, feature effects, and counterfactuals.
- **Fiddler AI / Truera (Commercial):** Enterprise platforms for monitoring and explainability.

Strengths: Broad toolkit availability, strong community support.

Limitations: Integration with enterprise workflows can be complex.

Choosing the Right Method

Selection depends on the audience, purpose, and model type:

- **Executives and Regulators:** Feature importance and summary plots.
- **Data Scientists:** SHAP, LIME, PDP, and ICE for technical debugging.
- **End users:** Counterfactuals, example-based reasoning, simple narratives.

Best Practices

- **Match Method to Stakeholder:** Avoid overwhelming business users with technical plots.
- **Combine Multiple Tools:** Use feature importance + local explanations for a fuller picture.
- **Document Explanations:** Maintain an audit trail of how models were explained.
- **Test for Bias:** Use explainability outputs to surface hidden discrimination.
- **Integrate into Lifecycle:** Apply tools during development, deployment, and monitoring.

Conclusion

Explainability methods and tools bridge the gap between powerful AI and human trust. By leveraging feature importance, local explanations, visualizations, and specialized toolkits, organizations can make AI more transparent and accountable. The most effective strategy combines multiple approaches, tailored to the needs of different stakeholders, ensuring AI remains a **responsible business asset rather than a black box of risk**.

Bibliography

Google AI. 2018. *What-If Tool.*

IBM Research. 2019. *AI Explainability 360 Toolkit.*

Microsoft Research. 2019. *InterpretML Documentation.*

Molnar, C. (2022). *Interpretable Machine Learning: A Guide for Making Black Box Models Explainable* (2nd ed.). Independently published. https://christophm.github.io/interpretable-ml-book/

Lundberg, S., & Lee, S. (2017). *A Unified Approach to Interpreting Model Predictions (SHAP)*. NeurIPS.

Ribeiro, M. et al. (2016). *"Why Should I Trust You?" Explaining the Predictions of Any Classifier* (LIME). KDD.

24

REGULATIONS AND EXPLAINABILITY STANDARDS

Artificial Intelligence is no longer an unregulated frontier. Governments and standards bodies around the world are introducing rules that demand transparency, accountability, and explainability. Organizations deploying AI must understand these evolving requirements to avoid legal penalties, reputational harm, and business disruption.

This chapter outlines the key regulatory frameworks and industry standards shaping AI explainability.

The Regulatory Imperative

Explainability has become a legal necessity, not just a best practice. Regulators increasingly recognize that opaque "black box" systems can lead to:

- **Discrimination and bias** in lending, hiring, and healthcare.
- **Lack of accountability** when AI harms individuals or businesses.
- **Erosion of consumer trust** in digital products and services.

DOI: 10.4324/9781003682530-29

As a result, laws now require organizations to **document, justify, and explain** AI-driven decisions.

Global Regulatory Frameworks

European Union

- **AI Act (2024):**
  - Classifies AI systems into risk categories (unacceptable, high, limited, minimal).
  - High-risk systems (e.g., healthcare, employment, finance, critical infrastructure) must meet explainability, transparency, and human oversight requirements.
  - Requires **technical documentation** and clear communication with end users.
- **GDPR (General Data Protection Regulation):**
  - Article 22 provides individuals with a *"right to explanation"* of automated decisions.
  - Companies must show meaningful information about logic, significance, and consequences.

United States

- **FTC Guidance:** Warns against "black box" AI that deceives consumers or fails to provide meaningful explanations.
- **NIST AI Risk Management Framework (2023):** Encourages explainability as part of trustworthy AI principles (transparency, accountability, fairness).
- **Sector-Specific Rules:**
  - **Healthcare (FDA):** Regulates AI-based medical devices, requiring clinical validation and interpretability.
  - **Financial Services (OCC, CFPB):** Demand explainable credit and risk assessment models.

Other Jurisdictions

- **UK AI White Paper (2023):** Promotes explainability and transparency across regulated sectors.

- **Singapore's Model AI Governance Framework:** Emphasizes explainability and accountability for AI adoption.
- **Canada's Directive on Automated Decision-Making:** Requires algorithmic impact assessments and user-friendly explanations.

Industry Standards

Standards bodies are codifying explainability into technical and governance frameworks:

- **ISO/IEC 42001:2023 (AI Management System Standard):**
  First international AI governance standard; mandates transparency and accountability processes, including explainability.
- **ISO/IEC TR 24027:2021:**
  Provides guidance on bias in AI systems and the role of interpretability in mitigating harm.
- **IEEE Standards (Ethically Aligned Design, P7001 Series):**
  Focuses on transparency, algorithmic accountability, and explainability requirements.
- **AICPA Trust Services Criteria (SOC 2):**
  Requires controls around transparency and responsible use of AI in audit reporting contexts.

Key Explainability Requirements across Frameworks

Despite differences, common regulatory, and standards themes emerge:

1. **Transparency:** Clear communication of AI's purpose, design, and limitations.
2. **Human Oversight:** Ability for humans to review, override, or appeal decisions.
3. **Documentation:** Maintaining records of data sources, model logic, and validation.
4. **Bias Mitigation:** Demonstrating fairness and non-discrimination.
5. **Auditability:** Providing regulators and auditors with meaningful model explanations.

Challenges for Organizations

- **Diverging Jurisdictions:** Different countries impose varying explainability requirements.
- **Technical vs. Legal Language:** Translating mathematical model outputs into legally defensible explanations.
- **Balancing IP Protection:** Companies may hesitate to reveal proprietary models while still needing to comply with explainability demands.
- **Operational Burden:** Continuous monitoring, retraining, and documentation of models requires resources and expertise.

Best Practices for Compliance

- **Adopt a Global Governance Framework:** Align internal policies with ISO/IEC 42001 and NIST AI RMF to cover multiple jurisdictions.
- **Embed Explainability Early:** Incorporate explainability checkpoints into project management and model development.
- **Maintain an AI Audit Trail:** Track data lineage, model versions, and explanation outputs for regulators.
- **Train Cross-Functional Teams:** Ensure legal, compliance, IT, and business leaders understand regulatory explainability expectations.
- **Engage with Regulators:** Proactively discuss explainability methods to avoid surprises during audits.

Conclusion

Explainability is no longer optional—it is a legal and ethical requirement for organizations worldwide. By aligning with global regulations and emerging standards, businesses can ensure compliance, build trust, and position themselves as leaders in responsible AI. Failure to prioritize explainability, by contrast, invites regulatory scrutiny, reputational damage, and operational risk.

Bibliography

American Institute of Certified Public Accountants (AICPA). (2017, revised 2022). 2017 *Trust Services Criteria for Security, Availability, Processing Integrity, Confidentiality, and Privacy* (with *revised points of focus — 2022*). AICPA & CIMA. https://www.aicpa-cima.com/resources/download/2017-trust-services-criteria-with-revised-points-of-focus-2022

European Commission. (2024). *Artificial Intelligence Act*.

European Parliament and Council of the European Union. (2016). *Regulation (EU) 2016/679 of the European Parliament and of the Council on the protection of natural persons with regard to the processing of personal data and on the free movement of such data (General Data Protection Regulation)*. Official Journal of the European Union, L 119, 1–88. https://eur-lex.europa.eu/legal-content/EN/TXT/?uri=CELEX:32016R0679

Government of Canada. (2019). *Directive on Automated Decision-Making*.

IEEE. (2021). *IEEE 7001-2021: IEEE standard for transparency of autonomous systems*. IEEE Standards Association. https://ieeexplore.ieee.org/document/9726144/

ISO/IEC JTC 1/SC 42. *ISO/IEC 42001:2023 Artificial Intelligence Management System Standard*.

ISO/IEC TR 24027:2021. *Bias in AI Systems and AI-Aided Decision Making*.

NIST. (2023). *AI Risk Management Framework*.

25

THE FUTURE OF AI EXPLAINABILITY

Explainability has moved from an academic discussion to a core business and regulatory requirement. Yet as AI grows more complex and deeply integrated into society, the need for **next generation's explainability** will intensify. The future of explainability will be shaped by innovative technologies, evolving regulations, and changing expectations from businesses, governments, and the public.

Drivers of the Future

Several forces will push explainability into the spotlight:

- **Complex AI Models:** Deep learning, foundation models, and generative AI make interpretability more challenging.
- **Expanding Regulation:** Laws like the EU AI Act, ISO/IEC 42001, and upcoming US federal guidance will require explainability by design.
- **Ethical Expectations:** Customers and employees increasingly demand fairness, transparency, and accountability.

DOI: 10.4324/9781003682530-30

- **Business Value:** Trustworthy AI will become a differentiator, with explainability as its foundation.

Trends Shaping Explainability

AI-First Governance

Explainability will be embedded in AI governance frameworks, with organizations adopting "explainability by design" alongside privacy by design.

Hybrid Models

Future systems may combine interpretable models with black-box approaches—using simple models where accountability is critical (e.g., finance, healthcare) and advanced models where accuracy dominates (e.g., image recognition).

Automated Explainability

Next-generation tools will automatically generate human-friendly explanations tailored to different audiences—executives, regulators, or end users.

Explainability as a Service (XaaS)

Vendors may offer cloud-based services that audit and explain third-party AI systems, similar to security scanning services today.

Explainability in Generative AI

With large language models and generative AI, explainability will expand beyond "why" an outcome was made to *what data influenced it* and *how outputs were constructed*.

Future Challenges

- **Scalability:** Explaining billions of decisions in real time will strain technical resources.
- **Adversarial Risks:** Bad actors may exploit explanation outputs to manipulate or attack models.

- **Balancing Transparency with IP:** Companies will need to reconcile disclosure requirements with protecting proprietary algorithms.
- **Human Comprehension:** Even the best technical explanations must be simplified to remain meaningful to non-technical audiences.

Research and Innovation

Active areas of research that will define the next decade of explainability include:

- **Causal Explainability:** Moving from correlations to understanding cause–effect relationships.
- **Interactive Explanations:** Allowing users to query AI systems with "what if?" scenarios in real time.
- **Multimodal Explainability:** Explaining decisions that combine text, images, audio, and structured data.
- **Ethical Explainability:** Ensuring explanations not only describe outcomes but also address fairness and social impact.

Strategic Implications for Businesses

Forward-looking organizations should:

- **Invest in Explainability Infrastructure:** Treat it as part of risk management, not just compliance.
- **Train Cross-Functional Teams:** Equip legal, compliance, and technical teams with explainability skills.
- **Engage in Standards Development:** Participate in ISO, IEEE, and regulatory consultations to shape future requirements.
- **Communicate Proactively:** Use explainability as part of brand strategy to build trust with customers and partners.

Vision for the Next Decade

In the future, explainability will not be an add-on—it will be a **core pillar of AI lifecycle management**, as fundamental as cybersecurity or privacy. Organizations that embrace explainability will gain trust, regulatory resilience, and market advantage. Those that ignore it will face legal penalties, reputational crises, and competitive decline.

Conclusion

The future of AI belongs to systems that are not only powerful but also transparent, fair, and understandable. Explainability will evolve from a technical challenge into a **strategic asset**. By anticipating regulatory shifts, investing in innovative tools, and embedding explainability into governance, businesses can ensure their AI remains a driver of value and trust in the digital age.

Bibliography

Doshi-Velez, F., & Kim, B. (2017). Towards a rigorous science of interpretable machine learning. *arXiv*.

European Commission. (2024). *Artificial Intelligence Act*.

ISO/IEC JTC 1/SC 42. ISO/IEC 42001:2023 *Artificial Intelligence Management System Standard*.

Molnar, C. (2022). *Interpretable Machine Learning: A Guide for Making Black Box Models Explainable*.

NIST. (2023). *AI Risk Management Framework*.

SECTION 6

AI AND PRIVACY—PROTECTING DATA IN THE AGE OF INTELLIGENT SYSTEMS

Artificial intelligence (AI) has fundamentally transformed the scale, speed, and sophistication of data processing—creating both unprecedented value and significant privacy risks. AI systems now collect, infer, and even predict sensitive personal information, often beyond the user's awareness or consent. This raises urgent questions around data rights, surveillance, autonomy, and the ethical limits of personalization. At the same time, AI is increasingly being leveraged to enhance privacy protection through techniques such as anonymization, differential privacy, and federated learning. The future of AI will depend heavily on its ability to preserve privacy while enabling innovation.

This section examines the evolving relationship between AI and privacy across six chapters:

- **Chapter 26: Data Collection & Consent**—analyzes how AI challenges traditional notions of informed consent, transparency, and lawful data processing.

DOI: 10.4324/9781003682530-31

- **Chapter 27: Data Security & Anonymization**—explores privacy-preserving mechanisms such as encryption, anonymization, synthetic data, and federated architectures.
- **Chapter 28: Surveillance & Ethical Concerns**—investigates AI-driven surveillance, facial recognition, behavioral tracking, and the societal implications of pervasive monitoring.
- **Chapter 29: AI & User Control**—evaluates mechanisms for user agency, explainable consent, data minimization, and self-sovereign identity.
- **Chapter 30: AI in Social Media & Advertising**—examines the ethical and regulatory implications of hyper-personalization, algorithmic profiling, and targeted influence.
- **Chapter 31: Emerging Solutions**—highlights next-generation privacy innovations, including zero-knowledge proofs, PETs, and AI architectures designed for privacy-by-design compliance.

This section equips readers to understand AI's dual role as both a threat and an enabler of privacy—a defining tension in the future of digital society.

26

DATA COLLECTION AND CONSENT IN AI SYSTEMS

Modern AI Systems Are Complex

Modern AI systems are complex ecosystems with several essential elements. Among all the elements, data and AI models are perhaps the two of the most critical components as they have a direct bearing on outcomes. A more nuanced view of AI systems suggests that the relative importance of components varies by application. For example, for research AI, data and models might indeed be most critical, whereas for production systems, infrastructure and monitoring become equally vital. Similarly, for user-facing applications, interfaces and user experience design may be crucial, while for regulated industries, governance and compliance frameworks are essential. That said, AI systems rely on the quality of data and the accuracy of models to produce expected results.

Why Data and Models Are Central

The very foundation of an AI system is the quality, quantity, and relevance of training data, which fundamentally determines what an AI

DOI: 10.4324/9781003682530-32

system can learn and how well it performs. Poor data leads to poor outcomes regardless of model sophistication. However, the data has to work in tandem with the architecture, algorithms, and learned parameters in a model encode the system's capabilities and determine how it processes inputs to generate outputs. These two components are indeed deeply interdependent—even the best model architecture will fail with inadequate data, while the richest dataset is useless without appropriate models to learn from it.

In order to get desired outcomes, AI systems require several other essential components:

- Computing infrastructure in the form of hardware (GPUs, TPUs, distributed systems) and software infrastructure for training, inference, and scaling are fundamental to system functionality.
- Data pipeline and processing systems for data ingestion, cleaning, preprocessing, feature engineering, and management are critical for translating raw data into usable training inputs.
- Evaluation and monitoring frameworks for testing, validation, performance monitoring, and detecting issues like drift or bias are essential for reliable operation.
- Human–AI interfaces for user interaction and APIs, which determine how effectively humans can work with the AI system.
- Governance and operations processes that ensure security controls, compliance frameworks, deployment pipelines, and operational monitoring that guarantee the system works safely and reliably in practice.

From a systems thinking perspective, modern AI is best understood as sociotechnical systems where technical components (data, models, infrastructure) interact with human elements (operators, users, stakeholders) and organizational factors (processes, policies, culture). The success of the AI system depends on how well all these elements work together. So, while data and models are undeniably central to AI system capability, treating them as the only critical components can lead to systems that are technically sophisticated but practically ineffective, unreliable, or unsuitable for real-world deployment.

Unresolved Consent in AI Systems Threatens Digital Trust

The triumphant march of AI systems is ongoing even through critical foundational issues such as data collection and consent remain largely unresolved. The reason is that these issues are fraught with fundamental contradictions between the technical requirements of AI systems and the practical realities of meaningful user control and privacy protection. This contradiction manifests in the following ways:

- AI systems need massive datasets to function effectively, but meaningful consent requires individual understanding and choice at a granular level that becomes practically impossible to implement at scale.
- The rapid pace of AI development and model iteration conflicts with the time needed for users to genuinely understand and make informed decisions about data use.
- AI applications involve sophisticated data processing that most users cannot reasonably be expected to understand, making well-informed consent largely notional or even fictional.
- Business models built on extensive data collection create structural barriers to implementing privacy-protective consent mechanisms that might limit data availability.
- AI systems operate across multiple legal jurisdictions with different privacy laws and consent requirements, creating compliance challenges that often default to the least protective standards.
- Consent frameworks designed for simpler data uses struggle to address AI systems that can repurpose data in ways not anticipated at the time of collection.
- Even when individuals can theoretically control their own data, AI systems trained on massive public datasets can still affect non-consenting individuals through algorithmic decisions.

These contradictions suggest that traditional consent models may be fundamentally inadequate for the AI era, requiring new frameworks that balance innovation benefits with meaningful protection of individual rights and societal values.

Data Collection and Consent Challenges

Many AI systems operate with limited visibility into what data is collected, how it is going to be used, and who has access thereby severely undermining informed consent. These issues directly impact user autonomy, transparency, and accountability in AI deployment. A majority of AI systems are opaque when it comes to data practices. To further compound the problem, they are supported by inadequate consent mechanisms. Often consent is often shrouded by legalese or is non-specific and fails to meet the standards of meaningful, granular, and revocable user control.

Data collection and consent in AI systems involve several interconnected challenges that span technical, legal, ethical, and practical aspects:

A basic issue involves collection and sourcing of data for training AI systems. Users often are not even aware that their data has been collected, let alone how it is being used. This includes data gathered through web scraping, social media harvesting, and aggregation from multiple sources without clear attribution. The original sources are usually unclear or undisclosed.

It is not surprising that due to such practices, major legal disputes over training data have emerged. Some prominent cases where AI systems lack desired transparency and provenance regarding their data collection and sources include the dispute between OpenAI and Meta Lawsuits and authors Sarah Silverman, Christopher Golden, and Richard Kadrey who filed separate lawsuits against Meta and OpenAI, arguing copyright infringement for training their engines on their works without permission (Davis 2023).

Another area where data collection and consent issues operate in a gray zone relate to web scraping without consent or attribution. Many AI companies scrape content from websites, social media platforms, forums, and digital libraries without clearly citing sources or obtaining explicit permission. This includes vast amounts of data relating to personal information, academic papers, social media posts, digitized books, and other content.

Thomson Reuters sued Ross Intelligence, alleging that Ross had infringed upon its copyrighted Westlaw headnotes by using them to train an AI legal tool through a third party called LegalEase (Cappuzzello 2025). This case shows how training data can be laundered through intermediaries, obscuring original sources.

Dataset laundering by intermediary services has become a common practice where companies urge them to source or buy pre-packaged datasets that obscure the ultimate sources of training data. It is no secret that most content used by AI models is obtained without authorization, prompting numerous lawsuits that typically include claims for copyright infringement.

AI systems use datasets like Common Crawl to aggregate web content without tracking original sources. Common Crawl has become one of the most extensively used datasets for training large language models (LLMs), more so in the generative AI space. It offers a wide-ranging snapshot of the public internet, including news, blogs, forums, and more and covers over 9.5 petabytes of web data, spanning billions of pages. Its popularity is also because it is freely available and maintained by a nonprofit, making it a go-to for startups, researchers, and even major AI labs. Reportedly, models like GPT-3 sourced over 80% of their tokens from Common Crawl. Another Mozilla study found that 64% of 47 major LLMs between 2019 and 2023 used Common Crawl as a core training source (Mozilla Report 2024).

LLMs typically do not disclose important information such as:

- The specific websites or publications in their training data
- If copyrighted books, articles, or other content was included
- What filtration methods were used for processing before training
- The nature of consent mechanisms that were used
- Which datasets were sourced/purchased from vendors who do not disclose collection methods
- Was the biometric and personal data with subject consent.

This represents a systemic lack of transparency about data sources and permission that has several implications related to intellectual property and copyright protection. Furthermore, researchers cannot verify AI system capabilities or limitations, users are unaware of potential biases or gaps in AI knowledge and regulators' struggle to assess compliance and safety issues.

Regulatory and Compliance Complexities

Over the past decade, data protection and privacy have become central pillars of digital governance, prompting a wave of regulatory frameworks across jurisdictions. Landmark regulations such as the General Data Protection Regulation (GDPR) in Europe and the California Consumer Privacy Act (CCPA) in the United States have set foundational standards for user consent, data minimization, and breach accountability. There are several clauses, which when interpreted in the context of AI systems, have important implications. The following tables highlight the provisions that directly impact how AI systems collect and process personal data:

However, these frameworks, while robust were largely conceived in a pre-AI paradigm, where data processing was deterministic, traceable, and human-directed. The rise of AI systems, particularly those powered by large-scale machine learning and autonomous decision-making, has introduced new layers of complexity that expose the limitations of existing laws.

Legal systems in the digital world are still grappling jurisdictional fragmentation with each region enforcing distinct definitions of personal data, consent, and algorithmic accountability, creating a patchwork of obligations for cross-border AI deployments. There are also legal issues such as opacity in data usage, synthetic and inferred data, model drift, and revoking consent or purging data, which need to be addressed through regulatory mandates. Governments around the world are engaged in understanding these gaps to address AI-specific governance frameworks that go beyond traditional data protection such as algorithmic accountability and consent-aware AI architectures. Even when regulations are created, their effectiveness will depend on practical mechanisms to exercise rights like data deletion, correction, or portability in AI contexts.

Data and Power Dynamics

The market power of big tech and other AI developers creates inherent imbalances in the consent relationship, where individuals have limited negotiating power. AI systems often involve complex ecosystems of data processors, cloud providers, and partners, making it difficult to track and control data flows even with initial consent. The most crucial of all factors related to power dynamics is the structure of business models of many AI companies, which depend on exploiting collected data for revenue, creating an asymmetry where user data becomes a commodity, consent is diluted into compliance, and control over digital identity shifts from individuals to opaque corporate algorithms.

Technical Implementation Challenges

Modern AI systems have become increasingly complex in terms of addressing issues such as data anonymization, consent management, intellectual

Provision	Description	Implications for AI
Article 5 – Data Processing Principles	Includes lawfulness, fairness, transparency, purpose limitation, data minimization, accuracy, storage limitation, integrity, and confidentiality	AI systems must justify data use, minimize unnecessary data, and ensure transparency
Article 6 – Lawful Basis for Processing	Requires a valid legal basis (e.g., consent, contract, legitimate interest)	AI training must align with one of the lawful bases, especially for sensitive data
Article 22 – Automated Decision-Making	Grants individuals the right not to be subject to decisions based solely on automated processing	AI systems making impactful decisions (e.g., credit scoring) must offer human intervention and explainability
Recital 71	Emphasizes safeguards against discriminatory effects of	AI models must be audited for bias and fairness
Data Protection by Design and Default (Article 25)	Mandates embedding privacy into system architecture	AI developers must integrate privacy-preserving techniques (e.g., differential privacy, federated learning)

Table 26.1 GDPR Provisions Relevant to AI Data Collection

Provision	Description	Implications for AI
Right to Know	Consumers can request details about data collected, sources, and	AI systems must log and disclose training data provenance and
Right to Delete	Consumers can request deletion of personal data	AI systems must support data erasure, even from training sets where feasible
Right to Opt-Out of Data Sale	Consumers can opt out of their data being sold	AI vendors must clarify if model training constitutes "sale" and offer opt-out mechanisms
Non-Discrimination	Businesses cannot discriminate against consumers exercising privacy	AI personalization must not penalize users who opt out of data
Sensitive Data Inference Restrictions (CPRA update)	Limits use of sensitive personal data (e.g., race, health, geolocation)	AI models must avoid inferring or using sensitive attributes without explicit consent

Table 26.2 CCPA Provisions Relevant to AI Data Collection

property protection and authentication. We shall deal with this in detail in the next chapter.

All these issues listed above are evolving rapidly as AI capabilities expand and regulatory frameworks develop. Solutions often require coordinated efforts across technical innovation, policy development, regulatory approaches, and industry standard-setting rather than isolated approaches to individual problems.

Current Regulatory Responses

Current regulatory responses to AI governance are exemplified by landmark initiatives such as the EU AI Act and the Generative AI Copyright Disclosure Act of 2024. These frameworks represent early attempts to impose guardrails on the development and deployment of AI systems specifically in areas of risk classification, transparency, and intellectual property attribution.

The EU AI Act introduces a tiered risk-based approach, mandating stricter compliance for high-risk applications (e.g., biometric surveillance, critical infrastructure, and employment algorithms). It also aims to harmonize AI governance across member states, with implications for global interoperability and enforcement.

The Generative AI Copyright Disclosure Act of 2024 is a federal US law that requires developers of generative models to disclose training data sources and ensure proper attribution for copyrighted content. It aims to balance innovation with creator rights, addressing growing concerns around unauthorized replication and derivative works.

China too has come out with its 2025 Action Plan on Global AI Governance, which outlines a comprehensive framework for inclusive, secure, and sustainable AI development. The Action Plan underscores the pivotal role of clean, high-quality data in shaping trustworthy and inclusive AI systems. It advocates for the lawful and secure flow of data across borders, encouraging the creation of global platforms for data sharing that respect privacy and national sovereignty. By promoting diverse and unbiased datasets, the plan aims to eliminate discrimination and preserve cultural richness within AI ecosystems. Further, it emphasizes robust safeguards for personal data throughout the AI lifecycle, right from collection to model generation, ensuring ethical integrity and public trust. This strategic focus on data quality and governance is positioned as a foundational enabler for equitable AI innovation worldwide.

However, it is early days yet and the true effectiveness of these regulations remains to be empirically validated.

Who Is Accountable for AI Data Collection and Consent?

The inevitable question that arises is who is indeed responsible for AI data collection and consent? This responsibility is a divided one and each of the following stakeholders must carry their share of it and fulfill their obligations:

- Developers and system architects of AI systems must design consent-aware architectures, embedding privacy-by-design principles.
- Deploying organizations such as corporates, governments, and institutions must ensure lawful data collection, transparent consent flows, and compliance with jurisdictional norms.
- Regulators and policy makers should frame enforceable standards for consent, data minimization, and cross-border data governance.
- End users and data subjects should exercise informed consent and data rights.

In future we may well see AI itself in the form of autonomous agents and models becoming responsible for their own governance and ensure that issues such as data collection, consent, transparency, and compliance are self-enforced and adaptable to meet changing requirements.

Bibliography

Davis, W. (2023, July 9). Sarah Silverman is suing OpenAI and Meta for copyright infringement. *The Verge*. https://www.theverge.com/2023/7/9/23788741/sarah-silverman-openai-meta-chatgpt-llama-copyright-infringement-chatbots-artificial-intelligence-ai

Cappuzzello, D. H. R. (2025, March 19). *Takeaways from Thomson Reuters v. Ross Intelligence: AI Litigation Risks and Insurance Solutions (via Passle)*. Passle. https://briefings.brownrudnick.com/post/102k566/takeaways-from-thomson-reuters-v-ross-intelligence-ai-litigation-risks-and-insu

Mozilla Report: How Common Crawl's Data Infrastructure Shaped the Battle Royale over Generative AI. (2024, February 6). Mozilla Foundation. https://www.mozillafoundation.org/en/blog/Mozilla-Report-How-Common-Crawl-Data-Infrastructure-Shaped-the-Battle-Royale-over-Generative-AI/

27

DATA SECURITY AND ANONYMIZATION

The Paradox of Data Dependency vs. Data Security in Artificial Intelligence

Unlike traditional IT systems, artificial intelligence (AI) not only stores and processes data but also learns from it, adapts to it, and sometimes even reveals patterns that were not explicitly encoded.AI systems are deeply reliant on large-scale data inputs to function effectively, yet, this very dependency exposes them to a wide range of security vulnerabilities. These risks range from data poisoning and unauthorized access to model inversion and privacy leakage. Often these risks overlooked or inadequately addressed, leaving critical gaps in trust, resilience, and governance. This dynamic nature makes securing AI data far more challenging.

AI systems often ingest sensitive personal, financial, or operational data. If access controls are weak or encryption is absent, this data becomes a prime target for unauthorized access. Malicious actors can inject deceptive or corrupted data during training, subtly altering model behavior undermining its integrity. This is especially dangerous in autonomous systems or

DOI: 10.4324/9781003682530-33

decision-critical environments. Over time, the data feeding AI systems may change in structure or source, introducing inconsistencies or vulnerabilities that go undetected without robust monitoring. Another security risk that can emanate from AI systems is related to the possibility of inadvertent exposure of personally identifiable information (PII) through outputs, especially in generative or predictive contexts, leading to privacy violations and compromise. Furthermore, AI models can be subject to reverse engineering by threat actors to infer sensitive training data, even if the data itself was never directly exposed.

AI data security and anonymization face several complex challenges that span technical limitations, practical implementation issues, and evolving threat landscapes shown in the following image:

Laws like GDPR and CCPA impose obligations related to data security such as purpose limitation, transparency, and data sharing with third parties after obtaining consent. In the context of AI systems, especially those deployed in regulated environments or handling sensitive personal data, these laws impose distinct but complementary obligations around user consent and third-party data sharing. GDPR, rooted in the EU's rights-based privacy framework, mandates that AI systems obtain explicit, informed, and purpose-specific consent before processing personal data. This means that any AI-driven profiling, personalization, or data enrichment must be preceded by a clear consent obtained from the user, with full transparency

Challenge	Description
Re-identification Risk	AI models can infer identities from seemingly anonymized data, especially when cross-referenced with external datasets
Federated Learning Models	While federated learning aims to keep data decentralized, it faces challenges including model poisoning attacks, gradient-based data reconstruction, and coordination security between participating nodes
Utility vs. Privacy Trade-off	Strong anonymization may degrade model perfomance by removing key features
Lack of Standardization	No universal benchmark for "effective anonymization" across jurisdictions
Inferential Leakage	AI can infer sensitive attributes (e.g., health status, ethnicity) even from anonymized inputs
High-dimensional data challenges	Modern AI often works with high-dimensional data (images, text, behavioural sequences) where traditional anonymization techniques become ineffective.
Dynamic Data Streams	Real-time AI systems (e.g., IoT, surveillance) complicate anonymization due to continuous updates
Multi-stage vulnerability	AI pipelines involve multiple stages (collection, preprocessing, training, inference, storage) where data can be compromised. Each stage requires different security measures, creating complex attack surfaces.
Operational Security Issues	Data lifecycle management and legacy integration

Table 27.1 Data Anonymization Challenges

Regulation	Provision	Key Highlights	Implications for AI Systems
GDPR (EU)	Recital 26[1]	Data is considered anonymous if individuals are "not identifiable."	Truly anonymized data falls outside GDPR scope; pseudonymized data remains regulated.
	Article 5[2]	Promotes data minimization and pseudonymization.	Encourages lean data practices and privacy-preserving techniques in AI workflows.
CCPA / CPRA (California)	Deidentified Data Definition[3]	Sets standards to ensure data cannot reasonably identify individuals.	AI systems must validate deidentification rigor and prevent re-identification risks.
	Disclosure & Deletion Rights[4]	Requires transparency in anonymization and deletion of	AI models must respect user rights even for derived or inferred personal data.
Emerging Frameworks	EU AI Act (2024)[5]	Mandates risk assessments and transparency for AI systems using personal data.	AI deployments must classify risk levels and disclose data usage and safeguards.
	India's DPDP Act (2023)[6]	Recognizes anonymized data as outside regulatory scope.	Places accountability on processors to ensure anonymization is robust and irreversible.

Table 27.2 AI Implications

about how their data will be used and with whom it will be shared. Moreover, AI developers and operators must maintain detailed records of consent and ensure that any third-party processors or data recipients adhere to GDPR standards through formal agreements and compliance audits.

CCPA follows a slightly different model that allows AI systems to process and share personal data by default but requires them to offer users a clear and accessible way to opt out. For AI applications that involve data monetization, behavioral targeting, or cross-context profiling, this means prominently displaying related links and honoring user requests to restrict data flows. While CCPA does not require prior consent for most adult users, it does impose stricter opt-in requirements for minors and holds businesses accountable for ensuring that third parties respect consumer privacy choices.

The focus of both GDPR and CCPA is on responsible AI by enforcing transparency, user agency, and accountability in data governance.

Data Anonymization

Data anonymization in AI systems refers to the transformation of datasets to protect individual privacy while preserving their usefulness for analysis and modeling. This process employs several techniques to reduce the risk of re-identification and unauthorized exposure. Data masking replaces sensitive information with fictional or scrambled values, effectively obscuring real identities. Pseudonymization substitutes personal identifiers with artificial ones, allowing limited analytical use while minimizing traceability. Generalization reduces data precision, for example, converting specific ages into broader age ranges so that records become less identifiable. Data perturbation introduces small, random variations into values, preserving statistical patterns while concealing individual details. Another method, data swapping, rearranges attribute values across records to break direct linkages without distorting overall dataset integrity. All these techniques form a strategic layer of privacy protection, enabling ethical and compliant AI deployment across sectors such as finance, healthcare, and governance.

Recent advancements in AI have ushered in more adaptive and intelligent approaches to data anonymization. AI-powered systems now automate the detection and safeguarding of sensitive information, dynamically adjusting privacy controls in response to emerging re-identification risks. One particularly impactful technique is synthetic data generation, where AI models produce entirely artificial datasets that mirror the statistical characteristics of real data without containing any actual personal identifiers. This synthetic data proves highly effective for model training and analytical tasks, offering strong privacy assurance without sacrificing utility. By striking a balance between data protection and operational value, AI-driven anonymization empowers organizations to meet regulatory requirements while leveraging data for innovation, strategic insights, and informed decision-making.

On the face of it, data anonymization provides a comprehensive solution to address challenges related to data security and privacy protection in AI systems. The objective of data anonymization is to retain analytical utility while eliminating identifiability. In the context of AI systems, which use data sets that include sensitive personal information, anonymization can enable training of AI models without violating any privacy laws, reducing risk of data breaches, sharing datasets across organizations and borders as well as harnessing the power of AI to uncover insights that fuel research and innovation.

Recent advancements in AI have ushered in more adaptive and intelligent approaches to data anonymization. AI-powered systems now automate the detection and safeguarding of sensitive information, dynamically adjusting privacy controls in response to emerging re-identification risks. One particularly impactful technique is synthetic data generation, where AI models produce entirely artificial datasets that mirror the statistical characteristics of real data without containing any actual personal identifiers. This synthetic data proves highly effective for model training and analytical tasks, offering strong privacy assurance without sacrificing utility. By striking a balance between data protection and operational value, AI-driven anonymization empowers organizations to meet regulatory requirements while leveraging data for innovation, strategic insights, and informed decision-making.

Threat	Description
Data Linkage Attacks	Combining anonymized data with public datasets to re-identify individuals
Model Inversion	Extracting training data from AI models (e.g., via adversarial queries)
Membership Inference	Determining whether a specific individual was part of the training set
Synthetic Identity Generation	Using AI to create realistic but fake identities that bypass anonymization safeguards
Third-palty processor risks	AI development frequently involves data sharing with vendors, contractors, and research partners, multiplying the number of entities with access and potential security vulnerabilities.
Prompt injection and data extraction	Large language models may inadvertently reveal training data through carefully crafted prompts, potentially exposing private information that was included in training datasets.

Table 27.3 AI Threats

Data Security Threat Landscape for AI Systems

The threat landscape for AI systems is rapidly evolving, marked by a convergence of technical, ethical, and geopolitical risks. Malicious actors are increasingly exploiting vulnerabilities in model training, data pipelines, and deployment environments, ranging from adversarial inputs and model inversion attacks to data poisoning and prompt injection.

Beyond technical exploits, AI systems face systemic threats such as bias amplification, misinformation propagation, and regulatory non-compliance, especially when operating across jurisdictions with divergent privacy and accountability standards. As AI becomes embedded in critical infrastructure, finance, and governance, the stakes escalate demanding robust threat modeling, crypto agility, and quantum-safe resilience to safeguard digital trust and societal stability.

Data Anonymization Helps, But Is Not Enough

Data anonymization is a critical component, but not a standalone solution for managing security risks in AI systems or achieving regulatory compliance. It plays a vital role in reducing exposure to sensitive information by protecting personally identifiable data (PII), thereby helping organizations comply with obligations under GDPR, HIPAA, and CCPA. However, anonymization alone cannot fully safeguard against the evolving threat landscape or meet the nuanced demands of modern AI governance.

Even where data anonymization is used by AI systems, advanced AI models can be used by threat actors to correlate anonymized data with external datasets to re-identify individuals especially when data granularity is high. Over-anonymization could also result in stripping data of critical features, reducing model accuracy and utility, thereby compromising contextual integrity. Furthermore, traditional anonymization is often a one-time process, while AI systems require continuous, context-aware privacy management.

To effectively manage AI security risks and meet compliance mandates, anonymization must be part of a multi-layered strategy, including:

- Combining pseudonymization, differential privacy, and synthetic data generation.
- Assessing re-identification risk based on data type, usage, and exposure vectors.
- Implementing differential privacy by adding mathematical noise to protect individual data points while preserving trends.
- Making use of secure enclaves and encryption to protect data at rest and in transit, especially during model training and inference.
- Embedding anonymization within adaptive data protection frameworks.
- Pairing anonymization with transparency protocols to ensure ethical accountability.
- Tracking data lineage, access, and usage for accountability and regulatory reporting.

In a multi-layered data protection strategy, anonymization serves as a foundational pillar for mitigating identification risks while enabling responsible data use. Techniques such as masking, pseudonymization, and generalization operate at the structural level to obscure direct identifiers by replacing sensitive fields, substituting personal tokens, and reducing data granularity. These methods reinforce compliance by embodying privacy-by-design and data minimization principles, signaling proactive governance to regulators and stakeholders alike. At a more adaptive layer, AI-powered anonymization introduces dynamic safeguards that preserve analytical utility without compromising individual privacy. Particularly in high-stakes domains like healthcare, finance, and public sector analytics, this intelligent layer ensures that data remains both secure and actionable while supporting innovation, policy development, and operational insight within a resilient privacy framework.

Bibliography

Art. 5 GDPR – Principles relating to processing of personal data - General Data Protection Regulation (GDPR). (2021, October 22). General Data Protection Regulation (GDPR). https://gdpr-info.eu/art-5-gdpr/

Article 50: Transparency obligations for providers and deployers of certain AI systems | EU Artificial Intelligence Act. (n.d.). https://artificialintelligenceact.eu/article/50/

California, S. O. (n.d.). Frequently asked Questions (FAQs) - California Privacy Protection Agency (CPPA). https://cppa.ca.gov/faq.html

IAPP. (n.d.). https://iapp.org/news/a/a-close-up-on-de-identified-data-under-the-ccpa/

Recital 26- Not applicable to anonymous data - General Data Protection Regulation (GDPR). (2019, September 2). *General Data Protection Regulation (GDPR).* https://gdpr-info.eu/recitals/no-26/

Taxmann. (2025, May 4). *Scope and key Definitions under DPDP Act.* Taxmann Blog. https://www.taxmann.com/post/blog/scope-key-definitions-under-dpdp-act

28

SURVEILLANCE AND ETHICAL CONSIDERATIONS

Artificial Intelligence Technologies Powering Surveillance Systems

Artificial intelligence (AI) has completely transformed surveillance from passive observation to intelligent monitoring with predictive capabilities. Modern surveillance and threat detection systems use multiple advanced AI technologies to deliver real-time intelligence and situational awareness. Computer vision enables machines to interpret visual data, powering applications such as facial recognition, object detection, and license plate reading. Complementing this, machine learning (ML) algorithms learn patterns from historical data to improve detection accuracy over time, supporting use cases like anomaly detection and predictive threat modeling. Beyond ML, deep learning can perform far more complex pattern recognition tasks, such as emotion analysis, gait recognition, and crowd behavior monitoring through the use of neural networks.

Additionally, natural language processing analyzes audio and text to extract intent and sentiment, facilitating voice surveillance and the

DOI: 10.4324/9781003682530-34

identification of threat-related keywords in communications. To ensure rapid response, Edge AI processes data locally on devices such as smart cameras and drones, enabling analytics without latency. Behavioral analytics adds yet another layer by tracking human movement and interaction patterns to detect loitering, trespassing, or suspicious behavior. Finally, multimodal fusion integrates inputs from video, audio, sensors, and biometrics to create a unified, high-fidelity picture of activity, which is critical for comprehensive situational awareness in environments like smart cities and airports.

Threat of Unauthorized Surveillance in the Age of AI

A new set of threats have been unleashed leveraging different AI technologies. AI-driven tools, such as facial recognition cameras and location trackers, enable continuous, often covert monitoring of individuals without their explicit consent. This mode of data collection violates individuals' fundamental rights to privacy and autonomy, blurring the line between legitimate security needs and intrusive surveillance practices. The shift to AI-driven surveillance systems from traditional modes of surveillance have introduced a new class of threats. These include:

- AI systems now monitor not just actions but intentions, emotions, and inferred beliefs that raise profound ethical concerns about autonomy and mental privacy.
- Individuals are increasingly subjected to algorithmic categorization that influences access to services, opportunities, and even justice—without their knowledge or recourse.
- Existing legal frameworks, rooted in pre-digital paradigms, are ill-equipped to address the velocity, complexity, and opacity of AI-driven surveillance.

Several surveillance technology vendors embed AI in their products, offering advanced capabilities like intelligent video analytics, real-time alerts, and facial recognition. These diverse AI technologies collectively transform traditional surveillance cameras into intelligent, automated security systems capable of continuous environment monitoring with heightened precision and efficiency.

Technology	Primary Applications
Facial Recognition	Real-time identification in law enforcement, border control, and retail security
Object & Weapon Detection	Detection of unattended bags, firearms, or restricted items in public spaces
Emotion & Gait Analysis	Infers emotional states and abnormal walking patterns to anticipate potential threats
Crowd Monitoring	Tracks crowd density, movement flow, and anomalies to prevent stampedes or civil unrest
Autonomous Surveillance	AI-enabled perimeter monitoring, search-and-rescue operations, and tactical

Table 28.1 Surveillance Technologies and Their Applications

Risk Dimension	Description & Implications
Function Creep	Data collected for one purpose (e.g., access control) is repurposed without consent and is used for tracking, profiling, or law enforcement.
Sensitive Inference	Biometric analytics can unintentionally reveal health status, emotional states, or political leanings, often without user awareness.
Demographic Bias	Higher error rates for racial minorities and women lead to wrongful identification and systemic discrimination.
Psychological Impact	Continuous biometric monitoring erodes autonomy, induces stress, and undermines trust in deploying institutions.
Privacy & Governance Gaps	Weak consent protocols and insecure data handling amplify risks, demanding robust regulatory and ethical safeguards.

Table 28.2 The Threat Landscape of Biometrics in AI Surveillance

The absence of strong safeguards in AI-biometric systems presents significant threats to individual privacy. Without rigorous regulatory oversight, these technologies can be deployed across sectors with little accountability, increasing the risk of misuse. A lack of informed consent mechanisms means that users may be unaware of how their biometric data is collected, used, or repurposed, often without the ability to revoke permissions. Insecure data governance mechanisms further compound the issue, exposing sensitive biometric information to breaches and unauthorized access.

AI Surveillance Systems—Ethics and Bias

AI-based surveillance raises critical ethical concerns by challenging the balance between security imperatives and the protection of individual rights and societal values. These systems often operate with minimal transparency, collecting and analyzing vast amounts of personal data—such as facial features, location patterns, and behavioral cues—without explicit consent, thereby eroding privacy and fostering environments of fear and self-censorship. The absence of bias-aware protocols and ethical design frameworks exacerbates the problem, leading to disproportionate misidentification and discrimination against marginalized groups, particularly women and racial minorities. Moreover, the lack of accountability in AI decision-making obscures responsibility when harm occurs, undermining public trust and user autonomy. Together, these issues demand urgent attention to governance, transparency, and human-centric design to ensure that surveillance technologies serve society without compromising its foundational freedoms.

When systems are designed without bias-aware protocols, they tend to disproportionately misidentify or discriminate against marginalized groups, particularly racial minorities and women. Moreover, the absence of ethical architecture such as privacy-by-design and human-centric principles undermines user autonomy and erodes trust in institutions that rely on these technologies. Together, these gaps create a landscape where privacy is routinely compromised, demanding urgent attention to governance, transparency, and ethical design.

AI surveillance systems frequently inherit and amplify social biases embedded in their training data. For example, facial recognition algorithms have been shown to misidentify women and people of color at higher rates, raising concerns about discrimination, wrongful targeting, and unequal treatment under the law. The lack of transparency and accountability within AI decision-making also complicates addressing errors and abuses, as it can be unclear who is responsible when technology harms individuals or communities.

Surveillance in the age of AI demands a reimagining of trust, governance, and the social contract itself: rights-centric, placing citizen agency, informed consent, and digital dignity at its core.

Bibliography

Brundage, M., Avin, S., Clark, J., Toner, H., Eckersley, P., Garfinkel, B., … & Anderson, H. (2018). The malicious use of artificial intelligence: Forecasting, prevention, and mitigation. *arXiv preprint arXiv:1802.07228*. https://arxiv.org/abs/1802.07228

Crawford, K. (2021). *Atlas of AI: Power, Politics, and the Planetary Costs of Artificial Intelligence*. Yale University Press.

Eubanks, V. (2018). *Automating Inequality: How High-Tech Tools Profile, Police, and Punish the Poor*. St. Martin's Press.

Latonero, M. (2018). *Governing Artificial Intelligence: Upholding Human Rights & Dignity*. Data & Society. https://datasociety.net/library/governing-artificial-intelligence/

Lyon, D. (2018). *The Culture of Surveillance: Watching as a Way of Life*. Polity Press.

Mittelstadt, B. D., Allo, P., Taddeo, M., Wachter, S., & Floridi, L. (2016). The ethics of algorithms: Mapping the debate. *Big Data & Society*, 3(2). https://doi.org/10.1177/2053951716679679

Richards, N. M., & King, J. H. (2014). Big data ethics. *Wake Forest Law Review*, 49(2), 393–432.

Zuboff, S. (2019). *The Age of Surveillance Capitalism: The Fight for a Human Future at the New Frontier of Power*. PublicAffairs.

World Economic Forum. (2022). *AI Governance Alliance: Responsible AI Framework*. https://www.weforum.org/agenda/2022/11/responsible-ai-framework-ai-governance-alliance/

29

AI AND USER CONTROL

Shifting Sands: The Erosion of User Control in the Age of AI

"*The real danger is not that computers will begin to think like men, but that men will begin to think like computers.*" (An Analysis of Sydney G. Harris' Popular Quote About Computers and Men | Kibin. n.d.) *Sydney J. Harris*

In earlier computing paradigms, users interacted with machines through clear, tangible interfaces such as keyboards, dashboards, and menus. Control was clearly in human hands; humans issued commands, and machines responded. But today's AI systems, from recommendation engines to autonomous vehicles and smart assistants, often operate invisibly, making decisions based on data patterns, behavioral cues, and predictive algorithms. The user's role shifts from being an active controller to passive participant, sometimes without full knowledge of how or why decisions are being made.

User control is a foundational concern in the development and deployment of AI systems, more so as these technologies are becoming increasingly

DOI: 10.4324/9781003682530-35

autonomous. As machines begin to make decisions without direct human input, it becomes essential to ensure that users retain the ability to guide, override, or audit those decisions. Prime concerns revolve around maintaining safety and accountability. Equally important is transparency and explainability; users must understand how and why an AI system behaves the way it does, otherwise any sense of control becomes superficial and ineffective. Moreover, AI systems must align with human intent by understanding underlying goals and not just interpreting commands literally. The unintended consequences arising from any misalignment can severely undermine trust and utility. There are also ethical boundaries that AI systems could fail to interpret and where a loss of user control in sensitive domains like surveillance, misinformation, or autonomous weaponry could have severe repercussions. Finally, while personalization can empower users by customizing experiences to their preferences, it could lead to exercising undue influence through subtle manipulation. Striking the right balance between helpful adaptation and undue influence is key to preserving genuine user agency in AI-driven environments.

This diminishing of control raises critical concerns. When interfaces become opaque and decisions are automated, users may lose the ability to question, override, or even understand the system's behavior. It challenges all recognized principles of transparency, accountability, and trust. Moreover, as AI systems personalize experiences and adapt in real time, they can subtly shape user behavior often nudging choices, filtering information, and reinforcing habits even without users realizing the extent of influence.

The paradox is that while AI promises convenience and efficiency, it also demands a new kind of watchfulness. Designers must rethink how to embed meaningful control, explainability, and ethical boundaries into systems that are increasingly autonomous. The future of human–AI interaction depends not just on smarter machines, but on smarter ways for humans to remain empowered within them.

Machines operate at a speed and scale far beyond human capability, enabling rapid data processing and decision-making. This efficiency often necessitates delegating control to automated systems, though it introduces trade-offs in transparency and oversight. As AI systems increasingly manage environments of immense complexity such as real-time fraud detection or dynamic pricing, they surpass the limits of manual human intervention.

Yet, their power is matched by their opacity: many models, particularly those based on deep learning, function as black boxes. Even their developers struggle to fully explain how decisions are derived, making accountability a persistent challenge.

Even as machines take over operational control, humans still design, deploy, and define the objectives of these systems. The challenge in this new era is to ensure that control remains firmly aligned with human values, users can exercise meaningful agency over outcomes and that systems are transparent and auditable. Traditionally, humans were *in the loop* by directly controlling systems and making decisions. Now, in many AI applications, humans are *on the loop* through monitoring or occasionally overriding systems that operate largely on their own.

The widespread use of AI systems is rapidly diluting human control. Other than user control, major challenges include guaranteeing data privacy, eliminating bias, and ensuring relatability of outcomes.

User Control in AI Systems: Navigating Autonomy and Agency

Autonomous vehicles are a forerunner in the future of user control on AI systems because they embody the most advanced and visible integration of AI decision-making, human oversight, and real-world accountability.

Operating in complex, dynamic environments, these vehicles must interpret road conditions, predict human behavior, and respond in real time, often without direct human input. Their architecture combines computer vision, sensor fusion, and deep learning, making them a testbed for explainable and controllable AI. Unlike passive systems, autonomous vehicles function in safety-critical contexts, demanding built-in mechanisms for ethical decision-making, regulatory compliance, and user override. At intermediate autonomy levels, users remain part of the decision loop, shaping hybrid control models that balance machine autonomy with human judgment. Moreover, the societal and ethical implications such as liability and moral choices in unavoidable accidents force developers to embed user values and norms into system design. In this way, autonomous vehicles are not just transforming mobility; they are pioneering how AI systems can be governed, trusted, and aligned with human intent.

Level	Name	User Control	Key Features	Challenges & Implications
Level 0–2	Driver Assistance	Human retains full control	Adaptive cruise control, lane-keeping assist, emergency braking	Requires constant supervision; preserves maximum user control with safety enhancements
Level 3	Conditional Automation	Human must be ready to take over when prompted	Vehicle drives under specific conditions; human intervention required on request	"Handoff problem"—humans struggle to regain situational awareness quickly; control ambiguity
Level 4–5	High to Full Automation	Minimal to no human intervention	Vehicle handles all driving tasks; no expectation of human takeover	Raises issues of agency, liability, and autonomy; paradoxically may be safer than Level 3

Table 29.1 Six-Level Autonomy Framework with Gradations of User Control

Source: SAE International—J3016 Taxonomy and Definitions for Terms Related to Driving Automation Systems for On-Road Motor Vehicles

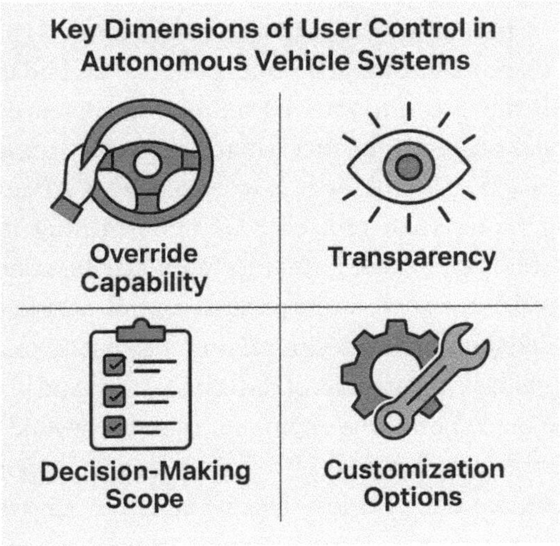

Image 29.1 Key Dimensions of User Control in Autonomous Vehicle Systems

Autonomous vehicles represent perhaps the most visible example of AI systems where control dynamics literally involve life-and-death decisions. Hence, even as autonomy of operation is the goal, user control is essential both in semi-autonomous and fully autonomous vehicles.

A human-centric and safety-centric approach to AI system control is vital for building technologies that are not only intelligent but also trustworthy, ethical, and resilient. Human-centric design begins with user empowerment, ensuring that individuals can understand, influence, and override AI decisions. This preserves autonomy and fosters confidence in the system. Interfaces must be cognitively aligned with human capabilities, especially in high-stakes domains like autonomous driving or healthcare, where overload or confusion can have serious consequences. Ethical responsiveness is equally critical; AI systems must reflect cultural norms, emotional context, and moral reasoning to ensure decisions are grounded in shared human values rather than opaque algorithms.

Complementing this is a safety-centric focus, which emphasizes robustness, redundancy, and graceful degradation to minimize harm even in failure scenarios. Systems must comply with legal standards and industry regulations to ensure public trust and safe deployment. By anticipating edge cases, adversarial inputs, and unintended consequences, safety-centric design helps mitigate risks and prevent catastrophic errors.

The synergy of human-in-the-loop and safety-by-design principles creates AI systems that are accountable, interpretable, and adaptive. This dual approach is not limited to autonomous vehicles; it applies equally to financial platforms, healthcare diagnostics, smart infrastructure, and educational technologies. In each case, the goal is to ensure that AI augments human decision-making rather than replacing or undermining it, reinforcing a future where technology serves humanity with clarity, control, and care.

To resolve this dilemma, we must rethink control paradigms. Meaningful transparency should focus not on technical minutiae but on clear disclosures of AI objectives, accessible explanations of decision factors, and visibility into how user inputs shape outcomes. Value alignment must go beyond superficial control features to embed user interests into system design, supported by business models and regulations that prioritize user welfare over engagement metrics.

Moreover, control should extend beyond individuals to collective and institutional frameworks. Proposals include democratic governance of impactful AI systems, regulatory oversight, third-party audits, and participatory design processes involving user councils. Finally, enhancing control literacy is essential. Users need conceptual understanding of AI, clarity on available control options, and guidance on exercising agency. This calls for better education, intuitive interface design, and perhaps standardized "control disclosures" akin to nutrition labels—making AI systems not just powerful, but also comprehensible and accountable.

Common Control Approaches Across AI Applications

An examination of current approaches to control in AI systems reveals a set of recurring strategies aimed at enabling user control, though each comes with its own limitations. Transparency and explainability are often flaunted as pillars of informed control, yet true transparency is shrouded in technical complexity, proprietary constraints, and users' perceptive limitations. Even when explanations are offered, they may be too abstract or inaccessible to foster genuine understanding.

Consent mechanisms such as opt-in or opt-out features are another common approach, but they frequently fall short of meaningful engagement. For consent to be effective, users must understand the implications of their choices, be offered viable alternatives, and have access to granular controls rather than binary decisions. In practice, these mechanisms often serve more as legal safeguards than as tools of empowerment.

Adjustable autonomy offers a more flexible model, allowing users to calibrate how much control they delegate to AI. Examples include smart home systems with manual overrides, email filters with tunable levels, and content moderation tools with customizable thresholds. This recognizes that optimal autonomy varies by context and user preference.

Human-in-the-loop design reinforces user agency by embedding human oversight into critical decision points. In domains like healthcare, recruitment, and content moderation, AI may assist but not replace human judgment, ensuring that consequential decisions remain under human control while benefiting from AI's efficiency.

Auditing and accountability mechanisms provide users with ways to review and contest AI decisions. Credit scoring systems, advertising platforms, and social media moderation tools increasingly offer explanations and appeal processes. However, these tools are often limited, unwieldly, and ultimately reinforce platform dominance rather than user empowerment.

Underlying all these approaches is a paradox: we want AI systems to be autonomous enough to deliver value by handling complexity, scaling decisions, and operating swiftly, yet they ought to be controllable enough to preserve human agency, ensure alignment with our values, and allow for intervention. These goals are inherently at odds; increasing autonomy often reduces user control, and vice versa.

To resolve this dilemma, we must think of new approaches and control paradigms. Meaningful transparency should focus not on technical intricacies but on clear disclosures of AI objectives, accessible explanations of decision factors, and visibility into how user inputs shape outcomes. Value alignment must go beyond superficial control features to embed user interests into system design, supported by business models and regulations that prioritize user welfare over engagement metrics.

Moreover, control should extend beyond individuals to collective and institutional frameworks. Proposals include democratic governance of impactful AI systems, regulatory oversight, third-party audits, and participatory design processes involving user councils. Finally, enhancing control literacy is essential. Users need conceptual understanding of AI, clarity on available control options, and guidance on exercising agency. This calls for enhancing user awareness, intuitive interface design, and perhaps standardized disclosure of controls such as nutrition labels making AI systems not just powerful, but also comprehensible and accountable.

Bibliography

An Analysis of Sydney G. Harris' Popular Quote About Computers and Men | Kibin. (n.d.). https://www.kibin.com/essay-examples/an-analysis-of-sydney-g-harris-popular-quote-about-computers-and-men-KL7Ipush

30

AI IN SOCIAL MEDIA AND ADVERTISING

The Era of AI in Social Media and Advertising Has Begun

We are firmly entrenched in the era of AI-powered advertising and social media, with 2025 being a critical inflection point in how digital engagement is strategized and executed. In advertising, AI has become the strategic tool driving hyper-personalization at scale. The integration of AI into advertising and social media has reached a transformative scale now, reshaping how brands engage, optimize, and build trust with audiences. In advertising, AI is now central to strategic execution, with 76% of marketing leaders reporting significant improvements in productivity and campaign effectiveness. Nearly half of global digital ad spend (47%) is now optimized through AI algorithms, which enhances targeting accuracy and reduces customer acquisition costs. Companies are leveraging AI for customer data analysis, A/B testing, and email campaigns are outperforming traditional methods. Overall, global spending on AI marketing technologies is projected to reach US$82 billion this year, up from US$67 billion in 2024 (Elad 2025).

DOI: 10.4324/9781003682530-36

AI, especially Generative AI, has profoundly transformed advertising and social media by shifting the focus from static campaigns to dynamic, hyper-personalized experiences. Brands now use Gen AI to generate customized content at scale, from ad copy and product descriptions to influencer-style videos and interactive chatbots, dramatically reducing production time and cost. Platforms like Meta Ads and Adobe Target now dynamically offer content based on real-time user behavior, preferences, and even emotional cues. Predictive analytics further empower marketers to forecast consumer trends and automate campaign adjustments, shifting the paradigm from reactive to proactive marketing. Generative AI is also transforming creative workflows, enabling brands to produce customized ad variations from copy and visuals to voiceovers for niche segments, significantly reducing production costs and boosting conversion rates by up to 30% (Sbiai 2025).

On social media, Gen AI powers real-time engagement through automated responses, sentiment analysis, and predictive targeting, enabling marketers to anticipate user behavior and deliver relevant messages with precision. It also fuels creative experimentation, allowing users and brands alike to co-create memes, filters, and viral content. As a result, advertising has become more conversational, adaptive, and immersive reshaping how audiences connect with brands across platforms. AI-driven and video-first has become a norm on social media. Short-form videos under 15 seconds, especially on platforms like TikTok and Instagram, are achieving up to 80% higher completion rates, with AI-optimizing hooks and calls-to-action for virality (Sbiai 2025). Influencers are evolving into AI-integrated creators, producing meta-content that not only entertains but educates audiences about AI itself, establishing new forms of digital engagement. Meanwhile, there is a grudging acceptance of ethical data practices to address rising privacy concerns. Brands are adopting transparent opt-in models and value exchanges such as offering exclusive content in return for data to align with emerging regulatory frameworks and build digital trust.

Given the overwhelming advantages for marketeers leveraging social media, it is not surprising that AI is powering over 80% of content recommendations, dramatically improving user retention and platform engagement. Businesses using AI for social media management report engagement rate improvements between 15% and 25%, translating into measurable revenue gains. Influencer marketing is also being reshaped, with 35% of investments now guided by AI, from identifying the right creators to optimizing campaign performance. Sentiment analysis tools powered by AI have enhanced brand campaign engagement by 25%, while real-time bidding systems have improved cost efficiency by 19% (Smith 2025). These figures reflect the strategic importance of AI not just as a technical capability, but as a foundational layer for personalization, and performance in the digital economy.

Recommendation Systems: The Illusion of Control

Recommendation algorithms are now deeply embedded across platforms, from Netflix's content suggestions to curated social media feeds and personalized e-commerce experiences. Users are increasingly embracing these systems, drawn to their ability to streamline decision-making, save time, and even reinforce the rationale behind their choices. Whether discovering a new show, product, or influencer, AI-powered recommendations are shaping user journeys with precision and convenience. Studies show that over 80% of consumer-facing companies now integrate AI-driven recommendations, with users reporting improved experiences in content discovery and decision-making (Smith 2025). Here, the risks are not physical safety but rather manipulation and loss of agency over one's information environment.

Most platforms offer users some apparent control mechanisms such as thumbs up/down buttons, "not interested" options, or rating systems that seemingly allow users to shape their recommendations. However, these inputs are just one factor among hundreds of factors that algorithms consider, and users rarely understand how their feedback actually influences outcomes. Users are also given options to indicate interests, block certain content types, or adjust privacy settings. Yet, the actual impact of these choices often remains opaque, and platforms may override user preferences when their business model benefits from doing so. Similarly, options to hide, block, or report content provide a sense of control, though they are typically reactive rather than proactive control mechanisms.

The basic problem with recommendation systems is that users do not truly understand what they are controlling. The algorithms operate as black boxes, incorporating thousands of elements such as your behavior, similar users' behavior, content characteristics, business objectives, and more. Here, even the engineers who built them cannot fully predict or explain the outputs. For example, when you tell Netflix you dislike a show, you are providing one data point that gets weighted against your viewing duration, completion rates, pause patterns, time of day, device used, and countless other factors. Your feeling of control may be illusory and may be overwhelmed by the implicit behavioral data the system collects automatically.

Recommendation systems present structural limitations that often undermine genuine user control. These include asymmetric information where platforms understand their algorithms, but users do not. This makes informed choices nearly impossible. Systems are optimized for engagement metrics like dwell time or clicks, which often are conflicting with user autonomy. Moreover, behavioral manipulation tactics exploit psychological triggers, nudging user behavior while giving the illusion of choice. Even opting out by leaving a platform is costly due to network effects and ecosystem lock-in, further defeating any form of meaningful control.

Surprisingly, even where attempts like offering chronological feeds were made to restore user agency, it has been observed that users frequently return to algorithmic curation, either because it genuinely adds value, has become indispensable, or because platform design subtly nudges them back. This creates a paradox: while users desire control, they also crave the efficiency and personalization that AI algorithms provide. Thus, the prevailing tension between autonomy and algorithmic convenience remains unresolved, highlighting a deeper challenge in designing systems that respect user agency without sacrificing usability.

Challenges and Solutions

AI's integration into social media and advertising brings a host of challenges, from privacy violations and algorithmic bias to the erosion of human creativity. Heavy reliance on personal data raises concerns about surveillance and data breaches, while biased training sets can result in discriminatory ad targeting and stereotype reinforcement. AI-generated content often lacks deeper emotional understanding, which contributes to impersonal user experiences. Furthermore, misinformation can be amplified by bots, and automation, giving rise to ethical dilemmas that are centered around behavioral manipulation and targeting vulnerable users.

This is further compounded by unreliable algorithms that misclassify or distort content.

To address these issues, a balanced approach is essential. Human–AI collaboration can preserve creativity while leveraging AI's efficiency for repetitive tasks. Bias mitigation can be addressed through rigorous audits and use of diverse datasets along with robust privacy safeguards. Organizational redlines based on their ethical values must be clearly articulated and aligned with broader societal values. Improving algorithm reliability through human oversight and continuous refinement, coupled with education for marketers and developers, ensures responsible deployment. Collectively, these strategies can unlock AI's potential in social media and advertising while minimizing its risks.

Bibliography

Elad, B. (2025, October 7). AI in marketing statistics 2025: ROI, tools & trends. *SQ Magazine*. https://sqmagazine.co.uk/ai-in-marketing-statistics/

Sbiai, F. (2025). AI-powered recommendation systems: Exploring their impact on customer-business interaction. *International Journal of Innovative Science and Research Technology*, 1332–1339. https://doi.org/10.38124/ijisrt/25apr623

Smith, J. (2025, February 1). *AI for Social Media Statistics 2025*. Saufter AI. https://saufter.io/ai-for-social-media-statistics/

31

EMERGING SOLUTIONS FOR TRUSTWORTHY AI

Developing Trustworthy AI Ecosystems

Fostering a trustworthy AI ecosystem is a key priority because trust is the foundation upon which sustainable, inclusive, and impactful AI adoption depends. As AI systems increasingly influence decisions in finance, healthcare, education, governance, and everyday life, users, regulators, and institutions must feel confident that these technologies operate transparently, ethically, and securely.

Without trust, AI adoption will repeatedly experience stalls as it will face users' resistance, greater restrictive control, and regulatory oversight. A trustworthy ecosystem ensures that data is collected with consent, algorithms are explainable and fair, and outcomes are aligned with societal values. It also mitigates risks such as bias, surveillance overreach, misinformation, and cybercrime, which can erode public confidence and cause systemic harm.

Moreover, in global contexts where digital sovereignty, privacy, and ethical governance are paramount, trust becomes a strategic asset. It enables

DOI: 10.4324/9781003682530-37

cross-border collaboration, responsible innovation, and the scaling of AI solutions that respect human rights and democratic norms. In short, trust is not a lofty ideal, it is an essential prerequisite for AI to fulfill its promise as a transformative force for good.

Trust is non-negotiable. Yet in the race to innovate, digital systems have historically prioritized features, speed, and functionality over foundational principles like transparency, accountability, and user agency. AI, with its immense potential and complexity, exemplifies this tension.

From predictive algorithms in healthcare to recommendation engines in social media, AI systems are often designed to optimize performance metrics such as accuracy, engagement, conversion without fully accounting for how they impact user trust. Data is collected invisibly, decisions are made opaquely, and users are frequently left out of the loop. This creates a paradox: the more powerful AI becomes, the more critical trust becomes; yet the very architecture of many AI systems undermines it.

Consider how personalization in advertising can morph into manipulation, or how surveillance tools can erode privacy under the guise of security. These are not just technical oversights; they are systemic design choices that reflect a misalignment between innovation and ethical stewardship. Trust, in this context, isn't a feature; it is a prerequisite. It demands explainability, consent, fairness, and resilience.

To course-correct, AI systems must embed trust as a design principle, not a retrofit. That means building with transparency from the ground up, enabling user control, ensuring data dignity, and aligning outcomes with societal values. In short, trust must become the architecture and not remain an aspiration of AI.

While addressing concerns at design stage is the best way to enhance trust and security of AI systems, in reality, we have to depend on a patchwork of solutions to 'bolt-on' trust mechanisms and frameworks. These include frameworks for informed consent and data transparency, ensuring users understand what data is being collected and how it is used. Ethical AI surveillance models to balance security with civil liberties, emphasizing accountability, bias mitigation, and human oversight. Advances in data anonymization, such as differential privacy and federated learning, to protect individual identities while enabling robust analytics. Simultaneously, creation of tools that enhance user control over AI systems, from algorithmic explainability to opt-out mechanisms, empowering individuals to reclaim agency and control in digital environments. In the realm of social media and advertising, regulatory and technical interventions are targeting manipulative practices, promoting ethical targeting, and curbing misinformation. These efforts do signal that as AI evolves key concerns within AI systems are being addressed based on their strategic relevance, technical depth, and ethical implications.

Top 10 Emerging Solutions for Building Trustworthy AI Systems

Solutions aimed at mitigating the negative implications of AI systems such as bias, misinformation, surveillance, and job displacement are emerging across technical, regulatory, and ethical domains. However, many of these interventions still resemble patchwork efforts rather than comprehensive safeguards. While tools like explainable AI, differential privacy, and adversarial testing offer promise, their scalability and maturity remain uneven. Similarly, policy frameworks such as the EU AI Act, and NIST's AI Risk Management Framework provide important direction but often lack global coherence and enforceability. China's Generative AI Regulatory Framework includes mandatory labeling of AI-generated content effective September 1, 2025. This involves the use of explicit labels in the form of clearly visible tags for text, audio, images, video, and virtual scenes and implicit labels that embed metadata to identify AI-generated content.

The deeper challenge lies in aligning stakeholders, including developers, regulators, educators, and civil society, around shared principles of digital trust, transparency, and resilience. Without systemic integration of these principles, AI systems risk becomes reactive rather than transformative. To move beyond patchwork, we must embed robust safeguards into AI architectures, foster collaborative governance, and scale pedagogical efforts that empower both decision-makers and citizens to navigate the AI landscape responsibly. Here are top 10 emerging solutions that can bridge the trust gap if integrated properly into an enterprise IT framework that on the one hand wants to address concerns related to AI systems and on the other hand also wishes to leverage AI to enhance trust:

1. AI-Powered Threat Detection and Response

   When AI systems are deployed within insecure enterprise IT environments, they become vulnerable to a wide array of threat vectors that can compromise both operational integrity and strategic outcomes. These risks extend far beyond conventional cybersecurity concerns. Hackers are increasingly relying on AI-enhanced tools to automate attacks and also develop advanced tactics to launch sophisticated attacks Attackers may manipulate training data, corrupt model parameters, or exploit algorithmic weaknesses to skew outputs, introduce bias, or trigger unintended behaviors. Such manipulations can lead to flawed decision-making, reputational damage, regulatory violations, and even systemic failure in critical domains like finance, healthcare, or national infrastructure.

Implementing AI-powered threat detection and response systems must happen before deploying sophisticated AI systems that handle core business operational tasks. For example, a global logistics firm used AI-driven Security Information & Event Management tools to detect and neutralize a polymorphic malware attack in real-time, preventing operational shutdown.

2. Behavioral Biometrics and Advanced Identity Verification

   Unlike traditional authentication methods, behavioral biometrics use unique user traits such as typing cadence, mouse movements, and navigation habits that can be used to continuously verify identity. Combined with AI-driven facial recognition, voice analysis, and digital ID verification, these systems offer robust protection against impersonation, deepfakes, and credential theft. They also support adaptive access control, triggering additional verification when anomalies are detected.

3. AI-Driven Zero Trust Architecture (ZTA)

   The concept of Zero Trust has been around for a while. ZTA is a Zero Trust concept that operates on the principle of "never trust, always verify." Every access request, whether from a user, device, or application is treated as potentially hostile until proven otherwise. This involves rigorous identity verification, least-privilege access controls, micro-segmentation of networks, and continuous monitoring of behavior and context. The goal is to minimize the attack surface and limit lateral movement within systems, especially in today's distributed environments where cloud, mobile, and remote work have blurred traditional boundaries.

   Despite its strategic appeal, widespread adoption of Zero Trust has been slow. Many organizations are hampered by legacy infrastructure that lacks the flexibility for granular access control or dynamic policy enforcement. Implementation complexity, high costs, and fragmented ownership across departments further complicate the transition. Security, compliance, and business units often operate in silos, making coordinated execution difficult. As a result, Zero Trust often remains a conceptual aspiration rather than an operational reality.

An emerging solution in the form of AI-driven Zero Trust can be transformative. Artificial intelligence enables real-time anomaly detection, predictive threat modeling, and automated response mechanisms that traditional systems struggle to deliver. Machine-learning algorithms can analyze vast telemetry data to enforce adaptive access policies based on behavioral patterns and contextual risk. In essence, AI turns Zero Trust from a static framework into a living, intelligent defense system, one that evolves with threats and adapts to organizational needs. Hence, AI-powered ZTA offers a compelling blueprint for resilience, agility, and trust in the digital age.

4. Deepfake & NLP-Based Threat Detection

A major concern around the world today relates to the way Gen AI enables hyper-realistic deception across media formats. The rampant misuse of Gen AI has left us vulnerable to AI-driven misinformation, fraud, and social engineering. AI-powered deepfake detection algorithms can be effectively used to analyze pixel-level inconsistencies, voice modulation, and facial dynamics to identify manipulated media. In parallel, NLP models can scrutinize email content, tone, and intent to flag phishing attempts and malicious communications. These tools are vital in combating social engineering, misinformation, and fraud. For example, a news outlet could use deepfake detection algorithms to identify manipulated political videos before they went viral, preserving public trust.

Generative AI can fabricate convincing falsehoods at scale. Platforms can now deploy AI models trained to detect hallucinations, misinformation, and coordinated disinformation campaigns. Fact-checking APIs, provenance tagging (e.g., C2PA standards), and watermarking of AI-generated content are emerging to verify authenticity. The C2PA standards have been developed by the Coalition for Content Provenance and Authenticity and represents an open technical framework designed to verify the authenticity and origin of digital content.

In today's world, this is essential for safeguarding democratic discourse, media integrity, and public trust in AI-generated content.

5. Ethical AI Surveillance Frameworks

   AI surveillance systems must balance public safety with individual rights. Emerging frameworks emphasize transparency, accountability, and bias mitigation. There are as yet no specific ethical guidelines with regard to AI-driven surveillance systems. Till such time globally accepted guidelines evolve, we must ensure that surveillance tools respect civil liberties, avoid discriminatory outcomes, and include mechanisms for redress and oversight. These are critical in contexts like smart cities, border control, and law enforcement.

   When applied to AI-driven surveillance, generic ethical AI frameworks offer essential guardrails to ensure that such systems are not only effective but also just, transparent, and accountable. For example, the EU Guidelines for Trustworthy AI emphasize human oversight, technical robustness, and fairness, principles that directly counter risks like biased facial recognition, opaque decision-making, or unchecked data collection. AI4People's focus on beneficence and non-maleficence reinforces the need for surveillance systems to serve public good without causing harm, while explicability ensures that individuals can understand how and why they are being monitored.

6. Federated Learning and Synthetic Data Generation

   Federated learning offers a decentralized approach to training machine-learning models that addresses data privacy, which is one of the most pressing challenges in AI. Traditionally, AI systems require centralized access to vast amounts of user data that are often collected from mobile devices, sensors, or enterprise systems. This centralization poses significant privacy risks, including unauthorized access, data breaches, and regulatory non-compliance. Federated learning flips this model by allowing AI algorithms to be trained locally on edge devices, with only model updates (not raw data) shared back to a central server. This ensures that sensitive data such as personal health records, financial transactions, or behavioral patterns never leave the user's device. Synthetic data generation, meanwhile, creates artificial datasets that mimic statistical properties of real data but contain no personal identifiers, offering a privacy-compliant alternative for model training and testing.

7. Homomorphic Encryption

   Homomorphic encryption (HE) offers a powerful advancement in AI data security by enabling computations directly on encrypted data, ensuring that sensitive information like medical or financial records remains protected even during processing. This capability is especially valuable for AI systems operating in cloud or third-party environments where data exposure risks are high.

However, fully HE faces practical limitations, including significant performance overhead and complex implementation requirements involving specialized cryptographic libraries and expert knowledge. As of now, these challenges have constrained its adoption in high-throughput AI applications such as real-time inference and large-scale model training even as regulatory support and hardware innovations are helping to bridge the gap. HE is currently best deployed as part of a layered-security strategy to enable privacy-preserving and resilient AI systems.

8. Dynamic Consent and Consent Management Platforms

   Traditional one-time consent models are being replaced by dynamic frameworks that allow users to update, revoke, or refine permissions over time. AI-powered platforms personalize privacy settings, adapt to regulatory changes, and manage consent for unstructured data (e.g., images, audio). These systems enhance user autonomy and enable regulatory compliance, especially under laws like GDPR, CCPA, and India's DPDP Act. These dynamic consent models restore user agency and also align with global privacy norms.

9. Unified Access Control and Permission Optimization

   In the context of AI security, next-generation permission management involves Unified Access Control and Permission Optimization represents a shift from static, role-based models to dynamic, context-aware governance. Traditional systems often rely on predefined access rules that are rigid and siloed, making them vulnerable to insider threats, privilege escalation, and compliance gaps. As AI systems become more pervasive and autonomous, managing who can access what, when, and under what conditions becomes a critical security challenge.

   Unified Access Control centralizes policy enforcement across diverse environments such as cloud, edge, enterprise while ensuring consistent and auditable permissions. Permission Optimization adds intelligence by adapting access rights based on behavioral signals, risk profiles, and operational context. This means permissions are no longer binary or permanent; they evolve in real-time to reflect trust levels, usage patterns, and threat indicators. These approaches reduce attack surfaces, prevent over-privileged access, and align AI operations with privacy and compliance mandates. They represent a foundational upgrade in securing AI systems, making access governance as dynamic and intelligent as the models themselves.

10. AI-Enhanced Social Media and Advertising Governance

Emerging solutions in AI-driven advertising are reshaping digital marketing by embedding ethical principles and adaptive intelligence into campaign design and delivery. Ethical targeting involves using consent-based data, contextual signals, and privacy-preserving techniques (such as differential privacy or federated analytics) to ensure that ads are relevant without being intrusive or manipulative. This marks a shift from behavioral profiling to value-aligned engagement, where users are targeted based on declared preferences, real-time context, and platform-specific norms.

Real-time ad adaptation leverages AI to dynamically tailor creative assets, messaging, and delivery timing based on user interaction, sentiment, and environmental cues. For instance, an ad may adjust its tone or format depending on whether the user is browsing casually or actively searching for a product. This responsiveness enhances relevance while respecting user autonomy. Meanwhile, cross-platform campaign integrity ensures that messaging remains consistent, compliant, and brand-safe across diverse channels such as social media, mobile apps, streaming platforms, and web environments. AI tools also monitor performance, flag anomalies, and harmonize content delivery to prevent fragmentation or misuse. All these innovations used appropriately can create a more respectful, intelligent, and accountable advertising ecosystem.

While a growing number of solutions are being developed to tackle AI-related concerns ranging from bias mitigation and data privacy to algorithmic transparency and accountability, a truly comprehensive framework that seamlessly integrates technological safeguards, ethical principles, and legal compliance remains elusive. Most current efforts tend to address these dimensions in isolation: technologists focus on robustness and explainability, ethicists advocate for fairness and human-centric design, and regulators enforce compliance through evolving data protection laws. However, without a unified structure that harmonizes these domains, AI governance risks fragmentation, inconsistency, and limited enforceability.

What is needed is an integrated framework that treats technology, ethics, and law not as parallel tracks but as interdependent pillars of responsible AI. Such a framework would embed ethical reasoning into system design, ensure legal mandates are operationalized through technical controls, and promote transparency and accountability across the AI lifecycle, from data collection and model training to deployment and impact assessment. It would also support adaptive governance, enabling organizations to respond to emerging risks, societal expectations, and regulatory shifts in real-time. Until this convergence is achieved, AI systems will continue to operate in a patchwork of partial safeguards, leaving gaps in trust, fairness, and long-term resilience.

Bibliography

AI Watch: Global Regulatory Tracker - China. (2025, May 29). *White & Case LLP International Law Firm, Global Law Practice.* https://www.whitecase.com/insight-our-thinking/ai-watch-global-regulatory-tracker-china

SECTION 7

ORGANIZATIONAL ALIGNMENT

As AI becomes a core strategic capability, organizations can no longer treat it as a series of isolated pilot projects or departmental experiments. A mature AI program requires a coordinated, cross-functional governance structure—one that integrates legal, technical, security, compliance, privacy, and operational stakeholders under a unified framework. This section provides a practical blueprint for how different teams within the enterprise contribute to responsible AI implementation, and how their efforts must be aligned to ensure both innovation and accountability.

This section is organized by key stakeholder functions, leading to a final synthesis of the governance model:

- **Chapter 32: Legal Team**—defines legal counsel's role in regulatory interpretation, liability management, contracts, and risk mitigation strategies.
- **Chapter 33: Chief Technology Officer (CTO)**—covers AI strategy, architecture decisions, and execution oversight from a technology leadership perspective.

DOI: 10.4324/9781003682530-38

- **Chapter 34: IT Governance & the Chief Data Officer (CDO)**—focuses on data stewardship, governance policies, and responsible data lifecycle management.
- **Chapter 35: Cybersecurity Team**—outlines security responsibilities for protecting AI systems from adversarial threats and ensuring operational resilience.
- **Chapter 36: IT Operations Team**—details system integration, infrastructure management, deployment pipelines, and ongoing performance monitoring.
- **Chapter 37: Compliance Team**—addresses alignment with frameworks such as NIST, ISO, GDPR, EU AI Act, and sectoral regulations.
- **Chapter 38: Privacy Team**—ensures data rights, ethical use, consent management, and privacy-by-design implementation.
- **Chapter 39: Project Management**—orchestrates coordination, governance cadence, stakeholder accountability, and operational execution.
- **Chapter 40: HR & Training**—manages AI literacy, responsible AI training, change management, and workforce readiness.
- **Chapter 41: Pulling It All Together**—synthesizes these functions into a scalable, interoperable enterprise AI operating model.

This section serves as a practical implementation guide for organizations seeking to operationalize AI responsibly—translating strategy into disciplined execution across every domain of the enterprise.

32

THE ROLE OF THE CHIEF TECHNOLOGY OFFICER IN CYBERSECURITY AND AI

Introduction

The Chief Technology Officer (CTO) plays a pivotal role in shaping an organization's technology vision, particularly as artificial intelligence (AI) and cybersecurity converge in today's digital enterprises. As threats grow more complex and AI becomes embedded in every facet of business, the CTO is not only a technical leader but also a strategic executive responsible for balancing innovation, resilience, compliance, and trust.

This chapter explores the evolving responsibilities of the CTO in overseeing AI-driven architectures and cybersecurity strategies, and highlights the leadership, governance, and execution duties that define this critical role.

Strategic Responsibilities of the CTO

- Define and execute the enterprise technology strategy with integrated AI and cybersecurity priorities
- Guide digital transformation efforts through secure AI-driven innovation

DOI: 10.4324/9781003682530-39

- Drive the adoption of emerging technologies such as machine learning, zero trust, and edge computing
- Ensure alignment of technology initiatives with regulatory and risk management frameworks
- Represent technology concerns in executive decision-making and board-level discussions.

Oversight of Cybersecurity Functions

The CTO often has direct or dotted-line oversight over the Chief Information Security Officer (CISO) or cybersecurity leadership. In this capacity, the CTO must:

- Integrate cybersecurity into product and platform design (security by design)
- Support secure software development life cycles (SSDLC)
- Ensure threat modeling, vulnerability management, and cloud security strategies are embedded
- Oversee identity, access, and data protection architectures
- Respond to major security incidents and support business continuity planning.

AI Governance and Deployment Leadership

As AI adoption scales, the CTO must ensure responsible AI development and deployment practices across the organization. Key responsibilities include:

- Define AI strategy aligned with business and ethical goals
- Oversee MLOps, model lifecycle management, and infrastructure scaling
- Collaborate with legal, risk, and compliance teams to enforce AI governance policies
- Lead initiatives on explainability, bias mitigation, and adversarial robustness.

CTO as a Cross-Functional Leader

To successfully lead AI and cybersecurity initiatives, the CTO must work collaboratively across functions:

- With the CISO: to ensure a cohesive risk-based security strategy
- With the CIO: to align infrastructure, data, and operations
- With Product Teams: to embed AI securely into offerings
- With Legal and Compliance: to navigate regulatory challenges
- With Data Science Leaders: to ensure scalable, trustworthy AI development.

CTO Role in Innovation and Vendor Ecosystem

CTOs play a key role in managing relationships with vendors, startups, and partners in the cyber and AI space. Their role includes:

- Evaluating and selecting secure, scalable AI and cybersecurity platforms
- Driving innovation programs, pilots, and proof-of-concept initiatives
- Representing the organization in standards bodies, consortia, and regulatory dialogues.

Skills and Attributes of a Modern Cyber-AI CTO

- Deep understanding of AI technologies, cybersecurity architectures, and regulatory frameworks
- Strategic vision with the ability to align tech with business value
- Strong communication skills to convey technical risks and opportunities to executives
- Leadership acumen to manage interdisciplinary teams
- Familiarity with frameworks such as NIST CSF, ISO/IEC 27001, AI RMF, and EU AI Act.

Training for the CTO on AI Governance, Security, and Risk

Training for the CTO on AI Governance, Security, and Risk

CTOs play a central role in the safe and effective deployment of AI systems within organizations. To fulfill this role responsibly, CTOs need comprehensive training that spans technical, legal, ethical, and risk domains. Below are key training areas CTOs should prioritize:

1. AI Governance Fundamentals
   CTOs must be fluent in leading AI governance frameworks such as the NIST AI Risk Management Framework (RMF), ISO/IEC 42001 (AI Management Systems), and the EU AI Act. Training should include principles of risk identification, proportional controls, auditability, and the difference between high-risk and general-purpose AI systems.
2. Cybersecurity for AI Systems
   CTOs should receive training on how AI systems introduce new threat vectors, including adversarial ML, model inversion attacks, and data poisoning. Collaborating with CISOs, CTOs must learn to embed AI-specific controls into the existing cybersecurity architecture.
3. Data Privacy and Governance
   Since AI systems depend heavily on data, CTOs should understand privacy regulations like GDPR, CCPA, HIPAA, and best practices for data minimization, anonymization, and data lineage tracking.
4. AI Lifecycle Oversight
   CTOs must be trained to supervise the full AI lifecycle:
   - Data Acquisition: Ensure datasets are lawfully sourced and ethically annotated.
   - Model Training: Validate training environments for security, fairness, and reproducibility.
   - Deployment: Confirm safe release practices, including red teaming, testing, and rollback plans.
   - Post-Deployment Monitoring: Implement model drift detection, risk flagging, and continuous impact audits.
5. Third-Party Risk in AI Supply Chains
   With many organizations integrating AI models or APIs from external vendors, CTOs must be able to evaluate third-party AI risks,

demand documentation (e.g., model cards), and negotiate contractual clauses ensuring explainability and audit access.

6. Incident Response for AI Failures

   CTOs should be trained in leading or co-leading incident response plans for AI-specific failures, such as unintended bias outcomes, hallucinations, or data leakage through generative models.

7. Cross-Functional Collaboration Skills

   Training should also enhance CTOs' ability to work with Legal, Privacy, Compliance, Product, and Audit teams—especially in documenting impact assessments and alignment with governance standards.

8. Where to Get Trained
   - Executive Certificate Programs from institutions like Pace University, Seton Hall University, or Oxford, focused on AI and ethics. www.cyberintelu.online
   - Industry Associations such as IEEE, ISACA, or IAPP offering targeted courses on AI compliance
   - In-House Trainings from legal, AI ethics, or compliance experts
   - Public Framework Workshops by NIST, ISO, or regional regulatory agencies.

Conclusion

In an age of digital acceleration, the CTO is no longer just a technologist—they are a steward of innovation, risk, and responsible AI integration. Balancing growth with governance, and cutting-edge technologies with cybersecurity best practices, the modern CTO plays a foundational role in enabling organizations to thrive securely in a data-driven, AI-enabled world.

Bibliography

Gartner. (2024). *The Strategic Role of the CTO in AI-Driven Organizations.*

Harvard Business Review. (2023). *How CTOs Can Lead Secure Innovation in AI and Cyber.*

ISO/IEC. (2023). *27001 and 23894 Standards.*

McKinsey & Co. (2024). *The Rise of the AI-Enabled CTO.*

NIST. (2023). *AI Risk Management Framework* (AI RMF) 1.0.

World Economic Forum. (2023). *Global Cybersecurity Outlook.*

33

CYBERSECURITY AND AI LEGAL TEAM ROLES

As artificial intelligence (AI) becomes foundational to digital transformation, it also creates complex legal and regulatory challenges—especially when integrated with cybersecurity operations. Legal teams now find themselves at the intersection of innovation, risk, and compliance. From ensuring ethical AI use to managing regulatory investigations after data breaches, legal professionals are pivotal in shaping how organizations govern AI and cyber risk.

This chapter expands on the evolving responsibilities of the legal function in a cyber-AI landscape. It presents a multi-disciplinary view of how General Counsel (GC), AI/cyber legal advisers, privacy counsel, and IP lawyers collaborate with security, compliance, and engineering teams to build trust and avoid liability.

Evolving Legal Challenges in Cyber and AI

Legal teams must adapt to new risk categories and operational complexity brought by AI. Some key challenges include:

DOI: 10.4324/9781003682530-40

- Regulatory Complexity and Fragmentation: Organizations must comply with overlapping regulations like the EU AI Act, GDPR, US Executive Order on AI, China's AI regulation, and Brazil's LGPD, often with conflicting requirements. For example, a company using facial recognition in Europe must navigate both data minimization (GDPR) and high-risk classification (EU AI Act).
- AI Liability and Autonomy: If an AI system makes a harmful decision (e.g., denying a loan, misdiagnosing a patient, causing a cyberattack through automation), legal teams must consider whether the developer, deployer, or model provider is responsible. Courts and regulators are actively shaping case law on "AI accountability."
- Third-Party Risks and Shadow AI: The use of third-party AI services raises IP, data leakage, and misuse concerns. For example, a marketing team uploading sensitive data into an unvetted AI tool can trigger both data breach liability and contract violations.
- Cybersecurity Incidents Involving AI: AI systems may be targets (e.g., model inversion, adversarial inputs) or vectors (e.g., AI-generated phishing). Legal must advise on breach notification, cross-border investigations, and eDiscovery risks.

Core Legal Roles in Cybersecurity and AI

- GC or Chief Legal Officer (CLO): Drives legal strategy on AI and cybersecurity. Advises the board and champions AI governance. For instance, the CLO of an insurer may convene an AI Risk Committee to evaluate LLM usage in claims processing.
- AI and Cybersecurity Legal Counsel: Interprets AI/cyber laws and ensures compliance in model and dataset reviews. For example, legal ensures a chatbot doesn't store PII illegally.
- Incident Response Legal Adviser: Coordinates breach disclosures under laws like the SEC's 4-day rule or NIS2. After a medical AI attack, legal would coordinate HIPAA disclosures.
- Privacy Counsel / DPO: Ensures AI and cyber efforts align with privacy laws (e.g., GDPR, HIPAA), advises on PETs, and reviews model risk. For example, using synthetic data in model testing.
- IP and Tech Transactions Counsel: Manages AI-related contracts, licensing, and open-source risk. Ensures IP protection for models and datasets. Drafts AI-specific indemnity and transparency clauses.

Legal Collaboration Across Teams

Legal teams must collaborate across business units:

- With Cybersecurity: Jointly review incident response plans and ransomware policies.
- With AI/ML Engineering: Conduct algorithm risk assessments and help ensure traceability.
- With Compliance and Audit: Review model inventories and classification under regulatory frameworks (e.g., EU AI Act).
- With Procurement: Standardize contract language for transparency, audit rights, and risk sharing with AI vendors.

Legal Responsibilities Across the AI Lifecycle

To ensure robust AI governance, legal professionals must be involved at each critical phase of the AI lifecycle. Below is a structured view of how legal engagement supports responsible AI development and deployment:

1. **Data Acquisition**
   - **Legal Focus Areas:**
     - Review data sources for lawful basis of collection, including consent, contracts, and regulatory exemptions.
     - Assess cross-border transfer implications and data localization mandates (e.g., China's PIPL, GDPR).
     - Evaluate IP ownership of datasets (e.g., scraped data from public platforms may violate terms of service or copyright).
   - **Illustrative Example:**
     - A voice assistant company collecting user voice data across regions must validate consent language across jurisdictions and ensure that biometric data laws (like Illinois' BIPA) are not violated.
2. **Model Training**
   - **Legal Focus Areas:**
     - Vet datasets for compliance with privacy, IP, and discrimination laws.
     - Conduct algorithmic bias assessments to avoid discriminatory outcomes.

    - Ensure appropriate licensing or rights for any third-party datasets or pre-trained models.
  - **Illustrative Example:**
    - Legal must review contracts when using foundation models like GPT or Stable Diffusion to ensure commercial use rights and indemnity provisions are clearly defined.
3. **Model Deployment**
  - **Legal Focus Areas:**
    - Review product terms, disclaimers, and user-facing documentation for accuracy and transparency.
    - Define contractual liability if models generate inaccurate or harmful outputs.
    - Ensure compliance with AI-specific regulations (e.g., risk tier classification under the EU AI Act).
  - **Illustrative Example:**
    - A bank deploying a credit scoring AI must disclose logic to regulators and ensure mechanisms for customer recourse, per Article 22 of GDPR and fairness mandates in the EU AI Act.
4. **Post-Deployment Monitoring**
  - **Legal Focus Areas:**
    - Collaborate on incident response plans for AI-related failures (e.g., hallucinations, model drift, cybersecurity exploits).
    - Define model change management policies with audit logs and documentation for regulators.
    - Prepare legal responses to government inquiries and data subject requests.
  - **Illustrative Example:**
    - After a generative model falsely generates defamatory information, legal coordinates takedown processes, responds to data subject complaints, and advises on litigation exposure.

Training Needs for Legal Professionals

As the legal landscape surrounding AI and cybersecurity becomes increasingly complex, legal professionals must pursue ongoing education to stay informed and effective. Training in the following areas is crucial:

1. AI and Machine Learning Fundamentals—Understanding basic AI concepts, types of models, and how algorithms function.

2. Data Privacy and Protection—Familiarity with GDPR, CCPA, and other global privacy regulations relevant to AI-driven systems.
3. Cybersecurity Law—Comprehensive knowledge of breach notification laws, incident response policies, and critical infrastructure protection.
4. Ethics and Bias in AI—Exploring fairness, transparency, accountability, and explainability issues in AI.
5. Contracting for AI Systems—Understanding unique provisions around IP ownership, liability, model explainability, and data use.

Recommended Training Pathways

– Online certifications such as Pace University: AI Governance Certification, Seton Hall University: AI Governance Certification. www.cyberintelu.online
– CLE programs on AI governance, digital compliance, and tech law.
– Internal training programs developed in collaboration with cybersecurity and data science teams.

Looking Forward: Legal Team's Role in Responsible AI

As AI regulations evolve, legal teams must shape governance policies, anticipate litigation risk, and define AI due diligence practices. Upskilling in adversarial ML, lifecycle oversight, and cross-border digital laws will be essential.

Conclusion

Legal teams are no longer just a backstop—they are enablers of safe innovation. By understanding cybersecurity threats, model behavior, and global legal frameworks, legal professionals help organizations deploy trustworthy technology with minimized liability.

Bibliography

European Commission. (2023). *EU AI Act*.

GDPR (General Data Protection Regulation). European Parliament and Council of the European Union. (2016). *Regulation (EU) 2016/679 of the European Parliament and of the Council* on the protection of natural persons with regard to the processing of personal data and on the free movement of such data (General Data Protection Regulation)*. Official Journal of the European Union, L 119, 1–88. https://eur-lex.europa.eu/legal-content/EN/TXT/?uri=CELEX:32016R0679

ISO /IEC 42001:2023 *Artificial Intelligence Management System.*

NIST. (2023). *AI Risk Management Framework.*

SEC. (2023). *Cybersecurity Disclosure Rule.*

U.S. Executive Order on Safe, Secure, and Trustworthy AI (2023).

34

THE ROLE OF IT GOVERNANCE AND THE CHIEF DATA OFFICER IN AI

Introduction

Artificial Intelligence (AI) has emerged as a transformative force across industries, offering opportunities for automation, innovation, and competitive advantage. Yet, with great power comes significant responsibility. AI systems are only as effective, trustworthy, and secure as the governance structures supporting them.

Two functions play a pivotal role in ensuring AI is deployed responsibly: **IT Governance**—providing the oversight, policies, and controls for technology use; and the **Chief Data Officer (CDO)**—ensuring that data, the fuel of AI, is accurate, ethical, and compliant. Together, they create the foundation for **trustworthy AI adoption**.

The Role of IT Governance in AI

Defining IT Governance

IT governance is the framework through which organizations align technology with business goals, manage risk, and ensure compliance. When

DOI: 10.4324/9781003682530-41

extended to AI, governance ensures these systems are secure, ethical, and aligned with organizational strategy.

Core Principles of IT Governance Applied to AI

- **Alignment**: Ensuring AI projects support business objectives.
- **Value Delivery**: Ensuring AI investments produce measurable ROI.
- **Risk Management**: Identifying and mitigating cybersecurity, compliance, and ethical risks.
- **Resource Management**: Efficient use of data, infrastructure, and skills.
- **Performance Measurement**: Continuous monitoring of AI accuracy, fairness, and outcomes.

Reference: ISACA COBIT Framework; ISO/IEC 38500 (IT Governance Standard)

IT Governance Mechanisms for AI

- **AI Steering Committees**: Overseeing AI strategy and prioritization.
- **Policy Frameworks**: Defining acceptable uses, prohibited practices, and review processes.
- **Control Systems**: Implementing guardrails against bias, drift, or misuse.
- **Audit and Assurance**: Independent validation of AI system integrity.

Example: A bank using AI for credit decisions may require governance approval for model changes, with regular audits for bias and compliance.

The CDO in the Age of AI

Evolving Role of the CDO

Traditionally, the CDO focused on data quality, management, and compliance. With AI, the CDO's role has expanded to include:

- **AI Data Strategy**: Ensuring the organization has reliable, accessible, and ethical data for AI.
- **Data Ethics**: Establishing principles for fairness, transparency, and non-discrimination.

- **Regulatory Compliance**: Ensuring adherence to GDPR, CPRA, HIPAA, and emerging AI-specific laws.
- **Data Security & Privacy**: Protecting sensitive and personal data used in training or inference.
- **Collaboration**: Working with CIOs, CISOs, and Chief Risk Officers to ensure responsible AI deployment.

Reference: Gartner Research on the CDO Role, 2023; ISO/IEC 42001:2023 (AI Management Systems)

Key Responsibilities of the CDO in AI

1. **Data Governance**: Establishing data stewardship programs.
2. **Bias Mitigation**: Monitoring and correcting imbalances in training data.
3. **Model Documentation**: Ensuring traceability and explainability.
4. **Third-Party Risk Management**: Evaluating AI vendors and data suppliers.
5. **Data Literacy & Culture**: Educating the workforce about responsible data use.

Example: A healthcare CDO ensures patient data used for AI diagnostic tools complies with HIPAA and is anonymized before use.

Synergy between IT Governance and the CDO

AI governance is most effective when IT governance and data leadership work hand-in-hand:

Reference: NIST AI RMF (2023); EU AI Act (2024)

Challenges and Future Outlook

Challenges

- **Fragmented Governance**: Disconnect between IT, compliance, and data functions.
- **Evolving Regulations**: Keeping up with the EU AI Act, US sectoral guidance, and China's AI rules.

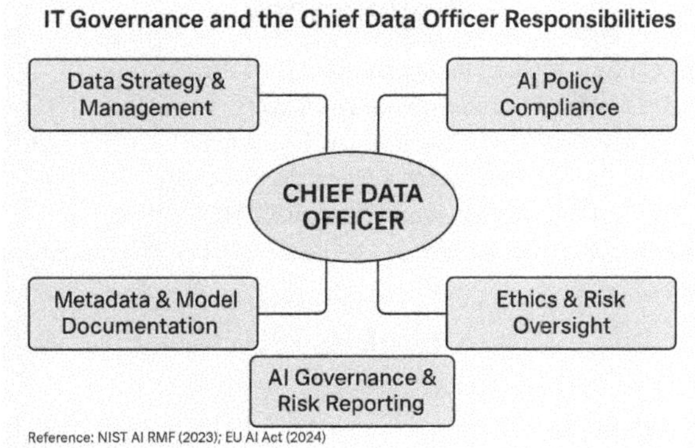

Image 34.1 AI Governance and Leadership

- **Cybersecurity Threats**: Data poisoning, model theft, and adversarial attacks.
- **Data Silos**: Poor data integration across departments.

Future Outlook

- **AI Governance Committees** that combine IT, data, legal, and ethics.
- **Integrated AI Risk Dashboards** for boards and regulators.
- **Increased Accountability** for CDOs in bias prevention and explainability.
- **Global Standards Adoption** (ISO/IEC 42001, OECD AI Principles) to unify compliance efforts.

Conclusion

AI success depends not only on algorithms but also on **governance and data leadership**. IT governance provides the framework for accountability, risk management, and alignment with business goals. The CDO ensures that the **fuel of AI—data—is ethical, accurate, and compliant**.

Together, they safeguard organizations against regulatory, cybersecurity, and reputational risks, while enabling responsible innovation. Companies that empower both IT governance and the CDO will build AI systems that are not just powerful, but also **trustworthy and sustainable**.

Bibliography

European Union. (2024). *Artificial Intelligence Act (EU AI Act)*.
Gartner. (2023). *The Evolving Role of the Chief Data Officer*.
ISACA. *COBIT 2019 Framework for IT Governance and Management*.
ISO/IEC 38500:2015. *Corporate Governance of Information Technology*.
ISO/IEC 42001: 2023. *AI Management System Standard (AIMS)*.
NIST. (2023). *AI Risk Management Framework 1.0*.OECD. (2019). *AI Principles*.

35

THE ROLE OF THE CYBER TEAM

Introduction

There is no "I" in *team*—a timeless adage that underscores the indispensable role of collaboration in achieving organizational success. A team is not merely a collection of individuals; it is a dynamic force that transforms vision into reality. While a single mind may conceive a brilliant idea, its execution and delivery invariably demand the coordinated efforts of a capable team. The realm of cybersecurity is no exception.

To effectively confront both current and emerging threats, a cybersecurity team must be strategically equipped to navigate the complexities of today's digital landscape and anticipate the challenges of tomorrow. Consequently, it is imperative for leadership and management to rigorously assess the team's readiness and evaluate the breadth and depth of its skill sets.

Given the relentless pace of innovation and disruption in the IT and cyber domains, continuous learning is not optional—it is essential. Team members must remain proficient and agile within their respective disciplines to ensure resilience and operational excellence.

DOI: 10.4324/9781003682530-42

In the sections that follow, we will delve into a curated selection of tools and developmental methodologies designed to fortify your cyber defense capabilities and elevate your team's strategic posture.

What Should a Team Look Like and What Tools Would They Need?

Toolset

The landscape of cybersecurity is populated by a plethora of vendors. While many offers superior products, one must discern that not all tools are necessary. An overabundance of technology can be paralyzing, and their management can become exacting. Consequently, teams often experience exhaustion and may eventually neglect crucial security alerts.

To establish a robust foundation, regardless of your current tool inventory, begin with a framework like CIS Critical Controls. The core task is to systematically map your existing or required tools to the appropriate CIS Controls. I know that many modern security solutions have functional redundancies. In these cases, it's paramount to focus on each tool's

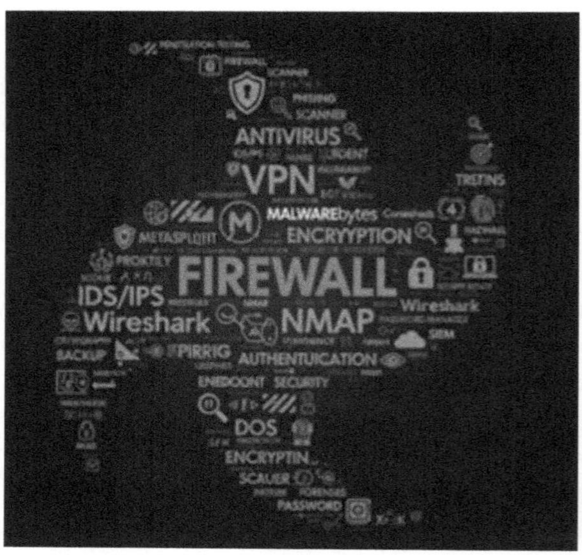

Image 35.1 Cybersecurity Tools

distinguishing strength. Although secondary features can be a welcome complement, always prioritize a tool's intended application, as that is where its efficacy lies.

A vulnerability management tool can effectively discover assets across your network, but is it as comprehensive and resilient as a dedicated IT helpdesk inventory management system? The answer is no. While such tools excel at pinpointing security vulnerabilities, asset management is not their forte.

Typically, IT asset management solutions are thoughtfully engineered and seamlessly integrated within standard helpdesk platforms. My recommendation is to primarily leverage your IT helpdesk software for managing assets and then cross-reference it with your vulnerability management tool to ensure a holistic and exhaustive scan of your entire digital ecosystem.

Skipping asset scans for the sake of convenience undermines the very essence of risk mitigation. The cornerstone of any robust cybersecurity strategy begins with accurate identification of environmental deficiencies. Without a clear understanding of what's amiss, remediation efforts are destined to fall short.

Assessment

Begin by conducting a comprehensive inventory of the tools within your cybersecurity arsenal. Once cataloged, map each tool to the CIS Controls framework. This exercise often reveals surprising insights—such as redundant solutions or critical gaps in control coverage. Such discoveries underscore the importance of aligning your toolset with a framework tailored to your organization's operational needs and regulatory obligations.

Understanding your organization's structure and the specific compliance mandates it faces—be it HIPAA, PCI DSS, ISO/IEC 27001, or other industry-specific standards—is paramount. Performing this strategic assessment not only illuminates deficiencies in your security architecture but also presents opportunities for cost optimization.

It's essential to recognize that tools are not merely acquired—they must be thoughtfully planned, meticulously engineered, and continuously nurtured. Procurement is a singular event; however, the true value of a tool is realized through sustained operational excellence and iterative refinement. This is where many teams falter, particularly when overwhelmed by an abundance of poorly integrated solutions. In such scenarios, tools often lack proper configuration, resulting in subpar reporting and ineffective dashboards.

When these flawed outputs inform critical decision-making, the consequences can be detrimental. Precision in engineering and clarity in reporting are not luxuries—they are necessities for sound cybersecurity governance.

A company initially presumed that their security stack—which included endpoint protection, a firewall, and email gateways—was adequate. While users' internet traffic was indeed passing through the firewall, a crucial element was absent. A firewall provides perimeter defense; it is not a substitute for a dedicated web gateway or proxy server. Although a firewall can be engineered to emulate a proxy, that is not its intended use case.

Once the company began mapping their existing tools to the CIS Controls, they discovered they lacked a proper web gateway, which offers significantly superior control and management of web traffic compared with a firewall. A dedicated proxy permits more fine-tuned policies, more flexible reporting, and excels at these tasks. We must, therefore, utilize appropriate tools for their designated functions.

CISO & Cybersecurity Team Responsibilities Across the AI Lifecycle

Role / AI Lifecycle Stage	Data Collection	Model Training	Deployment	Monitoring
CISO	Define policy & data classes Approve sources & DPIAs Risk acceptance criteria	Training risk governance 3rd-party model due diligence Data & model SLAs	Security go-live sign-of AI KRIs/KPIs definition Exception & waiver control	Board reporting AI incident escalation Audit & regulator interface
Security Engineering	DLP & encryption RBAC / ABAC access control Data quality gates	Hardened training environment Supply-chain scanning Poisoning & adversarial tests	Secure APIs & secrets Model registry & signing Rate limits & egress control	Attack surface monitoring Patch & rollback Backup & recovery
SOC	Exfiltration alerting Privileged access monitoring Playbooks & ticketing	Anomalous training jobs IAM misuse detection AI threat intelligence	WAF & bot protection Model abuse alerts SRE–SEC runbooks	Adversarial prompt alerts Drift & bias alerts Incident response & forensics

Table 35.1 Cyber Team Responsibilities

The Team

The size and composition of a cybersecurity team will vary across organizations, contingent upon their scale and operational complexity. Larger enterprises often maintain distinct engineering and operations teams, whereas smaller companies or startups may rely on a lean, multifunctional group responsible for managing every facet of their security posture.

So, what are the core focus areas? At a foundational level, teams must be equipped to manage and secure endpoints. This encompasses not only the deployment of antivirus and endpoint detection and response (AV/EDR) solutions but also the encryption of devices to safeguard sensitive data. If your organization utilizes a substantial number of mobile phones or tablets, the same principles apply—these devices must be systematically managed and encrypted.

To ensure continuity, especially within smaller teams, it is prudent to designate backup personnel who can step in should the primary individual be unavailable. This redundancy is vital across all domains, including perimeter security—firewalls, proxy servers, email gateways—and should follow a structured approach of assigning primary, secondary, and even tertiary custodians.

Equally critical are areas such as cloud security, privileged access management, and data loss prevention—domains where many small organizations encounter significant challenges. To mitigate operational disruptions, particularly when a team member departs, one indispensable practice is thorough documentation.

Mandate that all team members meticulously document system architecture, network diagrams, data flows, and other essential configurations—ideally within a centralized repository such as a SharePoint site. This documentation library not only serves as a reference point but also doubles as a training resource for onboarding new personnel.

By institutionalizing documentation, your organization becomes far more resilient to personnel changes. Knowledge is no longer siloed or at risk of being lost; instead, it is preserved and accessible, ensuring continuity and operational integrity even in the face of transition.

Furthermore, the following activities are highly encouraged:

- Cross-training: Encourages versatility and reduces single points of failure.
- Red and Blue Team Exercises: Simulate real-world attacks and defenses to sharpen skills.

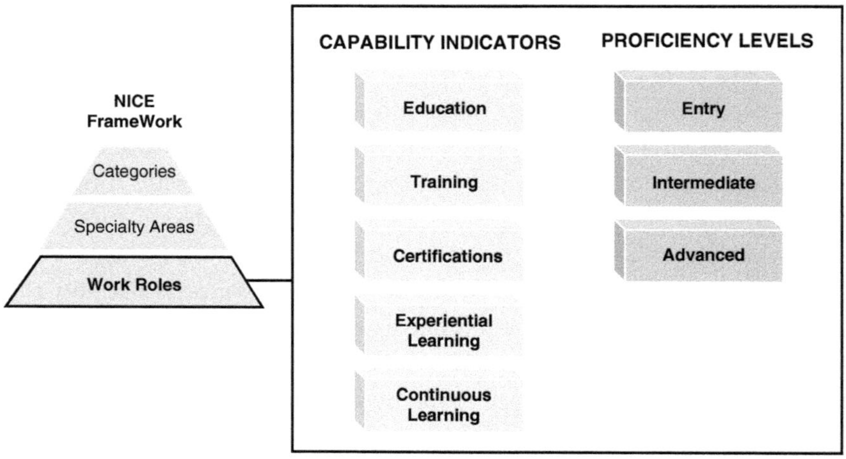

Image 35.2 Work Role Capability Indicators (NICE Framework)

- Threat Intelligence Platforms: Keep teams informed about the latest risks and trends.
- Collaborative Tools: Foster communication and coordination across departments.

Skillset

Having explored tools and team structure, it is now essential to turn our attention to one of the most critical pillars of cybersecurity success: human capital management—specifically, the continuous learning and development of your workforce.

It is imperative that team members remain well-informed and attuned to the latest trends, technologies, and threats in the cyber domain. As IT professionals, they should be expected to regularly engage with industry blogs, news outlets, and thought leadership content. This proactive consumption of information should be ingrained as a professional norm.

To facilitate structured learning, organizations can invest in site licenses for reputable educational platforms offering eBook libraries, technical training videos, and certification prep courses. These resources are not only cost-effective but also scalable across teams. However, merely providing access is insufficient. It is crucial to mandate a minimum number of training hours per month, with team members required to track and report their progress to management. Training can be self-directed or assigned based on project requirements or strategic priorities.

To foster a culture of shared learning and engagement, consider implementing a knowledge-sharing ritual. At weekly or monthly team meetings, each member should be encouraged—or required—to present, discuss, or demonstrate something they've learned since the previous session. This practice not only reinforces individual growth but also promotes cross-pollination of ideas and collective intelligence.

Another powerful incentive is subsidizing professional certification exams. Supporting team members in their pursuit of recognized credentials not only boosts morale but also enhances the organization's credibility and technical depth.

By investing in continuous education and cultivating a collaborative learning environment, organizations can transform their cybersecurity teams into agile, informed, and resilient defenders of the digital frontier.

Training Recommendations for the Cybersecurity Team

To remain resilient and ahead of evolving threats, cybersecurity teams should follow a structured training roadmap. The following are recommended training paths and certifications:

Foundational Training

- Security+ (CompTIA)—Ideal for junior team members or cross-trained IT staff
- Certified Ethical Hacker—For those beginning to engage in offensive security and vulnerability testing
- Network+ and A+ (CompTIA)—For foundational IT and networking knowledge.

Intermediate to Advanced Certifications

- CISSP (Certified Information Systems Security Professional)—Broad, vendor-neutral knowledge base suitable for senior roles
- CISM (Certified Information Security Manager)—Focus on management, governance, and risk

- GIAC Security Essentials (GSEC)—Intermediate security skills applicable across multiple domains
- OSCP (Offensive Security Certified Professional)—For penetration testers and red team members.

Cloud and Platform-Specific Security

- AWS Certified Security—Specialty
- Microsoft SC-200: Security Operations Analyst Associate
- Google Professional Cloud Security Engineer.

Ongoing Skill Development

- Subscriptions to platforms like Pluralsight, Cybrary, TryHackMe, or INE
- Regular participation in Capture the Flag and cyber ranges
- Attendance at conferences: Black Hat, DEF CON, RSA, or SANS events.

Internal Knowledge Transfer

- Monthly "knowledge shares" where team members present learnings
- Quarterly internal workshops or lunch-and-learns
- A mentorship program pairing junior staff with experienced team members.

Executive and Cross-Functional Awareness

- Non-cyber teams and executives should take short awareness courses such as:
    - NIST Cybersecurity Framework Introduction
    - Phishing & Social Engineering Awareness
    - Cyber Hygiene for Remote Work.

These trainings ensure the cyber team is not only prepared technically but also aligned with the business's risk posture and compliance requirements.

Conclusion

Achieving efficacy in the contemporary cyber landscape, as we can discern, demands a robust and proficient team, furnished with optimal tools. These elements must complement one another. We simply cannot afford the indiscretion of pairing inadequate tools with a high-caliber team, or effective tools with an ill-prepared team.

The strategic first step is to evaluate and verify the current suite of tools to identify any material deficiencies in control coverage. The subsequent effort should be concentrated on the professional development and upskilling of our teams. Once adeptly outfitted with the necessary technology, the team becomes the driver of success, fortifying your data and infrastructure. Indeed, it is markedly better to see a highly competent individual leave your organization than to retain one who is untrained. You must not devalue the imperative of capital investment in your human capital.

Bibliography

CIS Critical Controls. https://www.cisecurity.org/controls/v8-1

CISA Cybersecurity Best Practices. https://www.cisa.gov/topics/cybersecurity-best-practices

Microsoft Cybersecurity Reference Architectures. https://learn.microsoft.com/en-us/security/adoption/mcra

NICE Workforce Framework for Cybersecurity. https://niccs.cisa.gov/tools/nice-framework

36

CYBERSECURITY AND AI ROLES IN THE EVOLVING IT LANDSCAPE

Introduction

The integration of artificial intelligence (AI) into IT systems has fundamentally reshaped the landscape of cybersecurity. As IT infrastructure becomes more complex, the need for advanced threat detection, real-time response, and automated risk management has become imperative. Cybersecurity professionals are now required not only to defend traditional networks and endpoints but also to understand and oversee AI-driven systems that themselves introduce new attack surfaces and risk vectors.

This chapter explores the key roles at the intersection of cybersecurity, AI, and IT, highlighting how organizations are evolving their workforce, governance structures, and operational models to address emerging challenges.

DOI: 10.4324/9781003682530-43

The Convergence of Cybersecurity, AI, and IT

The Growing Complexity of IT Ecosystems

Modern IT environments span on-premises, cloud, edge, and hybrid infrastructures. With the proliferation of connected devices, SaaS platforms, and AI-driven systems, the attack surface has expanded dramatically. Traditional perimeter-based security models have proven inadequate, giving rise to a need for:

- Zero Trust architectures
- Identity-centric security
- Real-time anomaly detection
- Intelligent automation.

AI as a Force Multiplier in Cyber Defense

AI enhances cybersecurity capabilities through:

- Threat detection
- Incident response
- Fraud prevention.

According to Gartner (2023), over 40% of cybersecurity operations centers are now leveraging AI-driven solutions to augment human decision-making.

Core Roles and Responsibilities

Cybersecurity Data Scientist

Key Responsibilities:

- Analyze SIEM, EDR, and threat intelligence data.
- Train models for intrusion detection, anomaly detection, and malware classification.
- Work with red/blue teams to validate models.

AI Security Engineer

Key Responsibilities:

- Implement differential privacy and model watermarking.
- Detect adversarial inputs and data poisoning.
- Ensure compliance with AI risk and ethics standards.

Cyber Threat Intelligence Analyst with AI Focus

Key Responsibilities:

- Use LLMs to automate intelligence correlation.
- Leverage graph analytics for threat actor mapping.
- Feed structured threat intelligence into XDR/SOAR platforms.

IT Risk and Compliance Analyst (AI-Integrated)

Key Responsibilities:

- Conduct AI risk assessments aligned with NIST AI RMF or ISO/IEC 23894:2023.
- Evaluate third-party vendors' use of AI in their security operations.
- Monitor AI systems for ethical, legal, and regulatory compliance.

Organizational Models

Cyber-AI Fusion Teams

Progressive enterprises are forming integrated teams that combine AI engineers, cybersecurity experts, and IT operations personnel. These "fusion teams" support:

- Continuous monitoring and AI-enhanced SOCs
- Rapid response to model drift and threat evolution
- Joint development of secure AI/ML pipelines.

DevSecOps with MLOps Integration

AI pipelines must adhere to DevSecOps principles. MLOps engineers are increasingly tasked with:

- Automating security testing in CI/CD pipelines for ML models
- Versioning, logging, and rollback of model deployments
- Ensuring model reproducibility and auditability.

Future Trends and Emerging Roles

AI Governance Officer

This emerging executive-level role ensures responsible AI development and deployment. Responsibilities include:

- Policy development for AI use across IT and cybersecurity functions
- Oversight of AI fairness, accountability, and transparency
- Collaboration with legal, compliance, and audit teams.

Offensive AI Security Researcher

These professionals simulate adversaries using AI to test defenses. Common activities include:

- Building generative AI systems to simulate phishing attacks
- Conducting red teaming exercises with AI-generated malware
- Testing AI systems against prompt injection and jailbreaking.

Skills and Tools Landscape

Role	Key Tools	Certifications
Cybersecurity Data Scientist	Jupyter, Scikit-learn, Splunk	CompTIA CySA+, GSEC
AI security Engineer	TensorFlow Privacy, IBM ART	GIAC AI Security (emerging)
CTI Analyst	Maltego, MISP, OpenAI APIs	GCTI, MITRE ATT&CK Defender
Risk & Compliance Analyst	LogicGate, OneTrust, Power BI	CISA, ISO/IEC 27001

Table 36.1 Roles, tools, and certifications

Key Frameworks and Standards

- NIST AI Risk Management Framework (AI RMF)
- ISO/IEC 23894:2023
- MITRE ATLAS
- ISO/IEC 27001 & 27701
- EU AI Act & U.S. AI Executive Order (2023).

Recommended Training Programs

Seton Hall University, Pace University CDO Program. www.cyberintelu.online

Conclusion

As AI becomes embedded in every layer of IT infrastructure, cybersecurity professionals must evolve. Traditional security models are insufficient to address the dynamism and complexity AI introduces. The future of IT depends on hybrid roles that blend data science, security engineering, risk governance, and ethical oversight.

Building effective cyber-AI teams, supported by automation, continuous learning, and cross-disciplinary collaboration, will be key to defending against the threats of tomorrow.

Bibliography

Brundage, M. et al. (2020). *The Malicious Use of Artificial Intelligence.*
European Commission. (2024). *EU AI Act.*
Gartner. (2023). *Market Guide for AI-Based Cybersecurity Solutions.*
ISO. (2023). ISO/IEC 23894:2023 *Artificial Intelligence — Guidance on Risk Management.*
MITRE. (2023). *Adversarial Threat Landscape for Artificial-Intelligence Systems.* ATLAS.
NIST. (2023). *Artificial Intelligence Risk Management Framework* (AI RMF) 1.0.
U.S. Executive Order on Safe, Secure, and Trustworthy AI (2023).

37

CYBERSECURITY AND AI COMPLIANCE TEAM ROLES

Introduction

The growing use of artificial intelligence (AI) across digital systems has created new challenges for cybersecurity and compliance teams. As organizations integrate AI into core operations—from threat detection to customer profiling—regulatory scrutiny over AI ethics, data privacy, and algorithmic accountability is increasing. To ensure both regulatory compliance and responsible use of AI, organizations are forming cross-functional cyber–AI compliance teams that bridge legal, technical, and governance domains.

This chapter explores the key roles within such teams, their responsibilities, and how they collaborate to maintain trust, transparency, and risk control in AI-enabled environments.

The Need for Cross-Disciplinary Compliance Teams

AI compliance requires more than technical robustness; it also involves legal interpretation, ethical evaluation, privacy safeguards, and cybersecurity

DOI: 10.4324/9781003682530-44

controls. As a result, cyber–AI compliance teams bring together professionals from diverse fields to ensure that AI systems are secure, lawful, and aligned with organizational values.

Core Roles in Cyber–AI Compliance Teams

AI Compliance Officer

The AI Compliance Officer leads organizational efforts to ensure AI systems adhere to laws, regulations, and internal policies.

- Responsibilities:
- Translate AI-related regulatory requirements into internal controls and workflows.
- Oversee compliance with frameworks like the EU AI Act, NIST AI RMF, and ISO/IEC 23894.
- Conduct AI impact assessments and maintain documentation.

AI Ethics and Governance Lead

This role ensures AI use aligns with ethical standards such as fairness, transparency, and accountability.

- Responsibilities:
- Establish and operationalize ethical AI principles across teams.
- Conduct bias audits and fairness assessments.
- Serve on or support internal AI governance boards.

Cybersecurity and AI Risk Analyst

This role evaluates cyber risks associated with AI systems and ensures technical safeguards are in place.

- Responsibilities:
- Analyze model vulnerabilities such as adversarial ML, data leakage, or poisoning.
- Map AI risks to cybersecurity frameworks (e.g., NIST CSF, ISO 27001).
- Conduct red teaming, penetration testing, and threat modeling of AI systems.

Privacy Officer / Data Protection Officer (DPO)

The DPO ensures AI systems comply with data privacy laws such as GDPR, CCPA, and HIPAA.

- Responsibilities:
- Monitor the use of personal data in training and inference.
- Enforce data minimization, anonymization, and consent protocols.
- Handle data subject access requests involving AI-driven decisions.

Legal and Regulatory Counsel (AI & Cyber Focus)

This role interprets regulatory obligations and supports incident response and audits.

- Responsibilities:
- Provide legal guidance on AI, cybersecurity, and digital ethics regulations.
- Support contract reviews and vendor due diligence.
- Advise on regulatory reporting obligations and enforcement risks.

MLOps Engineer with Compliance Liaison Function

This technical role ensures machine-learning models are developed and deployed in line with compliance requirements.

- Responsibilities:
- Integrate auditability, traceability, and explainability into AI pipelines.
- Maintain model version control, monitoring, and rollback capabilities.
- Coordinate with compliance officers during model development and deployment.

Team Collaboration and Operating Models

Cyber–AI compliance teams typically operate through centralized governance frameworks supported by cross-functional committees. Best practices include:

- Defining clear roles and escalation paths
- Embedding compliance checkpoints in the AI lifecycle

- Leveraging risk registers and control libraries specific to AI systems
- Conducting joint scenario planning, tabletop exercises, and audit dry runs.

Courses/Certifications

- Seton Hall University and Pace University AI Governance Certification. www.cyberintelu.online
- Certified AI Compliance Professional (CAICP)—AI Governance Alliance.

Key Learning Areas

- AI regulations (EU AI Act, NIST AI RMF, ISO/IEC 23894)
- Compliance workflows and impact assessments
- Audit documentation standards.

Conclusion

Building effective cyber and AI compliance teams is critical as AI regulations evolve and cyber threats grow in sophistication. Organizations must foster collaboration among legal, ethical, technical, and operational leaders to ensure trustworthy AI deployment. These multidisciplinary teams will serve as the backbone of digital trust in the age of intelligent systems.

Bibliography

European Commission. (2024). *EU AI Act.*

Future of Privacy Forum. (2023). *Building and Sustaining AI Governance Programs.*

ISO. (2023). ISO/IEC 23894:2023 *Artificial Intelligence — Guidance on Risk Management.*

NIST. (2023). *AI Risk Management Framework* (AI RMF) 1.0.

OECD. (2021). *Principles on Artificial Intelligence.*

U.S. Executive Order on Safe, Secure, and Trustworthy AI (2023).

38

THE ROLE OF THE CPO AND PRIVACY TEAM

Privacy is not a bolt-on to AI—it's the quality bar for lawful, trusted systems. When privacy is designed as a system property, organizations unlock cleaner data, safer deployments, faster approvals, and durable trust. This chapter positions privacy as a strategic partner to security and AI governance and shows exactly how privacy collaborates with cyber and compliance teams to deliver outcomes that stand up to regulators, customers, and the board.

Reframing Privacy: From Policy to Product Property

Treat privacy like safety in aviation: it constrains design choices in ways that produce better systems. The core principles—lawfulness, purpose limitation, data minimization, storage limitation, integrity/confidentiality, accountability—become engineering constraints and product features, not legal fine print.

DOI: 10.4324/9781003682530-45

The Privacy–Security–AI Triangle

Security protects systems; privacy protects people; and AI governance protects outcomes. Mature programs weave all three together through shared processes—one intake, one risk pipeline, and aligned oversight. In practice, this means cross-functional collaboration and mutual visibility into how data, models, and people intersect.

Embedding Privacy Across AI Teams

Privacy must be represented at every layer of the AI governance structure. Privacy officers partnering with AI compliance leads to co-owned risk classification, working with ethics teams to assess fairness impacts, and aligning with cybersecurity teams to manage data exposure. Legal and MLOps teams depend on privacy specialists to clarify consent boundaries, minimize data retention, and ensure training and monitoring datasets are appropriately governed.

Privacy Engineering in Practice

Strong privacy engineering starts with data minimization. Collect less, keep it for less time, and anonymize wherever possible. When sharing or analyzing data, use privacy-enhancing technologies like differential privacy, secure multi-party computation, or federated learning. Complement these with privacy threat modeling methods such as LINDDUN to identify weaknesses before they surface.

Transparency and User Control

Trust grows when people understand and can influence how AI affects them. Design clear notices that explain what the AI system does and provide meaningful controls—not just toggles. Users should be able to access, correct, or delete their data and contest automated decisions. Human oversight must remain a real option, especially for high-impact use cases.

Vendor and Model Accountability

AI supply chains extend beyond your walls. Demand transparency from vendors about training data sources, fairness testing, and model updates.

Ensure contracts include obligations for privacy, incident reporting, and clear limits on secondary data use. Shared accountability prevents shared risk from becoming shared blame.

Measuring and Proving Privacy

Evidence matters more than promises. Maintain records of processing for each AI use case, conduct privacy impact assessments, and log decisions about data and model risk. Metrics like PII reduction percentage, response time to rights requests, or adoption of privacy-enhancing technologies can be tracked over time to demonstrate progress.

Culture and Collaboration

Privacy is everyone's responsibility, but it thrives when modeled from the top. Cross-functional collaboration between privacy, cybersecurity, and AI governance teams keeps objectives aligned. Regular communication, shared dashboards, and joint exercises create a culture where privacy isn't seen as an obstacle but as the foundation for trustworthy innovation.

Training Requirements for the Chief Privacy Officer (CPO) in the Age of AI

As AI technologies become deeply integrated into enterprise systems, CPOs must upskill to manage data privacy, compliance, and governance responsibilities effectively. They are now central players in shaping and enforcing AI governance frameworks, data protection strategies, and organizational accountability.

Essential Training Areas for CPOs

- **AI and Data Privacy Laws**
  In-depth understanding of evolving global and regional privacy regulations, including GDPR, CPRA, HIPAA, LGPD, and the EU AI Act.
  Example: The CPO must understand how Article 22 of GDPR restricts automated decision-making using personal data and ensure appropriate human review mechanisms exist.

- **AI Lifecycle Risk Awareness**
  Identify privacy risks at each phase of the AI lifecycle: data acquisition, training, deployment, and inference.
  Example: During model training, the CPO should verify if training data includes identifiable personal information and whether anonymization is applied.
- **Privacy-Enhancing Technologies (PETs)**
  Learn and evaluate PETs such as differential privacy, homomorphic encryption, federated learning, and synthetic data generation.
  Example: For a health dataset used in AI model training, applying differential privacy ensures individual-level data is protected.
- **Consent Management in AI**
  Build compliant consent mechanisms tailored for dynamic AI systems.
  Example: Enable opt-out features for users when their data is used in automated profiling models.
- **Cross-Functional Collaboration**
  Collaborate with cybersecurity, legal, compliance, and data science teams to integrate privacy into system design and audits.
- **Risk Quantification and DPIAs**
  Conduct privacy impact assessments (DPIAs) and implement privacy risk scoring models.
  Example: Before launching a chatbot that stores user inputs, a DPIA can flag risk areas like data retention and consent gaps.
- **Algorithmic Accountability**
  Understand mechanisms for explainability and challenge rights.
  Example: When a user is denied access to a loan by an AI model, the CPO ensures explainability tools are in place for appeal.

Recommended Learning Channels

- **Certifications**
  - *Pace University and Seton Hall University Certifications*
  - *IAPP CIPT / CIPM (Certified Information Privacy Technologist / Manager)*
  - *ISO/IEC 42001: AI Management Systems*
  - *NIST AI Risk Management Framework*
- **Conferences**
  - *IAPP Global Privacy Summit*
  - *IEEE Symposium on AI & Privacy*
  - *AI Governance Global Forum*

- **Internal Training and Workshops**
  - Joint simulations and incident response drills with engineering, legal, and security teams.
  - Policy walkthroughs of AI/ML use cases with vendors and internal developers.

Conclusion

When privacy is embedded deeply into AI systems, compliance becomes a byproduct of good design rather than a constraint on innovation. It bridges the gap between legal expectations, ethical aspirations, and technical realities—ensuring that AI systems are not only intelligent but also worthy of trust.

Bibliography

Council of Europe. (2024). *Convention on Artificial Intelligence, Human Rights, Democracy and the Rule of Law (CAI)*. https://www.coe.int

European Commission. (2021). Proposal for a regulation of the European Parliament and of the Council laying down harmonised rules on artificial intelligence (Artificial Intelligence Act) and amending certain Union legislative acts (COM(2021) 206 final). *Publications Office of the European Union*. https://eur-lex.europa.eu/legal-content/EN/TXT/?uri=celex:52021PC0206

European Data Protection Board. (2023). *Guidelines 03/2022 on Deceptive Design Patterns in Social Media Interfaces*. https://www.edpb.europa.eu

European Union. (2016). *General Data Protection Regulation (GDPR)*. Regulation (EU) 2016/679. https://eur-lex.europa.eu/legal-content/EN/TXT/?uri=CELEX:32016R0679

Future of Privacy Forum. (2023). *Building and Sustaining AI Governance Programs*. https://fpf.org

ISO/ IEC. (2019). *ISO/IEC 27701: Security Techniques — Extension to ISO/IEC 27001 and ISO/IEC 27002 for Privacy Information Management*. International Organization for Standardization. https://www.iso.org/standard/71670.html

ISO/ IEC. (2023). *ISO/IEC 42001: Artificial Intelligence — Management System*. International Organization for Standardization. https://www.iso.org/standard/42001

LINDDUN. (2021). *Privacy Threat Modeling: Methodology & Catalog*. https://linddun.org

National Institute of Standards and Technology. (2020). *Privacy Framework: A Tool for Improving Privacy through Enterprise Risk Management*. U.S. Department of Commerce. https://www.nist.gov/privacy-framework

OECD. (2019, updated 2024). *OECD AI Principles*. Organisation for Economic Co-operation and Development. https://oecd.ai/en/ai-principles

U.K. Information Commissioner's Office. (2023). *Guidance on Automated Decision-Making and Profiling*. https://ico.org.uk

U.S. Federal Trade Commission. (2024). *AI (and other) Companies Quietly Changing Your Terms Could Be Unfair or Deceptive* [Press release]. https://www.ftc.gov

39

CYBERSECURITY AND AI PROJECT MANAGEMENT ROLES

Introduction

As organizations increasingly adopt artificial intelligence (AI) and advanced cybersecurity solutions, project management plays a crucial role in aligning technical execution with business objectives, regulatory requirements, and risk management practices. Cybersecurity and AI projects are inherently complex, involving cross-functional teams, sensitive data, and evolving technologies.

This chapter outlines key project management roles within cyber and AI initiatives, including their responsibilities, required skills, and contributions to successful project delivery.

Unique Challenges in Cyber and AI Project Management

- High regulatory scrutiny and compliance needs (e.g., GDPR, EU AI Act, NIST AI RMF)

DOI: 10.4324/9781003682530-46

- Interdisciplinary coordination across IT, data science, legal, and risk teams
- Rapidly evolving technologies and threat landscapes
- Ethical, privacy, and security concerns surrounding data and model usage
- Integration of legacy systems with new AI-driven solutions.

Core Project Management Roles in Cyber and AI Projects

Cybersecurity Project Manager

Responsible for delivering cybersecurity initiatives such as SOC upgrades, vulnerability remediation, or threat detection implementations.

- Responsibilities:
- Define project scope, objectives, and risk mitigation strategies.
- Coordinate across security operations, IT, compliance, and vendors.
- Track deliverables, budgets, and KPIs related to security controls.

AI Project Manager

Leads initiatives involving machine learning, natural language processing, and AI-driven automation, often with a focus on risk management or business intelligence.

- Responsibilities:
- Manage data pipelines, model development, and deployment timelines.
- Align AI outcomes with ethical, legal, and governance requirements.
- Liaise between data scientists, IT, legal, and product owners.

Technical Program Manager (Cyber-AI Integration)

Oversees multi-project programs involving the integration of AI into cybersecurity workflows (e.g., SOAR automation, behavioral analytics).

- Responsibilities:
- Develop long-term roadmaps for AI adoption in security programs.

- Coordinate cross-domain initiatives and vendor collaboration.
- Ensure interoperability between AI tools and existing systems.

Governance, Risk, and Compliance (GRC) Program Manager

Drives initiatives that address AI and cybersecurity governance, audit readiness, and regulatory compliance.

- Responsibilities:
- Manage implementation of control frameworks (e.g., NIST, ISO, EU AI Act).
- Lead risk assessments and mitigation strategies for AI systems.
- Support internal and external audits with traceability and documentation.

Agile Delivery Manager / Scrum Master

Facilitates agile development practices for AI and cybersecurity product teams.

- Responsibilities:
- Organize sprints, retrospectives, and backlog prioritization.
- Remove blockers and promote team collaboration.
- Track velocity and deliver iterative project outcomes.

Skills and Tools Landscape

- Project management frameworks: PMP, PRINCE2, Agile/Scrum, SAFe
- Cybersecurity knowledge: CISSP, CISM, or equivalent familiarity
- AI/ML fundamentals and model lifecycle management
- Tools: Jira, Confluence, MS Project, GitHub, Miro, ServiceNow, Power BI.

Cross-Functional Collaboration

Successful cyber-AI project managers act as liaisons across:

- Security and operations teams
- Data science and engineering teams

- Legal, compliance, and risk management
- Product management and business units

They ensure alignment of stakeholder expectations while managing timelines, deliverables, and regulatory requirements.

Training Recommendations

Cybersecurity Project Manager

- *Recommended Training:*
  - Certified Information Systems Security Professional (CISSP)
  - CISM (Certified Information Security Manager)
  - NIST Cybersecurity Framework (CSF) workshops
  - MITRE ATT&CK training.

AI Project Manager

- *Recommended Training:*
  - Fundamentals of Machine Learning (Coursera, edX, etc.)
  - AI Governance Frameworks (EU AI Act, NIST AI RMF)
  - Ethical AI and Bias Mitigation (IEEE, OECD, PAI resources).

Technical Program Manager (Cyber-AI Integration)

- *Recommended Training:*
  - AWS/Azure AI Security Integration Labs
  - Data Engineering for AI Pipelines
  - AI-driven Threat Intelligence (MITRE + Gartner Labs).

GRC Program Manager

- *Recommended Training:*
  - ISO 27001, ISO/IEC 23894:2023
  - GDPR/CCPA/AI Act regulatory compliance training
  - AI Risk & Controls (NIST AI RMF deep dive, AICPA trust principles).

Agile Delivery Manager / Scrum Master

- *Recommended Training:*
    - Scrum Master Certification (CSM, PSM)
    - Agile for AI Projects specialization
    - DevSecOps frameworks for secure agile delivery.

General Skills Development (All Roles):

- *Soft Skills*: Risk communication, stakeholder negotiation, and regulatory translation
- *Technical Tools*: RiskQ, Jira, Miro, GitHub, Power BI for dashboards, MS Project for waterfall planning.

Conclusion

As cyber and AI initiatives continue to grow in scope and complexity, project management roles must evolve to meet the challenge. From traditional planning and coordination to AI governance and technical integration, project managers are vital to driving secure, ethical, and value-driven innovation. Organizations that invest in multidisciplinary project leadership will be better equipped to navigate regulatory landscapes and rapidly changing technologies.

Bibliography

Gartner. (2023). *Managing AI Projects in Cybersecurity: Key Skills and Strategies.*
ISO. (2023). ISO/IEC 23894:2023 *Artificial intelligence — Guidance on risk management.*
NIST. (2023). *AI Risk Management Framework* (AI RMF) 1.0.
PMI. (2021). *A Guide to the Project Management Body of Knowledge* (PMBOK® Guide) – 7th Edition.
Scrum.org. (2024). *The Scrum Guide.*

40

AI IN HR AND TRAINING

AI Has Reshaped the HR and Training Landscape

AI has profoundly reshaped HR and Training processes by transforming traditionally manual, reactive processes into intelligent, proactive systems that drive strategic value. In recruitment, AI has revolutionized how organizations handle structured inputs like job descriptions and resumes. Natural language processing and semantic matching now enable faster, more accurate candidate-job alignment. Screening logic, once reliant on human judgment, is now automated with precision, allowing enterprises to process thousands of applications in seconds, dramatically reducing time-to-hire and minimizing bias in early-stage filtering.

Candidate screening has evolved from static resume reviews to dynamic, data-driven assessments. AI models leverage historical hiring data, psychometric indicators, and behavioral signals to predict candidate success and cultural fit. Conversational AI tools conduct initial interviews, assess soft skills, and deliver consistent candidate experiences at scale. More

DOI: 10.4324/9781003682530-47

importantly, when designed ethically, these systems help mitigate bias by focusing on competencies and potential rather than demographic attributes.

Employee engagement has also been reimagined through AI-powered bots that offer real-time feedback loops, respond to HR queries, and escalate concerns, all while learning from interactions. Sentiment analysis tools are able to decipher emotional tone from employee communications, providing deeper insights into morale and well-being. With 24/7 availability, these bots enhance responsiveness and inclusivity across global teams.

Training platforms have shifted from static course delivery to adaptive, personalized learning ecosystems. AI personalizes content based on individual behavior, performance, and preferences, developing modules that align with career goals and skill gaps. These platforms foster continuous learning through feedback-rich environments that track progress, nudge learners, and dynamically adjust difficulty levels. The result is a more engaged, capable workforce—one that evolves in sync with organizational needs and technological change.

Data shows that as of 2025, 65% of HR departments globally have implemented at least one AI-based tool, with publicly traded companies leading the charge at 58% adoption, compared with 45% in private firms and 38% in nonprofits. Moreover, AI-enabled HR systems have reduced average time-to-hire by 23% (Elad 2025). Hence, AI has not just optimized HR and Training operations; it has redefined them.

AI in HR: Driving Scalable Talent Development and Organizational Resilience

HR and Training emerged as early adopters of AI because the technology delivers tangible, high-impact benefits across core functions. In high-volume, repetitive tasks like resume screening and interview scheduling, AI offers unmatched efficiency. It automates rule-based workflows, prioritizes applications, and matches candidate profiles to job descriptions, thereby significantly reducing time-to-hire and improving selection accuracy. This automation frees HR teams from administrative burdens, allowing them to focus on strategic engagement.

HR systems are often data-rich encompassing performance reviews, training logs, and engagement surveys, which makes them ideal for AI adoption. Analyzing these datasets can provide predictive insights into attrition risks, workforce planning, and personalized learning paths. Thus, AI transforms raw data into actionable intelligence, helping organizations proactively manage talent and optimize resource allocation.

Training, too, benefits from AI's scalability and personalization. Adaptive learning platforms customize content to address individual skill gaps and learning styles, enhancing retention and relevance. Enterprises use AI to automate onboarding, simulate real-world scenarios through chatbots or VR, and monitor learning outcomes, which helps create a dynamic, feedback-driven learning ecosystem.

Strategic talent development is another area where AI delivers value. It identifies high-potential employees, recommends career trajectories, and aligns training investments with business goals. This supports succession planning and ensures the workforce remains agile and future-ready, a critical advantage in fast-evolving industries.

Finally, AI drives cost and efficiency gains. Automating HR processes reduces operational overhead, while AI-powered training platforms lower content creation costs and boost learner engagement. The result is a more responsive, data-informed HR function that contributes directly to organizational resilience and growth.

Beyond Automation: AI's Expanding Role in HR

It is true that AI has delivered spectacular results in several areas of HR. Now, the use of Generative AI is becoming central to personalized learning journeys, skills-based hiring, and real-time performance coaching. However, there are some challenges that are already causing concern. One of the foremost challenges is algorithmic bias. AI systems trained on historical HR data can inadvertently reinforce existing disparities in hiring, promotion, and performance evaluation. Without proper oversight and bias audits, these AI tools risk amplifying systemic inequities rather than correcting them. Ensuring fairness and transparency will require robust governance frameworks and continuous monitoring.

Data privacy presents another critical concern. HR systems manage deeply personal information, from performance reviews to behavioral assessments, and AI tools must comply with evolving global regulations like GDPR, CCPA, and other national regulations. Organizations will need to ensure data security and privacy by implementing granular permission controls, secure data handling protocols, and transparent consent mechanisms to maintain trust and legal compliance.

Explainability is also essential. HR decisions directly impact careers and livelihoods, so AI-generated recommendations must be interpretable and accountable. Black-box models pose reputational and legal risks unless they are subjected to rigorous human oversight. Building trust in AI systems will depend on their ability to justify decisions in ways that not only HR professionals but also employees can understand.

Workforce readiness is another problem. Resistance to change and fear of job displacement remain real barriers, requiring thoughtful change management and upskilling initiatives. AI adoption demands not just technical skills but cultural adaptation. HR teams must be trained to collaborate with AI tools, interpret their outputs, and manage hybrid workflows.

Furthermore, fragmented HR ecosystems further complicate AI integration. Many organizations operate siloed platforms, making it difficult to harmonize data and deploy AI across the employee lifecycle. Interoperability and API-driven architectures will be key to unlocking the full potential of intelligent HR systems.

In the near future, we can expect to see AI agents embedded in several workflows such as onboarding flows, career pathing dashboards, and even mental wellness support systems. HR will increasingly rely on AI to predict attrition, optimize team dynamics, and align workforce capabilities with strategic goals. Meanwhile, training too will evolve into a continuous, context-aware experience, with AI curating personalized microlearning modules, simulating decision-making scenarios, and offering nudges for behavioral change. To unlock the full potential of AI in enterprise settings, organizations must prioritize human–AI collaboration. This means allowing AI to manage the cognitive load such as data processing, pattern recognition, and predictive analytics, while HR professionals focus on oversight as well as the human dimensions of work: empathy, ethical decision-making, and culture-building.

Training Recommendations for HR and Learning Teams in the AI Era

To ensure the effective, ethical, and strategic use of AI in HR and training, it is essential for HR professionals, learning and development teams, and

AI product owners to receive targeted education. The following training areas are recommended:

- AI Fundamentals: Understanding core concepts like machine learning, NLP, and neural networks.
- Algorithmic Bias & Fairness: How to identify, mitigate, and monitor bias in AI recruitment and performance systems.
- Data Privacy & Compliance: Understanding laws such as GDPR, CCPA, and emerging global privacy regulations as they pertain to employee data.
- Explainability & Transparency: How to interpret AI decisions and communicate them effectively to impacted employees and stakeholders.
- Ethical HR AI Use: Training on responsible AI principles tailored to HR contexts, including hiring, promotion, and employee monitoring.
- Vendor Risk Management: How to evaluate third-party AI tools for compliance, fairness, and alignment with organizational values.
- Adaptive Learning & EdTech Integration: How to deploy and manage AI-powered learning platforms effectively.
- Human–AI Collaboration: Building skills to work alongside AI tools while preserving the human element of empathy, ethics, and discretion in people management.

Recommended Training Programs

- Seton Hall University, Pace University CDO Program. www.cyberintelu.online

Bibliography

Elad, B. (2025, October 7). AI in HR statistics 2025: Uptake, impact & ethics. *SQ Magazine*. https://sqmagazine.co.uk/ai-in-hr-statistics/

41

FROM PRINCIPLES TO PRACTICE—THE ENTERPRISE AI GOVERNANCE PLAYBOOK

Introduction: Bridging the Governance Gap

Enterprises are no longer experimenting with AI—they're deploying it at scale across operations, customer experience, product development, cybersecurity, compliance, and finance. Yet many are still anchored in abstract "ethical AI" principles, struggling to translate them into operational reality. The goal of this chapter is to offer a concrete, actionable playbook that turns AI governance principles into enterprise practice—spanning policy, process, controls, accountability, and culture.

This playbook is designed for Chief Privacy Officers (CPOs), Chief Data Officers, Chief Compliance Officers, Chief Risk Officers, and Chief Information Security Officers working collaboratively to steer AI development and deployment responsibly. It connects governance to business value, trust, and resilience.

DOI: 10.4324/9781003682530-48

Step 1: Codify a Responsible AI Policy

Every enterprise AI governance framework must start with a foundational policy aligned to corporate values, sectoral regulations (e.g., GDPR, EU AI Act, DORA), and internal risk appetite. This document should:

- Define AI systems (including machine learning, LLMs, expert systems)
- Establish governance objectives: safety, fairness, transparency, privacy, security, and accountability
- Classify AI use cases by risk tier (low, moderate, high)
- Align with ISO 42001, NIST AI RMF, OECD principles, and other frameworks.

Tip: Include guiding questions such as "Is this AI system explainable to its users?" or "How will decisions be audited?"

A foundational **Responsible AI (RAI)** policy anchors the enterprise's approach to ethical and compliant AI deployment. This policy must translate high-level values and legal obligations into actionable controls, structured accountability, and continuous oversight across the AI lifecycle.

What Should the Policy Include?

A comprehensive Responsible AI Policy should:

1. **Define Scope & AI Systems:**
   - o Include classical ML, deep learning, LLMs (e.g., GPT, Gemini), reinforcement learning, generative AI, and hybrid systems.
   - o Clarify what falls under AI oversight vs. traditional automation.
2. **Set Governance Objectives:**
   - o Safety, Fairness, Transparency, Explainability, Privacy, Cybersecurity, Accountability, Sustainability.
3. **Classify AI Use Cases by Risk Tier:**
   - o **Low Risk**: Spam filters, auto-scheduling
   - o **Moderate Risk**: Credit scoring, AI hiring tools
   - o **High Risk**: Biometric identification, autonomous decision-making in healthcare or finance.

   (Refer to the *EU AI Act Annex III; NIST AI RMF Tiers*)

Role	Responsibility in Policy Codification
CPO (Chief Privacy Officer)	Ensures privacy-by-design is embedded; reviews data minimization and consent stuctures for training datasets
CISO (Chief Information Security Officer)	Reviews adversarial resilience, AI-specific threat modeling, and controls against model inversion/data leakage
CDO (Chief Data Officer)	Verfies data lineage, labeling integity, and AI data governance requirements
General Counsel / Legal	Maps legal obligations (GDPR, IP rights, liability), drafts enforcement language, and reviews third-party model usage risks
CTO / CIO	Ensures AI development aligns with enterprise architecture, software lifecycle: and DevSecOps practices
Board / Risk Committee	Approves overall risk appetite, receives periodic RAI briefings, and sets oversight tone

Table 41.1 Role-Based Responsibilities in Policy Formation

4. **Align with Global Frameworks:**
   - **ISO 42001:2023**—AI Management System
   - **NIST AI Risk Management Framework (AI RMF)**
   - **OECD AI Principles**
   - **EU AI Act, DORA, GDPR, U.S. Executive Order on Safe AI (2023).**
5. **Embed Guiding Questions:**
   - "Can this model's decisions be explained to affected users?"
   - "Has the training data been vetted for bias, consent, and provenance?"
   - "Who is accountable for adverse outcomes?"
   - "Can this model be paused or overridden in real-time?"

Real-World Example: Microsoft's RAI Policy Framework

Microsoft's RAI Standard (2022) breaks governance into **six pillars**: fairness, reliability and safety, privacy and security, inclusiveness, transparency, and accountability. Their **AI Assurance and Governance** team works cross-functionally to operationalize these principles into engineering processes.

Key takeaway: Microsoft integrates RAI into Azure development pipelines, requiring model documentation ("model cards") and red-teaming for high-risk systems.

Step 2: Embed AI Risk into Enterprise Risk Management (ERM)

AI introduces new risk categories (algorithmic bias, model drift, explainability failure) and amplifies existing ones (cybersecurity, legal, reputational). Enterprises must:

- Extend their ERM frameworks to include AI-specific risks
- Link AI risk scenarios to business impact (e.g., financial, regulatory, brand damage)
- Incorporate AI into RCSA (Risk Control Self-Assessments) and KRI (Key Risk Indicators).

Real-world example: A global bank added "unauthorized use of generative AI in client interactions" as a top operational risk after an internal incident exposed sensitive data in a prompt.

AI introduces both novel risks and amplifies existing enterprise risk vectors. Embedding AI risk into the **ERM** program ensures the organization proactively monitors, mitigates, and reports emerging threats from AI technologies across the lifecycle.

Why AI Needs a Dedicated ERM Lens

Traditional ERM frameworks (aligned to COSO or ISO 31000) typically focus on operational, financial, compliance, and strategic risks. However, **AI introduces new categories of risk** that must be explicitly captured, such as:

- **Algorithmic bias and discrimination**
- **Model drift and degradation**
- **Explainability failures**
- **Unauthorized use of LLMs or generative AI**
- **Synthetic content misuse (deepfakes, hallucinations)**

- **Intellectual property infringement**
- **Data poisoning and adversarial attacks.**

Key Actions to Integrate AI into ERM

1. **Extend Risk Taxonomies**
   - o Add AI-specific risk categories across operational, compliance, legal, and reputational domains.
   - o Example: Include "AI hallucination risk" or "non-deterministic outputs" in operational risk registers.
2. **Align AI Risk to Business Impact**
   - o Use quantitative and qualitative scoring for risks such as regulatory fines, downtime, reputational damage, and data exposure.
   - o Example: Tie explainability failures in credit scoring to potential loss of lending licenses.
3. **Update RCSAs and KRIs**
   - o Incorporate AI-specific controls into **RCSAs**.
   - o Define KRIs such as:
     - – % of models with incomplete model documentation
     - – of ungoverned generative AI prompts per quarter
     - – % of models reviewed by legal/compliance before deployment.
4. **Map AI Risks to Risk Appetite**
   - o Determine acceptable residual risk thresholds for high-impact AI systems.

Function	AI Risk Role in ERM
Chief Risk Officer (CRO)	Integrates AI risks into enterprise risk dashboards, board reports, and audits
CISO	Tracks adversarial AI threats and cyber-specific risks like model inversion, shadow AI tools
CDO	Identifies data quality, provenance, and drift issues that copromise AI reliability
Legal / Compliance	Reviews AI legal liabilities (e.g., FCRA, GDPR), monitors regulatory AI developments
CTO / CIO	Ensures technical mitigations like version control, sandboxing, rollback capabilities
Internal Audit	Validates ERM coverage of AI risks, including testing of AI-specific KRIs and control effectiveness

Table 41.2 Role-Based Responsibilities in AI Risk Governance

- For example, a bank may accept low transparency for internal fraud detection AI but not for customer-facing tools.

5. **Include Third-Party AI Risk**
   - Extend Third-Party Risk Management to capture risks from vendors using AI in their tools or decisioning pipelines.

Real-World Example

A **global bank** discovered an internal team used ChatGPT to generate customer email responses. A prompt inadvertently included a **copy/paste of PII**, resulting in a data exposure. The risk was escalated and prompted the bank to:

- Add "unauthorized use of generative AI in client communications" to its **Top Ten Operational Risks**
- Mandate mandatory AI tool logging across business units
- Update RCSA templates to include AI prompt risk scenarios.

Step 3: Operationalize Policies with Tools and Controls

Implement automated and manual controls to embed AI policies into daily workflows. For example, use AI model registries, bias detection tools, and approval checkpoints. The CISO ensures security and access controls, while legal integrates policy requirements into procurement and contract management. CPOs ensure privacy impact assessments are triggered by data model changes. Board oversight ensures that these controls are audited regularly.

Example: A global bank implements a mandatory "model card" registry tied to its MLOps pipeline, where legal reviews compliance tags before deployment.

Operationalize Policies with Tools and Controls

Having well-crafted RAI policies is only the beginning. Real-world AI governance depends on the ability to **translate principles into enforceable processes** using a blend of manual procedures, automated tooling, and multi-stakeholder ownership.

Key Actions to Operationalize AI Governance

1. **Establish Model Registries and Inventory Systems**
   - Maintain a real-time inventory of all AI models in use, under development, or deprecated.
   - Use **model cards** to document key attributes: purpose, training data, biases, explainability status, and legal reviews.
   - Connect model registries to MLOps pipelines for automated compliance checks before deployment.
2. **Automate Governance with AI Risk Management Tools**
   - Use platforms like IBM OpenScale, Fiddler, Arthur.ai, or Azure AI RAI dashboard for:
     - Bias and fairness detection
     - Drift detection
     - Explainability (e.g., SHAP, LIME-based visibility)
     - Risk scoring for model criticality.
   - Integrate alerts into SIEM or GRC platforms to trigger escalations for out-of-policy behaviors.
3. **Implement Cross-Functional Control Gates**
   - **Legal:** Mandates model documentation reviews for intellectual property, liability, and regulatory obligations.
   - **Compliance:** Requires Data Protection Impact Assessments before changes to training datasets involving personal data.
   - **Security:** CISO ensures secure environments for training/inference and access controls (IAM) on model endpoints.
   - **Privacy (CPO):** Verifies anonymization protocols, differential privacy, and consent tracking for personal data used in AI.
4. **Mandate Explainability Thresholds**
   - Embed explainability requirements into development sprints. For high-risk models, restrict deployment unless human-interpretable reasoning is available.
   - Example: Financial institutions must prove that loan denial reasons meet FCRA explainability standards.
5. **Include Governance Checks in Procurement**
   - Require AI vendors to complete standardized AI risk assessment questionnaires or NIST AI RMF mappings.
   - Insert right-to-audit, retrain, and termination clauses based on ethical breach thresholds.

Function	Operationalization Role
CISO	Implements access controls, endpoint protection, and cyber threat detection for AI systems
Legal	Reviews model documentation, vendor contracts, and IP/licensing risk; embeds AI clauses in SLAs
CPO (Privacy)	Triggers PIAs/DPIAs on model updates, enforces privacy-by-design
CTO	Ensures tools (model registries, bias checkers) are integrated into dev pipelines
AI Governance Officer	Oversees all governance workflows, reporting, and policy compliance checks
Internal Audit / Board	Validates control effectiveness and enforces governance through top-down oversight

Table 41.3 Role-Based Control Responsibilities

6. **Board Oversight & Auditing**
   - Boards should receive quarterly dashboards summarizing:
     - % of models with governance issues
     - Number of non-compliant model deployments blocked
     - Critical AI risk events and remediation timelines

Real-World Example: Model Registry with Legal Hooks

A **multinational bank** adopted a **Model Card Registry** integrated directly into its CI/CD DevOps pipeline. Before an AI model could be promoted to production, it required:

- Technical documentation (model versioning, drift score)
- Legal review of training data licenses and discrimination risk
- Approval from compliance if model outputs impacted customers
- Logging for every inference made by the model for audit trail.

This enabled the bank to block deployment of non-compliant or high-risk models and provided **audit-readiness** for regulators like the ECB and US OCC.

Step 4: Integrate AI Risk Management into Enterprise Risk Frameworks

AI-specific risks—such as model drift, hallucinations, or prompt injection—must be mapped into existing enterprise risk categories. This includes risk appetite thresholds and scenario planning. The CRO or risk officer, with the

AI Risk Category	Description
Model Drift	Over time, the model's accuracy and relevance degrade as input data or real-world conditions change.
Hallucinations	LLMs generate plausible but factually incorrect content, impacting trust, compliance, and safety.
Prompt Injection	Adversarial prompts Manipulate LLMs into producing harmful or unauthorized content.
Algorithmic Bias	Systematic disparities in outcomes across different user groups, often due to flawed training data.
Explainability Gaps	Difficulty justifying decisions made by black-box models to regulators or affected individuals.
Shadow AI / Unapproved Tools	Employees using AI systems outside official procurement or governance processes.

Table 41.4 Key AI Risks to Map into ERM

CISO and CTO, must align AI risk quantification models with existing loss events and mitigation controls.

Example: A healthcare provider adapted COSO ERM to include algorithmic bias as an operational risk, tracked with indicators monitored monthly. As AI evolves into a strategic enabler—and sometimes a critical liability—enterprises must fully embed AI-specific risks into their ERM systems. This integration ensures that AI risks are not treated in isolation but are quantified, monitored, and mitigated using the same rigor as financial, operational, or compliance risks.

How to Embed AI into ERM

1. **Expand the Risk Taxonomy**
   - Create a formal AI Risk Register aligned to the enterprise's existing COSO or ISO 31000 frameworks.
   - Add AI risk types as first- or second-tier risks, depending on the business model's AI reliance.

2. **Define Risk Appetite for AI Use**
   - o Establish thresholds for acceptable risk based on sector, use case, and stakeholder exposure.
   - o Example: A bank might tolerate moderate hallucination risk in internal productivity tools but set zero tolerance for hallucinations in consumer-facing chatbots.
3. **Align Risk Scenarios to Business Impact**
   - o Use stress-testing, red-teaming, and adversarial testing to simulate:
     - Biased loan approvals
     - Autonomous decisions harming users
     - Data exfiltration via prompt injection.
   - o Map these to potential business outcomes: lawsuits, regulatory fines, reputational loss, and customer churn.
4. **Integrate AI Risk into RCSAs and KRIs**
   - o Add AI-specific questions to **RCSAs** across business units.
   - o Track **KRIs** such as:
     - % of models reviewed for bias
     - Number of hallucination incidents
     - LLM prompt injection attempts flagged per month.
5. **Link AI Risk to Incident Management**
   - o Ensure AI-related incidents (e.g., unauthorized AI use, hallucination exposure) are logged and escalated via existing incident management processes.

Function	AI Risk Integration Role
Chief Risk Officer (CRO)	Owns the enterprise-wide AI risk taxonomy and leads integration into ERM systems
CISO	Ensures cyber risks from AI systems (prompt injection, LLM exposure) are tracked and mitigated
CTO	Provides the technical input on where and how models operate, ensuring model health and documentation
CPO	Maps privacy risks from AI outputs and data processing into GDPR, CCPA, or HIPAA risk categories
Legal / General Counsel	Monitors regulatory risk from AI misuse and litigation potential, especially around discrimination or harm
Internal Audit	Validates contols around AI risk registration, remediation, and continuous improvement

Table 41.5 Role-Specific Responsibilities

6. **Ensure Board-Level AI Risk Visibility**
   - The CRO must include AI risk in quarterly risk reports to the board, alongside financial and cyber risks.

Real-World Case Study: Healthcare + COSO ERM

A **leading US healthcare system** extended its **COSO-based ERM** framework to include AI use in diagnostics and personalized medicine. After discovering disparities in treatment recommendations for minority patients from an ML algorithm, it:

- Classified algorithmic bias as an operational risk
- Implemented **monthly KRI dashboards** for AI fairness and drift detection
- Integrated AI-specific incident reporting into its patient safety board process
- Required retraining protocols triggered by high drift or adverse patient outcome correlations.

This move aligned the AI governance strategy with both HIPAA obligations and Diversity, Equity, Inclusion goals.

Step 5: Enable Training and Awareness Across the Enterprise

Role-specific training is vital to operationalize governance. Legal teams need modules on AI liability and IP ownership. CISOs train on AI model security threats. Boards require strategic briefings and red team scenarios. HR must embed AI ethics into onboarding.

Example: A retail company rolled out a three-tier training program where engineers, managers, and executives each received tailored training aligned to their decision rights under the AI policy.

Why Training Is a Pillar of AI Governance

AI governance is only as strong as the people implementing it. Even the most robust policies and risk frameworks will fail without cross-functional

Tier	Audience	Focus Areas
Tier 1 (Foundational)	All employees (incl. HR, finance, sales)	Basic AI awareness, ethics, responsible use of GenAI, data privacy
Tier 2 (Role-Based)	Legal, Compliance, CISO, PM, CPO	Privacy, Security, Project Management, Legal

Table 41.6 Tiered Training Framework

understanding and behavior change. Therefore, **enterprise-wide AI training—tailored to roles and responsibilities—is a critical enabler** of RAI at scale.

Training ensures that:

- Decision-makers know their rights and limits under the AI policy.
- Developers and engineers understand compliance, explainability, and fairness requirements.
- Risk and legal teams can properly assess emerging AI-specific threats.
- Business users can identify when AI use cases deviate from approved norms.

Organizations should develop **multi-tiered training programs** aligned to internal decision rights, risk exposure, and AI usage intensity.

Step 6: Establish Monitoring, Auditing, and Incident Response

Monitoring for AI model behavior, data drift, and shadow AI usage must be constant. Compliance teams must define KPIs, and audit teams need playbooks to sample model outputs.

Example: A telecom operator set up a quarterly audit of generative AI model outputs and prompt logs, flagging prompts involving customer data for red-teaming and compliance review.

Step 7: Review, Adapt, and Report to Stakeholders

AI governance is not static. Regular policy refreshes, stakeholder reporting (including to regulators), and outcome assessments are essential. The CPO provides updates on data use trends, legal on evolving regulations, and CISOs on threat models. Boards require quarterly assurance reports.

Example: A SaaS provider embedded AI governance metrics into its Environmental, Social, and Governance (ESG) report, aligning with OECD AI Principles and showing explainability scores, model lifecycle status, and training audits.

AI Governance Is a Living Framework

AI governance cannot be a static policy document filed away in a compliance folder. As AI systems evolve—through new models, vendors, capabilities, and use cases—so must the controls that govern them. This step formalizes the **review cadence, adaptation triggers, and stakeholder reporting obligations** needed to maintain accountability, agility, and alignment.

A governance program that isn't reviewed regularly becomes obsolete, increases risk exposure, and fails to satisfy regulator expectations. Moreover, as stakeholder scrutiny (including investors, regulators, and the public) grows, transparent and auditable reporting becomes non-negotiable.

Governance Review Mechanisms

To institutionalize adaptability, leading organizations implement:

- **Quarterly AI Governance Reviews**: Conducted by a cross-functional AI Governance Council comprising legal, compliance, CISO, CTO, CPO, and business unit leads.
- **Annual Policy Refresh Cycles**: AI policies are updated annually to reflect:
  - Regulatory changes (e.g., EU AI Act, US EO on Safe AI, China's Algorithm Law)
  - New risk exposures (e.g., prompt injection, data poisoning, model inversion attacks)
  - Internal audit findings or near-miss events.
- **Use Case Re-Evaluations**: All high-risk AI applications (as classified under the AI policy) undergo periodic reassessment, especially when:
  - Training data changes significantly
  - Model behavior degrades or drifts
  - External incidents highlight new systemic risks.

Metrics That Matter

Effective reporting requires metrics that are:

- Decision-relevant
- Risk-aligned

Role-specific
Recommended metrics include:

- **Model Explainability Score** (avg. SHAP/LIME interpretability percentile)
- **Bias Detection Incidents** (per 100 models evaluated)
- **Training Data Source Coverage** (% verified for IP/licensing)
- **Model Registry Coverage** (% models registered with metadata)

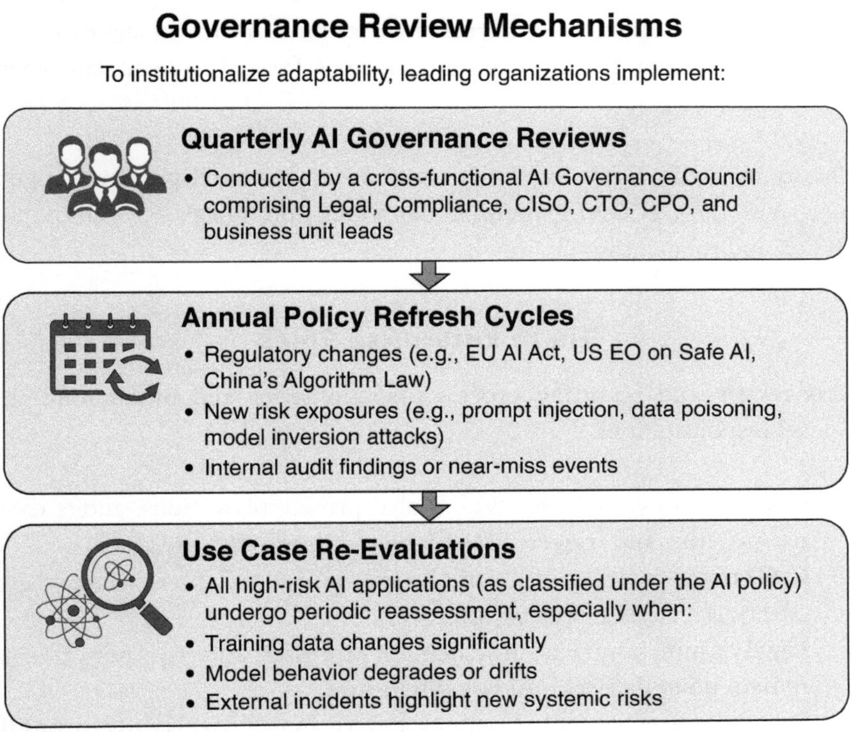

Image 41.1 Governance Review Mechanisms

- **Unapproved AI Usage Reports** (e.g., via generative AI monitoring tools)
- **Policy Violation Events** (triggers red team or legal review)
- **Audit Completion Rate** (models vs governance audit cycles)
- **Data Retention Violations** (flagged by CPO system scans).

Real-World Example: ESG Integration of AI Governance

A publicly traded SaaS provider aligned its AI governance KPIs with its **ESG** reporting framework. Its annual sustainability report included:

- A breakdown of all production AI systems by risk category (low/moderate/high)
- Metrics on explainability tooling coverage (80% of models > 75% explainability)
- An audit trail of model training datasets (with licensing provenance)
- Third-party assurance of fairness metrics for recruitment algorithms
- Documentation of red-teaming outcomes for LLM use in customer support.

This transparency built investor trust and demonstrated proactive alignment with the **OECD AI Principles**, particularly on transparency, accountability, and robustness.

Tie to Enterprise Roles

This review and reporting process operationalizes and unites multiple C-level responsibilities:

- **CPO** ensures compliance with global privacy obligations, audits data use patterns, and triggers PIAs for new training data use cases.
- **CISO** tracks evolving AI-specific attack surfaces and threat vectors (e.g., adversarial attacks, prompt leakage).
- **Legal** ensures contracts, procurement processes, and regulatory filings remain up to date with AI risk disclosures.
- **Board** receives strategic briefings and assurance dashboards to fulfill fiduciary responsibilities and prepare for upcoming AI legislation or enforcement trends.

INDEX

Note: **Bold** page numbers refer to tables and *italic* page numbers refer to figures.

For Product Safety Concerns and Information please contact our EU representative GPSR@taylorandfrancis.com
Taylor & Francis Verlag GmbH, Kaufingerstraße 24, 80331 München, Germany

www.ingramcontent.com/pod-product-compliance
Ingram Content Group UK Ltd.
Pitfield, Milton Keynes, MK11 3LW, UK
UKHW020156200926
475702UK00016B/2739

* 9 7 8 1 0 4 1 1 3 5 2 9 6 *